LATIN AMERICA IN COMPARATIVE PERSPECTIVE

Latin America in Global Perspective

The fundamental purpose of this multivolume series is to broaden conceptual perspectives for the study of Latin America. This effort responds to a perception of need. Latin America cannot be understood in isolation from other parts of the world. This has always been so; it is especially true in the contemporary era.

Accordingly, the goal of this series is to demonstrate the desirability and the feasibility of analyzing Latin America in comparative perspective, in conjunction with other regions, and in global perspective, in the context of worldwide processes. A subsidiary purpose is to establish a bridge between Latin American "area studies" and mainstream social science disciplines, to the mutual benefit of both. Ultimately, the intent is to explore and emphasize intellectual challenges posed by dynamic changes within Latin America and in its relation to the international arena.

The present volume, *Latin America in Comparative Perspective: New Approaches to Methods and Analysis*, explores theoretical and methodological issues involved in the comparative analysis of Latin America. Other studies in this series will include:

EnGENDERing Wealth and Well-Being: Empowerment for Global Change, edited by Rae Lesser Blumberg, Cathy A. Rakowski, Irene Tinker, and Michael Monteón;

Cooperation or Rivalry? Regional Integration in the Americas and the Pacific Rim, edited by Shoji Nishijima and Peter H. Smith;

Latin American Environmental Policy in International Perspective, edited by Gordon MacDonald, Daniel Nielsen, and Marc Stern;

Civil-Military Relations After the Cold War, edited by David Mares;

Institutional Design in New Democracies, edited by Arend Lijphart and Carlos Waisman.

This series results from a multiyear research program organized by the Center for Iberian and Latin American Studies (CILAS) at the University of California, San Diego. Principal funding has come from the Andrew W. Mellon Foundation.

LATIN AMERICA IN COMPARATIVE PERSPECTIVE

■

New Approaches to Methods and Analysis

edited by

Peter H. Smith

University of California, San Diego

Westview Press

BOULDER • SAN FRANCISCO • OXFORD

Latin America in Global Perspective

Copyright © 1995 by Westview Press, Inc.

Published in 1995 in the United States of America by Westview Press, Inc., 5500 Central Avenue, Boulder, Colorado 80301-2877, and in the United Kingdom by Westview Press, 12 Hid's Copse Road, Oxford OX2 9JJ

A CIP catalog record for this book is available from the Library of Congress.
ISBN 0-8133-2104-2. ISBN 0-8133-2105-0 (pbk.).

Printed and bound in the United States of America

The paper used in this publication meets the requirements
of the American National Standard for Permanence of Paper
for Printed Library Materials Z39.48-1984.

10   9   8   7   6   5   4   3   2   1

Contents

List of Tables and Figures   xi
Preface   xiii
List of Acronyms   xv

CHAPTER ONE
The Changing Agenda for Social Science
Research on Latin America
Peter H. Smith   1

PART ONE
ANALYTICAL STRATEGIES   31

CHAPTER TWO
Contending Paradigms for Cross-Regional
Comparison: Development Strategies and
Commodity Chains in East Asia and Latin America
Gary Gereffi   33

CHAPTER THREE
Purposes and Methods of Intraregional Comparison
Amparo Menéndez-Carrión and Fernando Bustamante   59

CHAPTER FOUR
Uses and Limitations of Rational Choice
Barbara Geddes 81

PART TWO
CONCEPTUAL ISSUES 109

CHAPTER FIVE
Rewriting the Scripts: Gender in the Comparative Study
of Latin American Politics
Jane S. Jaquette 111

CHAPTER SIX
Trajectory of a Concept: "Corporatism" in
the Study of Latin American Politics
David Collier 135

CHAPTER SEVEN
Assessments of State Strength
Evelyne Huber 163

CHAPTER EIGHT
Reassessing Political Culture
Frederick C. Turner 195

PART THREE
POLITICAL ROLES OF SOCIAL SCIENCE 225

CHAPTER NINE
Polls, Political Discourse, and the Public Sphere:
The Spin on Peru's Fuji-golpe
Catherine M. Conaghan 227

CHAPTER TEN
Public Opinion Research in Mexico
Miguel Basáñez   257

CHAPTER ELEVEN
Public Opinion Research in Russia and Eastern Europe
Elena Bashkirova   275

About the Book   293
About the Editor and Contributors   295
Index   299

Tables and Figures

Tables

1.1	Methods of agreement and difference	5
1.2	Most-Similar-Systems (MSS) and Most-Different-Systems (MDS) designs	5
1.3	Analytical strategies and methodological approaches	7
2.1	Comparative methods, generalizations, and variables	40
6.1	Subtypes and dimensions: Differentiating in terms of the locus of power	145
8.1	What people in different countries find to be very important, 1990–1991	199
8.2	Practices and attitudes relating to the transition toward democracy by social class: Mexico, 1990	202
8.3	The assignment of responsibility for political, economic, and social change by social class: Urban residents in Mexico, 1961	203
8.4	Practices relating to the transition toward democracy: Mexico, Argentina, and Chile, 1981–1991	213
8.5	Views of whether change should come through reform or through revolutionary action: Mexico, Argentina, and Chile, 1981–1991	214
8.6	Attitudes toward citizen participation, interpersonal trust, confidence in the legal system, and patriotism: Mexico, Argentina, and Chile, 1984–1991	215

9.1   Confidence in national institutions: Peru, 1990–1992   233
9.2   Approval rating of Alberto Fujimori as president,
       1990–1993   235
9.3   Conditions of continued approval/disapproval of
       Fujimori presidency, 1992   243

Figures

6.1   Effort to accommodate discussion of "concertation"
       leads to differentiation of overarching concept into
       two components   143
6.2   Classical versus radial subtypes   148

10.1   Party preferences in Mexico 1982–1993   265
10.2   Do you approve or disapprove of the way the
       president is handling his job? Mexico 1982–1983   266
10.3   Would you say your personal situation is better
       today, the same, or worse than it was a year ago?
       Mexico, 1987–1993   267
10.4   Do you think elections will be respected? Mexico,
       1988–1991   268

11.1   Perception of improvement in household finances:
       East European countries, 1992–1993   283
11.2   Perception of outlook for general economic situation:
       East European countries, 1993   284
11.3   Is the creation of a market economy right or wrong?
       East European countries, 1993   286
11.4   Are economic reforms proceeding too fast or too
       slowly? East European countries, 1993   287

Preface

This book results from extensive collaboration among numerous individuals and institutions over the past several years. Activities began in 1992 when the Inter-University Consortium for Political and Social Research (ICPSR) launched an initiative on Latin America in conjunction with its renowned Summer Program in Quantitative Methods held in Ann Arbor, Michigan. Colleagues from ICPSR and the University of Michigan and I then developed an intensive workshop on "Quantitative Research on Latin America," which is now offered on a regular basis. Select groups of students from Latin America, Europe, and the United States attend. In July 1992 we also held an exploratory two-day conference on "Prospects for Quantitative Research on Latin America." The following year we set out to organize a full-fledged conference and to convene an informal seminar where our ICPSR students could report on their research-in-progress. These efforts led to a meeting on "Latin America in Comparative Perspective: Issues and Methods" held in Quito, Ecuador, July 29–31, 1993.

This volume has emerged from all of these activities and addresses a broad range of analytical questions. After an introductory assessment of the state of the field, in Part One the authors explore methodological approaches to the study of Latin America: cross-regional comparison, intraregional comparison, and the application of rational choice. In Part Two contributors examine conceptual and substantive issues: women's movements, corporatism, state capacity, and political culture. And in Part Three the authors evaluate the status and usage of public opinion research in Latin America, Eastern Europe, and the former Soviet Union, thus providing insight on the roles of social science under conditions of political change.

As director of the Center for Iberian and Latin American Studies (CILAS) at the University of California, San Diego, I want to acknowledge the contributions of cosponsoring institutions: the Consejo Latinoamericano de Ciencias Sociales (CLACSO), the Facultad Latinoamericana de Ciencias Sociales Sede Ecuador (FLACSO/Ecuador), the ICPSR, and the Program in Latin American and Caribbean Studies at the University of Michigan. Financial support came from all these institutions and from the Andrew W. Mellon Foundation.

As project co-organizer I express gratitude to Claudia Leite, Amparo Menéndez-Carrión, Marcia Rivera, Richard J. Rockwell, and Rebecca J. Scott.

As volume editor I offer special thanks to Patricia Rosas, editorial assistant at CILAS, and to Barbara Ellington, our editor at Westview Press.

Peter H. Smith
La Jolla, California

Acronyms

AAPOR	American Association for Public Opinion Research
ACLS	American Council of Learned Societies
ADEX	Asociación de Exportadores (Association of Exporters, Peru)
AMAI	Asociación Mexicana de Agencias de Investigación (Mexican Association of Research Agencies)
APEIM	Asociación Peruana de Empresas de Investigación de Mercados (Peruvian Association of Market Research Companies)
APRA	Alianza Popular Revolucionaria Americana (Latin American Popular Revolutionary Alliance, Peru)
CARICOM	Caribbean Community and Common Market
CCD	Congreso Constituyente Democrático (Democratic Constituent Congress)
CEDYS	Centro de Estudios de la Democracia y la Sociedad (Center for the Study of Democracy and Society)
CEO	Centro de Estudios de Opinión (Center for Public Opinion Studies, University of Colima)
CEO	Centro de Estudios de Opinión (Center for Public Opinion Studies, University of Guadalajara)
CEOP	Centro de Estudios de Opinión Pública (Center for the Study of Public Opinion)
CIEPLAN	Centro de Investigación y Estudios para la Planificación (Center for Planning Research and Study, Chile)
CILAS	Center for Iberian and Latin American Studies
CIS	Commonwealth of Independent States
CLACSO	Consejo Latinoamericano de Ciencias Sociales (Latin American Council for Social Science)

CNN	Cable News Network
CONACYT	Consejo Nacional para Ciencias y Tecnología (National Council on Science and Technology, Mexico)
CPI	Compañía Peruana de Investigación (Peruvian Research Company)
CPSU	Communist Party of the Soviet Union
DESCO	Centro de Estudios y Promoción del Desarrollo (Center for the Study and Promotion of Development)
ECLAC	Economic Commission for Latin America and the Caribbean
EIU	Economist Intelligence Unit
EOI	export-oriented industrialization
EPZ	export-processing zone
ESOMAR	European Society for Opinion and Marketing Research
FLACSO	Facultad Latinoamericana de Ciencias Sociales (Latin American Faculty for Social Science)
FONDECYT	Fondo Nacional de Ciencias y Tecnología (National Fund for Science and Technology, Chile)
GCC	global commodity chain
GDP	gross domestic product
GEO	Gabinete de Estudios de Opinión (Survey Research Cabinet)
GNP	gross national product
ICPSR	Inter-University Consortium for Political and Social Research
IDB	Inter-American Development Bank
IDESP	Instituto de Estudos Economicos, Sociais e Politicos de São Paulo (The Institute of Economic, Social and Political Research of São Paulo)
IMF	International Monetary Fund
ISI	import-substituting industrialization
ISOP	Investigaciones Sobre Opinión (Public Opinion Research)
LASA	Latin American Studies Association
LASDB	Latin American Survey Data Bank
MDS	most-different-system
MERCOSUR	Mercado Común del Sur (Common Market of the South)
MSS	most-similar-system
NAFTA	North American Free Trade Agreement
NGO	nongovernmental organization
NIC	newly industrializing countries
OAS	Organization of American States
OBM	original brandname manufacturing

OECD	Organization for Economic Cooperation and Development
OEM	original equipment manufacturing
OP	Opinión Profesional (Professional Opinion)
PAN	Partido Acción Nacional (National Action Party, Mexico)
PCC	Partido Comunista de Cuba (Cuban Communist Party)
PEAC	Prospectiva Estratégica (Strategic Outlook)
PHARE	Aid for the Economic Reconstruction of Poland and Hungary
PM	Pulso Mercadológico (Market Pulse)
POP	Peruana de Opinión Pública (Peruvian Public Opinion)
PPS	probability proportional to size
PRD	Partido Revolucionario Democrático (Democratic Revolutionary Party, Mexico)
PRI	Partido Revolucionario Institucional (Institutional Revolutionary Party)
PSU	primary sampling unit
ROMIR	Russian Public Opinion and Market Research
SMEOP	Sociedad Mexicana de Estudios de Opinión Pública (Mexican Society for Public Opinion Research)
SSRC	Social Science Research Council
TACIS	Technical Assistance for Community of Independent States
TNC	transnational corporation
UNCTC	United Nations Centre on Transnational Corporations
USIA	United States Information Agency
USITC	United States International Trade Commission
VCIOM	All-Russian Center for Public Opinion
VLSI	very-large-scale integrated circuits
WAPOR	World Association for Public Opinion Research
WID	women in development

CHAPTER ONE

■

The Changing Agenda for Social Science Research on Latin America

Peter H. Smith

SOCIAL SCIENCE RESEARCH on Latin America stands at a crossroads. Sweeping transformations throughout the region and the world have brought new issues to the forefront. In the aftermath of brutal authoritarianism, the onset of "democratization" has sparked controversy over dynamics of political transition and regime consolidation. In the wake of the "lost decade" of the 1980s, the quest for economic development has prompted emulation of export-led strategies pioneered in the Pacific Rim and has led to widespread acceptance of the so-called Washington consensus. In the post–Cold War international arena, these concurrent trends in Latin America—political and economic liberalization—are commonly hailed as integral expressions of universal, worldwide trends that represent and celebrate the triumph of a new "neoliberal" orthodoxy. In the meantime, nations of Latin America are striving mightily to find appropriate niches amid rapidly shifting global arrangements.

These developments require rigorous investigation and analysis, instead of self-congratulation. And as such changes shape the substantive research agenda, they demand the application of two related methodologies. The first of these is comparative analysis, especially cross-regional analysis that can identify similarities and differences between changes in Latin America and other parts of the world. In order to assess the utility for Latin America of "Asian" development models, for instance, it is essential to comprehend the social and political conditions that led to their formulation and permitted their implementation—and to

1

acquire a precise understanding of their practical ingredients. In order to analyze the global impulse toward democratization, it is important to detect the specific properties of political transition and to evaluate differential prospects for institutional consolidation in such distant areas as Eastern Europe and Latin America.

The second methodology is quantitative research, especially statistical analysis that can provide the means for measuring the *extent* of political, economic, and societal change. In most instances, it is not just a question of *whether* a given phenomenon might be taking place, it is a question of *degree*. Besides, many specific items on the newly evolving agenda lead directly to matters of measurement. The study of political phenomena associated with "democratization"—elections, public opinion polls, and legislative coalitions—opens new possibilites for quantitative work. So does the examination of such contemporary social issues as income distribution, class structure, and gender inequality.

How to meet the demands of this agenda? What analytical strategies are most appropriate? Is it suitable to compare development policies in Chile with those of South Korea or Taiwan? What can be learned by comparing political transitions in Argentina with Poland or Hungary, or is it more fruitful to concentrate on comparisons within Latin America? To what extent can (or should) Latin Americanists make use of game theory and rational choice models? What are the intellectual benefits of quantitative research? How can statistical analysis be appropriately employed in the cultural and social contexts of Latin America? And how can statistical findings be usefully compared from one region to another? Such questions form the framework of this book.

In this chapter I explore relationships between substantive issues and analytical strategies. I begin with commentary on comparative and quantitative methodologies, offer an overview of recent trends in Latin American studies, assess resources in the field, and conclude with observations about current and future research challenges. I concentrate mainly on political questions and political science, but this focus should be relevant to other disciplines as well.[1] □

COMPARATIVE AND STATISTICAL ANALYSIS

Comparative and quantitative methodologies can go hand in hand. As Arend Lijphart pointed out some time ago, the two approaches are logically and practically linked to one another: "The comparative method resembles the statistical method in all respects except one. The crucial difference is that the number of cases it deals with is too small to permit systematic control by means of partial correlations. ... There is, consequently, no clear dividing line between the statistical and comparative methods; the difference depends entirely on the number of cases."[2] Moreover, quantitative analysis itself requires some form of comparative perspective: Only then is it possible to determine whether an empirical finding represents a high or low number—that is, in relation to some kind of standard—and to interpret the results accordingly.

Lijphart has made an important point, but it can be taken only so far. The distinction between comparative and statistical analysis does not depend merely on the magnitude of the N (the number of cases), nor is statistical analysis inherently superior or preferable to qualitative comparison. As Charles Ragin has forcefully demonstrated, qualitative approaches can have distinct advantages. Because they focus on "cases" rather than on "variables" qualitative comparisons deal with configurations of attributes; they respect particularity and apparent idiosyncrasy; they seek multiple, contingent, and complex forms of causality. Such work typically examines a small number of cases to establish meaningful generalizations about theoretically definable phenomena (the *opus classicus* of the genre is Barrington Moore's *Social Origins of Dictatorship and Democracy*).[3] In contrast, statistical analysis usually employs a large number of cases in order to measure "average" relationships between "variables" that are often taken out of context. Statistical methods look for general trends and probabilistic associations; deviant cases are regarded (and often dismissed) simply as "outliers." Qualitative methods usually insist on satisfactory explanation of every case under consideration.[4]

There are many different forms of comparative analysis. One of the most useful classifications has come from Charles Tilly, who distinguishes between several kinds of comparison:

- *individualizing comparison*, "in which the point is to contrast specific instances of a given phenomenon as a means of grasping the peculiarities of each case";
- *universalizing comparison*, which "aims to establish that every instance of a phenomenon follows essentially the same rule";
- *variation-finding comparison*, which purports "to establish a principle of variation in the character or intensity of a phenomenon by examining systemic differences among instances"; and
- *encompassing comparison*, which "places different instances at various locations within the same system, on the way to explaining their characteristics as a function of their varying relationship to the system as a whole."

This categorization represents differences in purpose rather than in method. As Tilly observed, "The four types of comparison differ ... with respect to the sorts of statements they yield rather than with respect to the logic of comparison as such. Their relative value depends on the intellectual task at hand."[5]

Additional classifications focus on methods and techniques of comparative analysis. Still relevant is the work of John Stuart Mill, who over a century and a half ago distinguished between two forms of comparative logic. Using the "method of agreement," cases with similar values on a dependent variable—the phenomenon to be explained, such as the outbreak of social revolution—are compared according to values on a theoretically determined set of independent variables. By a process of elimination, those independent variables with differing values are dismissed from consideration, leaving those independent variables with similar values as possible "causes" of common outcomes on the dependent variable. Mill's "method of difference" reverses the procedure, comparing cases with differing values on the dependent variable and eliminating independent variables with similar values from consideration as explanatory or potentially causal factors.[6] Table 1.1 depicts these methods in schematic form.

More recently Adam Przeworski and Henry Teune have offered an analogous distinction. On the one hand, comparisons based on a "most-similar-systems" (MSS) design involve a deliberate selection of cases with similar values on preselected variables, thus permitting close analysis of covariance between other variables. On the other hand, a "most-different-systems" (MDS) design utilizes cases with similar outcomes on the dependent variable but different values on a broad range of independent variables, leaving only those independent variables with similar values as possible explanatory or causal factors (Table 1.2).[7] (The concepts are similar to Mill's but the language is reversed: MSS is analogous to the "method of difference" and MDS is analogous to the "method of agreement.") MSS designs lend themselves especially well to intraregional comparisons, such as among nations or communities within Latin America, since location within a single region can operate as a "control" for the effects of a substantial range of potential independent variables. MDS designs are especially pertinent for cross-regional comparisons, such as among cases in Latin America and Eastern Europe or East Asia, since location within different regions can introduce variation in a broad range of independent variables. At the same time, MSS designs are especially helpful in the initial search for and elaboration of plausible hypotheses; MDS designs are particularly suited to testing and verification of established hypotheses.

There are further affinities between these methodological alternatives. As Gary Gereffi observes in Chapter 2 of this volume, MSS designs are especially appropriate for "individualizing" and "variation-finding" comparisons, whereas MDS designs lend themselves to "universalizing"

TABLE 1.1   Methods of Agreement and Difference

Method of Agreement	Case 1	Case 2	Case 3	
Variable I	a	b	c	overall differences
Variable II	d	e	f	
Variable III	g	h	i	
Variable X	x	x	x	crucial similarity
Variable Y	y	y	y	

Method of Difference	Positive Cases	Negative Cases	
Variable I	a	a	overall similarities
Variable II	b	b	
Variable III	c	c	
Variable X	x_1	x_2	crucial difference
Variable Y	y_1	y_2	

where $x_1 \neq x_2$ and $y_1 \neq y_2$

Source: Adapted from Theda Skocpol and Margaret Somers, "Uses of Comparative History in Macrosocial Inquiry," *Comparative Studies in Society and History* 22, no. 2 (April 1980): 174–197, esp. 184.

TABLE 1.2   Most-Similar-Systems (MSS) and Most-Different-Systems (MDS) Designs

	MSS Design		MDS Design	
	Case 1	Case 2	Case 1	Case 2
Variable I	a	a	a	b
Variable II	b	b	c	d
Variable III	c	c	e	f
Variable X	x_1	x_2	x_3	x_3
Variable Y	y_1	y_2	y_3	x_3

where $x_1 \neq x_2$, $y_1 \neq y_2$, $x_3 = x_3$, and $y_3 = y_3$.

comparisons. In effect, MSS strategies probe underlying and systematic differences between cases. MDS designs, by contrast, test the existence and durability of specified relationships between variables, regardless of values on other variables—that is, relationships that are "universal" and thus oblivious to context. As Carlos Waisman has also pointed out, MSS approaches can also serve a subsidiary function for universalizing comparisons, as can MDS designs for individualizing and variation-finding strategies.[8]

As Lijphart has maintained, statistical analysis can make major contributions to these efforts. I refer not to the straightforward accumulation of numerical data; this can often be a thoroughly simplistic exercise, although the judicious juxtaposition of quantitative information can play a useful role in qualitative, small N comparisons. Instead, I refer to the use of statistical methods that measure the form, strength, and significance of associations between variables across a relatively large number of cases. It goes without saying that fascination with statistical techniques can lend itself to methodological excess and substantive banality. Tilly has made this point with playful exageration:

> There is the abuse of the Great Blender, in which we take numerical observations on a hundred-odd national states, made comparable by the magic fact of appearing in parallel columns in a statistical handbook, and run multiple regressions or factor analyses in order to discern the dimensions of development, of modernity, or political instability, or some other ill-defined global concept. There is the abuse of the Ersatz Laboratory, in which survey teams establish themselves in a number of different countries, translate a common questionnaire into the various local languages, then send out interviewers to ask the questions of presumably comparable samples of individuals or households in each country, code up their results into standard categories, then pool the information thus manufactured into an analysis of cross-cultural variation in the relationship between X and Y, with Z controlled. Let us not forget the abuse of the Cultural Checkerboard, in which hired graduate students read stacks of ethnographic articles and monographs, recording for each "society" encountered the presence or absence of patrilocal residence, early weaning, male puberty rituals, couvade, and dozens of other traits, then transform their judgments into holes in Hollerith cards, so that someone else can run statistical analyses to determine either which "societies" resemble each other most, or which cultural traits vary together. ... I will not inflict any more dreary examples upon you.[9]

But as Tilly hastens to observe, these abuses do not constitute an indictment of statistical analysis per se. They reveal only the dangers of mindless application.

In fact, there exist statistical counterparts for each of the different forms of comparative analysis. Standard measures of statistical association (such as regression and analysis of variance) explore underlying patterns of variance and covariance, thus resembling the "variation-finding" type of comparison. Construction and comparison of individual scores, for single variables or composite scales, can assist "individualizing" comparisons. A variety of techniques, including time-series analysis, can promote the search for "universalizing" comparisons.[10] And network analysis, among other approaches, can make important contributions to the analysis of "encompassing" comparisons.[11]

As a heuristic device, Table 1.3 displays potential relationships between comparative and statistical methods. Columns in the table refer to conceptual goals of comparison: individualizing, variation-finding, universalizing, or encompassing. Row entries display corresponding modes of analysis: MSS, MDS, or global research designs.[12] Primary strategies are likely to be used for initial analysis of entire data sets; secondary strategies can be especially helpful for refinement of preliminary findings, often through application to subsets of the data. As presented in the bottom row, statistical techniques could be suitable for either primary or secondary analysis. The connections here are indicative, rather than restrictive; my purpose is to open up the range of methodological choice, rather than to narrow it. As Tilly and others have made clear, the most outstanding work in social science makes use of a broad variety of methods and techniques in order to focus on the intellectual task at hand.[13]

Recognition of these methodological and analytical concerns is essential to fulfillment of the newly emerging agenda for social science

TABLE 1.3 Analytical Strategies and Methodological Approaches

Mode of Analysis	Conceptual Purpose			
	Individualizing	Variation-Finding	Universalizing	Encompassing
Primary comparative strategy	MSS	MSS	MDS	Global
Secondary comparative strategy	MDS	MDS	MSS	MDS, MSS
Relevant statistical technique	Individual scores	Regression, analysis of variance, etc.	Regression, time series, etc.	Network analysis

research on Latin America. Are we ready to deal with these challenges? What tasks lie ahead? □

REVIEWING THE RECORD: TRENDS IN SOCIAL SCIENCE

What have been the predominant patterns in social science research on Latin America? In this brief overview I attempt to establish a baseline for assessing the state of theoretical and methodological preparedness within the field. This is by no means a complete survey of existing literature; citations are intended to be illustrative, rather than exhaustive.

Theoretical Debates

Social science on Latin America has evinced a cyclical tendency to embrace and discard grand theoretical schemes. Imbued with the optimistic hubris of the 1960s, students of Latin American politics, especially those from the United States, found ready and congenial answers in what had come to be known as "modernization theory." The argument posited simple causal connections: Economic development creates middle-class sectors, whose members, in turn, espouse political democracy, either as a tactical means of gaining power or as an expression of enlightened values (the difference did not seem to matter at the time). The greater the level of economic development, the greater the likelihood of democratic politics. This postulation appeared to find empirical support in rudimentary cross-national analyses. It carried implications for U.S. policy and foreign aid, and it offered hope for the future.

It proved too good to be true. Instead of dispensing prosperity, economic development (such as it was) accentuated the concentration of wealth and exacerbated existing inequalities. The middle strata, relatively privileged, forged little if any sense of class consciousness and, in critical moments of decision, joined with ruling classes in opposition to popular masses. Political outcomes took a decidedly authoritarian turn, as shown by the lamentable experiences of Brazil (1964), Argentina (1966), and Chile (1973)—three of the most-developed countries of the continent. Its postulates apparently disproven, modernization theory fell into widespread disfavor.

Into this vacuum came the *dependencia* approach, which accepted modernization theory's linkage of socioeconomic causes with political outcomes but which turned the answer upside down: Since Latin America's economic development was qualitatively different from that of North America and Western Europe, it produced different results. Specifically, according to this argument, Latin America's experience was determined by the pervasive fact of its "dependency." An inherent characteristic of dependent development is its tendency to intensify inequities, allocating benefits to sectors involved in the world market and denying them to marginal groups. As Guillermo O'Donnell asserted in the early 1970s, ruling elites eventually come to face a clear-cut choice: Sacrifice growth or pursue it through repression of the working classes (thus reducing wages, controlling inflation, and attracting international investment). The elites chose the latter course, thus precipitating vicious coups in Brazil, Argentina, and Chile. Repressive regimes did not emerge despite Latin America's economic development; they emerged because of it.[14] Bolstered by this explanation, the idea of *dependencia* became the dominant analytical paradigm throughout the field, especially in the United States.[15]

In the 1980s reality would challenge expectations once again. Just as Latin America was suffering its most protracted economic depression since the 1930s, countries of the region managed to jettison authoritarian regimes and embark on processes—however uncertain—of liberalization and/or democratization. Scholars seeking explanations for this unexpected (but welcome) turn of events, examined the roles of ideology rather than economics, agency rather than structure, volition rather than determination. Democracy came to be viewed as the achievement of courageous leaders and/or civil society, rather than an automatic consequence of economic performance. Events in Eastern Europe and the termination of the Cold War seemed to verify this general observation.

Dependency theory was dead. Yet the problems it addressed—inequality and underdevelopment—are still alive and well. In fact, it could be argued that dependency went out of fashion just as Latin America was becoming more, not less, dependent on the international "core" of the world system. As Barbara Stallings has observed, theory and reality have been persistently out of phase with one another. Dependency thinking emerged from Latin America in the 1960s and 1970s, just at a time when world developments were undermining the core argument. Multinational corporations were becoming less important, and developing countries were able to assert their independence through petrodollar borrowing and state-owned enterprises; as a result, Latin America was feeling less "dependent." Then, in the 1980s, the dependency framework was abandoned, just as constraints in the international economic system—particularly the debt crisis—were becoming more important and Latin America was becoming more "dependent." This enduring disjuncture between theory and reality helped discredit the dependency school.[16]

The *dependencia* idea also suffered from its policy implications. In contrast to the "realist" school of international behavior, the dependency approach focused its explanatory powers on problems of socioeconomic development as well as international relations. The realist school, however, pays very little attention to such issues. "It is also clear," as Richard Fagen has said, "that there was (is) a central prescriptive or normative dimension to dependencia. Here the key notion is that because dependency is a structural condition ... only structural changes can alleviate the ills associated with dependent development. In line with the national/international duality mentioned above, these structural changes must take place both 'at home' and 'abroad.'" The dismissal of *dependencia* stemmed precisely from the fact that its normative and policy prescriptions seemed so complete. And when its policies failed—largely because the problems were beyond the reach of any policy instrument— the whole apparatus fell out of favor.[17] The eventual exhaustion of import-substitution industrialization (after decades of success) and the demise of socialism have thus led to abandonment of what was essentially an analytical tool.[18]

As a result, the field of Latin American studies no longer has a preeminent paradigm. Paradoxically enough, however, the collapse of dependency theory may have the beneficial effect of promoting rigorous social research. In the absence of an overarching conceptual framework, scholars may turn their focus toward empirical hypothesis-testing and examination of questions at the so-called middle range of social science theory.[19] It has been asserted more than once that the "paradigm crisis" of the 1980s has stimulated primary research and that, in this sense, has been "healthy" for the social sciences. As Indalecio Perdomo Lafargue has maintained, it is precisely this development that has helped make the present outlook for social science "extremely promising."[20]

In the meantime, modernization theory has shown signs of coming back to life. One of its central precepts—the postulation of a systematic relationship between economic development and political democracy— appears to have gained broad support from processes of liberalization in Eastern Europe, Latin America, and elsewhere in the world. Samuel P. Huntington has argued that intermediate levels of development—measured by gross national product (GNP) per capita—establish a zone for transition from dictatorship toward democracy.[21] Mitchell Seligson has made a comparable case for Latin America throughout the 1980s.[22] Now couched in cautious terms, the proposition holds that economic development is only a *necessary prerequisite* for democracy, not a sufficient condition. But for proponents of the modernization school, the ultimate implication is clear: Modernization theory was essentially correct. It was merely ahead of its time.

Although there has been considerable tumult in the advancement and rejection of general theory, Latin American social science has made discernible progress in the formulation, application, and refinement of key analytical constructs. One has to do with social mobilization and political participation of underrepresented groups; as Jane S. Jaquette demonstrates in Chapter 5, the role of women and the place of gender issues constitute a defining feature for political systems. Another feature deals with the importance of social coalitions and of state-society relations, as David Collier argues in his examination and reassessment of the concept of "corporatism" in Chapter 6. Still another characteristic concentrates on the persisting and central role of the state, as Evelyne Huber reveals in Chapter 7. Despite its cyclical tendency, social science research on Latin America has thus reached consensus and clarity on a number of major conceptual questions.

Methodological Approaches: Quantification

Just as there have been cyclical patterns in theory, there has been a notable surge and decline in quantitative research on Latin America over the past generation. Prompted in part by the "behavioral revolution" in political science, a small group of scholars began to apply quantitative techniques in the 1960s and 1970s. James W. Wilkie, a historian, initiated the trend with his study of budget allocations and social indicators in the aftermath of the Mexican Revolution.[23] And a promising political scientist, Philippe C. Schmitter, issued a clarion call for statistical approaches to cross-national aggregate data.[24]

There followed a series of investigations on the origins and structure of political elites in Latin America. My own work on the composition and recruitment of political elites in Mexico employed contingency tables, mobility matrices, measures of association, and path analysis.[25] Roderic A. Camp has produced a stream of valuable studies about the social origins of Mexican leaders, though his approach tends to be somewhat descriptive and his methods rarely move beyond bivariate tables.[26] At a much higher level of technical sophistication, Peter McDonough made excellent use of network analysis to examine political elites in authoritarian Brazil.[27] And, more recently, Barry Ames has employed powerful statistical techniques to examine "survival" strategies of Latin American political leaders.[28]

In contrast to research on the United States and Europe, there has been very little attention to congressional behavior in Latin America. Using factor analysis and interactive analysis of variance, I once studied the determinants of roll-call voting and party coalitions in the Argentine Chamber of Deputies from 1904 to 1955.[29] Similarly, Wanderley Guilherme dos Santos performed a path-breaking analysis of fragmentation and radicalization in the Brazilian Congress from 1946 through 1964.[30] Taken together, these works articulate and to some extent verify a fundamental proposition: Increasing levels of political polarization among civilian political elites precede and may even provoke military intervention.

Electoral behavior has also attracted statistical research. Over the years, scholars have produced important studies on the social determinants of voting patterns in a variety of countries—Argentina,[31] Brazil,[32] and Ecuador.[33] Even in Mexico, where electoral outcomes have so often been determined well in advance, political conditions have prompted serious research on voting.[34] Such studies tend to rely on ecological analysis, matching the socioeconomic characteristics of census districts with aggregate election returns. Most analyses employ simple correlations, though some use multiple regression and path analysis.[35]

It is to be regretted that, even in its heyday, dependency theory promoted a conspicuously slim corpus of quantitative analysis. Though many of its propositions seemed amenable to statistical scrutiny through use of cross-national aggregate data, rigorous tests were few and far between. Robert Kaufman and his associates subjected a number of hypotheses to statistical tests, mainly through bivariate correlations,[36] and Kenneth Bollen used multiple regression to examine the political corollaries of peripheral and semiperipheral status in the world system.[37] In general, however, the dependency movement produced precious little empirical investigation.[38]

Throughout the 1980s, quantitative approaches fell into substantial disfavor. This rejection probably stemmed from a variety of reasons, from normative distaste for statistical neopositivism to intellectual disdain for its allegedly meager results. In some circles, quantification also came to be identified—incorrectly, in my view—with theoretical tenets of the then-discredited modernization school. And among *dependentistas*, conceptual debates drew attention to abstract and doctrinal issues, instead of primary research. After a promising start in the 1960s and 1970s, quantification was suddenly out of favor.

Technological innovation and political liberalization began to alter this picture during the 1980s, as research on public opinion began making giant strides. In Mexico, for instance, authentic public opinion polls first appeared in connection with the election of 1988. Since then, activity has flourished, as Miguel Basáñez shows in Chapter 10, and intense debates between progovernment *oficialista* cadres and independent (or opposition) groups have added to popular interest. In Argentina, too, the development of public opinion research has been closely related to the process of democratization. During the 1980s, public opinion research came to be widely used for candidate selection and campaign strategizing, and accuracy in predicting election results proved essential for gaining credibility; exit polls also established checks on official tabulation of election results. In her contribution to this volume,

Elena Bashkirova finds similar links between public opinion research and democratization in Russia and Eastern Europe; but as Catherine M. Conaghan argues in the case of Peru, polling results can also serve to stifle and "domesticate" the expressions of public opinion.

Many surveys were designed for short-term and practical applications, but they have begun to yield high-quality social science. The late Edgardo Catterberg carried out an outstanding study of continuity and change among political attitudes in Argentina during the 1980s.[39] And Frederick C. Turner, a longtime expert on public opinion research, has compiled a major collection of essays on the social determinants of political beliefs.[40]

In the future, quantitative approaches can make significant contributions to research on the newly evolving agenda for the region. Studies of political elites can shed much light on questions about turnover and continuity during periods of democratic transition. To what extent have new groups come to replace authoritarian cadres? On what bureaucratic levels? Do "democratic" leaders come from the same social background as their authoritarian predecessors? Such questions are of vital importance throughout Eastern Europe. They are critically pertinent to Latin America as well.

Legislative behavior also merits rigorous analysis. Disregard for this subject may have stemmed from the perception that legislatures were never genuinely important in Latin America, especially (and obviously) during periods of authoritarian rule. But that is not the case today. In democratizing countries, legislatures have assumed substantial roles, and executive-congressional relations pose questions of major political importance. Moreover, contemporary debates about the relative merits of presidentialism and parliamentarism—most evident in Argentina, Chile, and Brazil—entail conflicting visions of legislative performance. Implicitly or explicitly, propresidentialists minimize the capacities of congressional bodies; proparliamentarists tend to exaggerate them. Responsible advocacy of either position requires a clear and rigorous understanding of the determinants of legislative behavior in contemporary Latin America.

Elections offer additional subjects for study. If and as processes of democratization continue, there is urgent need for original research on a broad variety of themes: The debilitation of party systems, the impacts of electoral engineering, the determinants of electoral behavior, and the significance of voter apathy and abstentionism. Many of these topics can be analyzed through the use of quantitative methodology, and results of these analyses can be interpreted within cross-regional comparative frameworks. Moreover, elections can offer useful opportunities for the examination of political behavior beyond the act of voting itself—in such areas as political culture, elite-mass relations, and political learning.

Yet there has been remarkably little solid research on electoral behavior in the 1980s and 1990s. For all its imperfections, ecological analysis of aggregate data could greatly enhance understanding of the interaction of social and political structures. The resulting emphasis on sociopolitical context, rather than individual attitudes, illustrates an important connection between electoral studies and public opinion research. When they use political polls, researchers should make sharp and consistent distinctions between the study of *beliefs* and *behavior*. Voters may think one way but vote otherwise because of fear or other factors.

Similarly, there is much to be done in the field of survey research. It would be extremely useful to monitor public opinion along the lines of the well-established "EuroBarometer" project, to place Latin America within appropriate comparative context, and—as Frederick C. Turner displays in his chapter—to redefine the entire concept of political culture. Secondary analysis of existing survey material also provides considerable opportunity to examine the social basis and attitudinal correlates of political belief and to examine patterns of change over time. This is a wide-open field.

Methodological Approaches: Comparative Analysis

Comparative analysis of Latin America is most conspicuous by its scarcity. Scholars have tended to focus their investigative energies on the region itself, on selected subregions, or, most commonly, on one country at a time. In part, this reflects genuine respect for the complexity of national experience, as well as the need to gain command of substantial bibliographies. Yet it also reveals a widespread belief that every country is somehow "unique," that it stands apart, and that it defies comparison with other nations. (There is more than a little irony here, since the assertion of "uniqueness" itself represents a comparative judgment.) Whatever the reason, regional specialists, on the whole, have displayed substantial aversion to the comparative enterprise.

Of course, there have been some intraregional applications of comparative analysis, matching countries of the region against each other. A principal advantage of this approach is that it provides an opportunity to "hold constant" some variables and study patterns of covariation for the relatively small number of variables under examination. In keeping with the "most-similar-systems" method of comparative analysis, in other words, it is possible to control for experiences that countries of the region (or subregion) have in common—such as colonization, ethnic composition, economic structure, links with the United States—and to focus attention on relationships between variables that display substantial variance among the countries under study.

Along these lines, Amparo Menéndez-Carrión and Fernando Busta-mante argue in Chapter 3 that controlled, intraregional comparisons are especially suited to Latin American studies. A persistent feature of social science research on Latin America, in both the "modernization" and *dependencia* traditions, has been the tendency to concentrate on major countries—especially on Argentina and Brazil—and to apply resultant theoretical frameworks to the region as a whole. Now that these concep-tualizations have lost currency, there is increasing recognition of com-plexity and heterogeneity throughout the continent. This should, in turn, encourage comparative analyses on smaller nations as well.

Though few in number, there have been some excellent examples of intraregional comparison. Years ago, Carl Solberg wrote a monograph on ideological responses to immigration in Argentina and Chile.[41] More recently, fellow historian Charles Bergquist produced a remarkable study of labor organization and labor mobilization during the export boom of the late nineteenth and early twentieth centuries.[42] And the most ambi-tious, sweeping, and compelling demonstration of this method has come from Ruth Berins Collier and David Collier, who have offered a rich and provocative study of the way that labor movements have shaped political regimes in countries of Latin America.[43] On a much more modest level, Thomas Skidmore and I have attempted to draw explicit connections between class structures, social coalitions, and political outcomes in selected nations of the region.[44] And in an intriguing *tour de force*, Timothy Wickham-Crowley has applied principles of Boolean algebra (as recom-mended by Charles Ragin) to identify and analyze conditions responsible for the relative success of revolutionary movements from the 1950s to the 1990s.[45] Clearly, intraregional comparisons have a great deal to offer the field.

Even more scarce have been cross-regional comparisons—that is, comparisons between phenomena in Latin America and in other parts of the world. Such studies usually take one of two forms. One option is to devise a "paired comparison" between specific countries (or other units) that have similar values on specific variables—controlling, in effect, for these variables—in order to explore covariance between other variables. For example, it might be useful to investigate the evolution of party systems (the dependent variable) through a paired comparison of Turkey and Mexico (thus controlling for level of development, revolutionary experience, and formation of a one-party system) in order to explain dif-ferences in outcome (Turkey evolving to a multi-party system, Mexico remaining as a dominant-party system). Once again, this would consti-tute a version of the MSS approach.

An alternative would be to employ a "most-different-systems" ap-proach, matching countries with differing values on a series of variables, but similar values on one or two variables—the independent variable and/or the dependent variable. The purpose here is to discern if similar readings on the independent variable produce similar effects in widely differing contexts—in other words, where the units of analysis display differing values on other pertinent variables. This method can be employed in open-ended fashion, without a priori determination of the likely outcome for the dependent variable, or in closed-ended fashion, to examine the durability of a hypothesized relationship under differing conditions.[46]

Implicitly, if not explicitly, Latin Americanists have tended to rely on MSS designs for cross-regional comparisons. Historians have developed a substantial literature on the comparative study of slavery and race relations, most commonly focusing on the national experiences of the United States and Brazil—or, with greater control of exogenous variables, on regional experiences with common economic structures.[47] For example, the economic development of Argentina has prompted insightful comparisons with that of Australia[48] and, more recently, with Canada.[49] In my effort to achieve both "individualizing" and "variation-funding" comparisons, I have also placed my findings about Mexico's political elites within frameworks that included democratic and totalitarian as well as authoritarian types of regimes.[50]

What Tilly termed "encompassing" comparisons are particularly scarce. The "world-system" approach of Immanuel Wallerstein has offered a bold and ambitious scheme for the interpretation of economic developments in the colonial era.[51] And within the Latin American field, the path-breaking work of Fernando Henrique Cardoso and Enzo Faletto—still the most persuasive exposition of the *dependencia* school—employs at least two types of comparison: The "encompassing" approach, situating Latin America within the global structure of capitalist development, and the "variation-finding" approach, drawing distinctions between the socioeconomic structures of different zones and units of production within this overall framework.[52]

Cross-regional studies are, nonetheless, rare. The study of economic development strategies in Asia and Latin America, for instance, has received little systematic attention, despite its timeliness and topicality. Gary Gereffi and the late Donald Wyman brought out a collection of essays on this theme.[53] Articles concerning cross-regional studies have appeared from time to time.[54] And Stephan Haggard, an international political economist, produced an intriguing comparison between East Asian newly industrializing countries (NICs) and Mexico and Brazil.[55]

Comparisons with Europe are few and far between. Students of democratization have explored similarities and differences among transitions in Latin America and countries of southern Europe, especially Greece, Spain, and Portugal.[56] José Luis Rodríguez and Brian H. Smith, among others, have written a provocative essay on labor movements in Argentina, Italy, and Spain.[57] More recently, an international team of scholars has produced a comparative analysis of regional economic integration in the Western Hemisphere (North American Free Trade Agreement [NAFTA]; Mercado Común del Sur [MERCOSUR, or Common Market of the South]; and the Enterprise for the Americas Initiative) and in Europe.[58]

In perhaps the most powerful example of this genre, Dietrich Rueschemeyer, Evelyne Huber Stephens, and John D. Stephens have offered a provocative and systematic qualitative comparison of relationships between economic and political change in advanced capitalist countries (especially those in Europe) and Latin America, Central America, and the Caribbean. Having focused on the intersection of social class, the state, and transnational structures, they maintained that the working class—not the middle class, as is commonly argued—has constituted "the most consistently pro-democratic force." A major reason for the vacillating and incomplete nature of democracy in Latin America, therefore, has been the relatively weak position of the working class. Over time, the middle classes have managed to dominate the installation of a democratic form that has been restricted in character; only the active participation of the working class can lead to full democracy.[59]

In cross-regional analysis, as in other areas, there remains much to do. For example, continuing debates over the relative merits of parliamentarism and presidentialism rest upon implicit deductions from comparative analysis. Arguing that Western Europe provides a model for emulation, some analysts propose the adoption of a parliamentary form of government on the grounds that it would (1) facilitate executive succession, (2) impose restraints on presidential action, and (3) through proportional representation, encourage the formation of a loyal opposition instead of a disloyal one. Insisting that the European experience is inapplicable to Latin America, others argue that (1) strong executives provide the key to political stability, (2) legislative empowerment would create political stalemates, and (3) the political culture of Latin America does not promote the kind of tolerant, participatory citizenship that is required for parliamentary rule. Both cases rest upon the comparative assessment of hypotheses. Rigorous analysis could make an important contribution to resolution of this crucial debate.

There is considerable opportunity for fruitful comparison of political transitions in Latin America and Eastern Europe.[60] Subjects for comparison include the form and process of regime transition, the relations between economic and political change, and the uncertainty of change.

Not all transitions in these two regions will necessarily lead to full-fledged democracy. Might there emerge a brand of authoritarian populism akin to *peronismo* in Ukraine or other areas? And what is the connection between these transformations and trends in the global arena?

Access to data in Russia and Eastern Europe now makes it possible to provide rigorous tests for hypotheses derived from the Western European experience, as William Zimmerman has shown.[61] By U.S. and European standards, for example, levels of political participation in Lithuania are extraordinarily high. In general, in Russia, there tends to be a strong relationship between age and education and degree of preference for democracy. The most important criterion for popular evaluation of political rule, however, is neither representativeness nor participation; it is governmental performance. As these regimes face challenges of consolidation, Zimmerman suggests, additional questions will come forth for comparative analysis: the difference (if any) between postauthoritarianism and posttotalitarianism, the relative importance of internal evolution and international influence, and, finally, the role of external national actors (Slovenians in Cleveland, Cubans in Miami). Possibilities for research thus abound. □

RESOURCES ASSESSED:
THE STATE OF THE FIELD

Are Latin Americanists prepared to meet the challenges posed by the newly evolving agenda? Prospects are uncertain. There exists a serious shortage of institutional and human resources.

For a variety of reasons, including economic downturn and Reaganesque ideology, the United States has sharply reduced its own commitment to the development of social sciences. In constant dollars, U.S. federal expenditures for university-based research on foreign affairs shrank by nearly 60 percent from the late 1960s to the 1980s; funding for the Fulbright program fell by more than 50 percent. The number of government-funded Title VI fellowships for the study of Latin America dropped from an average of about 170 per year in 1960s to fifty-four in 1975, rebuilding by 1981 to eighty-one—less than half of the number available in the late 1960s. The 1980s also saw the termination of the Henry L. and Grace Doherty Charitable Foundation fellowship program for dissertation research on Latin America. By mid-decade there were, according to one reliable estimate, a maximum of 110 graduate fellowships per year for dissertation research on Latin America.[62]

Funding dried up not only for the U.S. academic community but also for the field as a whole. The Rockefeller Foundation closed down its area program on Latin America. The Ford Foundation, by far the largest and most consistent source of support for the field, slashed its spending on Latin America from about $27 million in the late 1960s to $15 million in 1970 to approximately $4 million per year in the 1980s. (Latin America accounted for 23 percent of Ford's international budget in 1970 and only 10 percent in 1981.) The American Council of Learned Societies and the Joint Committee on Latin American Studies of the Social Science Research Council (ACLS/SSRC), one of the most prestigious and prominent sources of support for collaborative research, found its budget reduced in current dollars from approximately $1 million per year in the mid-1970s to about $400,000 in the 1980s—and to just over $300,000 in 1989–1990.[63] By 1990 the total amount of funds for publicly available social science research in Latin America was significantly less than it was in the mid-1970s, both in real and nominal dollar terms.

These precipitous declines in support for traditional academic research were partially offset by an increase in resources for a different kind of work—proprietary research for private, usually profit-seeking, institutions. There was particular emphasis on marketing research and "risk analysis" for potential investors. The amount of support for proprietary research is difficult to measure, but it had several noticeable effects: First, it concentrated attention on specific segments of the social sciences (especially economics and marketing research); second, it focused on short-term analysis rather than on long-term investigation; and third, it failed to contribute to the public store of knowledge about the region.[64]

Within Latin America, the economic crisis of the 1980s had a catastrophic impact on social science research and on the training of young scholars. José Joaquín Brunner has painted a somber picture of this devastation: "Symptoms are various and evident: decline in salaries for university personnel in almost every country (not only the social sciences); reductions in scholarships for study abroad; cutbacks in local support for research; difficulties in financing international seminars; elimination of sabbatical leaves and other benefits and privileges; termination or drastic reduction in the creation of new institutions and programs in the social sciences; increasing difficultly in gaining access to international sources of research support, etc."[65] Reflecting these difficulties, the number of Latin American students in U.S. universities declined from nearly 57,000 in 1982 to fewer than 44,000 by 1986–1987.[66]

In Mexico, expenditures on higher education slipped from 0.79 percent of gross domestic product (GDP) in 1980–1981 to 0.54 percent in 1984 and continued to decline throughout the 1980s (that is, higher education received a declining proportion of a declining economy).[67] In 1980 and 1981 the nation's major source of research support, the Consejo

Nacional para Ciencias y Tecnología (the National Council on Science and Technology, CONACYT), financed 4,600 and 4,300 students, respectively. In 1982, however, as the debt crisis struck, the number plunged to 1,800. Between 1981 and 1982 the total number of scholarships for study within Mexico dropped from 8,226 to 2,309.

A similar pattern emerged in Chile, although the rhythm there tended to reflect political rather than economic conditions. Overall spending on education dropped sharply after the military coup of 1973, then recovered in the early 1980s—but with a marked de-emphasis on higher education. In 1982 the Chilean funding agency, Fondo Nacional de Ciencias y Tecnología (the National Fund for Science and Technology, FONDECYT), approved only four projects in the social sciences; over the following four years FONDECYT supported just twenty-four projects in the social sciences, which received merely 2.5 percent of total agency spending. Sites for independent study moved to private research and training centers, such as the Centro de Investigación y Estudios para la Planificación (the Center for Planning Research and Study, CIEPLAN), though these could scarcely compensate for drastic cutbacks in government funding.[68]

Democratization did not lead to much improvement. As observed by Marcia Rivera, executive director of the Consejo Latinoamericano de Ciencias Sociales (CLACSO), the return to elected civilian government has brought "a mixed bag of results" for the social sciences. Although the initial phases of democratization inspired great expectations, hopes are now diminishing. Private foundations in the United States and Europe apparently assumed that democratization would stimulate local support for social science, so they continued to scale back their activities throughout Latin America—concentrating instead on either domestic issues or Eastern Europe. The result has been clear and negative. Under severe financial constraints, newly democratic governments are unable to provide resources for training or research. Even though private universities have stepped in to fill part of this void, it remains extremely difficult for young scholars to develop professional careers. Academic infrastructure has, in the meantime, disintegrated. (The University of Buenos Aires is thirty times larger than Princeton University, for instance, but Princeton purchases thirty times as many books!)[69]

In some instances, economic pressure has led to distortions in the social science agenda, obliging researchers to accept consultancies with government agencies or to engage in "action-oriented" projects. Intense competition for scarce resources has discouraged collaborative work. Social scientists have often become *empresarios* instead of researchers. And there is a premium on journalism and campaign advising, usually on the basis of short-run polls, instead of the long-term focus that is essential to scholarly research.[70]

Argentina offers an illuminating case. To some extent, the development of professional political science was *part* of the political transition toward democracy. During and after 1983, political scientists came to play key roles in institutional development, helping to reorganize the universities, stimulating research efforts, training public officials, and shaping national debates through articles in major newspapers. Political science became not only "fashionable," as Edgardo Catterberg recalled, but also influential. And yet, just one decade later, public institutions and research centers throughout Argentina are suffering from protracted financial difficulties. There is little support for rigorous social science. The most prominent books on political issues in Argentina come from journalists. There continues to be a pressing need for serious and systematic research.

Brazil, for its part, reveals a paradoxical reality: According to Nelson do Valle Silva, academic research flourished under authoritarian rule but has languished under democratic government. During the economic expansion of the 1970s, Brazil's military regime supplied considerable financial support for social science. Continual elections provided ample opportunities for empirical analysis. Surveys on employment, social mobility, household consumption, and fertility generated rich data for the study of stratification. The return to democracy has been accompanied by economic crisis, however, so there has been a concomitant decline in governmental support.

For Latin America as a whole, there is an urgent need for institution-building. Marcia Rivera has stressed the importance of establishing national data banks on election results, for instance, and Frederick Turner has called for the creation of regional (or subregional) data banks on public opinion research. Such institutions could promote collaboration among colleagues from different countries, foster cross-national and cross-regional research projects, and, equally important, uphold appropriate standards for research. And as Amparo Menéndez-Carrión and Fernando Bustamante emphasize, it is essential to develop social science training programs for students and junior scholars, which could become a central mission for such agencies.

By contrast, the principal challenge for social science research in the United States stems not so much from a shortfall of institutional resources (though universities are now subject to intense pressure for budget reductions) but from deep-seated and long-standing barriers between Latin American "area studies" and mainstream social science disciplines. As John Coatsworth has described it:

> For half a century, the relationship between foreign area studies and the social science disciplines has generated controversy in the United States.

The charge is frequently made that U.S. area specialists do not contribute in proportion to their numbers to the theoretical and methodological development of the social science disciplines. Area studies journals contain many articles, and university presses publish innumerable monographs, that address issues of only passing interest to non-area specialists. Area studies scholars often seem obsessed with empirical research, more concerned with describing the exotic cultures they encounter than in attacking more general issues. Interdisciplinary area studies work is occasionally condemned as an excuse for mediocre social science. The better social scientists from the third world prefer to interact with the outstanding figures in their disciplines, rather than the U.S. area specialists with whom they are constantly thrown in contact. In sum, area studies are seen as vaguely humanist, primarily descriptive, and essentially boring. Area studies has an "image problem."[71]

One reflection of this gap appears in the use of divergent outlets for publication of research, which presents additional obstacles to communication between area studies and mainstream disciplines.[72]

Intellectual trends have reinforced these separatist tendencies. In particular, the adaptation of "rational choice" models has in recent years raised profound questions about the role of area studies. As described by Philippe Schmitter, this approach poses a central challenge for comparativists in general:

> The current fashion for rational choice and game theoretic explanations raises the specter of a possible return to universalistic premises. ... If completely successful, the approach would not only convert entire departments of political science into dependencies of orthodox liberal economics, but it would also wipe out the accumulated stock of comparativists' assumptions about the significance of cultural, institutional and obligational factors. History would be reduced to the passage of time and the iteration of exchanges; institutions would be contingent upon continuous calculation; preferences would be given rather than socially constructed; maximizing self-interest would be the only admissible norm.[73]

Though somewhat apocalyptic, Schmitter's vision captures a profound concern—and highlights a schism that afflicts many academic departments within the United States.

Instead of denouncing rational choice, however, area specialists and comparative experts should come to grips with it. Barbara Geddes makes a compelling case to this effect in Chapter 4.[74] More generally, Latin Americanists have not sufficiently engaged the theoretical and methodological discourse of the mainstream disciplines. Both sides have suffered as a result. Fulfillment of the new research agenda will require a closure of this gap between disciplines. □

MERGING SUBSTANCE AND METHODS

Contrary to popular myth, scholarship reflects society. Social science, in particular, attempts to explore the background, evolution, and complexity of contemporary issues. It responds to changes in real-world environments as well as to intellectual developments within disciplines, and research agendas undergo continuous alteration and adjustment. Virtually all studies seek to improve conceptual understanding of key issues in the public domain; many result in explicit policy prescriptions. Either way, social science exerts a significant impact on the pace, direction, and content of social change. Within this context of reciprocal causalities, therefore, a general rule holds: The greater the change in the society, the more sweeping the change in social science.

Accordingly, the scope and pace of transformation in Latin America have presented social scientists with a bold and expansive agenda for research. Meeting this challenge will require additional resources and new investigations.

In practice, of course, not every topic will lend itself to quantitative or comparative analysis. Limitations of data, time, and funding will make it unreasonable (if not impossible) to engage in statistical measurement or cross-regional comparison. More essential than execution, however, is the task of conceptualization. It is important to *think* in systematic social science terms, even in cases in which data and resources might be unavailable. Ultimately, it is imperative to construct research designs that are both imaginative and rigorous. At least on a conceptual level, this usually requires reference to questions of comparison and measurement.

Beyond this injunction, the new social science agenda will also entail significant changes in habits, assumptions, and outlooks by Latin Americanists. First, regional experts will have to discard the untested notion that Latin America is somehow "unique," unlike any other part of the world. This mystique often applies to individual nations as well—as in the well-known slogan, *como México no hay dos.* By definition, cross-regional comparative study jettisons this comfortable assumption and reformulates it as a proposition for empirical verification (or falsification). The uniqueness of a country or region thus becomes a subject for investigation, rather than an automatic premise.

Indeed, experts on Latin America, and comparativists in general, may have to reexamine the fundamental significance of geographic and regional boundaries. The concept of "Latin America" is, in fact, a cultural construct, not a timeless verity (more to the point, the term was invented by French imperialists in the late nineteenth century). There is equally good reason to reconsider the idea of the "Third World," which acquired specific ideological connotations during the course of the now-defunct

Cold War. As a result, Latin Americanists should give serious thought to the logical foundation for existing definitions and boundaries of their field.

Second, it will be necessary to overcome long-standing resistance to the use of statistical methodology. There is no question that quantitative approaches fell into much disfavor (or at least disuse) during the 1980s. Nor is there any question that quantitative methods can lead to abuse, obfuscation, and fallacies of misplaced concreteness. Contributors to this volume freely concede that mindless number-crunching serves no redeeming social purpose. At the same time, we contend that thoughtful application of statistical techniques can make a substantial contribution to the improvement of social science research on Latin America.

Finally, and perhaps most important, is a question of intellectual style. The surge and decline of theoretical and methodological orthodoxies has subjected understanding of Latin America to a pattern of cycles rather than to a pattern of cumulative growth. Regional analysts would do well instead to build upon previous contributions, rather than to denounce and discard competing theories à outrance. This is not a call for mindless eclecticism; it is an appeal for rigorous attention to empirical reality and to the analytical (rather than ideological) properties of alternative frameworks.

Especially in view of the contemporary complexity of Latin America, it now seems appropriate to construct theories and models gradually— block by block, from the bottom up, rather than in top-down fashion. The new agenda for social science research on Latin America not only offers an opportunity to explore new problems and test new methodologies, it also provides a chance to rebuild theory on solid empirical foundations. □

NOTES

I wish to thank David Collier, Evelyne Huber, and Carlos Waisman for comments and suggestions.

1. For additional commentary, see Julio Cotler, "Algunas reflexiones sobre el futuro de las ciencias sociales en América Latina," *Papers on Latin America*, no. 9 (New York: Institute of Latin American and Iberian Studies, Columbia University, 1989), and Ronald Chilcote, "Tensions in the Latin American Experience: Fundamental Themes in the Formulation of a Research Agenda for the 1990s," *Latin American Perspectives* 65, no. 17 (Spring 1990): 122–128.

2. Arend Lijphart, "Comparative Politics and the Comparative Method," *American Political Science Review* (1971) 65, no. 3: 682–693. See also Arend Lijphart, "The Comparable Cases Strategy in Comparative Research," *Comparative Political Studies* 8 (1975): 158–177.

3. Barrington Moore, *Social Origins of Dictatorship and Democracy: Lord and Peasant in the Making of the Modern World* (Boston: Beacon Press, 1966).

4. Charles C. Ragin, *The Comparative Method: Moving Beyond Qualitative and Quantitative Strategies* (Berkeley: University of California Press, 1987).

5. Charles Tilly, *Big Structures, Large Processes, Huge Comparisons* (New York: Russell Sage Foundation, 1984), with quotes from pp. 80–86 and 145.

6. See also Ragin, *The Comparative Method*, pp. 36–42.

7. Adam Przeworski and Henry Teune, *The Logic of Comparative Social Inquiry* (New York: John Wiley & Sons, 1970) esp. pp. 31–46. As these authors emphasize, MDS designs have the added advantage of employing individual or other subsystem data in order to test for the presence of system effects, whereas MSS designs tend to assume the existence of such effects.

8. Carlos Waisman, "Prospects for Interregional Comparisons: Political Processes in the Southern Cone and Eastern Europe" (paper prepared for the conference "Latin America in Comparative Perspective: Issues and Methods," Quito, Ecuador, July 29–31, 1993).

9. Tilly, *Big Structures*, pp. 116–117.

10. See Peter H. Smith, ed., *History, Statistics, and Epistemology*, special issues of *Historical Methods Newsletter* 17, 4–5 (Fall 1984 and Winter 1985), especially Smith, "Time as a Historical Construct."

11. David A. Smith and Douglas R. White, "Structure and Dynamics of the Global Economy: Network Analysis of International Trade, 1965–1980," *Social Forces* 70, no. 4 (June 1992): 857–893; and David A. Smith, "Overurbanization Reconceptualized: A Political Economy of the World-System Approach," *Urban Affairs Quarterly* 23, no. 2 (December 1987): 270–294.

12. A "global" research design would either (1) take all available cases from a universe, in order to enable an empirical search for networks among them, or (2) examine preselected cases on the basis of their known position in a given network. Both MDS and MSS designs are also compatible with encompassing comparisons.

13. Tilly, *Big Structures*, and Theda Skocpol, ed., *Vision and Method in Historical Sociology* (Cambridge: Cambridge University Press, 1984).

14. Guillermo O'Donnell, *Modernization and Bureaucratic-Authoritarianism: Studies in South American Politics* (Berkeley: Institute of International Studies, University of California, 1973).

15. Fernando Henrique Cardoso, "The Consumption of Dependency Theory in the United States," *Latin American Research Review* 12, no. 3 (1977): 7–24.

16. See Barbara Stallings, "International Influence on Economic Policy: Debt, Stabilization, and Structural Reform," in Stephan R. Haggard and Robert Kaufman, eds., *The Politics of Economic Adjustment* (Princeton: Princeton University Press, 1992), pp. 41–88, esp. pp. 44–48.

17. See Peter H. Smith and Peter Zung, "The Third World after the Cold War: A Conference Report," *CILAS Working Papers*, no. 1 (La Jolla: Center for Iberian and Latin American Studies [CILAS], University of California, San Diego, May 1992), p. 13.

18. For a much less sympathetic treatment of this subject, see Robert Packenham, *The Dependency Movement: Scholarship and Politics in Development Studies* (Cambridge: Harvard University Press, 1992).

19. See Peter H. Smith, "Crisis and Democracy in Latin America," *World Politics* 43, no. 4 (July 1991): 608–634.

20. See Claudia Leite and Peter H. Smith, "Social Science Research on Latin America: A Conference Report," *CILAS Working Papers*, no. 2 (La Jolla: Center for Iberian and Latin American Studies, University of California, San Diego, 1992), p. 4.

21. Samuel P. Huntington, *The Third Wave: Democratization in the Late Twentieth Century* (Norman: University of Oklahoma Press, 1991), pp. 59–72.

22. Mitchell Seligson, "Democratization in Latin America: The Current Cycle," in James M. Malloy and Mitchell A. Seligson, eds., *Authoritarians and Democrats: Regime Transition in Latin America* (Pittsburgh: University of Pittsburgh Press, 1987), pp. 7–9.

23. James W. Wilkie, *The Mexican Revolution: Federal Expenditure and Social Change Since 1910* (Berkeley: University of California Press, 1967); see also Thomas E. Skidmore and Peter H. Smith, "Notes on Quantitative History: Federal Expenditure and Social Change in Mexico since 1910," *Latin American Research Review* 7, no. 1 (Spring 1970): 71–85.

24. Philippe C. Schmitter, "New Strategies for the Comparative Analysis of Latin American Politics," *Latin American Research Review* 4, no. 2 (Summer 1969): 83–110.

25. Peter H. Smith, *Labyrinths of Power: Political Recruitment in Twentieth-Century Mexico* (Princeton: Princeton University Press, 1979).

26. See Roderic A. Camp, *Education and Recruitment in Twentieth Century Mexico* (Tucson: University of Arizona Press, 1980), *Entrepreneurs and Politics in Twentieth Century Mexico* (New York: Oxford University Press, 1989), and *Generals in the Palacio: The Military in Modern Mexico* (New York: Oxford University Press, 1992).

27. Peter McDonough, *Power and Ideology in Brazil* (Princeton: Princeton University Press, 1981).

28. Barry Ames, *Political Survival: Politicians and Public Policy in Latin America* (Berkeley: University of California Press, 1987).

29. Peter H. Smith, *Argentina and the Failure of Democracy: Conflict Among Political Elites, 1905–1955* (Madison: University of Wisconsin Press, 1974).

30. Wanderley Guilherme dos Santos, "The Calculus of Conflict: Impasse in Brazilian Politics and the Crisis of 1964" (Ph.D. diss., Stanford University, 1979).

31. Manuel Mora y Araujo and Ignacio Llorente, eds., *El voto peronista: Ensayos de sociología electoral Argentina* (Buenos Aires: Editorial Sudamericana, 1980).

32. Bolívar Lamounier, *Cem anos de eleiçoes presidenciais* (São Paulo: Instituto de Estudos Economicos, Sociais e Politicos de São Paulo, 1990); *Eleiçoes 1985: O voto em São Paulo* (São Paulo: IDESP, 1986); *Voto de desconfiança: Eleiçoes e mudança política no Brasil* (Petrópolis: Vazes, 1980); and Glaucio Ary Dillon Soares and Nelson do Valle Silva, "Urbanization, Race, and Class in Brazilian Politics," *Latin American Research Review* 22, no. 2 (1987): 155–176.

33. Amparo Menéndez-Carrión, *La conquista del voto: De Velasco a Roldós* (Quito: Facultad Latinoamericana de Ciencias Sociales, 1986).

34. Judith Gentleman, ed., *Mexican Politics in Transition* (Boulder: Westview Press, 1987), esp. Joseph L. Klesner, "Changing Patterns of Electoral Participation and Official Party Support in Mexico," pp. 95–152; and Edgar W. Butler and Jorge

Bustamante, eds., *Sucesión Presidencial: The 1988 Mexican Presidential Election* (Boulder: Westview Press, 1991).

35. Manuel Mora y Araujo and Peter H. Smith, "Peronism and Economic Development: The 1973 Elections," in Frederick C. Turner and José Miguens, eds., *Juan Perón and the Reshaping of Argentina* (Pittsburgh: University of Pittsburgh Press, 1983), pp. 171–188.

36. Robert Kaufman, Daniel Geller, and Harry Chernofsky, "A Preliminary Test of the Theory of Dependency," *Comparative Politics* 7, no. 3 (1975): 303–330.

37. Kenneth Bollen, "World System Position, Dependency, and Democracy: The Cross-National Evidence," *American Sociological Review* 48 (August 1983): 468–479.

38. Steven Jackson, Bruce Russett, Duncan Snidal, and David Sylvan, "An Assessment of Empirical Research on *Dependencia*," *Latin American Research Review* 14, no. 3 (1979): 7–28.

39. Edgardo Catterberg, *Los argentinos frente a la política: Cultura política y opinión pública en la transición Argentina a la democracia* (Buenos Aires: Planeta, 1989).

40. Frederick C. Turner, ed., *Social Mobility and Political Attitudes: Comparative Perspectives* (New Brunswick: Transaction Press, 1992).

41. Carl Solberg, *Immigration and Nationalism: Argentina and Chile, 1890–1914* (Austin: University of Texas Press, 1970).

42. Charles Bergquist, *Labor in Latin America: Comparative Essays on Chile, Argentina, Venezuela, and Colombia* (Stanford: Stanford University Press, 1986).

43. Ruth Berins Collier and David Collier, *Shaping the Political Arena: Critical Junctures, the Labor Movement, and Regime Dynamics in Latin America* (Princeton: Princeton University Press, 1991).

44. Thomas E. Skidmore and Peter H. Smith, *Modern Latin America*, 3d ed., rev. (New York: Oxford University Press, 1992), esp. pp. 382–394.

45. Timothy P. Wickham-Crowley, *Guerrillas and Revolution in Latin America: A Comparative Study of Insurgents and Regimes Since 1956* (Princeton: Princeton University Press, 1992), esp. pp. 302–326.

46. See Przeworski and Teune, *Logic of Comparative Social Inquiry.*

47. Rebecca Scott, for example, is now working on a comparison of slavery and liberation in northeast Brazil, Cuba, and Louisiana—all areas that concentrated on sugar production. See also Magnus Morner, Julia Fawaz de Vinuela, and John D. French, "Comparative Approaches to Latin American History," *Latin American Research Review* 17, no. 3 (1982): 55–89.

48. John Fogarty, Ezequiel Gallo, Héctor Dieguez, *Argentina y Australia* (Buenos Aires: Instituto Torcuato di Tella, 1979).

49. Carl E. Solberg, *The Prairies and the Pampas: Agrarian Policy in Canada and Argentina, 1880–1930* (Stanford: Stanford University Press, 1987).

50. Smith, *Labyrinths of Power*, pp. 20, 130–132, 176–183.

51. Immanuel Wallerstein, *The Modern World-System: Capitalist Agriculture and the Origins of the European World-Economy in the Sixteenth Century* (New York: Academic Press, 1974).

52. Fernando Henrique Cardoso and Enzo Faletto, *Dependency and Development in Latin America*, trans. Marjory Mattingly Urquidi (Berkeley: University of California Press, 1979).

53. Gary Gereffi and Donald L. Wyman, eds., *Manufacturing Miracles: Paths of Industrialization in Latin America and East Asia* (Princeton: Princeton University Press, 1990).

54. See Laurence Whitehead, "Tigers in Latin America?" *Annals AAPSS* 505 (September 1989): 142–151.

55. Stephan Haggard, *Pathways from the Periphery: The Politics of Growth in the Newly Industrializing Countries* (Ithaca: Cornell University Press, 1990).

56. Guillermo O'Donnell, Philippe C. Schmitter, and Laurence Whitehead, eds., *Transitions from Authoritarian Rule*, 4 vols. (Baltimore: Johns Hopkins University Press, 1986).

57. José Luis Rodríguez and Brian H. Smith, "Comparative Working-Class Political Behavior: Chile, France, and Italy," *American Behavioral Scientist* 18, no. 3 (September–October, 1974).

58. Peter H. Smith, ed., *The Challenge of Integration: Europe and the Americas* (Miami: North-South Center, 1993).

59. Dietrich Rueschemeyer, Evelyne Huber Stephens, and John D. Stephens, *Capitalism Development and Democracy* (Chicago: University of Chicago Press, 1992), with quote from p. 8.

60. See Arend Lijphart and Carlos Waisman, eds., *Institutional Design in New Democracies* (Boulder: Westview Press, forthcoming in this series).

61. Leite and Smith, "Social Science Research," pp. 22–23.

62. Paul W. Drake, "From Retrogression to Resurgence: International Scholarly Relations with Latin America in U.S. Universities, 1970s–1980s" (paper prepared for SSRC/CLACSO conference "International Scholarly Relations in the Social Sciences," Montevideo, Uruguay, August 15–17, 1989), esp. 37.

63. John H. Coatsworth, "International Collaboration in the Social Sciences: The ACLS/SSRC Joint Committee on Latin American Studies" (paper prepared for SSRC/CLACSO conference "International Scholarly Relations in the Social Sciences," Montevideo, Uruguay, August 15–17, 1989), 61.

64. See Louis W. Goodman, "Trends in North American Funding for Social Science Research on Latin America" (paper prepared for SSRC/CLACSO conference on "International Scholarly Relations," August 1989).

65. José Joaquín Brunner, "El financiamiento de las ciencias sociales en América Latina: Puntos de discusión" (paper prepared for CLACSO meeting in Recife, Brazil, November 1987), n.p.

66. Drake, "From Retrogression to Resurgence," pp. 30–32.

67. José Luis Reyna, "La educación superior en México: Tendencias y perspectivas dentro de los marcos institucionales e internacionales existentes." See also John H. Coatsworth, "Student, Academic, and Cultural Exchanges Between Mexico and the United States: A Report with Recommendations" (paper presented to the Bilateral Commission on the Future of United States–Mexican Relations, October 1987).

68. Manuel Antonio Garretón, "La evolución de las ciencias sociales en Chile."

69. Leite and Smith, "Social Science Research," pp. 4–5.

70. Leite and Smith, "Social Science Research," pp. 3–9.

71. Coatsworth, "International Collaboration in the Social Sciences," pp. 9–10.

72. See John D. Martz, "Political Science and Latin American Studies: Patterns and Asymmetries of Research and Publication," *Latin American Research Review* 25, no. 1 (1990): 67–86.

73. Philippe C. Schmitter, "Comparative Politics at the Crossroads," *Estudios/ Working Papers*, no. 27 (Madrid: Instituto Juan March de Estudios e Investigaciones, 1991), pp. 18–19.

74. See also George Tsebelis, *Nested Games: Rational Choice in Comparative Politics* (Berkeley: University of California Press, 1990).

PART ONE

Analytical Strategies

In this section, the authors explore three alternative strategies for the comparative analysis of Latin America. Their purpose is to demonstrate the feasibility of comparative work on Latin America and to illustrate the range of methodologies available.

In the opening chapter, Gary Gereffi offers reflections and recommendations for *cross-regional* comparisons. Using development strategies in Latin America and East Asia as a case in point, Gereffi argues for the use of diverse research methods. One option, he observes, is to compare the design and implementation of development programs by national governments in Asia and Latin America through the use of either most-similar-systems or most-different-systems research designs; a central challenge here is to examine these policies in sufficient detail so as to capture their truly salient features. Another general approach is to move beyond traditional units of analysis, such as the nation-state, and to explore the participation of economic units in what have come to be known as "global commodity chains"—which Gereffi defines as "the links between successive phases of raw material supply, manufacturing, distribution, and retailing that result in a final product available for individual consumption." This entails the use of "encompassing" comparisons and, above all, it underlines the importance of establishing suitable conceptual frameworks. Gereffi concludes the chapter with remarks on the utility of semistructured, in-depth "strategic interviews," as distinct from public opinion surveys.

Amparo Menéndez-Carrión and Fernando Bustamante address prospects for *intraregional* comparisons for the study of Latin American politics. Noting that the "increasing complexity" of political phenomena offers "a compelling rationale for intraregional comparison," they offer incisive critiques of long-standing tendencies to construct models of political transformation on the basis of extrapolation from one or two allegedly major countries; they also contest the whole notion of Latin

31

America as a definable "region." Although Latin American scholars have long resisted comparative approaches, they observe, the time has come for judicious application of comparative frameworks, even in the examination of individual cases—since the comparative approach is essentially "a question of method" rather than data-gathering. In ways similar to Gereffi, Menéndez-Carrión and Bustamante call for analysis of the multiple and reciprocal effects of "globalization." In particular, they identify three central issues that stand in need of comparative research: the meaning of democracy, especially at the level of micropolitics and culture; the question of human rights; and the nature of democratic consolidation.

In the following chapter, Barbara Geddes analyzes the uses and limitations of *rational choice,* an approach that has generated enormous controversy within the field of political science. Advocates sometimes appear to make imperious claims about the discovery of high theoretical truth; detractors often denounce its putative disregard for culture, history, and context. Systematically and thoughtfully, Geddes pierces through rhetorical debates on the subject and presents a cautious argument in favor of its application. The core of the rational choice approach, she says, stems from "the focus on the incentives facing individuals, the ruthless pruning of extraneous complexity, and the use of deductive logic." In the study of U.S. politics, rational choice has shed significant light on the (often counterintuitive) logic of collective action, on dynamics taking place within the "black box" of the state, and on processes of strategic interaction among actors. Carefully applied, the approach can offer comparable insights on Latin America and thus help locate regional phenomena within broad analytical frameworks.

CHAPTER TWO

■

Contending Paradigms for Cross-Regional Comparison: Development Strategies and Commodity Chains in East Asia and Latin America

Gary Gereffi

DEVELOPMENT STUDIES HAVE BEEN at the forefront of comparative analysis in the social sciences. Initially, much of this research was carried out by scholars who were imbued with the tools of the area specialist: facility with the appropriate foreign languages, an in-depth knowledge of local history and customs, and good contacts with indigenous experts and institutions. In some regions, such as Latin America, the commonalities of language and historical background led people quite naturally to think in terms of intraregional comparisons. In East Asia, however, where there are numerous languages and local dialects and where the cultural legacy of societies such as China and Japan spans many centuries, experts rarely strayed from their designated niches defined by individual countries and, within these, by specific historical periods, geographic locales, and economic sectors.

This regional insularity among development scholars seems to be diminishing, as evidenced by the recent spate of cross-regional projects involving Latin America, East Asia, and Europe. The theme of development strategies in East Asia and Latin America has been especially popular, with several volumes published in the past five years.[1] These studies use the logic of comparative analysis to derive meaningful conclusions about countries located in two regions, whose differences, at first glance, may appear to far outweigh their similarities. What does cross-regional research explain? What are the most appropriate comparative methods to use in this situation? How do these studies handle diversity within each region, as well as conspicuous contrasts between regions? Is it possible to make broad regional generalizations about development models? What are the limitations of this type of research? What new challenges lie ahead?

In this chapter I address these queries by focusing on two of my own cross-regional projects, which deal with development strategies and commodity chains. The arguments can be summarized as follows. First, diverse comparative research methods are appropriate, and indeed necessary, to improve the understanding of development strategies in East Asia and Latin America. Different disciplines feature variables that lead to generalizations of varying scope: commonalities across regions, contrasts between regions, and diversity within regions. Each type of generalization is associated with a distinct comparative method of analysis. These multiple approaches provide needed breadth and depth.

Second, studies of development strategies in Latin America and East Asia, though operating at different levels of analysis, nonetheless deal with the same unit: the nation-state. This becomes a problem when one tries to grapple with the multifaceted process of globalization, which has redefined the nature of development in the contemporary world. The most dynamic industries today are organized in production and trade systems that are transnational in scope. Therefore, one needs to find alternative development paradigms that systematically incorporate features of the international system into the analyses. One promising approach conceptualizes the organization of the world economy in terms of commodity chains, which are most simply defined as the links between successive phases of raw material supply, manufacturing, distribution, and retailing that result in a final product available for individual consumption. Instead of taking nation-states as the point of departure, as the development strategies literature does, the commodity chains framework focuses on firms and industries as the basic units of analysis and then asks how the position and mobility of countries within global commodity chains affect their development prospects.

Third, I address an issue, virtually ignored in discussions of comparative methods, that is an intrinsic feature of many of the best-known works on Latin America and East Asia, namely, the use of semistructured, in-depth interviews of political and economic actors in country and industry case studies. Unlike classic techniques of survey research or public opinion polling in which the respondents are selected with an emphasis on scientific sampling, standardized questionnaires, and the representativeness of their answers, most development studies in the

Third World rely on what I call "strategic interviews." This type of interviewing has very different objectives than survey research: Each respondent has a unique (not representative) stock of information that the researcher is trying to tap; access (not sampling) is the primary problem; and semistructured (rather than standardized) responses are the basis for conclusions. I briefly outline the utility of this research tool for cross-regional studies of development. □

DEVELOPMENT STRATEGIES IN EAST ASIA AND LATIN AMERICA

East Asia and Latin America have become the focal point of comparative thinking about development strategies in the Third World. Japan and the newly industrializing countries (NICs) of East Asia—South Korea, Taiwan, Hong Kong, and Singapore—were dubbed "miracle economies" because of their unparalleled accomplishments in the early decades of the postwar era. They not only registered record economic growth rates during the prosperous 1960s, when international trade and investment were expanding rapidly, but they also managed to sustain their dynamism through the 1970s and 1980s, in the face of several oil price hikes, a global recession, and rising protectionism in their major export markets. In addition, this rapid industrial growth was accompanied by a relatively egalitarian distribution of income.[2] By the mid-1970s, the four East Asian NICs had become the Third World's leading exporters of manufactured products, a status challenged in the 1980s only by the addition of another East Asian superexporter, the People's Republic of China.

Latin America seems to be a prime candidate for comparison with East Asia. These two regions are the most industrialized in the developing world. Extensive manufacturing in Latin America dates back to its first wave of import-substituting industries in the 1930s and 1940s, so the region has a relatively long record of industrial progress. By 1955, Brazil and Mexico were already entering a second dynamic phase of import substitution, a full decade before South Korea and Taiwan launched their initial export drives. By the mid-1970s, however, Latin America's growth rate had slowed, although East Asia's manufactured exports were thriving. The gap in economic performance between the two regions widened dramatically in the 1980s. Latin American nations found it difficult to maintain their previous levels of economic expansion as they confronted mountainous external debts, high rates of inflation, shortages of investment capital, and the social and economic marginalization of ever-larger segments of their population.[3]

The contrast in economic performance between Latin America and East Asia in the past two decades presents a challenge to academics and policymakers alike. How can we explain these differences? And if the East Asian model of development is indeed superior, how transferable is it to other regions of the world? For many observers, the most striking difference between the two regions lies in the realm of their development strategies. On one hand, Latin American nations followed the path of import-substituting industrialization (ISI), which relied on protectionist policies and a heavy infusion of foreign capital to build modern indus-tries to supply the needs of their sizable domestic markets. The East Asian NICs, on the other hand, in the mid-1960s turned to export-ori-ented industrialization (EOI), which depended on global markets to stoke demand for their labor-intensive manufactured exports. Neoclassi-cal economists and prominent international financial institutions, such as the World Bank and the International Monetary Fund (IMF) touted EOI as a successful development paradigm to be emulated by the rest of the Third World. The explicit message directed at Latin America and the other countries pursuing ISI was that policy reforms aimed at a greater outward orientation would promote development by simultaneously increasing exports, employment, and economic growth.[4]

Many scholars remained skeptical, however, that development strate-gies were the predominant reason for the divergent growth patterns in the two regions. Three alternative interpretations were offered to explain East Asia's success and Latin America's decline:

- *the institutional configuration of societies*: the developmental state, the spread of education, industrial structures in which local rather than foreign capital is in a privileged position, dynamic export-ori-ented subcontracting networks, and entrepreneurial familialism have all been cited as giving an edge to East Asia over other regions;[5]
- *linkages to the world-system*: the East Asian NICs benefited dispro-portionately from U.S. hegemony and the politics of the Cold War era, but Latin America's growth was hampered by its heavy reli-ance on transnational corporations and foreign debt;[6] and
- *the role of culture*: East Asia's Confucian, group-centered tradition is claimed to be more compatible with high-growth economies than Latin America's Ibero-Catholic tradition.[7]

In general, the transferability of the East Asian development model is viewed as progressively more difficult as one's identification of its key features shifts from economic policies to local institutions to world-system linkages to culture.

To subject these contending explanations of East Asian and Latin American economic performance to comparative scrutiny, the late

Donald Wyman and I brought together economists, sociologists, political scientists, and historians who were experts in at least one of these two regions. The gatherings led to our coedited volume, *Manufacturing Miracles*, which, in several important respects, challenges the conventional wisdom that Latin America can and should emulate the East Asian model of development. First, we demonstrate that the contrast between the outward-oriented and inward-oriented development strategies is frequently overdrawn. Each of the leading economies in the two regions has pursued a combination of both ISI and EOI approaches. Thus the Latin American and East Asian NICs are not as different as one has been led to believe. Export promotion always starts from ISI, but many Latin American nations are now pursuing EOI quite aggressively. This mix of development strategies helps one understand how industrial diversification (secondary ISI) has led to enhanced export flexibility and competitiveness (secondary EOI) in the East Asian and Latin American NICs in the 1980s and 1990s, indicating notable areas of convergence in the two regions.[8]

Second, both inward and outward approaches have inherent vulnerabilities that prevent either strategy from being a long-term solution to development problems. For example, the benefits of ISI are limited by the following conditions: (1) the size of the domestic market (which in Latin America is skewed by severe income inequalities); (2) ISI's import-intensive nature (ISI focused on consumer goods and displaces imports toward intermediate and capital goods industries, rather than reducing imports in an absolute sense); (3) its tendency to aggravate sectoral imbalances in an economy (industry is preferred over agriculture); and (4) its foreign exchange vulnerability (the overvalued exchange rates associated with ISI discourage exports). Similarly, EOI has its own drawbacks: (1) It is constrained by the technical impossibility of serving certain domestic needs through traded goods industries; (2) EOI employment in labor-intensive industries is unstable due to competition from low-wage nations; and (3) EOI is threatened by protectionism and slow growth in key overseas markets.[9] In addition, Albert Fishlow has cautioned against a "fallacy of composition"—namely, if all developing countries tried to pursue EOI at the same time, the ensuing competition would drive down the gains for all.[10]

Third, unique cultural and historical factors make it difficult to generalize from the East Asian experience. Various writers have argued that Confucianism confers certain advantages over other traditions, such as the Ibero-Catholic or Hispanic heritage in Latin America, in the quest for economic development. Because Confucian beliefs place a high value on hard work, loyalty, respect for authority, and education, these characteristics are thought to have facilitated the national consensus around high-speed economic growth evident in Japan and the East Asian NICs since the 1950s and 1960s.[11] Simplistic cultural arguments yielded a variety of problems, however.[12] First, regions are not culturally homogeneous. Taoism, Buddhism, and Christianity, along with Confucianism, all have large followings in East Asia. Second, timing is a problem. Both Confucian and Ibero-Catholic traditions have existed for centuries, but the dynamic shifts in economic performance that gave rise to the NICs have occurred in recent decades. Third, discussions of culture have been inconsistent. The same Confucian beliefs that are now claimed to facilitate rapid industrialization in East Asia were criticized by several generations of Western scholars for inhibiting economic development.[13] More sophisticated cultural representations are needed that see culture as historically situated and mediated through institutions.

Methods Used in the Cross-Regional Comparison of Development Strategies

Comparisons of East Asian and Latin American paths of industrialization reveal a wide array of similarities and differences. Although this dialogue is framed in terms of interregional and intraregional patterns, the basic unit of analysis is the nation-state. The concrete reference points for East Asian and Latin American development strategies actually are not "regions" at all, but only the most industrialized nations (the NICs) within these regions. Regional generalizations are usually achieved by aggregating the major conclusions drawn at the nation-state level. The focus on national cases from distinct regions of the world amplifies the theoretical and methodological complexity of the undertaking, however; scholars utilize an assortment of variables, multiple levels of analysis, and longitudinal as well as cross-sectional research designs to account for the determinants and consequences of East Asian and Latin American industrial trajectories. To interpret these findings, one needs to look more closely at the logic of comparative analysis employed in these studies.

The most useful typology of comparative methods was developed by Charles Tilly, who distinguishes four approaches: universalizing comparisons, variation-finding comparisons, individualizing comparisons, and encompassing comparisons.[14] *Universalizing comparisons* employ a most-different-systems (MDS) design to reveal that all cases of a phenomenon follow essentially the same rules.[15] As applied to the East Asian and Latin American NICs, a universalizing comparison shows that—despite their heterogeneity in terms of a wide variety of national and regional attributes (such as population size, land area, natural resources, cultural legacies, political regimes, social structures, per capita income, and economic policies)—South Korea, Taiwan, Brazil, and Mexico have several dynamic features in common that lead them to be widely perceived as industrial "success stories." These characteristics are relatively rapid and sustained economic growth, increasing levels of industrial diversification, and prominence as exporters, especially of manufactured goods.

The most-similar-systems (MSS) method of comparative analysis, which holds constant as many factors as possible in order to isolate a critical independent variable and match it with the dependent variable, is the logical choice for analyzing the cross-regional as well as the intraregional differences between the East Asian and Latin American NICs. Both variation-finding and individualizing comparisons adopt an MSS design, but with different objectives. *Variation-finding comparisons* strive for theoretical parsimony by focusing on a few key variables that explain particular comparative outcomes, like policy reforms or social revolutions. This approach is preferred for elaborating and testing middle-range theories that apply to a relatively small number of complex cases.[16] *Individualizing comparisons* contrast specific instances of a given phenomenon in order to grasp the peculiarities of each case. Theory is eschewed as a starting point, although individualizing comparisons may give rise to historically grounded concepts or typologies.[17]

Finally, Tilly's *encompassing comparisons* begin with a large structure or process. The practitioner then selects locations within the whole system and explains similarities or differences among those locations as a consequence of their relationship to the whole. According to Tilly, this approach is the most difficult for the comparativist to manage because he or she runs the risk of slipping into tautological functional explanations, in which a unit behaves in a certain way *because of* its consequences for the system as a whole.

The first three methods outlined by Tilly are utilized in *Manufacturing Miracles*, and each is linked to a particular type of comparative generalization: (1) universalizing comparisons help to establish the principal commonalities among the East Asian and Latin American NICs; (2) variation-finding comparisons emphasize the cross-regional differences between these NICs; and (3) individualizing comparisons stress the intraregional diversity of the NICs. Each of these generalizations, in turn, highlights specific variables: The common features of the NICs stem from their rapid economic growth and advanced levels of industrial development; the cross-regional differences between East Asia and Latin America reflect the predominance of EOI and ISI development strategies, respectively; and the main explanation for intraregional heterogeneity lies in distinctive institutional configurations at the national level (see Table 2.1). Since universalizing comparisons are used primarily to identify the NICs, my focus below is on the variation-finding and individualizing comparisons employed to explain cross-regional outcomes.

TABLE 2.1   Comparative Methods, Generalizations, and Variables

Comparative methods	Universalizing comparison	Variation-finding comparison	Individualizing comparison
Scope of generalizations	Commonalities across regions	Contrasts between regions	Diversity within regions
Key variables	Economic growth (the NICs)	Development strategies (ISI vs. EOI)	National institutional configurations
Representative authors in *Manufacturing Miracles*	Gereffi (chap. 1)	Bradford, Stallings, Fajnzylber, Dore, Ranis, Ellison, & Gereffi (chap. 14)	Kaufman, Cheng, Wade, Schive, Villarreal, Deyo, Gereffi (chap. 4)

Comparing Across Regions: Development Strategies as Cause and Effect

Variation-finding comparisons address a central issue in the field: How does one explain the contrasts between East Asia's and Latin America's development strategies? Here is a striking paradox: "Development strategies" are studied as both an independent and a dependent variable. As an independent variable, development strategies are linked to particular outcomes or patterns of development in each region.[18] This concern with the *consequences* of development strategies commands the most attention in public policy debates. When development strategies are used as a dependent variable, by contrast, the task is to identify their *determinants*. This has been the bailiwick of academic discourse.

The strength of development strategies as an *independent variable* is directly related to the role of the state in the economy. Development strategies are state-centered, that is, they are policies designed and executed primarily by national governments.[19] Although different groups in a society can and do influence economic issues, the formulation of a development strategy implies at least some degree of state leadership.[20] In contrast to the neoclassical interpretation of East Asia's success, which emphasizes the magic of the marketplace and accords governments a minor role, advocates of the "developmental state" perspective have argued convincingly that government policy has indeed been a key force in the postwar development of Japan and the East Asian NICs (with the exception of Hong Kong).[21] Robert Wade has documented that the governments of Taiwan, South Korea, and Singapore all exerted a significant degree of state leadership in promoting industrial growth.[22] Alice

Amsden shares Wade's skepticism about the neoclassical stance.[23] They both see market failures as pervasive, which offers a justification for governments to foster growth by "governing markets" (Wade) and "getting prices wrong" (Amsden) in order to accelerate industrial catch-up.

In Latin America, the developmental state argument was prefigured by the analysis of bureaucratic-authoritarian regimes, which emerged in the 1960s and 1970s to promote advanced ISI in much the same way as strong, centralized, and authoritarian governments in several of the East Asian NICs pushed EOI in the 1960s and ISI deepening in the 1970s.[24] However, development strategies in Latin America have not been as influential as in East Asia for at least two reasons. First, East Asia's authoritarian governments had far greater autonomy from local social groups and oppositional classes than their Latin American counterparts.[25] Second, foreign capital plays a more dominant role in Latin America than it does in East Asia, where it is a minor actor. This has limited the ability of Latin American states to formulate and implement national industrial policies.[26] Attention in Latin America has now shifted to whether the region's ballyhooed processes of redemocratization and structural adjustment in the 1980s can generate a new development model, combining economic growth with equity.[27]

Treating development strategies as a *dependent variable* means one must explain historical transitions or turning points in the East Asian and Latin American NICs. The transitions between development strategies involve policy reforms that raise three distinct questions: (1) Why does a given phase of ISI or EOI development come to an end? (2) What determines the choice of a particular development strategy from the array of available options? (3) How are new development strategies implemented and sustained? A detailed discussion of the substantive answers to each of these questions is beyond the scope of this chapter. However, in line with the logic of variation-finding comparisons, findings from the Gereffi-Wyman volume indicate that distinct levels of analysis are best suited for each of these questions.

Pressures emanating from the international system, such as economic shocks (the Great Depression of the 1930s and the oil price shocks of the 1970s), wars (World War II, the Chinese Revolution, the Korean War), and geopolitical realities (the hegemonic role of the United States during the 1950s and 1960s), are most important in discerning why given development strategies come to an end. The initial conditions of countries (such as natural resource endowments and domestic market size), the role of the state in responding to international opportunities and constraints, domestic political coalitions, and prevailing economic and political ideologies are critical factors in determining the choice of new strategies. Finally, the institutional and cultural levels of analysis are particularly

significant in understanding how development strategies are implemented and sustained. Sociocultural factors are embedded in decisionmaking and change at the local level because they include the most
proximate determinants of human behavior—ideas, incentives, and
values.

Diversity Within Regions

Individualizing comparisons abound in *Manufacturing Miracles*. They
tend to focus on closely matched intraregional pairs of NICs, which,
despite their regional proximity, follow distinct industrial paths. Tun-jen
Cheng, for example, found that South Korea and Taiwan exhibit systematic differences in how they implemented a common set of development
strategies (ISI, EOI, and EOI deepening): South Korea's approach was
hierarchical, unbalanced, and command-oriented while Taiwan's was
horizontal, balanced, and incentive-oriented. This contrast was elabo-
rated by a closer examination of each development strategy. South Korea
followed a "rent-seeking" approach to ISI, while Taiwan utilized a
"surplus-generating" model; EOI was "centralized" in South Korea and
"decentralized" in Taiwan; and with regard to EOI deepening, South
Korea pursued a "big push" approach, as opposed to Taiwan's "gradual-
ist" orientation.[28] Having examined the same two cases, Chi Schive indicated that Taiwan and South Korea built their very-large-scale
integrated circuits (VLSI) industries in contrasting ways: Taiwan developed the technology first and then moved into manufacturing; South
Korea inverted this sequence by initially forging its mass production
capacity, then acquiring the needed technology.[29]

Individualizing comparisons also apply to Brazil and Mexico. René
Villarreal has shown that Brazil, with the strongest capital goods industry in Latin America, has advanced further down the path of secondary
ISI than has Mexico. Furthermore, the energy crisis of the 1970s affected
the two Latin American NICs in opposite ways: Brazil gave top priority
to ISI deepening; Mexico became a prominent oil exporter, but in the
process the structural integration of its economy took several steps backward.[30] Individualizing comparisons within regions can even be used to
generate novel insights about cross-regional similarities. In my own
chapter on big business and the state, I show that the role of state enterprises is greater in Mexico and Taiwan than in their regional counterparts. Furthermore, there are sharp contrasts in how these cross-regional
pairs have internationalized their automobile industries. South Korea
and Brazil both stressed exports of finished vehicles, although via different kinds of corporate strategies and structures. Korea's auto exports
were produced by its domestically owned *chaebol*, but Brazilian-made

vehicles came from American, Japanese, and European transnational corporations. Taiwan and Mexico, alternatively, adopted component-supplier roles in the global auto industry, with their parts exports destined almost exclusively for the U.S. market. Whereas Mexico implemented this strategy through the intrafirm supply networks of the transnationals, Taiwan relied on its many small domestic auto parts companies.[31]

In summary, the development strategies literature is not primarily concerned with accounting for economic growth in the NICs. Both inward-oriented and outward-oriented development strategies have proven capable of spawning high-growth economies in distinct regions of the world. Rather, the literature's main emphasis has been twofold: (1) to explain the determinants of policy choice that have led the East Asian and Latin American NICs to adopt differing sequences of ISI and EOI development strategies; and (2) to demonstrate that similar development strategies have diverse institutional bases across societies, which shape the implementation, sustainability, and local consequences of these policies. This cross-regional agenda has diverted our attention, however, from a universal phenomenon, the globalization of production, which has redefined the roles of all nations in the world economy. The theoretical suppositions and comparative methods of this approach are fundamentally different from those used in studies of development strategies. □

GLOBAL COMMODITY CHAINS
AND REGIONAL DEVELOPMENT

Industrialization on a world scale has undergone significant shifts during past decades. In the 1950s and early 1960s, the world economy was an aggregation of distinct domestic economies, with production mainly organized within national boundaries. Since the 1960s, however, open international trade and an explosion of new products and new technologies have created a "global manufacturing system" in which production and export capabilities are dispersed to an unprecedented number of developing as well as advanced countries. Major breakthroughs in communication and transportation technologies have shrunk the world dramatically in terms of time and space, permitting manufacturers and retailers alike to establish transnational production and trade networks that cover vast geographical distances. The fragmentation and geographical relocation of manufacturing has resulted in novel patterns of specialization in the world economy. Organizationally, economic activities within nations are being reaggregated in global commodity chains (GCCs) and complex regional divisions of labor that alter the logic of comparative development research.

How can one study these processes of change? What conceptual and methodological tools can one use? What are the appropriate units and levels of analysis? How does globalization impinge on national development? To address these questions, I focus on a newly emerging framework for analyzing development issues in the world economy: the study of GCCs. As with my discussion of development strategies, I use my recent coedited book, *Commodity Chains and Global Capitalism*, to provide empirical backing for general points.[32]

The commodity chains perspective entails a fundamental departure from the development strategies approach in terms of its units and levels of analysis, its chief substantive concerns, and its principal research methods. Economic globalization has reduced the theoretical centrality of nation-states, which was the key unit of analysis in the development strategies literature. The global integration of goods, services, capital, and labor markets is eroding the power of states to set economic rules within their borders. Although protectionist policies still shape the international flows of investment and trade, national regulatory regimes are giving way to international agreements that cede sovereignty to broad regional trading blocs and transnational economic actors. As a result, crucial concepts in the social science lexicon, such as national development and domestic industries, are now rendered problematic.

The commodity chains framework targets the study of global capitalism, not national development. Industries and firms, not nation-states, constitute its primary analytical units. Different patterns of national development are an outcome, not the starting point, of this research. From a GCC perspective, diverse global industries, in which the dynamics of capitalist competition are played out, are taken as microcosms of the world economy. Firms and the economic networks that connect them are the essential building blocks of transnational production systems in which countries play a variety of specialized and shifting roles. Of course, firms do not exist in a vacuum. Their behavior is conditioned by factors operating at various levels: global economic and geopolitical conditions; regional integration schemes (de jure and de facto); the economic policies of national governments; the impact of domestic institutions and cultural norms on economic activity; and the wage rates, skills, productivity, and degree of organization of local labor forces. But nation-states are not free-floating actors either. The GCC approach argues that the development prospects of countries are conditioned, in large part, by how they are incorporated into global industries.

There are similarities as well as differences between the GCC perspective and world-systems theory.[33] Both approaches are global and encompass nations at all levels of development within their overarching conceptual frameworks; both assert that the world economy is organized in an international division of labor made up of vertical as well as horizontal linkages, whose geographical scope and modes of integration vary over time; both argue that global capitalism generates an unequal division of wealth between and within societies; and finally, both approaches try to explain the mechanisms of uneven development and its societal consequences.

Notwithstanding these affinities, there also are significant contrasts between the GCC and world-systems perspectives. First, the starting points of GCC studies are products, firms, and industries, rather than broad zones of development (core, semiperiphery, and periphery) in the world economy. Although firms are the main units of analysis in GCCs, world-systems theory is predominantly state-centric. Empirical explorations of world-systems theory often rely on measures of national wealth to define a state's position in the world economy.[34] Almost no attention is given to the structure of global industries, corporate strategies and rivalries, and economic and social networks. Second, world-systems theory favors a long view of history in which change usually is measured in centuries. The GCC framework, however, employs the tools of industry studies to focus on patterns of international competition that are contemporary and of much shorter duration. Third, GCC studies try to bridge the macro-micro gap in comparative research by highlighting the local social context of global production. Commodity chains "touch down" in communities and industrial districts where one can examine households, their connections to enterprises and states, and related issues of gender segmentation and racial and ethnic conflict in the workforce. From a GCC perspective, economic globalization actually strengthens, rather than weakens, the forces of localization in the world economy.

What does GCC analysis explain? How are regions dealt with in this approach? Commodity chains research, first and foremost, is concerned with explaining the governance structures of coordination and control in global industries. There exist two broad types of GCCs: "producer-driven" and "buyer-driven."[35] In producer-driven commodity chains, large transnational manufacturers play the central roles in coordinating production networks (including their backward and forward linkages). This is characteristic of capital- and technology-intensive industries such as automobiles, aircraft, computers, semiconductors, and heavy machinery. In buyer-driven commodity chains, large retailers, brandname marketers, and trading companies play a pivotal role in setting up decentralized production networks in exporting countries, frequently located in the Third World. This pattern of trade-led industrialization is common in labor-intensive consumer goods industries such as garments, footwear, toys, housewares, and consumer electronics. Although producer-driven chains controlled by giant industrial firms have been well established in the world economy for a long time, the emergence of buyer-driven chains dominated by commercial capital is newer and less well understood.

Second, instead of defining regions as the sum of geographically proximate nation-states, the GCC perspective allows one to document empirically the emergence and transformation of regional divisions of labor that vary by industry.[36] The linkages between countries within a region are the flows of investment capital, technology, goods, services, and people that make up commodity chains. Regional divisions of labor tend to be internally structured in similar ways: Core countries supply much of the technology, capital, and high-end services (communications, transportation, and banking); semiperipheral nations handle relatively advanced manufacturing and low-end services (e.g., quality control, component sourcing); and the periphery carries out low-wage, routinized production. In East Asia's division of labor, Japan is the core, the East Asian NICs are the semiperiphery, and Southeast Asian nations and the People's Republic of China constitute the periphery.[37] An analogous regional division of labor exists in North America, with the United States as the core, Canada and parts of northern and central Mexico as a semiperiphery (making a range of capital-intensive and high-technology products such as automobiles and their engines, computers, and electrical machinery), and southern Mexico, plus a number of Central American and Caribbean nations as the periphery.[38] A key conclusion that emerges from GCC research is that economic growth is not blocked by these regional divisions of labor; to the contrary, development can be fostered even within peripheral areas of the world economy under appropriate local conditions and linkage patterns.

Third, the GCC perspective explores many of the institutional mechanisms by which countries learn how to compete in world markets. Nations progress through fairly predictable industrial cycles in which organizational learning is continuous. At an early stage of an industry's development, people learn how to make and export products according to the price, quality, and delivery specifications of local and foreign buyers. Later, when initial exports are threatened by low-wage competitors or by protected or saturated overseas markets, local producers typically pursue several options to maintain a significant role in these industries. One option is domestic upgrading to improve the kinds of products a firm makes. Another option is direct foreign investment in low-wage countries to duplicate the products that no longer are competitive at home. A third mechanism is triangle manufacturing, whereby the erstwhile exporters become intermediaries to channel orders from established foreign buyers to new production sites in less-developed countries.[39] These patterns of adjustment to industrial decline reveal surprising regularities in the kinds of institutions and information that must be generated if sustained economic growth is to take place. This melding of development and organizational insights is facilitated by the GCC perspective.

Mapping Global Commodity Chains

One constructs global commodity chains by mapping economic networks along three related dimensions: products, countries, and organizations. At the *product level*, chains encompass the full production-consumption cycle: raw material supply, the design and manufacture of components and finished goods, exporting, distribution, and retailing. These products and services are connected in a sequence of value-adding economic activities. A distinctive feature of this product mapping is that it includes both backward and forward linkages from the production stage rather than focusing on manufacturing alone, as do many studies of industrialization. This broad scope allows one to show the relationship between industries ordinarily thought to be discrete. In apparel manufacturing, for example, one examines agriculture, petrochemicals, textiles, garments, shipping, wholesaling, and retailing.

At the *country level*, the geography of the GCC is superimposed on this production system. One needs to identify where each of the products in the commodity chain is made. An interesting finding here is that virtually all GCCs include countries at every level of economic development. For example, despite the fact that the apparel, automobile, and aircraft commodity chains represent widely varying levels of industrial sophistication, each of these chains involves core, semiperipheral, and peripheral nations in the world-system. Thus international divisions of labor are built into the very structure of GCCs.

Finally, at the *organizational level*, the focus shifts to the kinds of firms that make, distribute, and market the products. To what degree are these companies specialized or vertically integrated, large or small, transnational or domestic? Do they participate in interfirm networks across industry and country boundaries? The organizations that populate GCCs also mold the chain's governance structure—that is, the authority and power relationships that define how financial, material, and human resources are allocated and flow within a chain.

Varied data are used to construct GCCs. The raw materials, assorted components, and finished products in a GCC frequently are cataloged in textbooks or case studies of an industry, as well as in tomes on the global economy that contain sectoral profiles.[40] Once the products are known, the countries involved in GCCs can be identified via international production and trade statistics. Unfortunately, there are disparities in the classification systems for internationally traded goods over time. Supplementary trade figures often are available from national industry associations. The major firms in different segments of GCCs are mentioned in industry reports, investment surveys (like those provided by Standard and Poor's, Moody's, and Value Line), specialized trade journals, and numerous listings of the largest corporations around the world (such as those published annually by *Fortune* magazine).[41] In industry research, as in country studies, personal interviews remain one of the richest sources of information, for general and specific questions alike.

Export Roles and Their Impact on Regional Development

Countries are connected to GCCs through the goods and services they supply to world markets. These linkages can be conceptualized as export roles. This fits Tilly's notion of encompassing comparisons because one subsumes the cases (countries) in a conceptual map that outlines the entire system (a commodity chain), plus a mode of incorporation (export roles). One seeks to avoid the functionalist pitfalls of this method by recognizing that countries do not fill roles solely to meet the abstract needs of the international economy. To the contrary, choice, mobility, and the creation and restructuring of export niches are essential aspects of this model. Furthermore, the geography of GCCs is constantly shifting, which has important implications for national development.

There are five major export roles in the world economy: (1) primary commodity exports; (2) export-processing (or *maquiladora*) assembly operations; (3) component-supply subcontracting; (4) specification contracting of finished goods (also known as original equipment manufacturing or OEM); and (5) original brandname manufacturing (OBM).[42] These export roles are not mutually exclusive. Actually, most nations are tied to the world economy in multiple ways. The East Asian NICs have filled all five export roles between the 1950s and the early 1990s, although they currently are emphasizing the last three types of exporting. Most of the countries in Southeast Asia and Latin America are involved in the first three roles. The bulk of exports in South Asia and sub-Saharan Africa fit the first two roles, with many African countries limited only to mineral and agricultural exports. Each type of manufactured exporting (roles two through five) is progressively more difficult to establish because it implies a higher degree of domestic integration and local entrepreneurship; nonetheless, industrial development is enhanced as countries move from the second to the fifth option.

Burgeoning investments from Japan and the East Asian NICs in North America are leading to a deepening of multilateral ties between the two regions. In anticipation of the North American Free Trade Agreement (NAFTA), which took effect on January 1, 1994, Asian investors were eager to set up factories in Mexico and the Caribbean Basin in order to have preferential access to the U.S. market. NAFTA extends the regional division of labor to the poorest countries in the hemisphere, and it leads to a reevaluation of the impact of low-wage EOI strategies on Mexico and the Caribbean. Serious questions have been raised about the inadequate contributions made by these export industries to broader development objectives in the region, such as upgraded skills, technology transfer, backward linkages to local suppliers, and improved living conditions.

Until the last decade, Mexico's *maquiladora* plants were relegated to a low-wage, export-processing role in the world economy. A major concern for Mexico was how to push beyond the enclave model of EOI represented by its traditional, labor-intensive *maquiladora* plants in order to adopt a more dynamic, industrially upgraded development strategy. This strategy would generate higher incomes and better skills for Mexico's workers, and, at the same time, would allow Mexican exports to be internationally competitive in technologically advanced sectors. In the 1980s, a new wave of *maquiladora* plants began to push beyond this enclave model to a more sophisticated type of component-supplier production, making parts for capital- and technology-intensive consumer durables like automobiles and computers.[43]

In order to successfully carry out this shift from the "old" to the "new" *maquiladoras*, however, Mexico needs to move from its wage-depressing export strategy to more productivity-enhancing strategies. So far, it has taken the "easy road" to export expansion, since the sharp devaluations of the Mexican peso in the 1980s depressed real wages in the manufacturing sector by over 50 percent. The East Asian NICs, however, are moving in the opposite direction. They have diversified their exports in the face of a substantial appreciation (rather than devaluation) of their currencies, rising (not declining) real wages, and labor scarcity (rather than labor surpluses).

Today, many of Mexico's traditional *maquiladora* exports are shifting to Caribbean venues, which may become the favored locale for these low-wage activities. By the early 1990s, export-processing zones (EPZs) had become a leading source of exports and manufacturing employment in various Caribbean nations. In the Dominican Republic, for example, EPZs employed 142,300 Dominicans (primarily in garment assembly) in 1992 and generated $1 billion in trade, netting $300 million toward the balance of payments. In terms of employment, the Dominican Republic was the fourth largest EPZ economy in the world (the fifth if China's Special Economic Zones are included), and 11 percent of the more than

300 EPZ firms in the Dominican Republic were Asian.[44] Furthermore, East Asian projects were found to contribute more jobs, bigger investments, higher levels of local value added, and a greater utilization of skilled labor than the assembly oriented sewing operations by other foreign firms.[45]

Despite these gains, one should be skeptical of the role that labor-intensive EOI can play over time in the development of Caribbean nations. Export-processing activities, such as those that have grown so rapidly in Mexico and the Caribbean Basin in recent years, have undeniable benefits in job creation, foreign exchange earnings, and the fostering of industrial experience. They do not by themselves, however, constitute a sufficient basis for a long-term development strategy. Export-processing industries are best seen as a transitional phenomenon: the first stage in a process of moving to a higher level of industrial development, in which domestic inputs and diverse services also are required.

Although many Caribbean nations are just now making the basic transition from farm to factory, Mexico is moving further up the industrial export ladder from clothes to complex components to computers. But these countries have a long way to go before matching the success of the East Asian NICs. The latter nations are shifting from their role as the principal suppliers of OEM merchandise sold under the foreign buyers' labels in American and European department stores to making goods for export under their own brand names (the OBM role) with a growing emphasis on booming Asian markets. Hong Kong, Taiwanese, and Korean manufacturers thus are closing the commodity chains for consumer items, like apparel, by moving all the way from raw material supply through retailing within the Asian region. The North American consumer goods commodity chains, however, are still stymied by their weakest link—production. It is an open question whether Mexican or Caribbean manufacturers, or their U.S. or Asian counterparts, will step forward to fill this regional gap. □

DATA GATHERING
IN CROSS-REGIONAL RESEARCH

Data gathering for the cross-regional development strategies and commodity chains projects described above is a daunting task. At an individual level, my own work was facilitated because I was able to conduct interviews in both English and Spanish. For the Latin Americanist, Spanish allows one to do comparative research in most countries of the region. Though East Asia has a multitude of difficult languages and dialects, English is widely understood in business and academic circles. I also was fortunate to have local research assistants to help me in Hong

Kong, Taiwan, the People's Republic of China, and South Korea, where I do not speak the native languages. However, most of the nonwritten information I gathered in Asia was in English-language interviews that I conducted myself.

Although individual researchers can do cross-regional comparisons, they require substantial amounts of time and money to visit the countries included in their projects. A more feasible alternative for many scholars is to participate in collaborative research teams. The collaborative approach has two main advantages. One is the opportunity to find people with expertise in the different countries and areas of the world included in the research design. The second advantage of teams is the ability to bring together scholars trained in different academic disciplines. Today, many funding agencies have a preference for problem-oriented research. When one starts with an important problem or question, one generally discovers that the answers do not come in neat disciplinary packages. It often is necessary to find a diverse group of scholars with similar substantive interests to tackle the project.

Despite a personal preference for doing my own cross-regional fieldwork, the collaborative approach has been useful to me in a couple of ways. First, the pair of coedited books highlighted in this chapter are interdisciplinary volumes that allowed my coeditors and me to select scholars who were experts in particular regions (*Manufacturing Miracles*) or specific industries (*Commodity Chains and Global Capitalism*). The collective format of the edited book works best if you establish a common analytical framework at the outset and if you are able to bring together the participants for at least one joint meeting to present and discuss drafts of their chapters. Second, I also have found coauthors for articles who are knowledgeable about the industries or countries involved in my project.[46] Both forms of collaborative research—edited books and coauthored papers—tap the knowledge of experts. They are far less expensive and administratively cumbersome than a third option, which is to secure funds for a new research project by a group of collaborating scholars.

Secondary data analysis of written documents and statistics generally is an important part of any comparative study on industries or countries. Nonetheless, I also have relied heavily on in-depth interviews in all my research. Unlike surveys, which are instruments that require standardized questionnaires, fixed-choice response categories, careful sampling, pretests, statistical measures of reliability, and so on, the in-depth interview is often less systematic but equally valuable as a research tool. I employ two kinds of in-depth interviews in my research: the data probe and the strategic interview. The "data probe" is an open-ended interview, which I mainly use at the beginning of a project to orient myself to the issues, to refine my topic with academics and other local experts, and,

good

above all, to develop personal contacts for subsequent interviews. I use a snowball technique with both types of interviews to elicit the names of additional respondents.

The "strategic interview" is an indispensable tool for contemporary, actor-oriented comparative and case-based research. In strategic interviews, the value of a respondent's information is determined by his or her position in an organization, network, or historical process. These interviews are "semistructured": There are some central questions asked of all respondents and a number of other queries that are tailored to the unique position or experience of the respondent. Strategic interviews are frequently the only way to reconstruct complex decisionmaking processes, and they can be used to give a good first approximation of the actions of key groups and individuals in understanding historical events. For dependency studies, strategic interviews were used to uncover the bargaining that goes on between the state, transnational corporations, and domestic capital, in what Peter Evans calls the "triple alliance."[47] In the development strategies literature, this research method was employed in discussions with political and economic elites to determine why particular development strategies were pursued or abandoned and the problems encountered in implementing these policies.[48] Finally, strategic interviews are one of the best ways to trace corporate and social networks that connect the diverse organizations stretched across the world in global commodity chains.[49]

As with all research techniques, there are ways to augment the reliability of strategic interviews. First, it is important, whenever possible, to supplement oral accounts of events with written materials. Often one's respondents in strategic interviews are in a good position to provide this documentation or to tell you where it can be found. Second, when dealing with events about which there is no written record, such as closed-door negotiations or decisionmaking, one should try to triangulate sources in order to neutralize or reduce bias.[50] Third, when respondents are reluctant to reveal details about themselves or their organization, I ask them to tell me about other major individuals or groups who may be perceived as rivals. After an initial round of interviews, I will often return to the original respondents to get a fuller account of their side of the story. The more the interviewer knows about a situation, the more those involved feel a need to explain their actions. Finally, strategic interviews are an excellent way of getting feedback on one's interpretation of events while still in the field. The respondents in one's study often turn out to be astute problem-solvers.

Qualitative research methods such as strategic interviews are an essential feature of many cross-regional studies of development. Although the hypothesis-generating or inductive value of interviews is

widely recognized, my research on development strategies and commodity chains suggests that strategic interviews, if designed and done carefully, can also be used for hypothesis testing. Open-ended interviews are
frequently the only means to identify and assess the importance of historical contingencies, technological options, state policies, social networks, and particular economic conditions in shaping the choices made
by firms, governments, and other organizational decisionmakers. Information on key issues, such as the degree to which dynamic East Asian
forms of specification contracting can be transferred to such Latin American nations as Mexico or the Dominican Republic, is virtually impossible
to find in secondary sources or surveys. Strategic interviews, using a
sample of relevant firms, or well-crafted case studies, can help generate
data to test clearly specified causal connections about this kind of organizational learning. Multiple methods are recommended for complex
research projects, and interviews certainly belong in this mix. □

NOTES

I would like to thank Stephan Haggard, Lawrence Krause, and Peter H. Smith for
their detailed comments on an earlier version of this chapter, and Lisa Peloquin at
Duke University for her research assistance.

1. See Gary Gereffi and Donald L. Wyman, eds., *Manufacturing Miracles: Paths
of Industrialization in Latin America and East Asia* (Princeton: Princeton University
Press, 1990); Stephan Haggard, *Pathways from the Periphery: The Politics of Growth in
the Newly Industrializing Countries* (Ithaca: Cornell University Press, 1990); and the
essays by Albert Fishlow, Gary Gereffi, and Laurence Whitehead in "The Pacific
Region: Challenges to Policy and Theory," a special issue of *The Annals of the
American Academy of Political and Social Science* 505 (September 1989), edited by
Peter A. Gourevitch. A precursor of these recent comparative studies of East Asia
and Latin America is Fernando Fajnzylber, *La industrialización trunca en América
Latina* (Mexico City: Nuevo Imagen, 1983), followed by Fajnzylber's even broader
comparative study, *Unavoidable Industrial Restructuring in Latin America* (Durham,
NC: Duke University Press, 1990).

2. The disparities in income distribution between the Latin American and East
Asian NICs are dramatic. Brazil and Mexico have among the most inequitable
distributions of income in the world, but Taiwan and South Korea display relatively egalitarian patterns. Data from the 1970s show that the ratio between the
top and bottom quintiles of household income was 33:1 in Brazil, 20:1 in Mexico,
8:1 in South Korea, 5:1 in Taiwan, and 4.3:1 in Japan. See Gary Gereffi, "Paths of
Industrialization: An Overview," in Gereffi and Wyman, *Manufacturing Miracles*,
p. 16.

3. For a summary of these cross-regional trends, see Gereffi, "Paths of Industrialization," and Gary Gereffi and Stephanie Fonda, "Regional Paths of Development," *Annual Review of Sociology* 18 (1992): 419–448.

4. In its *World Development Report* for 1987, the World Bank claimed that "the economic performance of the outward-oriented economies has been broadly superior to that of the inward-oriented economies in almost all respects" (World Bank, *World Development Report 1987* [New York: Oxford University Press, 1987], p. 85). Also see Bela Balassa, *The Newly Industrializing Countries in the World Economy* (Elmsford, NY: Pergamon Press, 1981), pp. 1–26; and Bela Balassa, Gerardo M. Bueno, Pedro-Pablo Kuczynski, and Mario Henrique Simonsen, *Toward Renewed Economic Growth in Latin America* (Washington, DC: Institute of International Economics, 1986).

5. See Gereffi and Wyman, *Manufacturing Miracles*; Haggard, *Pathways from the Periphery*; and Peter L. Berger and Hsin-Huang Michael Hsiao, eds., *In Search of an East Asian Development Model* (New Brunswick: Transaction Books, 1988).

6. See Frederic C. Deyo, ed., *The Political Economy of the New Asian Industrialism* (Ithaca: Cornell University Press, 1987), and Gereffi and Wyman, *Manufacturing Miracles*.

7. See Roy Hofheinz, Jr., and Kent E. Calder, *The Eastasia Edge* (New York: Basic Books, 1982); and Berger and Hsiao, *In Search of an East Asian Development Model*.

8. There are five subtypes of outward and inward development strategies identified in *Manufacturing Miracles*: commodity exports, primary and secondary ISI, and primary and secondary EOI. Primary phases of ISI and EOI focus on consumer nondurable products, and secondary ISI and EOI include consumer durables, plus intermediate and capital goods. For evidence regarding convergence, see Gereffi, "Paths of Industrialization," and Colin I. Bradford, Jr., "Policy Interventions and Markets: Development Strategy Typologies and Policy Options," in Gereffi and Wyman, *Manufacturing Miracles*.

9. A fuller discussion of the natural limits of ISI and EOI development strategies can be found in Gary Gereffi, "International Economics and Domestic Policies," in Alberto Martinelli and Neil J. Smelser, eds., *Economy and Society: Overviews in Economic Sociology* (Newbury Park, CA: Sage Publications, 1990), pp. 242–246.

10. Albert Fishlow, "The State of Latin American Economics," in Inter-American Development Bank (IDB), *Economic and Social Progress in Latin America—External Debt: Crisis and Adjustment* (Washington, DC: IDB, 1985), p. 138.

11. See Lucian Pye, *Asian Power and Politics* (Cambridge, MA: Harvard University Press, 1985); and Berger and Hsiao, *In Search of an East Asian Development Model*.

12. See Christopher Ellison and Gary Gereffi, "Explaining Strategies and Patterns of Industrial Development," in Gereffi and Wyman, *Manufacturing Miracles*, pp. 394–397.

13. See Gary G. Hamilton and Cheng-shu Kao, "Max Weber and the Analysis of East Asian Industrialization," *International Sociology*, no. 2 (1987): 289–300.

14. Charles Tilly, *Big Structures, Large Processes, Huge Comparisons* (New York: Russell Sage Foundation, 1984).

15. Most-different-systems and most-similar-systems research designs are discussed in Adam Przeworski and Henry Teune, *The Logic of Comparative Social Inquiry* (New York: Wiley, 1970). Also see Chapter 1 in this volume. In their typology of methods used in comparative history, Skocpol and Somers refer to this

approach as the parallel demonstration of theory. This is the method utilized by most stage theories of social change as well as by standardized "natural histories" of different social phenomena such as civilizations, revolutions, and social movements. See Theda Skocpol and Margaret Somers, "The Uses of Comparative History in Macrosocial Inquiry," *Comparative Studies in Society and History* 22, no. 2 (1980): 174–197.

16. Classic exemplars of this approach are Barrington Moore, Jr., *Social Origins of Dictatorship and Democracy* (Boston: Beacon Press, 1966), and Theda Skocpol, *State and Social Revolutions* (New York: Cambridge University Press, 1979).

17. In Skocpol and Somers's tripartite framework, variation-finding comparisons are called "macro-causal analysis" and individualizing comparisons are referred to as "contrast of contexts" ("The Uses of Comparative History").

18. Fajnzylber shows how the reindustrialization debates in Japan and the United States highlight contrasting patterns of development in these two societies, which in turn serve as alternative industrial models for East Asia and Latin America, respectively. See Fernando Fajnzylber, "The United States and Japan as Models of Industrialization," in Gereffi and Wyman, *Manufacturing Miracles*.

19. Development strategies are defined as "government policies that shape a country's relationship to the global economy and that affect the domestic allocation of resources among industries and major social groups" (Gereffi, "Paths of Industrialization," p. 23). These policy choices may be open and negotiated (such as explicit tax and expenditure measures) or clandestine and imposed (such as inflation and overvalued exchange rates). See Gustav Ranis, "Contrasts in the Political Economy of Development Policy Change," in Gereffi and Wyman, *Manufacturing Miracles*.

20. Ronald Dore and Robert Kaufman remind us that development strategies do not necessarily mean comprehensive economic blueprints or grand designs of industrial transformation. Government decisionmaking in capitalist societies tends to be pragmatic and incremental, rather than strategic, responding to immediate crises and short-term dilemmas. Development strategies often gain coherence in a retrospective diagnosis of what, in fact, occurred incrementally. See Ronald Dore, "Reflections on Culture and Social Change," in Gereffi and Wyman, *Manufacturing Miracles*; and Robert R. Kaufman, "How Societies Change Developmental Models or Keep Them: Reflections on the Latin American Experience in the 1930s and the Postwar World," in Gereffi and Wyman, *Manufacturing Miracles*.

21. For a recent review of this debate in which the World Bank stakes out a moderate "market-friendly" position, see World Bank, *The East Asian Miracle: Economic Growth and Public Policy* (New York: Oxford University Press, 1993).

22. Robert Wade, "Industrial Policy in East Asia: Does It Lead or Follow the Market?" in Gereffi and Wyman, *Manufacturing Miracles*; and Robert Wade, *Governing the Market: Economic Theory and the Role of Government in East Asian Industrialization* (Princeton: Princeton University Press, 1990).

23. Alice H. Amsden, *Asia's Next Giant: South Korea and Late Industrialization* (New York: Oxford University Press, 1989).

24. See David Collier, ed., *The New Authoritarianism in Latin America* (Princeton: Princeton University Press, 1979).

25. On one hand, exclusionary bureaucratic-authoritarian regimes in Latin America emerged from the crises produced by periods of populist rule, when organized labor was one of the important bases of social support for the state. Authoritarian regimes in South Korea, Taiwan, and Singapore, on the other hand, never confronted an activated popular sector and were exclusionary from the outset. Furthermore, extensive postwar land reforms in South Korea and Taiwan, as well as in Japan, blunted the impact of large landowners, who were among the groups most likely to be affected by rapid industrialization. See Gary Gereffi and Donald Wyman, "Determinants of Development Strategies in Latin America and East Asia," *Pacific Focus* 2, no. 1 (Spring 1987): 25–28; and Frederic C. Deyo, "Economic Policy and the Popular Sector," in Gereffi and Wyman, *Manufacturing Miracles*.

26. The dominance of transnational corporations is a central theme of much of the dependency literature in Latin America. See Barbara Stallings, "The Role of Foreign Capital in Economic Development," in Gereffi and Wyman, *Manufacturing Miracles*.

27. This new development model is outlined in United Nations, Economic Commission for Latin America and the Caribbean (ECLAC), *Changing Production Patterns with Social Equity: The Prime Task of Latin American and Caribbean Development in the 1990s* (Santiago, Chile: ECLAC, 1990).

28. Tun-jen Cheng, "Political Regimes and Development Strategies: South Korea and Taiwan," in Gereffi and Wyman, *Manufacturing Miracles*.

29. Chi Schive, "The Next Stage of Industrialization in Taiwan and South Korea," in Gereffi and Wyman, *Manufacturing Miracles*.

30. René Villarreal, "The Latin American Strategy of Import Substitution: Failure or Paradigm for the Region?" in Gereffi and Wyman, *Manufacturing Miracles*.

31. Gary Gereffi, "Big Business and the State," in Gereffi and Wyman, *Manufacturing Miracles*.

32. Gary Gereffi and Miguel Korzeniewicz, eds., *Commodity Chains and Global Capitalism* (Westport, CT: Praeger, 1994). This interdisciplinary volume illustrates the structure and dynamics of GCCs in diverse industries, including steel, shipbuilding, automobiles, agriculture, apparel, footwear, cocaine, and services.

33. World-systems theory is most closely identified with Immanuel Wallerstein, who provided one of the earliest definitions of commodity chains: "A commodity chain is a network of labor and production processes whose end result is a finished commodity." See Terence K. Hopkins and Immanuel Wallerstein, "Commodity Chains in the World-Economy Prior to 1800," *Review* 10, no. 1 (Summer 1986): 159.

34. In Arrighi and Drangel's detailed study of stratification patterns between core, semiperipheral, and peripheral zones in the world economy, the indicator used to determine the zonal location of countries is GNP per capita (a distinctly national, rather than relational, measure of world-system position). See Giovanni Arrighi and Jessica Drangel, "The Stratification of the World-Economy: An Exploration of the Semiperipheral Zone," *Review* 10, no. 1 (Summer 1986): 9–74. For a relational assessment of world-system structure based on global "blockmodeling," which identifies trade patterns among nations for five major groups (blocks)

of commodities, see David A. Smith and Douglas R. White, "Structure and Dynamics of the Global Economy: Network Analysis of International Trade, 1965–1980," *Social Forces* 70, no. 4 (June 1992): 857–893. Another slant on zonal boundaries from a commodity chains perspective is offered by Roberto Korzeniewicz and William Martin, "The Global Distribution of Commodity Chains," in Gereffi and Korzeniewicz, *Commodity Chains and Global Capitalism*.

35. For a fuller discussion of this topic, see Gary Gereffi, "The Organization of Buyer-Driven Global Commodity Chains: How U.S. Retailers Shape Overseas Production Networks," in Gereffi and Korzeniewicz, *Commodity Chains and Global Capitalism*.

36. Jeffrey Henderson and Richard Doner conducted exhaustive firm-level research that identified the structure and dynamics of regional divisions of labor in the East Asian semiconductor industry and the Southeast Asian automobile industry, respectively. See Jeffrey Henderson, *The Globalisation of High Technology Production: Society, Space and Semiconductors in the Restructuring of the Modern World* (London: Routledge, 1989), and Richard F. Doner, *Driving a Bargain: Automobile Industrialization and Japanese Firms in Southeast Asia* (Berkeley: University of California Press, 1991).

37. The Greater South China Economic Region is a more specific subregional "growth triangle," which includes southern China's Guangdong and Fujian provinces, Taiwan, and Hong Kong. See Xiangming Chen, "The New Spatial Division of Labor and Commodity Chains in the Greater South China Economic Region," in Gereffi and Korzeniewicz, *Commodity Chains and Global Capitalism*.

38. See Gary Gereffi, "Global Sourcing and Regional Divisions of Labor in the Pacific Rim," in Arif Dirlik, ed., *What Is in a Rim? Critical Perspectives on the Pacific Region Idea* (Boulder: Westview, 1993).

39. Triangle manufacturing in the East Asian apparel commodity chain is discussed in Gereffi, "The Organization of Buyer-Driven Global Commodity Chains," and Gary Gereffi and Mei-Lin Pan, "The Globalization of Taiwan's Garment Industry," in Edna Bonacich, Lucie Cheng, Norma Chinchilla, Nora Hamilton, and Paul Ong, eds., *Global Production: The Apparel Industry in the Pacific Rim* (Philadelphia: Temple University Press, 1994).

40. An excellent volume with detailed chapters on the global textile, clothing, automobile, electronics, and service industries is Peter Dicken, *Global Shift: The Internationalization of Economic Activity*, 2d. ed. (New York: Guilford Press, 1992).

41. One of the best sources of information on the structure of global industries and the activities of the large transnational firms that operate within them has been the United Nations Centre on Transnational Corporations (UNCTC). The UNCTC was located in New York from 1975 to 1992, but in 1993 the work of this unit was transferred to the United Nations Conference on Trade and Development in Geneva as the Programme on Transnational Corporations, which now publishes an annual *World Investment Report*.

42. These export roles are discussed in Gary Gereffi, "Global Production Systems and Third World Development," in Barbara Stallings, ed., *Global Change, Regional Response: The New International Context of Development* (New York: Cambridge University Press, 1995).

43. See Gary Gereffi, "Mexico's Maquiladora Industries and North American Integration," in Stephen J. Randall, ed., *North America Without Borders?* (Calgary, Alberta, Canada: University of Calgary Press, 1992).

44. See Economist Intelligence Unit (EIU), *Dominican Republic, Haiti, Puerto Rico: Country Profile* (London: EIU, 1993/94), p. 20; Raphael Kaplinsky, "Export Processing Zones in the Dominican Republic: Transforming Manufactures into Commodities," *World Development* 21, no. 11 (1993): 1851–1865; and Alejandro Portes, José Itzigsohn, and Carlos Dore-Cabral, "Urbanization in the Caribbean Basin: Social Change During the Years of the Crisis," *Latin American Research Review* 29, no. 2 (1994): 3–37.

45. United States International Trade Commission (USITC), *Production Sharing: U.S. Imports Under Harmonized Tariff Schedule Subheadings 9802.00.60 and 9802.00.80, 1985–1988*, USITC Publication 2243 (Washington, DC: USITC, 1989), pp. 6-5.

46. Recent collaborative industry papers include Gary Gereffi and Miguel Korzeniewicz, "Commodity Chains and Footwear Exports in the Semiperiphery," in William Martin, ed., *Semiperipheral States in the World-Economy* (Westport, CT: Greenwood Press, 1990), and Gereffi and Pan, "The Globalization of Taiwan's Garment Industry." The value of collaboration for added country expertise is evident in Lu-Lin Cheng and Gary Gereffi, "The Informal Economy in East Asian Development," *International Journal of Urban and Regional Research* 18, no. 2 (June 1994): 194–219.

47. See Peter Evans, *Dependent Development: The Alliance of Multinationals, State and Local Capital in Brazil* (Princeton: Princeton University Press, 1979); Gary Gereffi, *The Pharmaceutical Industry and Dependency in Latin America* (Princeton: Princeton University Press, 1983); and Douglas C. Bennett and Kenneth E. Sharpe, *Transnational Corporations Versus the State: The Political Economy of the Mexican Auto Industry* (Princeton: Princeton University Press, 1985).

48. See Gereffi and Wyman, *Manufacturing Miracles*; and Haggard, *Pathways from the Periphery*.

49. See Gereffi and Korzeniewicz, *Commodity Chains and Global Capitalism*.

50. Numerous insights on the use of open-ended interviews as an indispensable tool in investigating corporate decisionmaking can be found in Erica Schoenberger, "The Corporate Interview as a Research Method in Economic Geography," *Professional Geographer* 43, no. 2 (1991): 180–189.

■

CHAPTER THREE

Purposes and Methods
of Intraregional Comparison

Amparo Menéndez-Carrión
and Fernando Bustamante

THE INCREASING COMPLEXITY OF POLITICAL CHANGE in Latin America poses a compelling rationale for intraregional comparison. Indeed, the accentuation of internal diversity—cultural, economic, social, and political—has become a fundamental feature of the region, with far-reaching implications for theoretical and empirical research. Recognition of this variability is essential for an adequate understanding of such issues as political identity, social conflict, and national as well as transnational integration.

The economic crisis of the 1980s exerted a differential impact on countries of Latin America and helped forge differential routes for exit from military rule. The consolidation of civilian government has further accentuated patterns of internal diversity. It is no longer feasible to incorporate within a single regional model the political economies of Chile and Mexico, or Brazil and Argentina—not to mention Ecuador and Peru. In recent years, Latin American nations have gone through a major restructuring of their models of capital accumulation, external trade, and sociopolitical structure. They have experienced drastic changes in their insertion in the global economy and in the international division of labor. They have responded to these challenges in differing ways: As a matter of deliberate strategy, Mexico, through NAFTA, has chosen to seek a closer association with the United States than with its neighbors to the south. Chile has expressed less interest in subregional integration through the Mercado Común del Sur (MERCOSUR, the Common Market of the South) than in the establishment of links with Europe, the Pacific Rim, and the United States. In addition, so-called "major" countries of the region have established goals that cannot be easily reconciled with such intraregional economic integration schemes as the Andean Pact, the Caribbean Community and Common Market (CARICOM), or the Central American Common Market.

Heterogeneity also tends to characterize cultural and political phenomena, as well as the practical outlook of Latin American political elites. Increasingly, these differences cast doubt upon the very concept of "Latin America." In some senses there are many Latin Americas today; in others there is none. What seems clear is that the umbrella notion of Latin America no longer has much analytical value for helping us to understand many facets of contemporary reality.

Complexity varies according to country, subregion, and subnational area, and it derives from specific historicocultural circumstances and patterns of societal change. To a certain extent this has always been so. What makes the present situation different is that the increasing internationalization of social and economic processes has had the effect of polarizing, fragmenting, and intensifying these long-existent heterogeneities. In other words, intraregional trajectories have the effect of inserting (or reinserting) various "parts" of Latin America in differing contexts. Countries such as Uruguay, Costa Rica, and Chile, for instance, may be more usefully understood in terms of Euro-Mediterranean *problematiques* and patterns, although Mexico—it could be suggested—increasingly belongs to a nascent "North American" political economy. Even subnational spaces may be reorganized according to influences from different international systems of functional action. Varying parts of the same nation-state can thus be connected at the same time to a variety of transnational sociopolitical networks, from which they derive their relevant behavioral rules and determinants.

At any rate, these increases in the internal differentiation of Latin America have strongly enhanced the relevance and role of comparative analysis. We begin this chapter by taking stock of past achievements and limitations in comparative political studies on Latin America. We then examine the present state of comparative work in Latin American political science. In the process, we show why we believe that comparative political studies can and ought to be stimulated in the future, particularly in light of contemporary changes in the world and in the region. We move on to a methodological and analytical discussion about the usefulness of intraregional comparison and its role in social science research. Finally, we discuss some topical areas in which comparative political studies can prove especially useful, and we conclude with some reflections on the institutional requirements that will be required for fulfillment of the research agenda that we propose. □

PAST LEGACIES AND FUTURE CHALLENGES

Comparative studies and approaches are relatively new to Latin American social sciences in general and to political science in particular.[1] Several factors account for the emergence of this interest. First, dissatisfaction has been mounting with studies and theoretical exercises derived from nation-centered perspectives, and especially with the formulation of grand generalizations based on allegedly "representative" features of major countries. All too often, as these critiques emphasize, the "homogeneity" of the region has been implicitly taken for granted; if some characteristic was found in any part of the region, it was presumed to apply to the rest. This type of reasoning is precisely what an adequate comparative framework can challenge, enrich, and refine.

Second, in the past fifteen years there has been an impressive surge of cross-national and cross-regional academic networks that stimulate exchange and cooperation between scholars inside and outside the region. This has resulted from significant efforts by such institutions as the Latin American Studies Association, the American Political Science Association, the Ford Foundation, the Inter-American Foundation, the Fulbright Commission, the Social Science Research Council, and Consejo Latinoamericano de Ciencias Sociales (CLACSO), and the Facultad Latinoamericana de Ciencias Sociales (FLACSO) in Latin America. Participants in these networks communicate with colleagues in Canada, Europe, and the United States as a regular part of their professional routines. These developments have fundamentally changed the way that Latin American scholars think about the region. They have also exposed them to the analytical methods that are commonly used in the United States and Canada, where comparative analysis has been encouraged since the 1950s by the "area studies" mode of teaching and research.[2] This contact and exchange has promoted new processes of socialization and mutual learning and has contributed to major collaborative endeavors. It has also revealed the dearth of comparative research on Latin America done by the Latin American scholarly community, at least in comparison with the impressive array of comparative studies produced by scholars in the North.[3] Third, the end of the Cold War and the disappearance of Latin America's intense suspicion and hostility toward anything that came from the United States have promoted a greater openness among Latin American scholars to comparative thinking and a greater willingness to abandon traditional attitudes that tended to see the North and South as hostile blocs, bound together only by historical antagonisms and by insurmountable cultural, political, and economic contradictions.

This growing receptivity to comparative analysis is particularly evident in the work of Latin American specialists who have written on such topics as the breakdown of democratic regimes and on processes of transition toward democracy and the challenges for consolidation of civilian rule.[4] Other Latin American authors have also recently taken a comparative approach toward civil-military relations.[5]

It is important to appreciate the significance of this new comparative work in Latin American social sciences. It must also be said that a good deal of this literature still suffers from the lack of a distinctively comparative method, however. So far it consists mainly of edited volumes with studies on specific countries, which appear to be linked by an introductory or final chapter in which one author attempts to extract general conclusions. In general, the chapters themselves do not incorporate comparative and contrasting references to other national experiences, which prevents these country studies from functioning as case-studies proper.[6] Despite the intrinsic value of such anthologies, they do not present national cases from a truly comparative perspective; it is left to the reader (or the volume editor) to extract the comparative implications from self-contained monographs.

This approach leads to serious methodological problems. Concentration on a single case may lead to the effect of reinventing the wheel over and over again, and thus to the endless discovery of "unique," "new," or "specific" features of national experiences—whereas these unique, new, or specific features might, in fact, appear only as a result of the failure to place the country-study within a suitable comparative framework. This problem may be found in much of the vast Latin American literature on urban poverty and popular sectors produced in the 1970s and 1980s.[7] This work shows a tendency to regard urban poverty as uniquely associated with the condition of underdevelopment, as a manifestation of a mode of modernization characteristic of the Third World—without any reference to slums and inner cities in Europe and the United States. Similarly, Latin American scholarship on urban popular sectors has eschewed intraregional comparison and has also ignored any reference to Europe, North America, Asia, and Africa.

These shortcomings stand in sharp contrast to the tradition of comparative analysis that has flourished in North American social science since the end of World War II. There is little doubt that scholars such as Gabriel Almond, James Coleman, David Apter, Lucian Pye, Seymour Martin Lipset, Charles Anderson, and Barrington Moore produced their work within a specific sociopolitical context that was influenced by the politics of U.S. global hegemony during the Cold War and by the struggles of continental Europe to confront and resolve colonial and postcolonial dilemmas. Despite its underlying strategic rationale, however, this wave of scholarship provided the initial impetus for a tradition that has gone beyond its limitations to promote fruitful questions, research, and debate about the social and political developments within the South.

Up through the 1970s, this Anglo-Saxon approach to comparative analysis tended to concentrate on the study of the "major countries" and to take these cases as representative of the region as a whole. The potential theoretical significance of certain cases was often disregarded because of their lack of geopolitical, demographic, or economic importance. This tendency has been traditionally shared by Latin American scholars as well. Awareness of the limitations of extrapolating features of Mexico or the Southern Cone to the entire region has only recently emerged. One of its positive impacts has been to stimulate the rise of a new comparative literature on Central America and on the Andean countries.[8]

Furthermore, it is well known that the "Anglo-Saxon" perspective has all too often been afflicted by ethnocentrism. This has led to problems in the literature on societal modernization and political development, which have been amply debated and discussed.[9] By contrast, comparative studies that are now being produced in the North reveal explicit attempts to overcome the theoretical as well as methodological—and ideological—implications of ethnocentrism.[10]

At present, the extensive development of comparative analysis in the North—particularly in the United States, Canada, and Britain—still highlights the relative shortage of comparative scholarship within the South. As a result, some of the major comparative material on Latin America is still coming from outside the region. It is quite clear that there is today in Latin America an emerging generation of scholars (many trained in the North) who are fully familiar with comparative methods of analysis. Nevertheless, the Latin American academic community as a whole faces the challenge of making comparative methods a major feature of its own development, lest the gap in the production of knowledge about its own region not only remains but widens. This would have serious implications for the ability of scholarly cadres to make a substantial endogenous contribution to their disciplines. □

APPROACHES TOWARD COMPARATIVE ANALYSIS

We now turn to several key issues in the development of comparative approaches to Latin American politics. As a point of departure, we wish to suggest that the presence or absence of comparative perspective is a question of method: A case study on the political process of a specific nation-state may or may not be comparative, depending upon whether it makes explicit reference to that which is known about other cases. Comparativeness, in other words, must be internalized within each case study. It is not just the number of cases under consideration that makes analysis comparative. It is the way in which cases are treated that makes them part of a comparatively constructed inquiry.

Comparative research does not consist in merely joining together particular cases in order to describe or illustrate differences and similarities. Each case must, from the outset, be approached in terms of other cases that (the researcher has theoretical and analytical reasons to believe) represent variants or instances of some processes that stand to be examined. The researcher must determine that whatever specific traits are found in each case are, in effect, peculiar to that case and, as such, should be understood in contrast to others. Likewise, similarities become useful, insofar as they are identified with reference to wider sets of phenomena that appear elsewhere.[11]

Comparative inquiry also entails awareness of the dangers of premature generalization. It is often tempting to extrapolate broad trends from one example or instance derived from one country or a group of countries, on the assumption that what is valid in one country or unit of analysis is valid for all others in the same region. This is, in fact, what often happened in development studies on Latin America. The model of import-substitution industrialization, for instance, was hailed as an adequate description for development processes in the entire region on the basis of the early experience of such countries as Argentina, Chile, Brazil, and Mexico. The concept of "bureaucratic authoritarianism," also, was too quickly and easily applied to contexts and regimes quite different to those that provided the original basis for its formulation.[12]

In the revision of traditional assumptions about Latin America, intraregional comparisons have become increasingly relevant. Awareness of the region's heterogeneity has several crucial implications for comparative work. Among them:

- There are issues that will be relevant to certain subregions and not to others. Such is the case, for instance, with the existence of fragmented or "incompleted" nation-states, of truncated or aborted neocorporative pacts, or of deep social, regional, ethnic, or cultural internal cleavages.
- There are also issue-areas that, if not specific to certain subregions, may be determined and affected by subregions; in the case of criminality or corruption, for example, specific factors within the local context may interact with general factors.
- In addition, fruitful comparative inquiry on Latin America may need to expand frames of reference to take account of accelerating processes of economic and technological globalization. Utilization of a global perspective should be done not in a quest for some

renewed form of "universalism" or "grand theory" but, rather, as an attempt to obtain a richer grasp on the specificities and variations of the phenomena under study. For a wide range of topics and issues, therefore, it would be desirable to begin by placing regional cases within a broad context of interregional inquiry.

- At the same time, it is necessary to recognize that questions that have traditionally been regarded as region-specific or subregion-specific may now have to be viewed as part of increasingly globalized dynamics and processes. Examples include such topics as political culture, political corruption, and the crisis of the nation-state—phenomena that are taking place on a global scale.

Methodological implications of the contemporary process of globalization deserve special attention. We think it useful to regard globalization as a double movement whereby some problems and issues are internationally and interregionally integrated and, in that very process, acquire strong national, regional, subnational, and local specificities. At the same time, this internalization of transnational issues may generate a wider gap in each country between social-action systems linked to global processes and other intranational systems that are unable or unwilling to integrate. Many countries may thus become polarized between cosmopolitan areas and local spheres. Studies that seek to understand the impact of international migration on politics in countries of the North, for example, may need to consider within their framework not only general features of the national political system of the migrants' country of origin but also the local micropolitical networks of specific "sending" communities.[13] Migrants often retain very strong links with their place of origin. They do so in organized ways, transferring to their new habitat practices, conflicts, demands, and operational structures that can be fully understood only in terms of their original context. Simultaneously, informal networks of family, friends, relatives, and partners are being projected at a transnational level and are increasingly affecting the internal dynamics of nation-states—particularly their economies, labor relations, and culture.[14] Far from implying a trend toward homogeneity, these new trends suggest complex phenomena of differentiation as a result of the increasing presence of informal transnational links that bypass state-centered channels. We believe that they require careful scrutiny.

Thus it will be increasingly important to carry out local and community-level studies, as well as urban and micro-regional studies, since the latter are especially affected by global changes in an increasingly differentiated and heterogeneous manner. Many international links no longer involve the nation-state as chief protagonist; rather, they tie directly in to local networks without regard for state frontiers. Articulations and feed-back circuits between local and supranational phenomena pose new challenges for comparative analysis. For example, the political relationships involving migrant communities extend from villages in Latin America to pressure groups in U.S. cities to transnational corporate interests.

Specialists in international relations have in recent years become fully aware of these developments and their implications.[15] Phenomena that formerly were encapsulated within nation-state boundaries have gained weight in foreign spheres and are being affected by them in turn. Labor negotiations in Philadelphia, for instance, may become crucial to politics in Chile. A strike by rural workers in California may have direct impact on labor relations and social policy in Mexico. Conversely, political violence in Guatemala may create domestic problems in the United States and Mexico. This process occurs because actors engaged in domestic conflicts can increasingly project their actions and ideas across borders and use foreign countries as sanctuary, as destination, or as relevant audience and potential ally. And, as recent experience in Europe aptly illustrates, refugee movements can have crucial political consequences for sending and host societies.

As a result, contemporary international politics is processed not only through the traditional channels of the past but also through growing networks between social segments and sectors located in different nation-states. This has given rise to the new realm of so-called "intermestic" relations.[16] Intermestic phenomena do not simply reveal domination or exploitation, as dependency theory would suggest; instead, they represent complex games among diverse actors at several levels, in variable-sum situations that feature indeterminate coalitional behavior. Interdependencies, in such instances, are best captured through concepts relevant to social action, to "agency," and to the concrete and situated historical performance of groups that operate through interacting networks composed of multiple channels and pluridirectional exchanges. □

ISSUES IN RESEARCH DESIGN

We believe that fruitful approaches to comparative analysis require careful attention to appropriate definition of the units of analysis—at subnational, national, regional, and transnational levels—and to their evolving interaction. Such customary categories as "nation," "country," "subregion," "region," "global," "intraregional," or "interregional" must be systematically questioned and scrutinized. This is essential for proper identification of units of analysis and levels of aggregation.

In particular, we believe that the concept of "region" requires reexamination. Upon reflection, the standard assumption that it refers to a set of geographically proximate countries seems rather trivial. Geographical propinquity itself does not generally have much descriptive or explanatory significance. In fact, it is worth asking: Why it is that geographical proximity has become such an important feature in modern social scientific thought? We suspect that, up through the 1960s, most variables deemed relevant to foremost questions of the day appeared somehow to be "lumped together" in spatial terms. Thus modernization and development looked like exclusive traits of closely situated countries or societies, in what later came to be known as the "North," though tradition or backwardness were defined as everything outside the real or imaginary boundaries of the developed or modernized areas. Substantive social characteristics were seen as strongly associated in both a spatial and a statistical way. Cultural traditions of area-studies programs reinforced this tendency. Ever since the eighteenth century, in fact, scholars and writers had attempted to define and understand the nature of European culture through its opposition to the East, to the South, or to "uncivilized" territories and peoples elsewhere in the world. Thus Montesquieu and others chose to interpret cultural differences as a result of climate, latitude, and topography. This general legacy has repeatedly permeated modern social science.

At present, social scientists need to take a closer look at the analytical core that lies behind the concept of region. Contemporary research has directly challenged the notion that concrete processes, variables, and behaviors can be seen as strictly associated with sociogeographical space. Concepts of modernity/tradition and development/backwardness are no longer seen as physically descriptive categories, but as heuristic devices that can help illuminate complex processes of social change. As a consequence, the connection between cultural area and societal modernization can no longer be taken at face value.

In fact, the notion of region tends to mask an assumption that geographical proximity actually represents a proxy variable or prima facie indicator of similarity with regard to some substantive dimension. This assumption should not be entirely discarded out of hand, but it should be subjected to careful scrutiny. We maintain that when social scientists employ the idea of "region" as a unit of analysis, they are, in fact, asserting that proximity may cause (or at least indicate) specific tendencies that homogenize political or social processes within a particular geographical realm. For the sake of consistency, then, scholars are obliged to specify the bases for such an assumption and make them explicit. In order to do so one must (1) establish precise hypotheses connecting propinquity with relevant and observable phenomena, and (2) state which common traits make the component units of the region part of a distinguishable common realm. Proximity itself, or even intense interaction, may or may not make the units part of a relatively self-enclosed system of action that displays distinctive features vis-à-vis comparable macro-units or regions.

When one engages in comparative intraregional analysis, therefore, one is not necessarily engaging in most-similar-system (MSS) analysis; instead, one may be (1) testing the hypothesis that we are in fact dealing with a region; and (2) testing specific hypotheses about the connection between spatial proximity and sociopolitical similarity. MSS analysis is more strictly analytically bounded. It assumes that prior questions about similarity have been resolved and that scholars have solid descriptive statements that allow them to believe, at least provisionally, that their cases belong to some relevant common universe or set. Therefore, they may find themselves applying MSS analysis to countries or political systems that are widely separated in space, or most-different-systems analysis (MDS) to countries or political systems located within the same geographical region. For instance, one may find it possible to compare the political systems of Costa Rica and Nicaragua from a MDS perspective, or Uruguay and Austria as most-similar cases. Intraregional comparisons are not necessarily tied to either MSS or MDS designs. Proximity is relevant only if it can be translated into or related to specific connecting processes, that is, through common exposure to some political trend or experience whose diffusion has been meaningfully helped by propinquity.

Let us point out briefly the types of variables that may be most interestingly treated through intraregional comparisons. We note, at the outset, that it is impossible to "control" for the given dimensions of region (historical, cultural, geographical) in this kind of research design. This is because the dummy variable "region" takes only one possible value (in statistical terms, it is usually coded as 0 = not present, 1 = present). One does not really know whether those variables or clusters of variables operate as they do in the specific region under study simply because they occur only in this particular context or because they represent a localized manifestation of more general trends. For instance, if one assumes that Latin America—as has been widely suggested in the literature—is a region in which clientelism is a pervasive feature of social and political transactions, one would be able to establish this point meaningfully only if one examines some cases outside the area—in order to determine whether "Latin American" clientelism and its correlates are unique or, on the contrary, appear in other regions as well.

Intraregional comparisons are useful for testing general hypotheses concerning causal or interpretive statements originally formulated without reference to region. A general proposition about elections and clientelism worldwide can be examined using cases from a single region.

If there turns out to be meaningful intraregional differences between countries regarding the relevant variables, one can proceed to falsify the universal hypothesis. If the expected relationship appears, however, one still cannot be certain that the general hypothesis is valid. This is so because although only one instance of inapplicability is needed in order to falsify the hypothesis, one cannot truly confirm the proposition on the basis of one region because there exists the logical possibility that it might prove false in other regions.

We think that all intraregional comparisons must begin with a critical appraisal of the analytical plausibility of the putative region. It is essential to show that geographical factors are relevant in accounting for observations and that the referent units are commonly affected by particular processes or causes associated with propinquity. For different issues one may encounter different clusters of units, and regions accordingly may take different shape.

Additionally, one could use intraregional comparisons to search for variations in common processes or problems. This approach can enhance the heuristic power of comparisons through utilization of an MSS research design. For instance, one interesting exercise is to focus upon a group of countries that appear at one point in time to be similarly situated regarding certain variables and then to observe differences in their subsequent trajectories. Study of the differentiation of originally similar cases can help social scientists to identify new relevant variables and intervening factors, as well as to weed out spurious correlations.[17] In his study of *Modern Social Politics in Britain and Sweden*, for example, Hugh Heclo attempted to show how civil servants and public bureaucracies can shape the social agenda of nations with relative autonomy from civil society and political parties.[18] For that purpose he examined old-age assistance and unemployment insurance in the two countries. Although he showed that civil servants framed the terms of discussion and policy-making, Heclo detected a difference in the capacity of the two states to control the shape of the social debate: The Swedish bureaucracies are much more efficient and adroit than their British counterparts. This difference is attributed to the fact that Sweden had a well-entrenched and premodern but centralized public administration prior to industrialization and democratization, whereas centralization of the British civil service came afterward. From the beginning, therefore, the Swedish civil service was in a better position to steer and adapt to social and economic changes.

In other words, Heclo took two relatively similar countries within a given geographical area and then proceeded to uncover (1) a "common trait," namely, the ability of central bureaucracies to act independently from social pressures; and (2) a meaningful difference of degree in this ability. Once the difference had been established, he employed a heuristic process to search for some hitherto unforeseen factor that might account for the difference—and in this instance, Heclo fastened on the sequential relationship between institutionalization of a central public service and the parallel processes of democratization and industrial development. This kind of "paired comparison" works by keeping most factors equal (Sweden and Britain can be seen as roughly equivalent along a number of societal and political dimensions). If differences emerge, there remains a fairly limited set of alternative explanations that can logically account for the divergences.

Though not an area study, Peter Katzenstein's edited volume *Between Power and Plenty: Foreign Economic Policies of Advanced Industrial States* further illustrates both the rationale for intraregional comparison through an MSS design and the ways that boundaries of a region may be contingent upon the research problem in question.[19] Katzenstein and his coauthors brought together country studies on developed nations to examine the nations' ability to manage the international aspects of their economies and interdependence. He compared the performance of Japan and continental European polities, on one hand, with that of Britain and the United States, on the other. The studies revealed that Japan and Europe were able to use policy instruments that enabled them to intervene effectively in specific industrial sectors, but Britain and the United States were able to manipulate only aggregate macroeconomic variables. This difference is explained by the global macrohistory of the countries involved.

The Katzenstein interpretation does not point toward a single factor but to a holistic constellation of elements. In this instance, the advanced industrial countries can be seen as analogous to a region (the North), and what is kept constant is the variable "level of development." The difference that emerges among them is the ability of states to micromanage adaptation to the international political economy. These studies are not designed to "prove" a relationship between "level of development" and "availability of policy instruments." (One can easily find that so-called less-developed countries, such as Brazil, have used the same tools in order to adapt to the world economy.) What is to be explained, instead, is the differential availability of specific policy instruments among several industrialized countries—whatever might be the relationship between these instruments and level of development. The most plausible explanation is found in the global and aggregate history of relationships between state and society. In any event, the methodological procedure is clear: A group of countries is selected on the basis of their similarity regarding "level of development" in order to compare their management of international economic relations. Differences are then uncovered that cannot depend on level of development, so the researchers turn toward other types of explanations, which can, in turn, give rise to new hypotheses.

One question that we regard as increasingly important for future consideration concerns the ways in which it may be valid to compare subregions-within-a-region with other subregions-outside-the-original-region—for instance, the Andean and the Balkan countries. The subregional units to be compared in such cases ought to be chosen according to the type of problem and according to theoretical considerations, and not, as frequently occurs, for reasons of geographical proximity or putative sociocultural similarity. In a comparison of the Andes and the Balkans, for instance, one important similarity might be the unresolved and potentially explosive plurinational character of many countries in the two regions. This comparison would enhance the explanatory "visibility" of differentiating factors, which may, in turn, permit more precise identification of what does or does not make ethnic conflict so potentially explosive.

Another way to compare political systems and processes is to take specific topics as points of departure. For instance, it is not particularly enlightening to assert that clientelism exists within many political systems and can be found in countries as dissimilar as Italy, the United States, Brazil, or Ecuador. Such statements run the risk of becoming trivial. The comparative challenge consists in specifying how this theme is present in each case and how it interacts with specific political processes. It is essential to show how these factors interact in different countries, regions, or subregions. These factors should be stated in terms of level-specific variables, since they may have different kinds of relevance at different levels of aggregation: Variables can operate in diverse ways, depending on whether they are observed in local, subregional, regional, or global spheres, and these diversities may also vary between regions and subregions. Thus, for example, political links that the general phenomenon of clientelism articulates at local and national levels may vary sharply by region. In other words, the way that "level of aggregation" interacts with relevant variables is itself a factor that varies. These efforts to specify links between categories, concepts, regions, and levels of analysis can serve a very useful heuristic role, opening up new questions about the essential content of broad theoretical statements and enhancing the empirical depth of otherwise abstract generalizations and concepts.

In sum, the development of new comparative approaches for the study of Latin American politics requires a link of conceptual issue-areas with units of analysis at different levels of aggregation. No doubt some topics are not relevant to an entire region; others can be researched at the national, subregional, or intraregional level. This conclusion should be reached as a result of comparative analysis, however, not on the basis of a priori supposition. Intraregional comparisons can thus be employed to test the analytical plausibility of the concept of region itself, to falsify generalizations about a group of countries, to identify new relevant variables, to form new hypotheses, and to discover previously unknown sources of variation. This may be accomplished through either spatial or issue-centered approaches. Intraregional comparisons do not entail a necessary commitment to either MSS or MDS research designs. □

CENTRAL THEMES FOR RESEARCH

Here are some preliminary suggestions about key topics that could be fruitfully examined through comparative intraregional analysis and that lend themselves to cross-regional methods of inquiry as well. This brief inventory presents only a small sample of some of the most relevant and pressing issues that might be included in a future research agenda for Latin America.

The Question of Democracy

The question of democracy in its classic sense and as it has developed in advanced industrial countries of the North may be relevant to certain Southern Cone countries—for example, Chile and Uruguay—as well as to Costa Rica. For other countries of Latin America, however, and specifically for countries in the Andes, researchers encounter severe difficulties that spring at least partly from the fact that concrete political practices, the civic ethos, and the nature of micropolitics in these nations seem to be grounded on very different routines, assumptions, and norms. The way in which political agents in the Andean subregion construe democracy and politics appears to lack some of the rock-bottom traits that make democracy "feasible" in the classical mode. This is not just a matter of "infant," "incomplete," or "incipient" democracy. Most of the Andean and South American republican political systems are at least as old as their European counterparts; they are by no means as "new" as emerging states in Africa or parts of Asia. Latin American nation-states have been around for a long time. Their inability to produce classic forms of political democracy cannot be attributed to youth or "immaturity." The character of these political systems, therefore, must be due to some other factor.

We believe that part of the explanation might be found in the realms of micropolitics, in the self-rationality of everyday practices, and in political culture and habits at large—whose examination requires scholars to go beyond the limitations of conventional cultural determinism. A comparative approach to these issues might combine several analytical modes. Among these, we would like to emphasize the potential relevance of a neo-Tocquevillian approach, together with rational choice and game theory as well as historicocultural instruments of analysis. Such lines of inquiry might be fruitfully merged with comparative institutional analysis and with studies of the nature of Latin American political structures, dynamics, and agencies at the intraregional level in order to ground the nature of "the common" and "the specific." Comparisons of "European-type" systems—that of Chile, Uruguay, and Costa Rica—with the Andean systems, and between relatively stable and unstable systems within the Andes, could yield numerous insights about the practice of politics in Latin America.[20]

Another topic worthy of renewed comparative analysis at the intraregional level is the question of authoritarianism. For this purpose researchers can distinguish between liberal democracies, inclusionary authoritarian regimes (e.g., Mexico), and exclusionary authoritarian polities (i.e., bureaucratic-authoritarian). There are also indications that hybrid systems that combine traits of authoritarianism and democracy are emerging in Latin America. Alberto Fujimori's regime in Peru, and certain aspects of Carlos Menem's administration in Argentina and Fernando Collor de Mello's administration in Brazil, display this type of hybrid profile. These systems are authoritarian but not bureaucratic or inclusionary or strictly populistic (in the sense in which populism has been described since the 1920s, that is: as a set of procedures and policies that incorporate interests of the middle classes plus selected segments of the working strata, articulated through a nationalistic discourse). This new breed of still vaguely defined authoritarian tendencies that coexist with democratization efforts and ideologies together with the survival of older authoritarian institutions and practices presents rich opportunities for the discovery of new forms of political legitimacy, regulation, integration and for the formulation of new hypotheses concerning the unsolved questions of governance and democratic consolidation in the region.

Beyond the description and analysis of authoritarianism at the macropolitical level, we also advocate comparative analysis of specific institutions, practices, and micropolitical relations. This can reveal the various ways in which authoritarianism and participatory tendencies coexist, struggle, and adapt to each other within specific settings. Authoritarianism can be seen not only as a characteristic of entire systems but also as a set of entrenched political habits, rationalities, and routines that shape the everyday business of government and politics. Authoritarianism can, moreover, be seen as a "way of life" below and beyond the institutional structures—in the authoritarianism of everyday relations, in other words, and in the definition of what constitutes "common sense."[21]

The Question of Human Rights

The ethical and practical meaning of human rights looks very different from the point of view of Central American, Andean, or Luso-American politics than from the highly institutionalized political systems and cultures of Europe, the Southern Cone, and the Anglo-Saxon world. These differences ought to be studied in terms of the constitution of subjectivity in different types of political environments. They should be examined in terms of notions of "subject" and "citizen," to include not only individual participation and "rights" but also collective rights and duties and systems of conviviality, which can provide key mechanisms for social change.[22] A relevant comparative endeavor is to study the ways in which people socially construct their public and private personae in different political contexts, both between and within countries. On the basis of previous work, we suggest that subjectivities in the Andean world are ethically, psychologically, and communicatively constructed in ways that differ sharply from the rational assumptions associated with the European Enlightenment. This has key implications for political culture-related dimensions of social coexistence, as well as for understanding the nature and prospects of governance throughout the region.

In the Andean world, for instance, it seems difficult to legitimize and support self-perceptions of people on the basis of the post-Kantian canon of personhood as constituted around a hard core of universalistic rights and duties. This is because wide segments of the population and of the elites have not been thoroughly acculturated in the post-Enlightenment world of rationality and practicality. Notions of human, political, and civil rights presuppose culturally determined ideas about personhood and subjective self-images that are absent from (or strongly distorted among) vast segments of the nominal citizenry of these countries. Comparative research could delve into the social construction of citizenship in different environments and explore their implications for democratic governance, authoritarianism, and the enforcement of human, civil, and political rights.

Concepts of governability, legitimacy, and social contract have proven useful for the study of political change in Latin America and, in particular, for the study of the consolidation of civilian republican rule. Yet there is considerable variation in the significance and meaning of these issues among the Andean region, Central America, and the Southern Cone. Efforts to build nation-states on the basis of classical "continental" models of governance or Anglo-Saxon ideas about democracy may lead to unexpected outcomes and trajectories if the social and cultural preconditions for their implementation are missing. The "Napoleonic" and post-Jacobin ideal of a homogeneous, rationally centralized, and unitary nation-state may not be feasible in countries that have been fractured from the outset by deep and unsolved ethnic, regional, cultural, and social cleavages. Such rifts cast doubt upon the possibility of articulating and elaborating the common and egalitarian ideals of social solidarity that lie at the core of modern nationhood. Comparative analysis may help illuminate ways in which the political and cultural prerequisites of the classic nation-state may or may not be present in different social systems. At the same time, it may help show the most probable and feasible forms of democratic governance—even if those trajectories depart considerably from classical models. Comparative research can also broaden our comprehension of the meaning of republicanism and of the very concept of the "nation-state."

The Question of Consolidation

The consolidation of democracy in contemporary Latin America poses a series of political challenges that can, in turn, help define a critical agenda for research. We mention only three specific topics that lend themselves to intraregional comparative analysis. First, many Latin American political systems are currently undergoing deep electoral realignments, and several are in a state of considerable flux. Others, however, display a good deal of stability and resilience, for example, in Chile, Uruguay, Costa Rica, Honduras, and Colombia. Intraregional comparative research may improve our understanding of the dynamics behind crystallization, dealignment, and realignment in political party systems. This was not possible before the wave of electoral democratization in the 1980s, but most countries now have a sequence of regular electoral events that can provide the empirical foundation for such research. Second this increase in the regularity and breadth of elections in Latin America can open the door for more and better comparative electoral research. Many studies of European and Anglo-Saxon democracies can be replicated and enhanced by adaptation to this region. This can help scholars expand the number of cases generated by research on electoral systems outside Latin America and thus create an enlarged database for hypothesis testing. This strategy will also permit researchers to identify the impact of the Latin American "region" on correlations found elsewhere in the world. Finally, civil-military relations deserve intense and careful scrutiny. The future political development of Latin America still depends to a great extent on the ability of political systems to find new ways of institutionalizing the role of the military and of establishing civilian control over the armed forces. Democratic consolidation requires confrontation with the legacies of military interventionism and authoritarianism in politics. The deepening and improvement of the democratic "qualities" of Latin American governments also are linked to the reform of civil-military relations. They are also connected to the formulation of new doctrines of national defense that are compatible with external peace and with increased popular participation in debates about national security. In such areas, comparative intraregional studies can support the region's efforts to prevent future rounds in the secular cycle of coup-democracy-breakdown-coup.

These are just a few of the most pressing topics for comparative research on Latin American politics. There are many other interesting and important subjects for investigation, as suggested by the increasingly complex nature of the region and the problems it will be facing in the future. The prospects for intraregional research are promising indeed. □

THE TASKS AHEAD

Intraregional comparisons have acquired renewed relevance for understanding and "reproblematizing" conditions in contemporary Latin America—a region whose dramatic changes have profound implications for the definition of its very identity. At the same time, vigorous discussions about the theoretical and methodological assumptions of modern social science should instill social scientists with a healthy skepticism vis-à-vis traditional premises and also encourage them to search for fresh approaches toward the old and new features of Latin America.[23]

This situation leads us to emphasize the need to subject research practices to a permanent process of reexamination and redefinition. In particular, units of analysis should be determined according to the thematic requirements of the problem at hand, not on the basis of a priori assumptions about the nature of the world and its component parts. We think it especially appropriate to set aside the common tendency to take for granted the "substantial" existence of entities such as region and subregion and, instead, to regard the definition of such units as a question worthy of verification. And, depending upon the topic, of course, relevant units of analysis may change. For some purposes it may be useful to imagine the existence of an entity called Latin America—but this is something that, increasingly, research will have to demonstrate. Scholars must keep themselves open to the possibility of new and unsuspected forms for the definition of region and subregion.

Here we call attention to the proposition that relevant units of analysis may be defined in terms of relatively stable networks of interaction, endowed with some defined degree of self-containedness and "thickness." In this context Anthony Giddens's efforts to develop a theory of social structuring may be useful to bear in mind.[24] As he pointed out, units of analysis may be determined on the basis of certain hypotheses *ex ante* about systems of sustained and frequent interaction. This concept of systems can help draw the limits of relevant comparable units of analysis.

Comparative inquiry on Latin America must not only move beyond premature universalization and ethnocentrism, the most blatant manifestations of which have long been overcome, but also move toward a systematic reexamination of the intellectual assumptions. On one hand, we suggest that comparative approaches should contain a strong component of transcultural enrichment of perspectives and of systematic self-criticism of the initial points of theoretical departure. In order for comparative analysis to be meaningful and relevant, one should go beyond the mere empirical verification of specific hypotheses and taxonomies. At the same time, one must attempt a balance between generalization and specificity. On the other hand, scholars' premises are inevitably bounded by professional disciplinary and cultural environments. Awareness of the limits on their individual perspectives, perceptions, and biases does not, however, constitute a reason to jettison the endeavor as a whole. Instead, it provides an opportunity to enrich the understanding of the complexities inherent in all social science research. Furthermore, this awareness can help disciplinary specialists to widen their horizons and to establish a partial safeguard against possible confusion and plain error, which can sometimes lie within their theoretical and methodological frameworks.

Finally, we must point out that the adoption of comparative methods and of comparative analysis for Latin American research is not only a matter of awareness and will. It is also a matter of training. Up to now, the comparative approach has been conspicuous by its absence from university curricula in Latin America. Present debates on the reform of higher education should make explicit reference to the issue of comparative methods and social science training, particularly at the postgraduate level. There should be open and lively academic discussion about the appropriate place for comparative theory and methods in graduate-level social sciences in Latin America.

The presence of a new generation of scholars, trained mostly in the United States and Canada, provides a critical resource for intellectual development throughout the region. The willingness is there; the training lags behind. Institutional strategies necessary to bridge this gap merit serious attention, and international donors would be wise to take this into account. The establishment of strong comparative programs in Latin American centers of higher learning can provide excellent opportunities for the joint education, within the region, of future social scientists. They could acquire the tools for approaching national issues rigorously, systematically, and creatively and could then jointly develop, regardless of national boundaries, new attitudes toward the understanding of regional, intraregional, national, and global issues from fresh and original endogenous perspectives.[25] Here is a mission and a purpose for academic leadership. □

NOTES

1. This statement refers to the study of comparative politics in Latin America. There are some important exceptions to the relative neglect of comparative studies by Latin American scholars. Some of these are: Fernando Henrique Cardoso and Enzo Faletto, *Dependency and Development in Latin America*, trans. Marjory Mattingly Urquidi (Berkeley: University of California Press, 1979); Gino Germani, *Authoritarianism, Nationalism, Populism, and Fascism* (New Brunswick, NJ: Transaction Books, 1977); Jorge Hardoy, Richard Morse, and Richard Schaedel, *Ensayos históricos-sociales sobre la urbanización en América Latina* (Buenos Aires: Ediciones SIAP, 1978); Jorge Hardoy and Richard Schaedel, *Las ciudades de América Latina y sus áreas de influencia* (Buenos Aires: Ediciones SIAP, 1975); Helio Jaguaribe, *Political Development: A General Theory and a Latin American Case Study* (New York: Harper and Row, 1973); Claudio Veliz, *The Centralist Tradition in Latin America* (Princeton: Princeton University Press, 1979); Guillermo O'Donnell, *Modernization and Bureaucratic-Authoritarianism: Studies in South American Politics* (Berkeley: Institute of International Studies, University of California, 1973); Guillermo O'Donnell, Philippe C. Schmitter, and Laurence Whitehead, eds., *Transitions from Authoritarian Rule: Comparative Perspectives and Tentative Conclusions* (Baltimore: Johns Hopkins University Press, 1987).

2. Ronald Chilcote provides a very useful bibliography of comparative studies on Latin America in *Theories of Comparative Politics* (Boulder: Westview Press, 1981).

3. The problem is not a shortage of competent scholars in Latin America; rather, it is the absence of an infrastructure in place to support the creation of communities of scholarship within the region.

4. See David Collier, ed., *The New Authoritarianism in Latin America* (Princeton: Princeton University Press, 1979); Germani, *Authoritarianism, Nationalism, Populism, and Fascism*; O'Donnell, Schmitter, and Whitehead, *Transitions from Authoritarian Rule*; Fernando Henrique Cardoso, *Autoritarismo e democratizaçao* (Rio de Janeiro: Paz e Terra, 1975); Marcelo Cavarozzi, *Autoritarismo y democracia, 1955–1983* (Buenos Aires: Centro Editor de América Latina, 1983); Manuel Antonio Garretón, "Proyectos, trayectorias y fracasos de los regímenes militares del cono sur, un balance," *Alternativas* (CERC, Santiago de Chile), no. 7 (January–April, 1984); José Labastida Martín del Campo, ed., *Dictadores y dictaduras* (Mexico City: Siglo XXI, 1986); Norbert Lechner, *Estado y política en América Latina* (Mexico City: Siglo XXI, 1981); Francisco Rojas, ed., *Autoritarismo y alternativas populares en América Latina* (San José, Costa Rica: FLACSO, 1982).

5. See, for example, Fernando Bustamante, "Algunas conclusiones e hipótesis en torno al problema del control civil sobre las FFAA y la consolidación democrática en los paises andinos," Documento de Trabajo, no. 333 (Santiago de Chile: FLACSO, 1987), "El Desarrollo de las FFAA de Ecuador y Colombia: Una

revisión comparativa," Documento de Trabajo, no. 346 (Santiago de Chile: FLACSO, 1987), and "Los militares y la creación de un nuevo orden democrático en Perú y Ecuador," Documento de Trabajo, no. 370 (Santiago de Chile: FLACSO, 1988). See also Augusto Varas, ed., *Paz, desarme, y desarrollo en América Latina* (Buenos Aires: GEL, 1987), *La autonomía militar en América Latina* (Caracas: Nueva Sociedad, 1988), and *Democracy Under Siege: New Military Power in Latin America* (New Haven, CT: Greenwood Press, 1989); Louis Wolf Goodman, Joanna Mendelson, and Juan Rial, eds., *Los militares y la democracia* (Montevideo: PEITHO, 1990).

6. Single-country case studies can be methodologically comparative if the single case is treated with reference to other contexts and if those contexts illuminate specific problems being investigated.

7. Alejandro Portes and John Walton, *Urban Latin America: The Political Condition from Above and Below* (Austin: University of Texas Press, 1975); Irving Louis Horowitz, *Masses in Latin America* (New York: Oxford University Press, 1970); Janice Perlman, *The Myth of Marginality: Urban Poverty and Politics in Rio de Janeiro* (Berkeley: University of California Press, 1976).

8. Arturo Escobar and Sonia E. Alvarez, eds., *The Making of Social Movements in Latin America: Identity, Strategy and Democracy* (Boulder: Westview Press, 1992); Alfred Stepan, *The State and Society: Peru in Comparative Perspective* (Princeton: Princeton University Press, 1978); Edelberto Torres-Rivas, *Centroamerica hoy* (Mexico City: Siglo XXI, 1975).

9. See, for example, David Apter, *The Politics of Modernization* (Chicago: University of Chicago Press, 1965); Samuel Huntington, *Political Order in Changing Societies* (New Haven: Yale University Press, 1968); John Johnson, *Political Change in Latin America: The Emergence of the Middle Sectors* (Stanford: Stanford University Press, 1958); Seymour Martin Lipset and Aldo Solari, *Elites in Latin America* (New York: Oxford University Press, 1967).

10. See, for example, Charles Anderson, *Politics and Economic Change in Latin America* (Princeton, NJ: VanNostrand and Co., 1967); Collier, *The New Authoritarianism in Latin America*; Liisa North, *Civil-Military Relations in Argentina, Chile, and Peru* (Berkeley: University of California, Institute of International Studies, 1966); Stepan, *The State and Society.*

11. Although here we are not specifically interested in interregional comparisons, it is possible that extraregional references may potentially constitute an excellent tool. The specificity of regional processes may be better understood if they are contrasted with a more universal range of cases and spatial and time spheres. It could lead to finding new and distinctive features that may easily escape observation due to their common presence in the region.

12. O'Donnell, *Modernization and Bureaucratic-Authoritarianism.*

13. On migrants and squatters, see Frank Andrews and George W. Phillips, "The Squatters in Lima: Who They Are and What They Want," *Journal of Developing Areas* 4, no. 2 (January 1970), Wayne Cornelius, *Politics and the Migrant Poor in Mexico City* (Stanford: Stanford University Press, 1975); and Portes and Walton, *Urban Latin America.*

14. See James Caporaso, ed., *The Elusive State: International Comparative Perspectives* (Newbury Park, CA: Sage Publications, 1988).

15. Robert Keohane and Joseph Nye, *Poder e interdependencia: La política mundial en transición*, Colección Estudios Internacionales (Buenos Aires: GEL, 1988).

16. See Stephen Krasner, *Structural Conflict: The Third World Against Global Liberalism* (Berkeley: University of California Press, 1985); Jeannie Lincoln and Elizabeth Ferris, eds., *The Dynamics of Latin American Foreign Policies: Challenges for the Eighties* (Boulder: Westview Press, 1984); and Abraham Lowenthal, *Partners in Conflict: The United States and Latin America* (Baltimore: Johns Hopkins University Press, 1987).

17. Bustamante compared the development of military professionalism in Ecuador and Colombia through the nineteenth and twentieth centuries. These countries experienced similar stages of military warlordism, and their political structure looked similar, but their civil-military relations evolved in diverging directions. By knowing which variables were constant it was possible to develop new insights on what caused these differences. Bustamante, "El desarrollo de las FFAA de Ecuador y Colombia."

18. Hugh Heclo, *Modern Social Politics in Britain and Sweden* (New Haven: Yale University Press, 1974).

19. Peter Katzenstein, *Between Power and Plenty: Foreign Economic Policies of Advanced Industrial States* (Madison: University of Wisconsin Press, 1978).

20. On the importance of questioning the concept of "democracy," see Amparo Menéndez-Carrión, "Democracias pendientes y representación política en América Latina," in Margarita López Maya, ed., *Desarrollo y democracia* (Caracas: Editorial Nueva Sociedad, 1992), and "Para repensar la cuestión de la ciudadanía. Dilemas, opciones, y apuntes para un proyecto," *Revista Latinoamericano de Ciencias Sociales* (FLACSO) 1, no. 1 (1991).

21. Menéndez-Carrión, "Para repensar la cuestión de la ciudadanía."

22. Menéndez-Carrión, "Para repensar la cuestión de la ciudadanía."

23. See Heinz Sonntag, *Duda/certeza/crisis: La evolución de las ciencias sociales en América Latina* (Caracas: UNESCO, 1988).

24. Anthony Giddens, *Las nuevas reglas del método sociológico* (Buenos Aires: Amorrortu 1987), and Anthony Giddens, Jonathan Turner, et al., *La teoria social hoy* (Mexico City: Alianza Editorial, 1993).

25. Menéndez-Carrión, "Para repensar la cuestión de la ciudadania."

CHAPTER FOUR

———————— ■ ————————

Uses and Limitations of Rational Choice

Barbara Geddes

As LONG AS MOST DEVELOPING COUNTRIES remained mired in authoritarianism, scholars tended to focus their work on efforts to understand the causes of economic development and the reasons for initiation and breakdown of authoritarian regimes. While observers of developing countries concentrated their political and intellectual attention on the dynamics of these crucial issues, however, a series of important theoretical breakthroughs occurred elsewhere in the study of democratic politics. These successes were associated with an approach that was not new; indeed, a version of it had been used by economists since the nineteenth century. But scholars had more recently adapted this method in ways that made it useful for the study of elite actors in democratic political systems. This approach is usually called rational choice.[1]

In contrast to most arguments in the dependency, new institutionalist (as defined by March and Olsen), and comparative historical sociology traditions, rational choice arguments use the individual, or some analogue of the individual, as the unit of analysis.[2] They assume that individuals, including politicians, are rational in the sense that, given goals and alternative strategies from which to choose, they will select the alternatives that maximize their chances of achieving their goals. Institutions, along with other structural features, such as ethnic divisions or the size of the peasantry, and immediate political circumstances enter rational choice arguments as factors that shape second-order preferences (that is, strategies employed to attain goals). These factors determine the alternatives from which individuals may choose their strategies. Factors that shape first-order preferences, goals, are outside the deductive structure of rational choice models (in the sense that models do not attempt to explain their origins), but goals, nevertheless, play a crucial role in rational choice arguments. The most compelling use of this approach results from the creative synthesis of the rational actor assumptions with, one, a plausible attribution of goals and, two, a careful interpretation of the effects of institutions and other factors on the feasible strategies available to actors for achieving these goals.

In this chapter, I show first, why those using the rational choice approach have had so much success constructing theories of democratic politics; and second, which parts of this theoretical literature can be most easily and fruitfully adapted to the context of politics in developing and newly democratic countries. Only a few years ago, Robert Bates lamented that due to the dearth of democracies in the developing world, knowledge of the advances made by rational choice theorists in explaining democratic politics merely added to the frustrations facing students of developing countries.[3] Now, however, with democratic processes squarely at the center of politics in most Latin American countries and becoming important in more and more African, Asian, and former communist countries, it is time to look closely at these theoretical developments to see what they have to offer. □

MISPERCEPTIONS ABOUT RATIONAL CHOICE

Many who have worked outside the rational choice tradition hold misperceptions that interfere with using the insights and methods associated with it. So, before considering the applicability of some of these ideas outside the context in which they emerged, the most common misperceptions need to be examined. They include contentions that rational choice arguments:

- are inherently conservative;
- assume that all people are motivated by material interests (the economists' famous *homo economicus*);
- assume that people's preferences are stable or unchanging;
- are based on unrealistic assumptions—since people are not really rational, and they lack the information and calculating ability assumed by rational choice theory;
- are ahistorical and fail to take context into account; and
- are deterministic.

In the following paragraphs, I discuss each of these misperceptions in turn, including the grain of truth upon which each pearl of misperception has been accreted. This section aims to clear away some misunderstandings and to delimit the domain in which rational choice arguments are likely to be useful. Although none of the statements listed above is generally true, some are true in some instances; and, when they are true, rational choice arguments are not likely to provide much leverage for understanding events.

Ideology

Although a number of scholars whose sympathies cluster to the left of the political spectrum use rational choice models (e.g., John Roemer, Amartya Sen, Michael Taylor, Adam Przeworski, David Laitin, Michael Wallerstein, and George Tsebelis), one continues to hear the claim that rational choice arguments have a conservative bias. This stems, apparently, from the prominence of University of Virginia and University of Chicago economists in the development of the public choice subfield, which often focuses on the economic inefficiencies caused by government interventions in markets. It is true that many economists, especially those associated with the public choice literature, show a touching faith in markets and a deep suspicion of government involvement in economic matters. And some of these economists have helped to build the current structural adjustment orthodoxy now having such a major impact on developing country economies. Public choice is only one subfield, however, in what has become a very large field of rational choice arguments applied to many aspects of politics. As the work of the individuals listed above shows, the tools of the rational choice approach can be used to serve many different ideals.

Goals

A second misperception is that rational choice arguments assume that human beings are motivated by material interests. This is simply false. The "rationality" assumed by rational choice arguments is of the narrowest means-ends kind. No assumptions are made about the goals held by individuals. The approach only assumes that people (1) choose the means they consider most likely to result in desired ends; (2) can weakly order their goals (that is, given any set of alternatives, they will prefer one or the other or be indifferent); and (3) hold consistent preferences (that is, if they prefer Bill Clinton to George Bush and Bush to Ross Perot, then they prefer Clinton to Perot). Although one can think of situations in which the second or third condition might not hold, they are not common. If one limits the domain of rational choice arguments to areas in which these conditions seem plausible, the domain remains extremely broad.

Because the rational choice approach makes no assumptions about goals, the analyst who seeks to apply it to a particular problem must identify the goals of the actors involved. This is an empirical question. The analyst cannot usually offer direct proof, such as survey data, to show that actors really do have the goals imputed to them, since actors may have good reasons to lie about their goals. Nevertheless, checks on the analytic imagination are built into the rational choice approach: If the analyst misperceives actors' goals, then their behavior will differ from that predicted. Inconvenient facts will cast doubt on empirical elements of the argument, as they would within the framework of any other approach.

In practice, analysts often make plausible assumptions about the goals of actors, but these assumptions are supplied by analysts, not by the approach per se. For most arguments in economics, and for some in political science, it is entirely plausible to attribute goals of material self-interest to actors. If one wants to explain how firms set their prices or which industries lobby for tariffs, it is reasonable to assume that material interests shape these decisions. There is, of course, nothing unique to rational choice in the idea that much of human behavior is motivated by material interests. It is an idea shared by most Marxist, neo-Marxist, pluralist, corporatist, ad hoc, and journalistic accounts of political behavior.

Many of the most interesting rational choice arguments about democratic politics, however, do not conceptualize the salient actor as *homo economicus*. Instead, they attribute to democratic politicians the goals of reelection, political survival, and career advancement. In some countries, the advancement of a political career may be the surest road to amassing a fortune, but, more commonly, officeholders could make more money doing something else. A rational choice argument might not offer a satisfactory account of why certain individuals choose politics though others choose business or professional careers. Once the choice has been made, however, it seems reasonable to attribute the goal of survival in office to those who have previously demonstrated a preference for officeholding, and rational choice arguments have had substantial success using this assumption to explain the behavior of politicians.

The theoretical bite of rational choice arguments depends both on the plausibility of the goals attributed to actors and on the ability of analysts to identify the goals a priori, that is, without reference to the specific behavior to be explained. Most of the time, analysts are on firm ground when they assume that actors prefer more material goods to less or that politicians prefer continuing their careers to ending them. It is obviously not true that all politicians prefer continuing their careers since some retire before every election, but if the average politician has this goal, then the argument that assumes the goal will explain average behavior. Rational choice arguments tend to become less persuasive and less useful as goals become more idiosyncratic. Thus rational choice arguments do a good job of explaining why most members of the U.S. Congress cater to the interests of their constituents, but they would not, in my view, do a good job of explaining why a few Russian intellectuals joined Lenin in his apparently hopeless struggle to overthrow the czar. It is possible to construct a rational choice explanation for this behavior, but it would leave unexplored one of the most puzzling factors needed to explain Lenin's followers: the origin of their unusual goals.

Plausibility of the a priori attribution of goals to actors thus limits the domain within which rational choice arguments are useful. Because the approach sets no limits on what the goals may be, it is possible to construct rational choice explanations for apparently irrational (in the everyday sense of the word) behavior by claiming that actors were rationally pursuing their own (idiosyncratic) goals. The person who, for instance, gives all his or her possessions to a religious cult can be said to be rationally pursuing the goal of self-abnegation. But when goals are directly inferred from observed behavior, rational choice arguments slide from "creative tautology," to use Brian Barry's phrase, into mere tautology.

Consequently, the appropriate domain for rational choice arguments, in my judgment, includes only situations in which plausible goals can be attributed to actors a priori. Rational choice arguments are not usually useful for explaining acts of extraordinary heroism, stupidity, or cruelty, which are usually motivated either by highly idiosyncratic goals or by momentary lapses of means-ends rationality. (They can, however, deal reasonably well with run-of-the-mill cruelty and stupidity, such as that occurring in Bosnia.) They are not useful in situations in which goals must be inferred from the specifics of the behavior one seeks to explain. Such "explanations" are vacuous.

Some examples from the study of revolution may help to clarify when plausible goals can be attributed to actors a priori, thus making rational choice arguments useful, and when they cannot. Powerful rational choice arguments have been suggested to explain why peasants, who can plausibly be assumed to maximize their own welfare, sometimes join revolutionary movements; why members of radical organizations, who can plausibly be assumed to maximize their chance of achieving power, choose particular political strategies; and why postrevolutionary regimes, which can plausibly be assumed to maximize survival in power, choose particular economic policies.[4] In these instances, the analyst can identify goals that are, on one hand, plausible, and that, on the other, motivate many behaviors, not just the one the analyst seeks to explain.

In contrast, there is, to my knowledge, no rational choice argument to explain why a few educated, middle-class individuals ignore family responsibilities and more secure and lucrative career opportunities in order to join nascent revolutionary movements in which the likelihood of achieving power is far lower than the likelihood of ending up dead or in jail. We know that such individuals play an important role in the early stages of revolutionary movements, regardless of the objective chances for movements' success. They can be incorporated within the rational choice framework as people who have unusual goals, and they are sometimes taken as a given in rational choice arguments that explain why people with more average goals sometimes join movements.[5] But rational choice arguments have not, and I suspect never will, offer a persuasive explanation for the goals of such exceptional individuals. Only their strategies, *given their goals*, are good grist for the rational choice mill.

Stable Preferences

The claim that rational choice arguments assume unchanging preferences is a misunderstanding born of a failure to distinguish everyday language from technical language. Rational choice arguments require only that preferences remain stable during the time it takes actors to choose strategies. This can be for the minute or two it takes an actor to decide how to vote in a committee, or it can be a period that covers many years if the analyst believes that actors faced the same situation repeatedly over a long period of time. The duration of stable preferences depends on how the analyst interprets the situations facing actors. If the analyst's reading of history suggests that preferences changed over time or in reaction to external shocks, then he or she can easily incorporate such a change into the rational choice argument through a change in payoffs.

Some discussions of the implausibility of unchanging preferences arise from a confusion between preferences as used in the rational choice idiom—what I have called "goals" here—and second-order, or strategic, preferences. The first-order preferences, or goals, commonly used in rational choice arguments are extremely simple and, in fact, are relatively stable (e.g., people prefer more to less material goods, politicians prefer to continue their careers). Second-order preferences are, as explained, choices of strategies for achieving first-order preferences. Politicians' policy preferences (in everyday language) may alter radically in response to changed circumstances. In the rational choice idiom, however, those everyday-language preferences are not referred to as "preferences," but instead as "strategies" for achieving actors' goals.

In short, the objection that rational choice arguments make implausible assumptions about unchanging preferences arises from a misunderstanding. The assumptions actually necessary to rational choice arguments about the stability of preferences are minimal and substantively innocuous.

Information and Calculating Requirements

A fourth objection to the use of rational choice arguments is that they make unrealistic assumptions about human calculating ability and information acquisition; it is argued that although people may try to pursue their goals efficiently, they lack sufficient information and calculating ability to do it. There is a sizable grain of truth in these claims, but it is mitigated by three circumstances. First, the information requirements are more implausible in some situations than in others. Rational choice arguments are most likely to be useful in situations in which these requirements do not strain credulity, and it is in these areas, as I show below, that they have been most successful. Second, for several reasons (also discussed below), people can sometimes behave as if they had sufficient information and calculating ability even when they do not. That is, they make the same choices they would have made if they had had full information and unlimited mental ability. Rational choice arguments also work pretty well when the analyst can demonstrate reasons to believe that people behave as if they were making rational calculations, even if they are not. Finally, although the simplest rational choice arguments usually assume complete information, techniques exist for incorporating incomplete information into models. Models that assume incomplete information can get complicated, but they pose no problem in principle.

Rational choice arguments work best in situations in which actors can identify other actors and know their goals, and in which the rules that govern interactions among actors are precise and known to all.[6] Many situations in democratic politics exhibit these characteristics, and, consequently, rational choice arguments have successfully explained a number of democratic processes. Interactions in legislatures, between legislatures and the bureaucracy, within party leaderships, within ruling coalitions, and in other political bodies established in democratic settings tend to involve easily identifiable actors whose goals are easy to establish and whose interactions are governed by precise, well-known procedural rules.

Rational choice arguments can even be used successfully in democracies that differ substantially from the ideal, as do many of the democracies in Latin America. Limitations on effective participation, representation, or party competition do not reduce the usefulness of rational choice arguments, as long as there is some competition in the system and interactions among political actors remain reasonably predictable and transparent to all involved.

Rational choice arguments are also more likely to be useful when explaining outcomes of high salience to the individuals involved. Actors spend more time and effort acquiring information when the results of their decisions have important consequences. The average citizen is often "rationally ignorant" about politics; his or her vote will have almost no effect on political outcomes, and therefore it would not be rational to spend time learning all about the issues and candidates. In contrast, the average legislator, whose career depends on making electorally correct choices, has good reason to use time and energy to stay well informed. Because of the visible and well-structured nature of governing institutions in established democracies and the importance to the careers of elected officials of making the right decisions, rational choice arguments have proved especially useful in explaining behaviors in these institutions.[7]

Whether rational choice arguments can be used successfully to explain decisionmaking within authoritarian regimes depends on their level of transparency, stability, and predictability.[8] Rational actor assumptions are likely to be plausible in regimes in which the rules governing survival and advancement are clear to both participants and observers and relatively unchanging, but not in regimes in which many decisions are made in secret by a small group of individuals and in which rules and rulers change frequently, radically, and unpredictably.[9]

Rational choice arguments can be useful in some circumstances even when actors lack crucial information. Actors can sometimes learn through trial and error to choose the same strategies that they would have chosen if they had had full information and the unrestricted ability to calculate. Thus, if situations are repeated over and over again, people can be expected to learn over time to understand the situation and to make more effective decisions. The more important the outcome to the person, the more effort will be expended on learning. It has been suggested that rational choice arguments will not work in very new or transitional democracies because the rules and players have not become established and actors have had no time to learn about the new system. Recent research suggests that this concern is overstated. The electoral incentives created by democracy are so powerful and transparent, and the results of decisions so important to hopeful politicians at the birth of democracy, that they spend whatever effort is necessary to acquire information and update it constantly to keep up with the fluidity of the political situation. To judge by their decisions, they are about as well informed and can calculate about as well as politicians in more institutionalized democracies.[10]

A plausible argument can be made, however, that voters in new democracies have fewer incentives than would-be politicians to learn about the options available in the new system and thus learn more slowly. As a result, substantial numbers of new voters may fail to vote for the parties that would best represent their interests. Modest support for this argument can be found in recent analyses of electoral behavior in

Eastern Europe. Voters in Hungary tell survey researchers that they prefer social democratic policies, but they do not vote for parties that offer this option.[11] The strongest vote for Communist successor parties in Bulgaria, Romania, and Poland comes from the most backward rural areas, not from the regions with a concentrated blue-collar vote that former Communist campaign promises have tried hardest to attract. In general, the association between socioeconomic status and party vote is substantially lower in Eastern Europe than in Western Europe. Although the evidence is not strong enough to prove that this is caused by incomplete information and various other explanations have been suggested, incomplete information is a plausible contender.[12] If so, then the tendency of rational choice arguments to be more useful for predicting elite behavior (because elites are more likely to approximate the information requirements of the model) than mass behavior may be exaggerated in transitional or fluid political situations.

Actors may also behave as if they were rational without conscious learning if some selection mechanism exists to weed out behaviors that lead to outcomes different from those a rational actor would have chosen. Just as differential survival rates eliminate less-efficient mutations in evolutionary theories, they can eliminate actors in other arenas who follow strategies that fail to converge with the outcomes that would have been produced by rational (that is, efficient) choices. It has been argued, for example, that firm managers do not actually think about profits when they make most decisions.[13] Nevertheless, existing firms behave as though they were profit-maximizers because competition drives out of business those that deviate too far from profit-maximizing behavior.[14] The same kind of argument can be made for politicians. Politicians may sincerely believe that they are ignoring constituency and interest-group pressures and are voting according to conscience, but if they deviate too far from behavior that maximizes their chances for reelection, they are likely to be defeated in the next election. As with learning, natural selection requires repetitions. Neither learning nor evolution can be used to support a claim that actors behave as if they were rational in unrepeated situations.

To summarize, the information and calculation requirements of the rational choice model are stiff. Rational choice arguments are more likely to succeed in explaining behavior when actors closely approximate these requirements. The appropriate domain of rational choice arguments thus includes situations in which outcomes are very important to actors, since that impels gathering knowledge; situations in which the rules governing interactions are clear and precise; and situations that occur repeatedly so that actors can learn, or efficient strategies can evolve even in the absence of conscious learning.[15] Where choices have few consequences (e.g.,

"cheap talk," such as survey responses) or little effect on overall outcomes (votes in elections), we should expect scant investment in information gathering, and rational choice arguments may not predict actors'
behavior very well. Where information is kept hidden from actors or the
rules that govern interactions change frequently and unpredictably (as in
some authoritarian regimes), rational choice arguments will probably not
be useful. Where situations are not repeated or no plausible selection
mechanism can be identified, rational choice arguments are likely to offer
less-explanatory leverage. Despite these numerous limitations, however,
much of politics remains inside the rational choice domain.

History and Context

The claim that rational choice theories ignore history and context is true
to the same degree that it is true about all theories. All theories identify
causes that can be expected to have the same effect, with some probability, within a specified domain. History and context may determine the
domain within which a theory is useful. Or they may determine the
values of the variables that enter the theory as independent variables. Or
they may supply the other variables that impinge on the relationship of
interest and thus affect the probability that the cause will actually have
the predicted effect. History and context enter into rational choice arguments in the same ways. If there is any difference, it is that the rational
choice approach provides criteria for selecting specific elements from the
vast rococo of reality for use in arguments, rather than leaving the choice
entirely to the observer's intuitions.

Contrary to the claims of critics, most rational choice arguments
about political behavior actually give primacy to institutions and other
contextual circumstances as causes of outcomes. "The rational-choice
approach focuses its attention on the constraints imposed on rational
actors—the institutions of a society. ... Individual action is assumed to be
optimal adaptation to an institutional environment, and interaction
between individuals is assumed to be an optimal response to each other.
Therefore, the prevailing institutions ... determine the behavior of the
actors, which in turn produces political or social outcomes."[16]

A couple of examples may clarify the integral relationship between
context and rational choice arguments. In a recent article that treats Catholic hierarchies as rational actors attempting to maximize the number of
the faithful, Anthony Gill found that the amount of competition from
Protestant evangelists, along with a few characteristics of the historic
church-state relationship in each country, predicted whether the Catholic
Church opposed authoritarianism.[17] In other words, the behavior of
interest (opposition to authoritarianism) is explained by a circumstance

(level of Protestant competition) and a small set of institutions (that structure church-state relations) in conjunction with the assumption that the church hierarchy acts rationally to pursue its goal (of maximizing the faithful). In a second example, using an argument that treats Latin American legislators as rational actors bent on reelection, Nancy Lapp found that institutional changes that increase the importance of the peasant vote (e.g., illiterate suffrage, secret ballot, or easy registration) lead to land reform.[18] In these and other rational choice explanations of political phenomena, variations in institutions (e.g., changes in electoral laws) and other contextual circumstances (e.g., the amount of competition from Protestants) cause differences in the incentives faced by rational actors, who then make decisions in accordance with the incentives they face. Far from being ahistorical or acontextual, rational choice arguments about politics depend heavily on context.

Determinism

The rational choice model, that is, the deductive logic that connects the choice of means to preexisting goals, is deterministic. This does not, however, imply that rational choice arguments make deterministic predictions of behavior. The most useful way to think of rational choice arguments is as if-then statements of the form: *if* actors have the goals the observer claims, *if* the information and calculation requirements are plausible (for any of the reasons noted above), and *if* the actors actually face the rules and payoffs the observer claims they do, *then* certain behavior will occur. Some slippage can occur at each *if* without necessarily eviscerating the whole argument. A few actors may have goals that differ from the majority's. For example, a few members of Congress may not care about reelection. If most do, however, the argument will still explain the behavior of most of them and therefore the outputs of the legislature. Some actors may lack information or the ability to calculate. For example, freshman legislators may not yet have "learned the ropes," but if most legislators are not freshmen, the argument will still hold. Or the observer may misunderstand the situation that faces some actors even though the situation facing most of them has been correctly interpreted. For example, the observer may incorrectly assume that payoffs to members of small parties are the same as payoffs to members of large parties. If so, the argument will still explain the behavior of members of large parties. In all of these examples, an empirical test of the argument (if one is possible) should show that the argument explains a substantial part of the outcome, though not every individual case. In other words, the argument results in probabilistic predictions and explanations, just as other social science arguments do.

This section has dealt with a series of misconceptions about rational choice arguments. It has shown that several of them are simply that: misunderstandings that should not be permitted to muddy the waters any longer. Other misperceptions bring to light serious impediments to using rational choice arguments to explain all conceivable human behaviors. I have argued that these objections should be taken seriously and used to delimit the domain within which rational choice arguments can be expected to be useful. I now turn to a different question: What really distinguishes the rational choice approach from others? □

THE RATIONAL CHOICE APPROACH

The defining features of the rational choice approach are (1) methodological individualism, usually applied to individual people but sometimes also to organizations that can plausibly be expected to behave as unitary rational actors;[19] (2) explicit identification of actors and their goals or preferences; (3) explicit identification of the institutions and other contextual features that determine the options available to actors and the costs and benefits associated with different options; and (4) deductive logic. The rational choice approach has no monopoly on any of these features. Furthermore, most arguments originally posed within other frameworks can be translated into rational choice idiom. Advocates of structuralist arguments, for example, believe that structural conditions cause outcomes. They consider it unnecessary to spell out explicitly how structures determine the incentives facing particular individuals and thus determine their choices and, through their choices, social outcomes. Nevertheless, the analyst who wants to incorporate these intervening steps into a structuralist argument usually has no trouble doing so.

In short, there is nothing very unusual about the assumptions or structure of rational choice arguments. Nevertheless, the focus on the incentives facing individuals, the ruthless pruning of extraneous complexity, and the use of deductive logic have together resulted in a cluster of theoretical results both novel and fruitful (discussed below).

The rational choice literature in political science is now so enormous that it would be impossible even to catalog it briefly. Rather than attempting a comprehensive survey, I focus on the developments within rational choice theory that seem most potentially fruitful for the study of democratic (and quasi-democratic) politics in developing countries. I deal with three categories of arguments: those that depend on the unintended and nonobvious results of aggregating individually rational choices; those that unpack the black box of the state by looking explicitly at the individuals who actually make state decisions, the goals that shape their behavior, and the incentives they face; and those that treat political decisions as strategic interactions among actors rather than as decisions under external constraint. □

THE CONSEQUENCES OF AGGREGATION

The theoretical development within the rational choice framework that has had the most radical and far-reaching effect on our understanding of the political world is the series of proofs that group decisions will not necessarily, or even usually, reflect the interests of the majority in the group, even if members of the group are entirely equal and decisions are arrived at democratically. Among a number of nonobvious and sometimes perverse aggregation effects,[20] two stand out in terms of their political and theoretical consequences: the proof that majority rule does not necessarily result in policies that reflect majority preferences; and the demonstration that individuals who would benefit from public goods will not, if they are rational, usually help achieve them.

Cycles Under Majority Rule
and the Effects of Intralegislative Institutions

Kenneth Arrow developed the original proof that the aggregation of preferences through majority rule (given a set of plausible conditions) may lead to policy cycles.[21] Arrow's results have been extended, developed, and revised by a number of scholars, most notably Richard McKelvey, Amartya Sen, and Thomas Schwartz.[22] The theoretical work in this area is mathematical, and I am not the person to summarize it adequately. Instead, let me note some of the substantive implications that flow from it.

First, majority rule is no guarantee that the interests of the majority will be reflected in policy. A series of votes in a representative institution, such as a legislature, can result in any possible policy outcome, depending on the *sequencing* of votes on different options—usually called agenda control.[23] Thus one need not posit powerful interest groups that buy votes through campaign contributions or hegemonic classes to explain the failure of legislatures to represent the interests of the majority of voters. Powerful groups *may* greatly influence policy—whether they do is an empirical question—but the mere existence of unrepresentative policies does not show that they do. The consequence of this result is to focus attention on the leadership and institutions within representative institutions in order to figure out who controls the agenda and how, and to figure out what causes policy stability when Arrow's proof leads to the expectation of cycling.

An enormous rational choice literature has arisen, most of it focused on the U.S. Congress, that seeks to explain how congressional institutions and procedures lead to relatively stable policy outcomes.[24] Implicitly or explicitly, these arguments also address the question of how representative legislatures are likely to be under different institutional arrangements (especially rules governing the role of committees, assignment to committees, and amendments from the floor). Some comparative work on the effects of intralegislative institutions has been done, but almost none, to my knowledge, on legislatures in developing or former Communist countries.[25]

Research in this area could help to explain differences in representativeness across countries, tendencies toward immobilism versus legislative effectiveness, and biases in policy outcomes. It would also, by broadening the range of institutions across which comparisons could be made, make an important contribution toward the development of theories about the effects of intralegislative institutions. In order to apply these models to legislatures in developing countries, assumptions about the functioning of the institutions themselves would obviously have to be revised. Since Latin American political systems resemble the U.S. system in terms of the fundamental division of power between the president and the legislature, however, there is reason to believe that models developed to explain outcomes in the United States would provide a useful starting point for the study of intralegislative institutions in Latin America.

Collective Action Problems

Nearly thirty years ago, Mancur Olson demonstrated the political consequences of combining standard assumptions about individual rationality with the notion of public goods developed by economists.[26] Public goods have the following properties: Once supplied to a target group, no member of the group can be excluded from enjoying them, whether the person helped to create them or not; and use of the good by one individual does not reduce its availability or usefulness to others. The standard example is clean air. Once laws limiting pollution have been passed, clean air (the public good) can be enjoyed by all. Whether or not a person did anything to bring it about—work to pass a clean-air law, pay for an antipollution device for his or her car, or do whatever might be necessary to create clean air—no one can be denied its use, and, in most circumstances, the fact that many other people are breathing it does not crowd anyone out or reduce the air's healthful effects.

Consequently, it is not rational for any individual to contribute toward attaining the good. If, on one hand, enough people are already willing to do the work or pay the cost to bring about the public good, there is no reason to do anything oneself, since one will enjoy its benefits when it arrives regardless of whether one worked for it. But if, on the other hand, there are not presently enough individuals at work to produce the public good, there is still no reason to contribute, since any one person's efforts are extremely unlikely to make the difference in whether the public good is produced. There are, as it turns out, certain conditions under which it is rational for individuals to band together in collective action, but the conditions are somewhat stringent and often go unmet. Hence effective collective action toward a commonly held goal often fails to develop, even when it seems to a casual observer that it would be in everyone's interest to cooperate.

The logic of collective action leads to devastating revisions of some standard ideas about politics. It breaks the link between individual interests and group political action that underlies virtually all interest-based understandings of politics, from Marxist to pluralist. The failure of lower-class groups to organize to defend their interests, for example, is transformed from an anomaly to be explained by false consciousness or Gramscian hegemony into the behavior expected of rational actors from the lower-classes.

The effects for democratic theory are equally serious. The logic of collective action leads to the expectation that the interests of average citizens are unlikely to influence policymaking, since ordinary people are unlikely to organize to express their interests effectively. In general, government policies that supply benefits to groups are public goods for the group, even if the goods themselves are privately consumed. Organizing to press for benefits is costly to the individuals who could benefit from the goods if they were supplied, and, because the goods are public, it is not rational for individuals to bear these costs if they can "free ride" instead.

The logic of collective action has a number of frequently observed but—prior to Olson—misunderstood substantive consequences. Groups in which resources are distributed unequally, for example, are more likely to be able to organize than are groups in which members are more equal; inequality increases the likelihood that one member of the group will receive enough benefits from a public good to be willing to shoulder the costs of lobbying, regardless of the free riding of others. This argument has been used to explain why industries that contain one or a few very large firms are more likely to be protected by tariffs.

Small groups are more likely to be able to organize to press for the policies they prefer than are larger groups. In small groups, members can recognize whether others are contributing and punish those who free ride. As a result, they can solve the collective action problem by changing the incentives facing individual members. This explains why special interest groups are often effective in the policy arena even when most citizens disagree with them or could benefit from different policies. The relationship between group size and the ability to organize also helps explain the prevalence of agricultural pricing policies in Africa that benefit the relatively small number of urban consumers (and their employers, since low food prices reduce the demand for wages) at the expense of large numbers of rural producers.[27]

Previously organized groups are more likely to achieve the policies they want than are the unorganized. Because organization is costly, groups that have already paid start-up costs have an advantage over groups that have not. It is easier to change the purpose of an existing group than to form a new group. This argument has been used to explain why political leaders in new states often mobilize followers along ethnic lines. It is more difficult to form new groups than to turn to new purposes ethnically based organizations that already exist.[28]

Most of these substantive arguments have been made in the context of either the United States or Africa. Nevertheless, their implications for other countries are obvious. Tariffs elsewhere have also tended to protect large industries. Pricing and other policies affecting the relative welfare of urban and rural dwellers have, on average, disadvantaged the less-organized rural inhabitants. The barriers to the entry of new parties representing recently enfranchised groups have, on average, been high. The logic of collective action implies that policies, *even in fair and competitive democracies*, will tend to benefit the rich and well organized at the expense of the more numerous poor and unorganized, simply because the former are more likely to be able to exercise their rights effectively; it thus offers a possible explanation for one of the central characteristics of policy choice in most of the world. □

INSIDE THE BLACK BOX OF THE STATE

The paradoxical effects of aggregation discussed above result from the pursuit of individual interests by actors in society. Their representatives in government are either assumed simply to reflect constituency interests (as in the cycling and intralegislative institutional literature) or never discussed with care (as in the collective action literature). In the collective action literature, elected representatives tend to reflect the interests of whichever groups lobby hardest or make the largest campaign contributions.

A second stream of rational choice theorizing has moved further from its roots in economics to focus on the actors inside the black box of the state.[29] Despite the emphasis placed on the state recently by new institutionalists and others, rational choice arguments are the only ones that make systematic links between particular institutional characteristics of states and the behavior of elected and appointed officials. Practitioners of rational choice were not the first to notice the autonomy of the political (or the state), but they have been the most successful at producing theories that use state or political characteristics to explain policy outcomes.

Rational choice arguments about state or government actors begin with explicit attention to their goals and then consider the ways that various behaviors and choices can affect the achievement of goals in given institutional settings. The keystone of the approach is a simple model of politicians as rational individuals who attempt to maximize career success. In the U.S. context, this is often simplified to maximizing the probability of reelection, but somewhat broader conceptions of what it is that politicians maximize have been suggested and successfully used by comparativists.[30] Using this one simple assumption about goals and a small number of characteristics of the U.S. political system, rational choice arguments have explained many of the behaviors that characterize members of Congress: the devotion of large amounts of resources to constituency service; the preference for pork; position taking and credit claiming; the avoidance of votes on controversial issues; and the assiduous pursuit of media coverage.[31]

Other rational choice arguments link election-seeking or survival-maximizing to particular kinds of policy outcomes. Anthony Downs has argued that parties trying to maximize the probability of election in a two-party system offer policy platforms that converge to the center of the electorate's preferences.[32] James Buchanan and Gordon Tullock, followed by a long series of books and articles in the public choice tradition, have claimed that various inefficient government interventions in the economy can be explained as results of the efforts of election-seeking politicians to secure support from constituents and campaign contributions from special interests.[33] Anne Krueger demonstrated the political benefits and general welfare losses associated with import quotas and other forms of state intervention in the economies of developing countries.[34] Robert Bates showed that African agricultural policies, chosen in part to consolidate political support, lead to reduced food production, reduced agricultural exports, and recurring balance-of-payments crises.[35] In all these cases, analysts have shown how clear political incentives lead state actors to adopt economically inefficient policies. Barry Ames went a step further and claimed that presidents in Latin American countries generally choose policies in order to maximize their chances of survival in office.[36]

Still other rational choice arguments examine coalition formation, the relationship between politicians and bureaucrats, and the creation of new political institutions. William Riker's seminal analysis of coalition formation began a long and fruitful inquiry into the study of coalitions.[37] A variety of rational choice arguments have shown that the relationship of election-oriented politicians to self-interested bureaucrats affect legislative oversight, policy implementation, and the supply of both public goods and constituency services.[38] Buchanan and Tullock were the first to argue explicitly that political institutions are political creations, and that their creation and operation can be understood only by understanding the individual purposes they serve. Since then, changes in many other political institutions—innovations in the committee system of the U.S. Congress, changes in the nominating procedures for British members of Parliament and in French electoral laws, and the choice or representative institutions and electoral rules during transitions to democracy in Latin America and Eastern Europe—have been explained as results of the efforts of politicians to maximize their long-term electoral success.[39] In short, a set of extremely simple arguments that begin with the assumption that politicians are self-interested maximizers of the probability of political survival or reelection, along with a context supplied by the institutions of a given political system, provide explanations of many of the political outcomes scholars would most like to understand.

Of special interest during the current debate in developing and former Communist countries over which democratic institutions would best serve the interests of citizens are rational choice arguments that compare the effects of different institutions on stability and economic policymaking. The advantage of institutional comparisons based on the rational choice approach over other kinds of institutional comparisons is that they examine the *incentives* created by institutions, not simply the outcomes associated with different institutions. When only outcomes are compared—as, for example, when analysts argue that parliamentarism leads to greater stability based on a comparison between European parliamentary systems and American presidential systems—it is often impossible to tell if the institutional difference is really the cause of the difference in stability. The difference might be caused by level of development or any one of a number of other characteristics that distinguish European countries, on average, from American. The rational choice approach cannot "prove" which institutions work better any more than any other approach can, but it has the advantage of spelling out rigorously and deductively why particular institutions can be expected to have particular effects.

The comparative study of the effects of political institutions has a long and distinguished history.[40] But until recently, most of this literature focused on the effect of electoral institutions on either the number of parties in the system or the fairness of the translation of votes into seats, and these were not issues of great interest outside Western Europe.[41] Now, with constitutional changes taking place in many developing and former Communist countries and discussion of constitutional change going on in nearly all of them, institutional questions have taken on new salience as academics and politicians try to figure out what the effects of different institutional choices are likely to be on issues ranging from long-term political stability to rapid growth and the distribution of income. Although little work has so far been done in this area, it is one in which major advances can be expected as comparativists become more familiar with the rational choice idiom and methodology. □

STRATEGIC INTERACTIONS AMONG POLITICAL ACTORS

The final subset of rational choice arguments to be discussed here is game theory. To the standard apparatus of rational choice arguments in which individuals respond to a particular set of institutional incentives, game theory adds the idea that individuals strategically interact with each other to produce social outcomes. That is, game theory "seeks to explore how people make decisions if their actions and fates depend on the actions of others."[42] In nongame theoretic arguments individuals are assumed to pursue their goals within constraints imposed by the environment. In game theory, actors decide how best to pursue their goals after taking into account both environmental constraints and the equally rational and strategic behavior of other actors. Since strategic behavior and interdependence are fundamental characteristics of politics, game theory offers a particularly useful approach to understanding political actors and processes.[43]

Game theoretic explanations of politics have emerged from the study of elections and legislative decisionmaking, mostly in the United States. Much of this literature, like that on intralegislative institutions, is both abstract and highly technical, and I do not discuss it here. Indeed, a shortcoming of much game theory is that, because of the great complexity of interactions among strategic players, many game theoretic studies are heavy on mathematical theorizing and short on credible empirical results. Here, therefore, I focus on less technical and less abstract applications of game theory that have proved fruitful in substantive terms.

One of the most revolutionary contributions of game theory to thinking about politics is the prisoner's dilemma. The prisoner's dilemma game describes the logic of situations in which two or more individuals would all end up better off if they could agree among themselves to cooperate, but, if binding agreements are impossible, each will be better off if he or she chooses not to cooperate. Since it is rational for each individual to refuse to cooperate, none do; the goal is not achieved and all are worse off than they might have been had they cooperated. This may have a familiar ring to it, and it should. The prisoner's dilemma game is a generalization of the collective action problem discussed above.[44] Much of the work on prisoner's dilemma games has focused on the difference between single interactions and interactions that are repeated (or "iterated") over time. Although it is always rational for all players to defect in single games, under some circumstances cooperation is rational when games are repeated.

Prisoner's dilemma games have been used to explain many situations in international relations. They can also offer leverage for explaining domestic political outcomes, for example: interactions among coalition partners; pacts such as the Colombian National Front, in which traditional enemies agree to cooperate to limit competition in order to secure the democratic system that benefits both and to exclude other potential competitors; and the pervasiveness of patron-client relationships. Other simple games illuminate the logical structure of other situations.[45]

One of the earliest nontechnical game theoretic arguments of relevance for students of Latin American countries is Guillermo O'Donnell's analysis of the game between Argentine parties between 1955 and 1966.[46] Game theory has also been used to explain the initiation of civil service reform in Latin America.[47] George Tsebelis's game theoretic analysis of interactions between party elites and masses, and between elites of different parties in Belgium, has obvious implications for understanding politics in other divided societies. His treatment of electoral coalitions in France should be read by anyone interested in countries such as Poland, Peru, Brazil, and Chile, which have multiparty systems and runoff elections.

In my opinion, game theory is the most exciting and potentially fruitful strand of the rational choice approach. Its strategic and interactive image of politics is realistic, and it can be used to illuminate political situations without recourse to advanced mathematics.[48] Although theoretical developments in game theory will continue to be made by the mathematically gifted and trained, substantive progress can be made using the simple logic that game theory provides. □

RATIONAL CHOICE AND THE LATIN AMERICAN RESEARCH FRONTIER

To some extent, the choice of which intellectual perspective to embrace is simply a matter of taste. A taste for rational choice arguments may involve little more than a preference for the austere over the rococo. It is often suggested that an attraction to the rational choice approach implies a (naive) belief in human rationality, or at least a belief that if people are not rational, they should be. Some practitioners may feel this way, but I, at any rate, do not. The appeal of the rational choice approach, in my view, lies in its substantive plausibility in numerous political situations, its theoretical coherence, the fruitful simplification of "buzzing blooming" reality it offers, which facilitates comparative work, and its capacity to explain puzzling outcomes and generate nonobvious conclusions.

Rational choice arguments deal only with systematic patterns of incentives that lead to systematic patterns in outcomes. In contrast, more contingent political arguments, such as those that characterize the Juan Linz and Alfred Stepan series on the breakdown of democracy and the Guillermo O'Donnell, Philippe Schmitter, and Laurence Whitehead series on redemocratization, focus on the specific conjunctural circumstances that make particular decisions understandable.[49] The strength of such contingent political explanations is that they offer a very complete treatment of events; their weakness is that they do not easily lend themselves to the construction of general theories. Rational choice arguments have the opposite strengths and weaknesses. They invariably omit from the analysis colorful and arresting details that some observers consider important. But, by abstracting from the specifics of particular cases, they make theory-building possible and facilitate comparisons across cases that may at first appear too different to compare.

Many criticize rational choice models on the grounds that they simplify reality to such a degree that the model seems to bear no resemblance at all to the real world. And some work unquestionably deserves this stricture. Rational choice arguments can easily cross the line from simple to simplistic. Persuasive and useful applications of the rational choice approach, however, take into account the most important features of the social and institutional setting. They also draw insights from important abstract arguments. The bite of good rational choice arguments comes from the synthesis of empirical evidence from the cases under examination and abstract deductive logic.

Using rational choice models requires the analyst to identify relevant actors, to determine their preferences, and to present a plausible justification for the attribution of preferences. Observers can, of course, make mistakes in their attribution of preferences, but rational choice models do "have the advantage of being naked so that, unlike those of some less explicit theories, [their] limitations are likely to be noticeable."[50] The rational choice approach does not prescribe any particular methodology for testing hypotheses, but persuasive work combines deductive rational choice arguments with examinations of evidence to see if it conforms to the expectations generated by the deductive model.

This summary of rational actor explanations has dealt only with some of the best-known arguments that directly address questions fundamental to understanding democratic politics. Even this brief survey shows that there is a well-developed rational choice literature replete with theories that have only begun to be extended and modified for use in Latin

American countries. Analysts so far have made use only of the simplest of the theories about parties and legislatures that have emerged in the context of U.S. politics. With increasing democratization, this literature should begin to seem more relevant to scholars interested in understanding politics in Latin America.

Recent events set the agenda for future applications of the rational choice approach by students of Latin American politics. Because institutions determine available options and affect strategic choices, the institutional fluidity of democratizing and recently democratized countries poses a challenge and opportunity for the rational choice approach. This fluidity determines the research frontier.

Two areas seem to me especially overdue for systematic attention from rational choice practitioners. The first is the emergence and consolidation of democracy. Scholars working on developing countries have in the past focused so heavily on economic, cultural, and social structural causes of political outcomes that many have found themselves at a loss to come up with systematic explanations of democratization—since underlying economic and cultural conditions have changed little—and thus they have fallen back on ad hoc inductive generalizations. Rational choice arguments that focus on the incentives facing political actors during democratization have the potential for producing much more satisfying explanations. A start has been made on the task of illuminating democratization through the use of rational choice arguments and game theory, but much remains to be done.[51] Little analysis of legislatures and party systems in new democracies has been carried out, and most of what exists is theoretically primitive. Some interesting and insightful studies of particular parties exist, but these studies do little to explain the interactions among political actors that determine how political systems work.

The second and, to my mind, most exciting area for new research involves the creation of new institutions. Rational choice arguments about the creation of institutions are in their infancy.[52] Most explanations of institutional change by economists assume that efficiency gains explain changes, without considering who reaps the benefits of efficiency gains and who loses as a result of changes. The challenge for rational choice theorists is to revise such economic arguments by incorporating the effects of different actors pursuing their own, often inconsistent goals, and the nonobvious effects of the aggregation of individual choices.

Current events in Latin America and Eastern Europe provide a great opportunity for building theories to explain institutional creation precisely because so many institutions are being created, changed, and destroyed. Struggles over the design of new political institutions have recently taken place in several countries, and many more can be expected during the next few years. Compelling explanations of such important institutional changes would have a tremendous impact not only in our own field but in political science as a whole, reflecting back on how Western Europe and the United States arrived at the institutions that now rigidly structure their politics. We have a large and sophisticated theoretical literature on which to build. Progress should be rapid, once work begins. □

NOTES

I am grateful to Peter H. Smith, David Collier, Jonathan Hartlyn, and John Zaller for comments on earlier versions of this chapter, and to the National Science Foundation, Institutional Reform and the Informal Sector, and the Latin American Center of the University of California at Los Angeles for support while it was being written.

1. Rational choice arguments have also been used to explain the behavior of authoritarian governments. Douglass North, Margaret Levi, and Mancur Olson, for example, have used the assumption that monarchs or autocrats maximize revenue as the basis for important arguments about economic transformation and the development of democracy. Douglass North, "Framework for Analyzing the State in Economic History," *Explorations in Economic History* 16 (1979): 249–259; Margaret Levi, *Of Rule and Revenue* (Berkeley: University of California Press, 1988); Mancur Olson, "Dictatorship, Democracy, and Development," *American Political Science Review* 87 (1993): 567–576, and "Autocracy, Democracy, and Prosperity" (paper prepared for the American Political Science Association meetings, Washington, DC, 1991). But the immense proliferation of rational choice explanations has occurred in the context of democratic politics. It is these theories that I think have the most to offer Latin Americanists trying to understand current political processes.

2. James March and Johan P. Olsen, "The New Institutionalism: Organizational Factors in Political Life," *American Political Science Review* 78 (1984): 734–749.

3. Robert Bates, "Macropolitical Economy in the Field of Development," in James Alt and Kenneth Shepsle, eds., *Perspectives on Positive Political Economy* (Cambridge: Cambridge University Press, 1990), p. 46.

4. Samuel Popkin, *The Rational Peasant* (Berkeley: University of California Press, 1979); James DeNardo, *Power in Numbers* (Princeton: Princeton University Press, 1985); and Forrest Colburn, *Post-Revolutionary Nicaragua* (Berkeley: University of California Press, 1986).

5. For example, Susanne Lohmann, "Rationality, Revolution and Revolt: The Dynamics of Informational Cascades" (Graduate School of Business research paper, no. 1213a, Stanford University, 1992); and "A Signaling Model of Informative and Manipulative Political Action," *American Political Science Review* 87 (1993): 319–333.

6. George Tsebelis, *Nested Games: Rational Choice in Comparative Politics* (Berkeley: University of California Press, 1990), p. 32.

7. For example, John Ferejohn, *Pork Barrel Politics* (Stanford: Stanford University Press, 1974); Morris Fiorina, *Congress: Keystone of the Washington Establishment* (New Haven: Yale University Press, 1977); Morris Fiorina and Roger Noll, "Voters, Bureaucrats and Legislators: A Rational Choice Perspective on the Growth of Bureaucracy," *Journal of Public Economy* 9 (1978): 239–254; Thomas Hammond and Gary Miller, "The Core of the Constitution," *American Political Science Review* 81 (1987): 1155–1174; David Mayhew, *Congress: The Electoral Connection* (New Haven: Yale University Press, 1974); Kenneth Shepsle and Barry Weingast, "Structure-Induced Equilibrium and Legislative Choice," *Public Choice* 37 (1981): 503–519.

8. The point being made here has to do with the plausibility of the information requirements of the rational choice model for individuals operating in different kinds of political systems. When the analyst treats the state itself as a rational actor, authoritarianism has little effect on the plausibility of assumptions about information and may make more plausible the unitary actor assumption.

9. Peter H. Smith, for example, has used motivational assumptions consistent with the rational choice approach (though without explicit rational choice jargon) to explain the behavior of officials in Mexico's Partido Revolucionario Institucional (PRI). See Peter H. Smith, *Labyrinths of Power: Political Recruitment in 20th Century Mexico* (Princeton: Princeton University Press, 1979). This kind of analysis would have been much harder to do in Kampuchea.

10. Barbara Geddes, "The Initiation of New Democratic Institutions in Eastern Europe and Latin America," in Arend Lijphart and Carlos Waisman, eds., *Institutional Design in New Democracies* (Boulder: Westview Press, forthcoming).

11. Tamás Kolosi, Iván Szelényi, Szonja Szelényi, and Bruce Western, "The Making of Political Fields in Post-Communist Transition (Dynamics of Class and Party in Hungarian Politics, 1989–90)," in András Bozóki, András Körösényi, and George Schöpflin, eds., *Post-Communist Transition: Emerging Pluralism in Hungary* (New York: St. Martin's Press, 1992); László Bruszt and János Simon, "The Great Transformation in Hungary and Eastern Europe" (paper prepared for the Southern California Workshop on Political and Economic Liberalization, University of Southern California, Los Angeles, 1992).

12. Some have suggested that East European voters have longer time horizons than are usually attributed to voters in the West, and that they vote for candidates who offer radical reform despite short-term costs because they expect that they or their children will benefit in the long run. This argument seems less plausible now than it did a couple of years ago, since the vote for candidates and parties that actively support radical economic reform during their campaigns has fallen in more recent elections. Others, most notably Kenneth Jowitt ("The Leninist Legacy, in Ivo Banac, ed., *Eastern Europe in the 1990s* [Ithaca: Cornell University Press, 1991], and *The New World Disorder: The Leninist Extinction* [Berkeley: University of California Press, 1992]), argue that citizens in the new democracies of Eastern Europe have goals different from the essentially materialist ones usually attributed to voters in established democracies. If Jowitt's view is correct, East European voters are not inefficiently pursuing the goal of policies that will improve their material situations because they lack sufficient information about the new system, but rather are pursuing, perhaps efficiently, some other goal.

13. Richard R. Nelson and Sidney G. Winter, *An Evolutionary Theory of Economic Change* (Cambridge, MA: Harvard University Press, 1982).

14. Armen Alchian, "Uncertainty, Evolution, and Economic Theory," *Journal of Political Economy* 58 (1950): 211–222; Sidney G. Winter, "Economic `Natural Selection' and the Theory of the Firm," *Yale Economics Essays* 4 (1964): 225–272.

15. Tsebelis, *Nested Games*, pp. 31–39, makes a similar but more emphatic argument.

16. Tsebelis, *Nested Games*, p. 40.

17. Anthony Gill, "Rendering unto Caesar? Religious Competition and Catholic Political Strategy in Latin America, 1962–1979," *American Journal of Political Science* 38 (1994): 403–425.

18. Nancy Lapp, "The Extension of Suffrage and Land Reform in Latin America" (paper prepared for the Latin American Studies Association meeting, Atlanta, March 1994).

19. In my judgment, not shared by all practitioners, a further limitation on the appropriate domain of rational choice arguments is that they are only likely to be useful when the unit of analysis is either the individual or a hierarchical and well-organized group. The reason for the need for hierarchy and organization is that, as Kenneth Arrow (*Social Choice and Individual Values* [New Haven: Yale University Press, 1950]) and Richard McKelvey ("Intransitivities in Multidimensional Voting Models and Some Implications for Agenda Control," *Journal of Economic Theory* 12 [1976]: 472–482) have shown, nondictatorial methods for aggregating preferences within groups lead to cycles, and thus violate the consistency requirement of rationality. See also Jon Elster, ed., *Rational Choice: Readings in Social and Political Theory* (New York: New York University Press, 1986), pp. 3–4. Extensive research on the U.S. Congress shows that institutional arrangements within groups can prevent cycling and lead to stable outcomes, and thus it may be reasonable to treat even democratic states as unitary actors in some circumstances. But these kinds of institutions do not exist in unorganized groups such as classes. It seems reasonable to treat unions, states in the international arena, and parties (in some circumstances) as rational unitary actors, since the analyst can usually discover the institutions that lead to stability. In general, however, unorganized groups such as classes or interest groups do not behave as rational unitary actors. One can use rational choice arguments to explain the behavior of members of these groups, and of groups as aggregates of these individuals, but not of such groups as corporate units.

20. See Thomas Schelling, *Micromotives and Macrobehavior* (New York: W. W. Norton, 1978) for other aggregation effects.

21. Arrow, *Social Choice and Individual Values*.

22. McKelvey, "Intransitivities"; and Richard McKelvey, "General Conditions for Global Intransitivities in Formal Voting Models," *Econometrica* 48 (1979): 1085–1111; Amartya Sen, *Collective Choice and Social Welfare* (San Francisco: Holden Day, 1970); Thomas Schwartz, *The Logic of Collective Choice* (New York: Columbia University Press, 1986).

23. McKelvey, "Intransitivities"; Norman Schofield, "Instability of Simple Dynamic Games," *Review of Economic Studies* 45 (1976): 575–594.

24. For example, Kenneth Shepsle, "Institutional Arrangements and Equilibrium in Multidimensional Voting Models," *American Journal of Political Science* 23 (1979): 27–36; Shepsle and Weingast, "Structure-Induced Equilibrium"; Kenneth Shepsle and Barry Weingast, "Uncovered Sets and Sophisticated Voting Outcomes with Implications for Agenda Institutions," *American Journal of Political Science* 28 (1984): 49–74; Kenneth Shepsle and Barry Weingast, "The Institutional Foundations of Committee Power," *American Political Science Review* 81 (1987): 85–114; and Kenneth Shepsle and Barry Weingast, "Reflections on Committee Power," *American Political Science Review* 81 (1987): 935–945; Arthur Denzau and Robert MacKay, "Structure-Induced Equilibria and Perfect-Foresight Expectations," *American Journal of Political Science* 25 (1981): 762–779, and Arthur Denzau and Robert MacKay, "Gatekeeping and Monopoly Power of Committees: An Analysis of Sincere and Sophisticated Behavior," *American Journal of Political Science* 27 (1993): 740–761. See Keith Krehbiel, "Spatial Models of Legislative Choice," *Legislative Studies Quarterly* 13 (1988): 259–319, for an extremely useful review of some of the most important arguments and how they fit together.

25. For example, John Huber, "Restrictive Legislative Procedures in France and the United States," *American Political Science Review* 86 (1992): 675–687. The first steps in this direction have been taken in a series of recent papers by Barry Ames, "Disparately Seeking Politicians: Strategies and Outcomes in Brazilian Legislative Elections" (paper prepared for the Latin American Studies Association, Los Angeles, 1992); and "Wheeling, Dealing, Stealing, and Appealing: Bases of Voting in the Brazilian Congress" (manuscript, Washington University, 1993); Barry Ames and David Nixon, "Understanding New Legislatures: Observations and Evidence from the Brazilian Congress" (paper prepared for the American Political Science Association, Washington, DC, 1993). Barry Ames, *Political Survival: Politicians and Public Policy in Latin America* (Berkeley: University of California Press, 1987) contains some discussion of the committee system and procedures for appointing committee members and chamber leadership in Brazil between 1946 and 1964. A number of descriptive studies of Latin American legislatures were carried out during the 1970s; for example, Gary Hoskin, Francisco Leal, and Harvey Kline, *Legislative Behavior in Colombia* (Buffalo: Council on International Studies, State University of New York at Buffalo, 1976); Weston Agor, *The Chilean Senate: Internal Distribution of Influence* (Austin: Institute of Latin American Studies, University of Texas Press, 1971); Weston Agor, ed., *Latin American Legislative Systems: Their Role and Influence* (New York: Praeger, 1972); Robert Packenham, "Legislatures and Political Development," in Alan Kornberg and Lloyd Musolf, eds., *Legislatures in Developmental Perspective* (Durham: Duke University Press, 1970); Peter H. Smith, *Argentina and the Failure of Democracy: Conflict Among Political Elites, 1904–1955* (Madison: University of Wisconsin Press, 1974). Many observers currently follow legislative activities closely in their respective countries. I know of no one besides Ames, however, who has tried to extend, adapt, or disconfirm the models developed to explain the effects of legislative institutions in the United States in developing or former Communist countries.

26. *The Logic of Collective Action: Public Goods and the Theory of Groups* (Cambridge, MA: Harvard University Press, 1965).

27. Robert Bates, *Markets and States in Tropical Africa* (Berkeley: University of California Press, 1981).

28. Bates, "Macropolitical Economy."

29. The word "state" is not often used in literature dealing with the United States. Nevertheless, within the standard terminology of comparative politics, arguments that focus on the causes of decisions by presidents, legislators, and government bureaucrats open up the black box of the state to see how the mechanisms inside work.

30. Ronald Rogowski, "Rationalist Theories of Politics: A Midterm Report," *World Politics* 40 (1978): 296–323. See also Ames, *Political Survival*.

31. Mayhew, *Congress: The Electoral Connection*; Ferejohn, *Pork Barrel Politics*; Fiorina, *Congress*; Kenneth Shepsle and Barry Weingast, "Political Preferences for the Pork Barrel: A Generalization," *American Journal of Political Science* 25 (1981): 96–111.

32. Anthony Downs, *An Economic Theory of Democracy* (New York: Harper, 1957).

33. James Buchanan and Gordon Tullock, *The Calculus of Consent* (Ann Arbor: University of Michigan Press, 1962).

34. Anne Krueger, "The Political Economy of the Rent-Seeking Society," *American Economic Review* 64 (1974): 291–303.

35. Bates, *Markets and States.*

36. Ames, *Political Survival.*

37. William Riker, *The Theory of Political Coalitions* (New Haven: Yale University Press, 1962).

38. William Niskanen, *Bureaucracy and Representative Government* (Hawthorne, NY: Aldine, 1971); Douglas Arnold, *Congress and the Bureaucracy: A Theory of Influence* (New Haven: Yale University Press, 1979); Fiorina and Noll, "Voters, Bureaucrats and Legislators"; Barbara Geddes, *Politician's Dilemma: Building State Capacity in Latin America* (Berkeley: University of California Press, 1994).

39. Gary W. Cox and Mathew McCubbins, *Legislative Leviathan: Party Government in the House* (Berkeley: University of California Press, 1993); Tsebelis, *Nested Games*; Barbara Geddes, "New Democratic Institutions as Bargains Among Self-Interested Politicians" (paper prepared for the American Political Science Association meeting, Washington, DC, 1990); Barbara Geddes, "A Comparative Perspective on the Leninist Legacy in Eastern Europe," *Comparative Political Studies*, forthcoming.

40. Maurice Duverger, *Political Parties: Their Organization and Activity in the Modern State* (New York: Wiley, 1954); Arend Lijphart, "The Political Consequences of Electoral Laws, 1945–85," *American Political Science Review* 84 (1990): 481–496; Arend Lijphart and Bernard Grofman, eds., *Choosing an Electoral System: Issues and Alternatives* (New York: Praeger, 1984); Douglas Rae, *The Political Consequences of Electoral Laws* (New Haven: Yale University Press, 1967); Rein Taagepera and Matthew Shugart, *Seats and Votes: The Effects and Determinants of Electoral Systems* (New Haven: Yale University Press, 1989).

41. Notable exceptions are Bruce Cain, John Ferejohn, and Morris Fiorina, *The Personal Vote* (Cambridge, MA: Harvard University Press, 1987); Gary W. Cox, "Centripetal and Centrifugal Incentives in Electoral Systems," *American Journal of*

Political Science 34 (1990): 903–935; Matthew Shugart, "The Effects of Timing of Elections for President and Assembly," in Scott Mainwaring and Matthew Shugart, eds., *Presidentialism and Democracy in Latin America* (forthcoming); and Matthew Shugart and John Carey, *Presidents and Assemblies* (New York: Cambridge University Press, 1992).

42. Peter Ordeshook, *Game Theory and Political Theory: An Introduction* (Cambridge: Cambridge University Press, 1986), p. xii.

43. Extremely good, moderately technical introductions to game theory can be found in Ordeshook, *Game Theory* and in Herve Moulin, *Game Theory for the Social Sciences* (New York: New York University Press, 1982).

44. Russell Hardin, *Collective Action* (Baltimore: Johns Hopkins University Press, 1982).

45. See Tsebelis, *Nested Games*, for a description of the most commonly used simple games and the relationships among them.

46. Guillermo O'Donnell, *Modernization and Bureaucratic-Authoritarianism* (Berkeley: Institute of International Studies, University of California, 1973).

47. Barbara Geddes, "A Game Theoretic Model of Reform in Latin American Democracies," *American Political Science Review* 85 (1991): 371–392.

48. See David Collier and Deborah Norden, "Strategic Choice Models of Political Change in Latin America," *Comparative Politics* 24 (1992): 229–242, for a discussion of other work on Latin American politics that uses elements of game theory without necessarily embracing the full technical apparatus.

49. Juan Linz and Alfred Stepan, eds., *The Breakdown of Democratic Regimes* (Baltimore: Johns Hopkins University Press, 1978); Guillermo O'Donnell, Philippe Schmitter, and Laurence Whitehead, eds., *Transitions from Authoritarian Rule* (Baltimore: Johns Hopkins University Press, 1986).

50. Thomas Schelling, *Choice and Consequence: Perspectives of an Errant Economist* (Cambridge, MA: Harvard University Press, 1984).

51. Especially, Adam Przeworski, "Some Problems in the Study of the Transition to Democracy," in O'Donnell, Schmitter, and Whitehead, eds., *Transitions*; Adam Przeworski, *Democracy and the Market: Political and Economic Reforms in Eastern Europe and Latin America* (Cambridge: Cambridge University Press, 1991); Przeworski, "Games of Transition," in Scott Mainwaring, Guillermo O'Donnell, and Samuel Valenzuela, eds., *Issues in Democratic Consolidation* (Notre Dame: University of Notre Dame Press, 1992); Gretchen Casper and Michelle Taylor, "A Game Theoretic Analysis of Elite Cooperation and the Prospects for Democratic Consolidation" (paper prepared for the American Political Science Association, Washington, DC, 1993).

52. Besides the works cited above, very important contributions to the study of institutional change have been made by Douglass North, *Structure and Change in Economic History* (New York: Norton, 1981); Douglass North, *Institutions, Institutional Change and Economic Performance* (Cambridge: Cambridge University Press, 1990), Douglass North and Robert Thomas, *The Rise of the Western World: A New Economic History* (Cambridge: Cambridge University Press, 1973); Levi, *Of Rule and Revenue.*

PART TWO

Conceptual Issues

In this section the authors examine substantive issues that are central to the newly emerging agenda for social science in Latin America. In addition to offering methodological insight, they reveal the complex ways that political and societal transitions can affect priorities for scholarly research.

Reflecting upon the close interaction between women's movements and feminist scholarship, Jane S. Jaquette stresses the need for "new ways of thinking about gender, from the inclusion of sex as a variable to the radical rethinking of what is political." Sparse and often condescending references to women constitute "a devastating weakness in the mainstream literature" on comparative politics. At the same time, Jaquette observes, recent trends in feminist writing—postmodernism, critical theory, difference feminism, and the emphasis on social movements—have perhaps moved too far from basic political questions. There is reason to focus "on the development of a women's agenda [and] on what would be needed to get new policies adopted and implemented." Ultimately, this means that women's roles should become a central topic for political analysis: The result promises to be mutual enrichment of both women's studies and comparative politics.

David Collier follows with a perceptive examination of the multiple meanings of "corporatism," a concept that rose to prominence during the authoritarian era of the 1960s and 1970s. He traces the evolution of the concept and its analytical refinements "as a form of interest group politics," then assesses the very different utilization of the idea as a guide to underlying predispositions in Latin American culture. In the contemporary context of democratization, Collier observes, the notion of corporatism has fallen out of fashion—though its practices are still in evidence and its legacies are bound to affect processes and patterns of political consolidation. In a general sense, this chapter offers important messages for methodology—about recognition of historical continuity, about the need for conceptual precision, about the meanings of typologies, and about the dangers of what Collier calls "theoretical stretching."

If current trends have drawn attention away from the study of corporatism, Evelyne Huber points out that they have intensified the need for reconsideration of the state, especially in the face of mounting poverty, inequity, and lawlessness. This task is particularly urgent for nascent democracies throughout Latin America. Toward this end, Huber defines state strength as "the capacity to achieve the goals set by incumbents in chief executive positions" in four distinct arenas: imposition of the rule of law, promotion of economic growth, achievement of popular compliance with authority, and distribution of societal resources. State strength depends on structural characteristics of the state apparatus and upon its relationship to other actors (in civil society, in the economic realm, and in the international arena). The "most reasonable methodology to measure state strength," according to Huber, "is qualitative comparative analysis. The linear and additive assumptions of quantitative analysis, and its inability to deal with conjunctural causation, make it an inappropriate approach to the problem." Quantitative measures can serve to operationalize specific attributes of state power, but assessments of overall capacities call for qualitative analysis "grounded in a thorough historical knowledge of the cases."

Frederick C. Turner discusses public opinion research on political culture. Often dismissed as a self-indulgent artifact of U.S. social science, the study of public opinion has acquired immediate and pressing relevance for the understanding of Latin American transitions toward democracy. As Turner demonstrates, there now exists a sufficient body of empirical data to test and refine numerous hypotheses about the meaning and structure of "culture." Sophisticated use of quantitative methodology can yield important findings about determinants and patterns of attitudes, beliefs, and values, and comparative analysis can help determine the extent to which political cultures vary by nation, subregion, or region. To echo a question that reverberates throughout the chapters in Part Two: What is distinctive about "Latin America" as such? What is the meaning of its regional identity?

———————— ■ ————————

CHAPTER FIVE

Rewriting the Scripts: Gender in the Comparative Study of Latin American Politics

Jane S. Jaquette

METHODOLOGIES HAVE EMERGED in the past twenty years to analyze gender and politics and discuss their applicability to the comparative study of Latin America. In this chapter, I trace the evolution of gender methodologies in the North, as well as examine the contributions of Latin American researchers and women-led political activities. This discussion reflects the rich international debate about how women participate in politics and how politics should be construed and studied. I examine in detail two specific research areas, women in development and women's social movements, to show how the Latin American experience has reinforced the now widely held view that women seek different political goals, using distinct political strategies, and that women's experiences provide new criteria to measure the health of the body politic.

By gender methodologies I do not mean new empirical research techniques but rather new ways of thinking about gender, from the inclusion of sex as a variable to the radical rethinking of what is political. I am convinced that the incorporation of gender analysis can strengthen virtually all comparative work on, for example, the changing role of the state, or democratic transitions and consolidations, or public policy. But I am critical of some trends in contemporary feminist research, and I believe that the divisions among feminists themselves, and between feminist and mainstream researchers, are not helpful either to feminism or to democratic practice.

Since what I have to say runs counter to major trends in research on women, I confess my analytical biases at the start. Although I value the search for a model of citizenship that is not male-biased, I am suspicious of the essentialism that is evident in most discussions of "difference" feminism, despite its obvious relevance in a region that has a long tradition of sharply differentiated sex roles. I believe that feminists must make egalitarian claims to achieve social justice and that positivist methodologies are essential to doing so. Unlike many feminists (and others), I do not reject rational choice theory out of hand as hopelessly individualistic, wrongly concerned with practical reason, or necessarily male-biased.[1]

Yet I am frustrated by a persistent blindness to gender in mainstream research on Latin American politics.[2] Despite the obvious fact that women's votes count equally in democratic elections (and that women voters often outnumber men); despite the evidence of a surge of women's political participation at all levels of society in the past twenty years; despite the adverse impact of neoliberal economic policies on women and children; and despite the central role of women's labor in the new global economy, references to women in the contemporary political literature on Latin America remain sparse. In my view, this is a devastating weakness in the mainstream literature, which will become more apparent as democratic politics in the region continue to evolve.

Sins of commission also occur. When the political behavior of women and men is compared, women are usually viewed as deviant. Women's opinions are dismissed as moralistic, emotional, or uninformed; women are portrayed as unpredictable or irrational because they do not act like "self-interested" men. They are condemned for being too conservative by some, or too naive and utopian by others.

I suggest, drawing by analogy on James Scott's moral economy of the peasant, that research should begin with the assumption that women's political behavior is rational; in any democratic system in which women vote, join parties and organizations, and have political interests, women's behavior also has significant political consequences. Although critical of postmodernist approaches, I agree with many of their criticisms of barefoot empiricist methodologies that universalize and label behavior in irresponsible ways; that incorrectly assume an "objective" viewpoint and submerge differences; that distance the researcher from those researched, facilitating social engineering rather than empowerment; and that ignore history. For me, the aim is not to abandon all positivist methodologies but to transform them.[3] □

THE EVOLUTION OF GENDER METHODOLOGIES

The analysis of the evolution of feminist methodologies presented here links developments in the North—primarily in Anglo-American and French feminism—with methodologies used by Latin American researchers. This analysis is too brief to trace all the connections or even to explore most of the issues. My intent is to provide initial observations that may provoke others to do more research in this area.

Feminist methodologies in the North have evolved in three stages. The first made women visible, filling in the gaps left by decades of ignoring women's political participation. The second criticized the conventional definitions of politics as male-biased and emphasized the ways in which women understood politics differently and sought political ends distinct from those of men. In the third phase, feminist revisions of such terms as "citizen," "contract," and "authority," and feminist analyses of the relationship between the public and private spheres were employed to redefine the political realm, for men as well as women.[4]

First-phase researchers added the gender variable to empirical analyses of mass and elite behavior, such as voting and legislative styles, which in turn facilitated cross-national comparisons. Evidence of male/female inequalities were used to fight discrimination against women, in keeping with the egalitarian feminist agenda of the early 1970s.

In the same period, Latin American researchers, influenced by Marxism, were beginning to focus on women, using empirical methodologies to study women's economic roles. Their data supported a radical critique of Latin America's economic condition. Poor working conditions and low wages for women, evidence that women were hired to weaken unions, and the fact that the single largest category of paid work for women was domestic service all illustrated how effectively the capitalist system exploited labor. For dependency theorists, there was overwhelming evidence of women's marginalization: Women were the ultimate "periphery."[5] Using this approach, researchers could focus on the condition of women without risking the label of "feminist."

In the mid-1970s, Northern feminism, strongly influenced by new trends in Europe, was shifting into a second stage. Egalitarian feminism came under attack for assuming that women should be "just like men." Studies of male/female differences, such as Carol Gilligan's *In a Different Voice*, Nancy Chodorow's *The Reproduction of Mothering*, and the writings of French feminists Julia Kristeva and Luce Irigaray, emphasized not only the persistence but the value of *difference*, as such political theorists as Jean Bethke Elshtain and Nancy Hartsock played out the implications of "difference" feminism for the study of politics.[6]

Methodological issues were at the heart of this revaluation of the feminine. Earlier behavioral studies were dismissed as "add women and stir." They were replaced by in-depth interviewing, oral histories, and personal testimonials, which were put forth as more authentically feminist ways of knowing. The role of the author was no longer that of objective or impartial observer; researchers often began their books with an introductory discussion of their class background and political commitments. The possibility that social science research might be used to manipulate or otherwise harm the women studied became an issue, and there was much discussion of how to give women more say in the uses made of research results.

In keeping with this trend, testimonial autobiographies by Domitila Chungara and Rigoberta Menchú became the standard classroom texts and thus the major sources by which the experiences of Latin American women were known in the North. Their particularity and emotional appeal, exactly what made them suspect to the empiricists, were prized. Earlier testimonial literature, notably Margaret Randall's anthologies reporting women's lives in Cuba, seemed ideologically motivated in comparison with the more sophisticated and open-ended use of testimonials and personal histories by women researchers in the 1980s to portray the lives of women, especially domestic servants and women of urban shantytowns. These studies looked at how women constructed their lives and their identities, and, as the decade came to a close, they documented the impact of structural adjustment policies on the lives of poor and middle-class women.[7]

Meanwhile, some Latin American researchers began to identify themselves as feminists. The UN Decade for Women (1975–1985) and the influence of returned women exiles—many of whom had been active in women's groups in Europe, Canada, and the United States—created a new wave of feminist consciousness in the region and a growing audience for feminist research. At the same time, women's human rights and popular women's organizations were becoming visible in prodemocracy opposition movements, especially in the Southern Cone. Taken together, these developments reinforced a shift from the dominant focus on women's economic roles to studies of women and politics.[8]

As had occurred in the North, evidence that women's political attitudes and behavior were different from men's was interpreted favorably. Women's greater concern with moral issues, their greater tendency to reject violence on the left and on the right, and their involvement in local politics and "domestic" issues were portrayed as positive norms rather than as signs of women's lack of interest in the real business of politics or as political naiveté. It soon became clear that, although there were a few self-identified feminist groups, most activist women rejected any feminist label. Instead, women often justified their political activities and described their growing political consciousness as arising out of their roles as mothers, whether they were involved in human rights groups, such as the Madres of the Plaza de Mayo, or in neighborhood associations, such as the Glass of Milk and communal kitchens programs in Peru, or in the day care and health movements in Brazil.[9]

As the activities of the Madres became more widely known, the argument was developed that women defend the values of the family against the state, that women are "Antigone's Daughters," to quote the title of an essay by Elshtain (which circulated among feminists, particularly in Argentina). The Madres became a focus of intense international feminist interest, not only because of their unlikely origins and their heroic dissent but also as a real world example of how "difference" politics could face off against the most masculine form of power—a military junta—and emerge victorious. That women could enter politics through their roles as mothers was also taken as proof that the self-regarding individual at the core of liberal theory is not the only viable model for the democratic citizen. Not everyone agreed that the Madres's example augured well for the future of feminist politics or democratic participation. María del Carmen Feijoó questioned whether the Madres's strategy could be extended to other issues. She observed that, by putting themselves "above politics," the Madres had painted themselves into a corner: They could not then turn to women's rights or poverty without becoming "political" and thus losing the clarity of their moral appeal.[10] Maxine Molyneux, looking at women's efforts to influence policy in revolutionary Nicaragua, noted that most women making demands on the Sandinistas were pursuing their "practical gender interests" as mothers—that is, the improvement of material conditions for their families—and that such mobilization did not easily translate into support for their "strategic" interests in promoting gender equality.[11]

The third phase of feminist methodology-building used the insights of the second phase to reconstruct both politics-as-a-discipline and politics-in-the-world. Conventional definitions of politics—that it is a public-sphere activity, carried out in recognizably "political" institutions; that it is about the control of the state, or even that it is about the "authoritative allocation of values"—are rejected as too narrow and too biased in favor of men's political activities and interests. Some have countered that there is politics in everything, that to study politics is "to analyze relations of dominance" in all settings, including the family. Others, in a new post-structuralist trend, defined politics as a "text": They saw that women could more easily manage and manipulate symbolic politics than tanks and guns. Still others, following the work of Jürgen Habermas, explored politics as a "communicative action," or, with Hannah Arendt, defined politics as people coming together to accomplish commonly agreed-upon goals.

In third-phase analysis, all concepts were contested, and women's political knowledge was taken as a means to rethink political processes in order to create new political outcomes. In Chile, for example, the history of militarism and the prevalence of hierarchical, coercive power relations in Chilean society was linked to the persistence of authoritarian power relations in the family, opening new avenues for thinking about ways to strengthen democracy.[12]

Many Latin American researchers, reflecting on their own social science training and on their political commitments, concluded that positivist methodologies, though useful in painting the larger picture of women's oppression, were inadequate. To narrow the distance between research and political action, they developed study-action groups, which combined research with work in women's popular organizations.[13]

An important context for the elaboration of a "difference" perspective and the rejection of behavioral research methods was the theoretical ferment in the social sciences in response to the rise of poststructuralism, postmodernism, and critical theory, particularly the work of Habermas. In addition to the usefulness of these approaches to those who are critical of behavioral methodologies and their manipulation by the state, these perspectives are very appealing to feminist scholars who seek radical changes in gender relations. The poststructural/postmodern view that all forms of knowledge are "texts" and its acute sensitivity to the way in which science's claims to objectivity legitimate power relationships serve to reinforce the feminist desire to counter arguments that women are inferior because of their "natures." The notion that politics is a text not only plays to women's relative abilities to manipulate the symbolic arena but also opens up the possibility of "rewriting the texts" to reflect more closely what women bring to and want from political life. As language replaces coercion as the basis of power, feminist methodology "shift[s] its attention from social analysis to discourse analysis, from power itself to the politics of its representation."[14]

These new methodologies have also influenced Latin American analysts who, for example, have used poststructural analysis to deconstruct both the militarized discourse of the right and the hierarchical vanguardism of the left.[15] "Rewriting the texts" means creating new political space and new political identities for marginalized groups.

Postmodernism has also brought new issues to the fore. It underlines the persistence of colonial mentalities and scrutinizes the ways in which the "self" constructs the "other." Postmodernism rejects the "Enlightenment project," which links the natural sciences, capitalism, and liberalism in a tightly knit "meta-narrative" of "reality." It seeks alternative futures by looking to the "submerged discourses" of native peoples—and women.[16]

From this perspective, liberal egalitarian feminism is just another Enlightenment narrative, one that suppresses race, class, and generational differences among women. Sarah Radcliffe and Sallie Westwood decry most feminist discourses as being "universalizing and essentializing accounts of 'woman.'" Instead, feminist research should "contextualize women's protest, not only in terms of pre-existing political organizations, socioeconomic structures and reproductive responsibilities, but also to uncover some of the 'internalities' of political protest, like gender and political identities, images and practices that shape everyday behaviour, symbolism and place in political culture."[17]

Like postmodernism, critical theorists are dissatisfied with capitalism and liberal politics, which they view as distortions of the promise of the Enlightenment rather than as its natural end. Habermas described the condition of modern political institutions as a "legitimacy crisis." New social movements have formed—in Latin America, Europe, Eastern Europe, and North America—to respond to this crisis, which arises from the commodification and bureaucratization of the "lifeworld"—the world of the family and the neighborhood, of everyday life. Although there are important differences between postmodernism and critical theory—foremost among them the inability of postmodernism to provide the vision for a new political project (since there is no standpoint that cannot be deconstructed)—it is obvious that feminist methodologies overlap postmodernism and critical theory on a number of crucial points.[18] □

RESEARCH ON LATIN AMERICAN WOMEN: "WOMEN IN DEVELOPMENT" AND "NEW SOCIAL MOVEMENTS"

In order to illustrate these observations about the evolution of gender methodologies and their relationship to issues of comparative politics, I examine two topics that have been widely studied. The first, women in development (WID), is an interdisciplinary field that has maintained its behavioral methodological core because it is policy oriented: Its raison d'être is to provide guidance to policymakers. By contrast, the study of women and social movements has been oppositional from the start; it is addressed to scholars and political intellectuals who may have the power to rewrite the texts, and to women all over the world who might become activists as a result of seeing politics, and their roles in it, in new ways.

Women in Development

In the 1970s, the comparative social science framework for studying women (when they were studied at all) was conceived in regard to the comparative "status" of women across nations.[19] These studies relied primarily on census data and household surveys and tended to reinforce the common wisdom of modernization theory: that low levels of women's education, poor quality of life, large family sizes, and restrictions of women's legal and political rights are correlated and are typical of under-development, and that modernization produces better outcomes for women—higher levels of education, smaller families, and greater recognition of women's legal and political rights.

Marxist feminists quickly noted flaws in this analysis: Women's economic participation did not correlate with other indicators of development, and high levels of education and literacy did not guarantee that women had access to either political or economic power. They pointed out that a higher percentage of elected officials in socialist countries are women (over 30 percent in the Eastern bloc and over 20 percent in the Nordic countries, compared with fewer than 5 percent in the United States and Britain), which proved, they argued, that you could not have feminism without socialism. Even liberal feminists were uncomfortable with a methodology that seemed to make women just one more "indicator" of development and that failed to capture women's struggles for equality; they agreed that, despite centuries of liberal egalitarianism, women were still second-class citizens in the most advanced countries.[20]

In 1970 Ester Boserup's *Women's Role in Economic Development* untied the issue of women's work from its Marxist moorings and made it available as a gender critique within liberal development theory.[21] Her argument (based primarily on African data) was that, far from liberating women, modernization had reduced women's power and status. Colonial administrators, reproducing the gender relations of Northern Europe, had introduced new technologies and cash cropping to men on the assumption that women did not or should not have a major role in agricultural production. This upset the traditional distribution of resources and responsibilities between men and women. It also jeopardized subsistence food production, which was still in the hands of women—who were increasingly disadvantaged in their access to land and technology. Boserup wrote that African agriculture had been a "female farming system" in which women had enjoyed high status and relative equality with men, but under colonialism women had fallen farther and farther behind.

The publication of *Women's Role* marked a watershed and launched "women in development" as an academic and policy field. Its arguments were quickly adopted by feminists in the developed (donor) countries to argue for improving women's incomes as a matter of justice (because colonialism had deprived women of their former status) and as a matter of efficiency (development could not be expected to occur when half the population was excluded). Feminists gained some allies who were convinced that enhancing economic opportunities for women would serve their goals, including reducing the birth rate, increasing food production, and managing the environment.

Women and development became an international issue at the first UN Conference for Women held in Mexico City in 1975.[22] It subsequently was incorporated, although grudgingly, into the policies and programs of multilateral and bilateral aid agencies (and of several foundations with international programs). Because UN member states were required to document the status of women, the Decade for Women created a new demand for gender analysis and for data on women.[23]

As statistical work progressed in Latin America, it soon became clear that women's economic activity had been grossly undercounted, particularly in agriculture. This, in turn, had implications for development policies: Few development goals could be reached without taking women's roles in production and family decisionmaking into account. Debates arose about how women's unpaid family labor should be represented in national accounts. Dramatic social changes, such as the rapid increase in female-headed households in the region, were documented and became policy issues.[24]

The WID approach had its critics, among them Lourdes Benería and Gita Sen, who attacked Boserup for assuming a capitalist framework for development and for ignoring—as did most Marxists—the relationship between women's roles in production and reproduction.[25] Nonetheless, the gap between the discourse of the North (based on legal rights) and of the South (based on economic justice) had narrowed. From 1975 until the present, there has been a virtual explosion of studies on women's economic activities from a variety of perspectives. In Latin America they include historical studies of women's roles in nineteenth-century export industries and in agricultural development, the exploitation of women in the *maquiladora* industries, and on women in the informal sector.[26]

These studies provided some interesting data on the effects of international economic policies, showing, for example, that the industries on the U.S.-Mexico border were hiring women at low wages and not reducing male employment as the program intended; that agrarian reform could disadvantage women unless they had rights to own land or to participate equally as cooperative members; and as the decade moved forward, how women were responding to the economic crisis and to the loss of jobs and services as a result of structural adjustment policies.

WID produced new methodological innovations in censuses and household surveys, and "gender-integrated" programs added new dimensions to project planning and evaluation. However, WID's role as a handmaiden to development policymaking did not allow its analysts to raise the most difficult issues. WID studies documented the terrible human costs of structural adjustment policies, but WID researchers were not in a position to challenge the neoliberal consensus. WID research on the informal sector showed that there was little upward mobility for women and that women were increasingly being asked to shoulder a triple burden of housework, informal sector activities, and political participation. This evidence did little, however, to dampen official enthusiasm for the informal sector as an economic panacea.[27] WID analysts could show why women should have access to aid as producers, not just as reproducers (through maternal and child health programs), and how to reach women more effectively, but WID researchers could do little about the social-engineering orientation of foreign assistance programs.

This weakness was especially visible in the field of population and family planning. U.S.-backed population control programs in Brazil eventually produced a strong counterreaction, led by Brazilian feminists. Having rejected outside interference in population programs, these researcher-activists headed a movement that put population issues firmly in the context of women's health and women's choices. In so doing, they identified and publicized the issue of violence against women, an issue pioneered by Brazilians, which has now mobilized women across class and racial lines throughout the region.[28]

New Social Movements

The study of women in social movements shows a very different methodological trajectory from that of WID. Although Latin America has had a long history of women's movements, a number of factors—the sheer numbers of women involved in contemporary movements;[29] the participation of women of all classes; and the visible role of women's groups in the politics of democratic transitions in the Southern Cone—have made women's movements a major focus of research.

Several recent books have explored various aspects of contemporary women's movements.[30] The experiences of the Madres of the Plaza de Mayo, the communal kitchens movements in Chile and Peru, and the day care and health movements in Brazil are widely discussed in international forums and are viewed as models throughout the world. They are part of a global shift toward women's greater political participation.

The rise of women's movements in Latin America has taken place in the context of the rapid expansion of social movements in many countries and regions of the world. This has also meant that they have been described as part of the wave of new social movements in the postindustrial world, using categories originally developed to describe dissident movements in Eastern Europe and the former Soviet Union, the Greens, and human rights and student movements in the West. Alain Touraine, Eduardo Viola and Scott Mainwaring, Susan Eckstein, and Sonia Alvarez and Arturo Escobar, among others, have analyzed the ideological and organizational characteristics of new social movements in Latin America and have speculated about their role in future social and political developments.[31] Much of this research has emphasized the role of social movements in democratic transitions, countering the tendency to see the transitions primarily in terms of elite pacts and civil-military relations rather than in terms of popular mobilization.

The political and solidarity activities of the new social movements have been characterized as "new" because they differ from earlier revolutionary and millenarian movements, corporatist associations, and interest groups. Jean Cohen distinguished these movements by the fact that they seek "collective goods" rather than furthering "narrow self-interests," by their interest in radically redefining politics to accommodate more communal and "postmaterial" values, and by their autonomy from political parties and the state.[32] Others have emphasized the reliance of new social movements on symbolic politics and the importance of media technologies that enable them to reach large audiences and to communicate with each other. It is argued that new social movements have new agendas, that they "write new scripts."

New social movements have emerged in several countries, and comparisons with Eastern and Central Europe are particularly provocative. In both regions, social movements successfully opposed authoritarian rule, and both regions have experienced the dislocations caused by privatization and structural adjustment. In both regions, the transitions from authoritarianism provided optimal conditions for movement politics. Social movements reinvigorated democratic ideals without having to take responsibility for governing. The media provided a platform, which meant that groups did not need the support of other political institutions or leaders to be heard. Movements united by the goal of ending authoritarian rule provided a strong sense of solidarity and unity.[33]

In Latin America, women's organizations and women members of "mixed" organizations were the backbone of the new social movements. The Madres of the Plaza de Mayo are the most striking example, but many other groups sprang up, with a wide range of goals. Because of their response to the economic crises of the 1970s and 1980s and their effectiveness as voices for human rights, women's groups became a visible sign of the resistance of civil society to the military state.

The methodologies used to study women's social movements are good examples of second- and third-phase analysis. Very little quantitative data or conventional survey research has been done, and there has been no systematic attempt to make cross-national or cross-regional comparisons. Personal histories, interviews with women leaders and activists, and participatory observation document the organization, goals, leadership styles, and differences among these groups, and these methods have been used to trace their roles in transitions toward democracy. Studies have been done on how women come to political awareness and how they see themselves as citizens; researchers have investigated the distinct ways in which women have changed the vocabulary of politics. Organizational issues have also received considerable attention: how women come together despite cultural and familial resistance; how women's organizations relate to other neighborhood groups and to international agencies and nongovernmental organizations (NGOs); and how new forms of protest and resistance have been conceived and implemented.[34]

Many of these studies analyze how the attitudes and political strategies of these movements reveal a distinctly female approach to politics: Women often explicitly reject the idea of self-interest and are wary of party politics based on interests; they usually see their political activity as justified by the need to help their families and communities. Women emphasize the solidarity of their groups (compared to neighborhood groups led by men); they criticize the *machismo* and *caudillismo* of male leaders.[35] Women understand their political attitudes and beliefs in terms of concrete personal histories rather than as commitments to abstract principles or party platforms.

Women's strategies are also different. In Venezuela, for example, women's groups have found new ways to frame ecological issues, using symbolic politics to mobilize popular support. Jennifer Schirmer contends that the activities of human rights groups in El Salvador and Guatemala have created a "kind of collective citizenry of political motherhood," and Yvonne Corcoran-Nantes argues that the innovative politics of the new social movements are simply women's political practices.[36]

It is a short step from recognizing that new kinds of politics are possible to making the case that women's attitudes and practices should become the basis for reconstituting the political system. Annie Dandavati and Patricia Chuchryk have documented how feminists in Chile, seeing the displacement of social movements elsewhere once democracy was reinstalled, took out ads in Santiago newspapers to argue that democracy itself should be structured to guarantee more access to women and more responsiveness to women's issues.[37] In Brazil, the National Council on the Condition of Women succeeded in getting much of its agenda into the Constitution. In response to similar pressures, some political parties in the region have adopted quotas to ensure that a certain percentage of women will be nominated in each election, not solely on the grounds that women deserve equal representation but based on the rationale that women bring something unique to the political arena, which is lost if they remain underrepresented. □

EVALUATING GENDER METHODOLOGIES

The results of studying women's organizations, political participation, and changing economic roles have proven immensely useful. WID studies have strengthened demands for women's economic rights and increased access to resources; WID studies have been used by activists in legislatures and in state bureaucracies and by women's organizations themselves. The study of women's movements has put the issue of women and citizenship on the table in debates about democratization. Study-action approaches (linking groups that study women and social problems with the women they are studying) have ensured a more effective connection between analysis and practice.

However, it is appropriate to step back and reassess contemporary methodological trends and their implications for future research and political practice. Critics have, for example, attacked women in development research and its advocacy for unquestioning acceptance of capitalism and unimaginative reliance on bureaucratic interventions that strengthen the state. It is true that virtually all WID research accepts the market as a given: Support for income generation projects and women's employment opportunities—the essence of the WID agenda—begins with the assumption that women are better off in the market than they are when relying on a male "head of household." Indeed, Amartya Sen has shown that women have more rights within the family when they have economic opportunities outside of it.[38] It is also true that, as a field, WID legitimates "experts," who then exercise power over "beneficiaries," and it may increase women's dependence on the state or on international sources of funding. As was the case in the Progressive era in U.S. politics, policies to improve the quality of life increase the likelihood that the state will penetrate the "lifeworld," with bureaucrats rather than clients deciding what is "good for women."

Some of these criticisms can be countered. Others offer insights about how foreign assistance programs could be designed and administered if empowerment and equality were given priority over efficiency, the main criterion used to measure the success of (and thus to design) aid programs.

The idea that the lifeworld should be protected comes from Habermas; it can be criticized on feminist grounds. If the lifeworld is equated with the family, it must be observed that the private sphere is not a realm of freedom or a site free from exploitation and commodification. This is not a function of modernity but of patriarchy. Amartya Sen's research has shown that, in contrast to every other region, in South Asian societies men outnumber women in all age cohorts; because patriarchal family structures deny women equitable access to resources, more women die.

Where women have economic opportunities outside the home, the sex ratios are more like those in the rest of the world. Then, too, domestic violence occurs in pre-modern as well as modern societies, and state intervention seems a necessary part of the solution. The answer cannot be to rely on the lifeworld of the community: Historically communities have not prohibited domestic violence and have often condoned it. A community powerful enough to regulate human behavior by imposing its values cannot tolerate a private realm of freedom. The issue is not whether the state will penetrate the lifeworld, or regulate the family, but *how*, and who will decide.

To take the second criticism, WID experts may have relative power over women "beneficiaries," but they are largely powerless in donor bureaucracies. In comparison with market forces, donor assistance programs determine few of the economic parameters and opportunities of women's lives. Yet WID research could be more ambitious in its goals by being more radical in its methods. Postmodern critiques suggest the importance of recognizing differences among women and the need to "level the playing field" between donors and those who participate in the programs they fund. Questioning the positivist methods used in project design, monitoring, and evaluation could make it possible for women recipients to become coplanners and implementers. If WID methodologies cannot do this, they cannot really respond to the needs, interests, and values of the women who participate.

The women in development field has been enriched by its multidisciplinary composition, but there are costs as well. WID expertise tends to be highly specialized, with case studies focused on a single issue: how to create credit programs, how to increase the productivity of the agricultural household, or how to assess the impact of an irrigation project. The recent priority given to democratization as a development goal has had the positive effect of adding a political dimension in which results must be measured in terms of participation, not productivity. This shift legitimizes the empowerment of women. Nevertheless, it has also added yet another group of experts who compete for scarce resources: donor funding and the time and energies of the women who participate.

Because of specialization, all issues tend to be addressed separately, using researchers and methods from divided disciplines. There are no overarching analyses or frameworks to assign priorities or to assess the interactive aspects of projects and policies. This is inadequate from several standpoints. For women recipients, the possibility of getting microenterprise credit, for example, is part of a larger calculation involving who in the family can work, who controls the household's money and access to the market, the way the state taxes and regulates such activities, how much time will be taken from other important tasks, and the crisis that may throw off all the other calculations. One aspect of decisionmaking that is virtually absent from the literature is any discussion of how participation in a program may affect more intangible but very significant "utilities," such as the moral standing a woman has in her community, or her own sense of dignity and self-worth.[39]

The logic of efficiency has worked against multidimensional analysis. The interactions between different kinds of projects, or between projects and macrolevel policies, often adopted under pressure from donor agencies, have not been explored at conferences or in the scholarly literature. This makes it much more difficult for WID projects to empower women. It also means that WID is missing an opportunity to increase its usefulness to development studies. As Monique Cohen has observed, family decisionmaking provides an ideal perspective from which to do intersectoral analysis, a major issue in the field, but its potential is unrecognized. Research in this area could also bolster our understanding of women's decision-rules. In the development studies of the 1950s and 1960s, women were often seen as the carriers of "traditional" (i.e., noneconomic) values in the family, and the family itself was seen as a bulwark against the adoption of "modern" values.[40] Jeanne Marie Col has suggested deepening our understanding of women's rationality by using the theory of nested games to reflect the multiple contexts that women must take into account.[41]

But the potential of these approaches has not been recognized by mainstream development or WID researchers. One problem is that WID research is done for a highly specialized audience and often with immediate project goals in mind, and in that sense its method falls almost entirely within the parameters of phase one: Researchers adding women to comparative analysis rather than challenging the foundations of development theory or the standard operating procedures of development practice. WID researchers and practitioners have devoted their energies to redistributing resources within aid programs (which often lack domestic political support within donor countries), and challenging these programs runs the risk of further undermining the support for foreign aid.

If WID suffers from being too close to the state, then postmodernism, critical theory, and difference feminism have moved too far away. The tension between difference politics and feminist goals is increasingly resolved in favor of difference politics, just as the study of "texts" has displaced the study of power. This helps explain why most of the work done on women's political participation in Latin America has focused on human rights and on neighborhood solidarity organizations, not on the development of a women's agenda or on what would be needed to get new policies adopted and implemented.

The current debate over the distinction between practical versus strategic gender interests is illustrative. Molyneux has been taken to task for imposing "binary" categories and a Northern definition of feminism on the political practices of Latin American women. Yet Molyneux's point seems to me to be incontrovertible: There is a difference between women's political action to provide for the needs of their families (or to protect their children from state violence) and women's actions to improve their status as women vis-à-vis male power long-reinforced by tradition and law. Each is worthy and useful, but the difference between them is conceptually and politically important, even when, in practice, the pursuit of practical gender interests forces women to raise strategic gender questions, as when women must go out to political meetings; or when women develop managerial expertise that puts them in conflict with their husbands; or when, in order to participate, women must convince the men to take care of the house and children. Similarly, I would argue that symbolic politics can open up new issues and create space for women as political actors, but it is not equivalent to changing political outcomes for women.

Women's movements did help restore democratic governments to the region, and they continue to broaden traditional patterns of representation, which are class and race as well as gender biased. But much of what women have accomplished for themselves and their families in this recent wave of mobilization has been marginal redistribution or self-help. With the exception of the issue of violence against women, political progress on a woman's agenda—including such crucial issues as reproductive rights and family law—has been less than one might expect, given the extent and intensity of women's political engagement.

Under these circumstances, it is perhaps not surprising that so little research has been done on comparative public policy and women. The virtues of social movements—their autonomy, their distance from party politics, their face-to-face approach to organizing, and their unwillingness to negotiate moral positions—puts women in the role of a permanent opposition and reduces their effectiveness. The distance between social movements, on one hand, and political parties and the state, on the other, may jeopardize the prospects for participatory democracy, itself the vision that once united the different sectors of the opposition.

The new wave of women's political mobilization in Latin America has drawn women into social movements, not into parties or interest groups; there is no institutionalized way of linking women's political concerns to the political system and no established means by which parties and governments can be held accountable. The study of what happens to social movements after the transitions are over is thus a critical area for research.

Unfortunately, neither mainstream scholars nor feminist researchers are likely to take up this topic. Postmodern and difference feminists and those who have viewed women through the lens of new social movements are hostile to the empirical and institutional analyses that could increase the likelihood that democratic politics in the region will become more representative and responsible. As daughters of Antigone (or of Foucault or Habermas), many women and feminist activists are highly suspicious of the state. Like Marxists during much of this century, they have adopted the role of critical outsiders.

Mainstream scholars who are put off by the polemical claims of much feminist research (and men who may fear they will be punished if they invade women's turf) are also unlikely to view gender methodologies as promising. Rational choice theorists, who have provided many of the tools used to analyze the transitions, have ignored gender, and feminists have returned the favor by arguing that women do not operate according to the narrowly individualistic assumptions of the theory.

Both mainstream and feminist research would benefit from a less-strict gender division of labor. With half of Latin America's electorates composed of women, and with electoral volatility and "populism" a major concern of those studying the future for democracy in the region, the need for more work on women's attitudes and women's organizations seems self-evident, especially since survey data suggest that significant gender gaps exist. Women are contributing to the demand for greater morality in politics (which can have costs as well as obvious benefits), and they are more likely than men to reject neoliberal policies and to support candidates who would "bring the state back in."

But there is also some evidence that more women than men support plebiscitary governments in times of crisis, which may increase the chances of a new wave of authoritarianism. Women's attitudes and behavior will surely be an important factor in determining the course of democracy over the next decade, and women's organizations have established themselves as recognized political actors in virtually every nation. Gender should become a topic for mainstream analysis, not for academic affirmative action reasons, but because gender is essential to understanding contemporary politics throughout the region.

Feminists of all persuasions have much to gain by encouraging mainstream empirical and institutional research and by expanding the assumptions of rational choice theory. Postmodern critiques can improve the quality of behavioral and institutional research and help rectify the imbalance that currently exists between data gathering and theory building. The political visions that have emerged from the new gender methodologies can add to the older empirical methodologies, but they cannot replace them.

Egalitarian arguments—that women should enjoy legal, economic, and political rights and opportunities and that they should not be deprived of dignity, bodily integrity, or moral respect—are still central to feminism. To make these arguments effectively, advocates must rely on empirical work to make—and remake—their case. Maintaining the current "gender division of research labor" virtually ensures that we will have politics as usual. We could settle for more. □

NOTES

1. "Difference" feminism has been the most important theoretical development in feminist theory, edging out the egalitarian feminism of the late 1960s and early 1970s; see, for example, Iris Young, *Justice and the Politics of Difference* (Princeton: Princeton University Press, 1990); Hester Eisentein and Alice Jardine, eds., *The Future of Difference* (New Brunswick: Rutgers University Press, 1985). For persuasive counterarguments, see Anne Philips, *Engendering Democracy* (University Park: Pennsylvania State University Press, 1991), and Mary Dietz, "Citizenship with a Feminist Face: The Problem with Maternal Thinking," *Political Theory* 13, no. 1 (1985): 19–38.

2. In an exhaustive review of the literature on democracy in Latin America by Jonathan Hartlyn and Arturo Valenzuela, there are no references to women's roles and only one citation on social movements ("Democracy in Latin America Since 1930," in Leslie Bethell, ed., *The Cambridge History of Latin America*, vol. 6, *Latin America Since 1930: Economy, Society and Politics* [Cambridge, England: Cambridge University Press, 1994]); most of the well-known studies on transitions have no references to women. Latin American theorists exploring the implications of women's participation for democratic theory include José-J. Brunner and Norbert Lechner (see particularly the latter's *Los patios interiores de la democracia: Subjetividad y política* [Santiago, Chile: Fondo de Cultura Económica, 1988]). For bibliographic essays, see Lynn Stoner, *Latinas of the Americas: A Source Book* (New York: Garland Publishing, 1989).

3. On feminism and postmodernism, see Linda Alcoff and Elizabeth Potter, eds., *Feminist Epistemologies* (London: Routledge, 1993), and Linda J. Nicholson, ed., *Feminism/Postmodernism* (London: Routledge, 1990).

4. Jean Bethke Elshtain, *The Sexual Contract* (Stanford: Stanford University Press, 1988); Jean Bethke Elshtain, *Public Man/Private Woman* (Princeton: Princeton University Press, 1981); Nancy Hartsock, *Money, Sex and Power: Toward a Feminist Historical Materialism* (New York: Longman, 1983); Kathleen B. Jones, *Compassionate Authority: Democracy and the Representation of Women* (New York: Routledge, 1993); Nancy J. Hirschmann, *Rethinking Obligation: A Feminist Method for Political Theory* (Ithaca: Cornell University Press, 1992).

5. For example, Heleith I. B. Saffioti, *A mulher na sociedade de classes: Mito e realidade* (Petropolis, Brazil: Vozes, 1976); Marianne Schmink, "Dependent Development and the Division of Labor by Sex: Venezuela," *Latin American Perspectives* 4, nos. 1–2 (thematic issue, 1977); Verena Stolcke, "The Exploitation of Family Morality: Labor Systems and Family Structure of São Paulo Coffee Plantations, 1950–1979," in Raymond T. Smith, ed., *Kinship, Ideology and Practice in Latin America* (Chapel Hill: University of North Carolina Press, 1984); Magdalena León

de Leal and Carmen Diana Deere, eds., *La mujer y la política agraria en América Latina* (Bogotá: Siglo XXI, 1986); Lourdes Benería, *Women and Development: The Sexual Division of Labor in Rural Societies* (New York: Praeger, 1982); Latin American and Caribbean Women's Collective, *Slave of Slaves: The Challenge of Latin American Women* (London: Zed Press, 1980); June Nash and María Patricia Fernández-Kelly, *Women, Men and the International Division of Labor* (Albany: State University of New York Press, 1983).

6. Carol Gilligan, *In a Different Voice: Psychological Theory and Women's Development* (Cambridge, MA: Harvard University Press, 1982); Nancy Chodorow, *The Reproduction of Mothering* (Berkeley: University of California Press, 1978); Hartsock, *Money, Sex and Power*; and Elshtain, *Public Man/Private Woman*.

7. *I, Rigoberta Menchú* (London: Verso, 1983, edited by Elizabeth Burgos-Debray) received the Nobel Peace Prize in 1992. On testimonial literature, see Georg Gugelberger and Michael Kearney, "Voices for the Voiceless: Testimonial Literature in Latin America," *Latin American Perspectives* 18, no. 3 (1991): 3–14. Testimonials have been extremely important in the human rights movement to document the experiences of political prisoners and of their families, for example, Marjorie Agosin, *Scraps of Life: Chilean Arpilleras* (Trenton: Red Sea Press, 1987), and Ximena Bunster, "Surviving Beyond Fear: Women and Torture in Latin America," in June Nash and Helen Safa, eds., *Women and Change in Latin America* (South Hadley, MA; Bergin and Garvey, 1980). Personal histories also served to underline the human costs of structural adjustment policies. See, for example, Dagmar Raczynski and Claudia Serrano, *Vivir la pobreza: Testimonios de mujeres* (Santiago, Chile: CIEPLAN, 1985); Neuma Aguiar et al., *Mujer y crisis: Respuestas ante la recesión* (Rio de Janeiro: DAWN/Editorial Nueva Sociedad, 1990); Maruja Barrig, *Seis familias en la crisis* (Lima: Asociación Laboral para el Desarollo, 1993).

8. See Ana María Portugal, ed., *The Latin American Women's Movement: Reflections and Actions* (Santiago, Chile: ISIS International, 1986). Important early works on women and politics are Armand Mattelart and Michele Mattelart, *La mujer chilena en una nueva sociedad* (Santiago, Chile: Editorial Pacífico, 1968), an extensive survey of women's political attitudes; Fanny Tabak and Meoma Toscano, *Mulher y política* (Rio de Janeiro: Paz e Terra, 1982); Elsa Chaney, *Supermadre: Women in Politics in Latin America* (Austin: Institute of Latin American Studies, 1979); Jane S. Jaquette, "Female Political Participation in Latin America," in June Nash and Helen Safa, *Sex and Class in Latin America* (Brooklyn: J. F. Bergin, 1980); Marysa Navarro-Aranguren, "The Construction of a Latin American Feminist Identity," in Alfred Stepan, ed., *Americas: New Interpretive Essays* (Oxford: Oxford University Press, 1992).

9. This was noted of political elites by Chaney, *Supermadre*; see also the more recent literature on participation in groups, for example, Beatriz Schmukler, "Gender and Authority in Lower Class Working Families in Buenos Aires" (Ph.D. diss., Yale University, 1985); Jennifer Schirmer, "The Seeking of Truth and the Gendering of Consciousness: The Comadres of El Salvador and the Conavigua Widows of Guatemala," in Sarah A. Radcliffe and Sallie Westwood, eds., *Viva: Women and Popular Protest in Latin America* (London: Routledge, 1993), pp. 30–64; Patricia M. Chuchryk, "Subversive Mothers: The Women's Opposition to the Military Regime in Chile," in Sue Ellen Charlton, Jana Everett, and Kathleen Staudt,

eds., *Women, the State and Development* (Albany: State University of New York Press, 1989), pp. 130–151.

10. María del Carmen Feijoó, "The Challenge of Constructing Civilian Peace: Women and Democracy in Argentina," in Jane S. Jaquette, ed., *The Women's Movement in Latin America: Participation and Democracy*, 2d ed.(Boulder: Westview Press, 1994).

11. Maxine Molyneux, "Mobilization Without Emancipation? Women's Interests, the State and Revolution in Nicaragua," *Feminist Studies* 11, no. 2 (1985): 227–254.

12. Patricia M. Chuchryk, "Feminist Anti-Authoritarian Politics: The Role of Women's Organizations in the Chilean Transition to Democracy," in Jaquette, *The Women's Movement*, pp. 149–184.

13. See Navarro-Aranguren, "The Construction of a Latin American Feminist Identity"; Nancy Saporta Sternbach, Marysa Navarro-Aranguren, Patricia Chuchryk, and Sonia E. Alvarez, "Feminisms in Latin America: From Bogotá to San Bernardo," *Signs* 17, no. 2 (1992): 393–434, and in Arturo Escobar and Sonia E. Alvarez, eds., *The Making of Social Movements in Latin America: Identity, Strategy and Democracy* (Boulder: Westview Press, 1992), pp. 207–239.

14. Cited in Patricia Cordova, *Mujer y liderazgo: Entre la familia y la política* (Lima: Yunta, 1992), p. 25; see also Alison Brysk, "Hearts and Minds: Symbolic Politics and Collective Action," unpublished manuscript.

15. María Elena Valenzuela, *Todos ibamos a ser reinas: La mujer en el Chile militar* (Santiago: Ediciones Chile y America, 1987); Maruja Barrig, "The Difficult Equilibrium Between Bread and Roses," in Jaquette, *The Women's Movement*, pp. 114–148.

16. Nicholson, *Feminism/Postmodernism*, and Steven Connor, *Postmodernist Culture* (London: Basil Blackwood, 1989), chaps. 1–2; Jean Franco, "Remapping Culture," in Stepan, *Americas*, pp. 172–188.

17. Sarah A. Radcliffe and Sallie Westwood, "Gender, Racism and the Politics of Identities in Latin America," in Radcliffe and Westwood, *Viva*, p. 1. See also Chandra Mohanty, Ann Russo, and Lourdes Torres, eds., *Third World Women and the Politics of Feminism* (Bloomington: Indiana University Press, 1991).

18. See Lois McNay, *Foucault and Feminism* (Boston: Northeastern University Press, 1994); Nancy Hartsock, "Foucault on Power: A Theory for Women?" in Nicholson, *Feminism/Postmodernism*, pp. 157–175.

19. A good example of the comparative status literature is Janet Zollinger Geile and Audrey Chapman Spock, eds., *Women: Their Role and Status in Eight Countries* (New York: John Wiley, 1977).

20. See Jane S. Jaquette, "Women and Modernization Theory: A Decade of Feminist Criticism," *World Politics* 34, no. 2 (1982): 267–284.

21. Ester Boserup, *Women's Role in Economic Development* (London: Allen and Unwin, 1970).

22. See Irene Tinker and Michele Bo Bramson, eds., *Women and World Development* (Washington, DC: Overseas Development Council, 1976).

23. For a discussion of bureaucratic resistance to women in development in the U.S. Agency for International Development, see Kathleen Staudt, *Women, the State and Foreign Development Assistance* (New York: Praeger, 1985).

24. An excellent review essay is Lourdes Benería, "Accounting for Women's Work: The Progress of Two Decades," *World Development* 20, no. 11 (1992): 1547–1560; see also Susan Tiano, "Women and Industrial Development In Latin America," *Latin American Research Review* 21, no. 3 (1985): 157–170.

25. Lourdes Benería and Gita Sen, "Accumulation, Reproduction and Women's Role in Economic Development: Boserup Revisited," in Eleanor Leacock and Helen I. Safa, eds., *Women's Work: Development and the Division of Labor by Gender* (South Hadley, MA: Bergin and Garvey, 1986).

26. See extensive bibliography in Stoner, *Latinas of the Americas: A Source Book*; essays by Patricia Fernández-Kelly, Helen Safa, and Lourdes Arizpe and Josefina Aranda in Leacock and Safa, eds., *Women's Work*; Susan Tiano, "Maquiladoras, Women's Work and Unemployment in Northern Mexico," *Aztlan* 15 (1985): 396–412. On women and agrarian reform, see Elizabeth Croll, "Rural Production and Reproduction: Socialist Development Experiences," in Leacock and Safa, *Women's Work*; Sarah Radcliffe, "'People Have to Rise Up—Like the Great Women Fighters'—The State and Peasant Women in Peru," in Radcliffe and Westwood, *Viva*, pp. 197–218. A pro-Senderista study of rural women in Peru is that of Carol Andreas, *When Women Rebel: The Rise of Popular Feminism in Peru* (Westport, CT: Lawrence Hill, 1985).

27. Caroline O.N. Moser, "Adjustment from Below: Low Income Women, Time and the Triple Role in Guayaquil, Ecuador," in Radcliffe and Westwood, *Viva*; and Benería, "Accounting for Women's Work," pp. 1550–1551.

28. See Carmen Barroso and Cristina Bruschini, "Building Politics from Personal Lives: Discussions on Sexuality Among Poor Women in Brazil," in Mohanty, Russo, and Torres, *Third World Women and the Politics of Feminism*, pp. 153–172; Sonia Alvarez, *Engendering Democracy in Brazil* (Princeton: Princeton University Press, 1990); Kathleen Staudt and Jane Jaquette, in "Gender and Politics in U.S. Population Policy," in Kathleen B. Jones and Anna Jonasdottir, *The Political Interests of Gender* (London: Sage Publications, 1988).

29. See Francesca Miller, *Women in Latin America: The Search for Social Justice* (Hanover: Northeastern University Press, 1992), and Julieta Kirkwood, *Ser política en Chile* (Santiago, Chile: FLACSO, 1986); Alvarez, *Engendering Democracy in Brazil*.

30. Elizabeth Jelín, ed., *Women and Social Change in Latin America* (London: UNRISD and Zed Books, 1990); Regina Rodríguez et al., eds., *Transiciones: Mujeres en los procesos democráticos* (Santiago, Chile: ISIS International, 1990); Susan C. Bourque and Donna C. Divine, eds., *Women Living Change* (Philadelphia: Temple University Press, 1985); Jaquette, *The Women's Movement in Latin America* (1994); Radcliffe and Westwood, *Viva*; Alvarez, *Engendering Democracy in Brazil*; Jo Fisher, *Out of the Shadows: Women, Resistance and Politics in South America* (London: Latin America Bureau, 1993); a recent brief review, focusing on Central America, is that of Norma Stolz Chinchilla, "Women's Movements in the Americas: Feminism's Second Wave," North American Congress on Latin America (NACLA) *Report on the Americas* 17 (thematic issue, July–August, 1993): 1; and several articles on women's organizations in the Caribbean are in Janet H. Momsen, ed., *Women and Change in the Caribbean* (Bloomington, IN: Indiana University Press, 1993). On

132 JANE S. JAQUETTE

women's organizations and political development assistance projects, see Dorrit Marks, ed., *Women and Grass Roots Democracy in the Americas* (Miami: University of Miami/North-South Center, 1993).

31. Susan Eckstein, ed., *Power and Popular Protest: Latin American Social Movements* (Berkeley: University of California Press, 1989); Escobar and Alvarez, *The Making of Social Movements in Latin America*; Eduardo Viola and Scott Mainwaring, "Novos movimentos sociais: Cultura, política e democracia no Brasil e Argentina," in Ilse Scherer-Warren and Paulo J. Krischke, eds., *Uma Revolucão no Cotidiano? Os novos movimentos sociais na America do Sul* (São Paulo, Brazil: Brasiliense, 1987). Annie G. Dandavati, "The Women's Movement and the Transition to Democracy in Chile" (Ph.D. diss., University of Denver, 1993) reviews the social movements literature and its relevance to Latin America.

32. Jean Cohen, "Strategy or Identity: New Theoretical Paradigms and Contemporary Social Movements," *Social Research* 52, no. 4 (1985): 663–716.

33. See Brysk, "Hearts and Minds: Symbolic Politics and Collective Action," p. 6; Alberto Melucci, "The Symbolic Challenge of Social Movements," *Social Research* 52, no. 4 (1985): 789–816; Russell J. Dalton and Manfred Kuechler, *Challenging the Political Order: New Social Movements in Western Democracies* (London: Oxford University Press, 1990).

34. See essays in Jaquette, *The Women's Movement*, Jelín, *Women and Social Change in Latin America* (especially Blondet), and Radcliffe and Westwood, *Viva*; see also Susan C. Bourque, "Gender and the State: Perspectives from Latin America," in Charlton, Everett, and Staudt, *Women, the State and Development*, pp. 114–129; María del Carmen Feijoó, *Alquimistas en la crisis: Experiencias de mujeres en el Gran Buenos Aires* (Buenos Aires: UNICEF, 1991).

35. There are deep divisions among feminists about whether women have, or should have, "interests"; Caroline Moser, for example, has argued that women have strategic and practical gender needs. See Jones and Jonasdottir, *The Political Interests of Gender*; Jane S. Jaquette, "Gender and Justice in Economic Development," in Irene Tinker, ed., *Persistent Inequalities* (Oxford: Oxford University Press, 1990), pp. 54–69. There is evidence that women are alienated from interest-based politics (e.g., Teresa Caldeira, "Women, Daily Life and Politics," in Jelín, *Women and Social Change in Latin America*). For a Latin American–based perspective, see Jeanine Anderson, *Intereses o justicia?* (Lima: Flora Tristan, 1992). On *machismo* and competition, see Patricia Cordova, *ed.*, *Mujer y liderazgo: Entre la familia y la política* (Lima: Yunta, 1992).

36. María Pilar Garcia-Guadilla, "Ecología: Women, Environment and Politics in Venezuela," in Radcliffe and Westwood, *Viva*, pp. 65–87; Schirmer, "The Seeking of Truth and the Gendering of Consciousness"; Yvonne Corcoran-Nantes, "Female Consciousness or Feminist Consciousness: Women's Consciousness Raising in Community-Based Structures in Brazil," in Radcliffe and Westwood, *Viva*, pp. 136–155.

37. Dandavati, "The Women's Movement and the Transition to Democracy in Chile"; Chuchryk, in Jaquette, *The Women's Movement*.

38. Amartya K. Sen, "Gender and Cooperative Conflicts," in Tinker, *Persistent Inequalities*, pp. 123–149.

39. One concept that does reflect some of these concerns, though it equates the women's moral status with that of the family, is Hanna Papanek's notion of "status production" ("To Each Less Than She Needs, From Each More Than She Can Do: Allocations, Entitlements, and Value," in Tinker, *Persistent Inequalities*, pp. 162–184).

40. Monique Cohen, personal communication, October 1993.

41. Jeanne Marie Col, personal communication, October 1993; George Tsebelis, *Nested Games: Rational Choice in Comparative Politics* (Berkeley: University of California Press, 1990).

CHAPTER SIX

■

Trajectory of a Concept: "Corporatism" in the Study of Latin American Politics

David Collier

BEGINNING IN THE 1970s, "corporatism" came to be a major focus of attention in research on Latin America.[1] Analysts employed the concept to refer both to a pattern of interest group politics that is monopolistic, hierarchically ordered, and structured by the state and to a broader cultural and ideological tradition of the region that they viewed as patrimonial and statist. The concept commanded great attention, as it seemed to provide a valuable analytical tool for scholars concerned with the authoritarian regimes emerging in Latin America during this period. In addition, the understanding of political relationships suggested by this concept appeared to offer a useful alternative, or at least an important supplement, to pluralist models widely used in the United States. Hence, corporatism has been subject to much theoretical debate, and the concept has been applied in many empirical studies.

In this chapter I explore the trajectory of corporatism as a concept in the Latin American field. The analysis is based on the premise that scholars should occasionally step back and take stock of the major concepts with which they work. In any area of research, new concepts may initially be embraced with great enthusiasm, and, at times, with unrealistic expectations about the degree of insight they will provide. Subsequently, these concepts may be relegated to the domain of outmoded ideas, sometimes with considerable loss of learning and neglect of accumulated insight. In the face of this potential problem, it is useful periodically to assess the evolution of concepts and attempt a codification of what has been accomplished.

135

In the first two sections of this chapter, I focus on the body of literature that treated corporatism as a form of interest group politics. The initial section explores the overall contribution of the concept and the shared empirical understanding of corporatism that emerged. The second section considers refinements introduced in the literature. These refinements include efforts to situate corporatism both in relation to the overarching concepts of which it may be seen as a specific type and also in relation to parallel concepts, such as clientelism, concertation, consociationalism, pluralism, monism, and syndicalism. Attention then turns to the more fine grained understanding achieved through identifying subtypes and elaborating dimensions of corporatism. It appears that once the initial insight introduced by the concept became familiar, the further analytic contribution came, in important measure, from refinements that provided sharper differentiation of corporatism as a distinctive political phenomenon. This section concludes by distinguishing between "conceptual stretching," a traditional concern in the field of comparative analysis, and "theoretical stretching," arguing that both issues arose in the literature on corporatism.

The next section examines the debate generated by the thesis—identified above all with Howard J. Wiarda—that corporatism in twentieth-century Latin America can be seen as deriving from an Iberic-Latin historical tradition of hierarchical, statist authority relations. This literature focused not only on twentieth-century structures of group politics but also on this longer political tradition. This thesis commanded wide interest, in part because it advanced a type of cultural explanation that ran against some of the main intellectual currents in the Latin American field. The result was a debate that, as is suggested below, remains in important respects unresolved.

A concluding section discusses what may be called the "normalization" of the concept of corporatism and the partial erosion of corporative practices that has occurred recently in many Latin American countries. Corporatism remains a useful concept that refers to important political phenomena, but it is less central both to scholarly debates and to day-to-day politics than it was two decades ago. □

EMERGENCE OF THE CONCEPT:
CORPORATIVE FORMS OF INTEREST GROUP POLITICS

The concept of corporatism began to attract wide attention in the Latin American field in the first half of the 1970s.[2] Earlier writers such as Robert J. Alexander and Charles W. Anderson had previously made passing reference to the corporative character of state-group relations.[3] Likewise, authors such as Richard M. Morse had described a Latin American tradition of hierarchical, state-centric authority relations that has much in common with some conceptions of corporatism, although Morse did not use this label.[4] However, it was Philippe C. Schmitter who first placed corporatism more centrally on the intellectual agenda with his book *Interest Conflict and Political Change in Brazil.* He explored the corporative policies toward interest groups introduced in Brazil under Getúlio Vargas in the 1930s and 1940s, focusing on the elaborate system that emerged for creating, structuring, subsidizing, and controlling these groups. Although the Vargas administration fell in 1945, Schmitter argued that the corporative policies of that period had "struck deeper roots" and that corporatism had become a fundamental feature of Brazilian interest politics.[5] Anyone attempting to analyze the Brazilian political system needed to come to grips with this legacy.

Corporatism soon became a common theme in the Latin American field.[6] As scholars attempted to deal analytically with the wave of military regimes that began in the 1960s, the concept offered a valuable new perspective for understanding the authoritarian political relationships that seemed so prevalent in the region. Within this framework, analysts focused attention very centrally on monopolistic, hierarchically structured patterns of interest group politics. These patterns were generally the product of a strong state role in sponsoring the formation of groups, granting them a monopoly of representation, shaping their internal organization, controlling or at least influencing their demand making, and channeling their interaction with public institutions and with one another. Through such initiatives, actors within the state sought to "harmonize" relations among groups, classes, and sectors, although this harmony was often founded on a strong bias in favor of some groups and against others.

Scholars who studied group politics from the perspective of corporatism addressed the misgivings shared by many analysts about employing a pluralist perspective, which emphasized the free competition of autonomously organized groups.[7] Periodic expressions of pluralism are unquestionably an important feature of Latin American politics: for instance, the efforts, initiated "from below," to constitute or reconstitute social and political groups and to organize new efforts at protest and demand making. Yet the central role of the state in structuring group politics has been reflected in the recurring tendency over many decades for new groups and new demands to be subordinated to state-regulated networks of group representation and state-established frameworks for demand making. By calling attention to this tendency toward subordination and state regulation, the concept of corporatism yielded new insight.

Definition and Conceptualization of Corporatism

Within the literature on corporative patterns of interest group politics, a basic set of shared understandings emerged. In terms of formal definitions, the most widely cited was that of Schmitter:

> Corporatism can be defined as a system of interest representation in which the constituent units are organized into a limited number of singular, compulsory, noncompetitive, hierarchically ordered and functionally differentiated categories, recognized or licensed (if not created) by the state and granted a deliberate representational monopoly within their respective categories in exchange for observing certain controls on their selection of leaders and articulation of demands and supports.[8]

Other scholars had their own, slightly different, "checklist" definitions.[9] Notwithstanding some differences in emphasis, a rough consensus developed regarding the constellation of attributes within the sphere of group politics on which attention should focus. These attributes can be organized under three broad headings, with specific corporative provisions fitting under each: (a) The *structuring* of representation, involving the official recognition of groups, which are organized into well-defined functional categories and enjoy a monopoly of representation within their respective categories; (b) the *subsidy* of groups, which can occur through direct state subvention and, especially in the case of labor unions, through mechanisms that provide for compulsory membership and that facilitate dues collection; and (c) state *control* over leadership, demand making, finances, and internal governance.[10]

A broader conceptual understanding of the relationship among these three sets of defining attributes also emerged in the literature. Philippe Schmitter and Alfred Stepan suggested that the advantages bestowed by both structuring and subsidy are granted "in exchange for" the acceptance of state control.[11] Ruth Berins Collier and David Collier, in a related argument, maintained that corporatist political relationships entail an interaction between "inducements" and "constraints." Structuring and subsidy represent organizational benefits (inducements) for the groups and their leaders, in exchange for which they accept the controls (constraints) associated with corporatism.[12] Obviously, in order for a genuine exchange to occur, the state must be actively involved in seeking to control, or at least to strongly influence, the groups. Yet the groups must also have some degree of autonomy so that their leaders have a margin of choice in accepting the initiatives of the state.

Stepan, in his analysis of this power relationship between groups and the state, argued that the possibility of an imbalance in the relationship constitutes a "generic predicament" of corporatism.[13] On the one hand, power may shift toward the *state* to such a degree that corporatism is simply transformed into a system of state domination of groups. On the other hand, power may shift toward the *groups* to such a degree that central coordination, an essential attribute of corporatism, is lost or is fundamentally weakened. Thus, the two underlying components of corporatism are in opposition. Not surprisingly, there is no inherently "correct" balance between these components. However, if an imbalance reaches either extreme, it is reasonable to ask whether one is still in the presence of corporatism. This issue will prove important in discussing subtypes of corporatism below.

Shared Empirical Understanding

Along with this conceptualization of corporative forms of group politics, one also finds in the literature a shared empirical understanding of corporatism in Latin America. Obviously, further insights emerged as more research was carried out, yet a significant degree of common understanding may be identified that had emerged roughly by the time of the publication in 1977 of James M. Malloy's *Authoritarianism and Corporatism in Latin America*. Key elements of this understanding are outlined here, several of which are drawn from chapters in that book.

First, although many specific corporative provisions have been found in Latin America, the literature did not presume the existence of full-blown corporative systems. No country provided for well-institutionalized mediation among labor, business, and the state at the pinnacle of the corporative system, although the region has seen unsuccessful attempts to establish such mediation and scholars have identified some partial approximations.[14] Even Brazil, with its elaborately developed corporative system, did not allow for an overarching labor confederation. Consequently, Kenneth P. Erickson described the corporative system for organized labor in Brazil as a "truncated pyramid,"[15] and at this peak level, actors in the state sought to control worker politics not through corporative mechanisms for channeling worker organization but through the noncorporative mechanism of *preventing* such organization. A quite different departure from a full corporative model was found in cases where a political party, closely linked to a corporatively organized labor movement, was banned from the political arena. This pattern was, for example, a fundamental feature of Argentine and Peruvian politics in the late 1950s and 1960s.

Another feature that might be viewed as an element of a full-blown classical model of corporatism in Latin America, nonpeak organizations that combined labor and business, was rare indeed. One of the few instances in which such organizations appeared was in Peru in the post-1968 period. The Peruvian government established "industrial communities" in which workers were to play an important role in the management of enterprises, thus creating a "classless corporative structure."[16] Yet the initiative failed, and this form of organization has not been a significant feature of Latin American corporatism.

A second part of the shared empirical understanding was the recognition among scholars who analyzed corporatism within the general framework of the defining attributes discussed above that such a large set of attributes would not always be present in any particular instance. Schmitter's book on Brazil, which played a central role in stimulating scholarly interest in this phenomenon, was based on an extreme case. Scholars did not necessarily assume that other Latin American countries had as fully developed a corporative system as Brazil. Thus, in relation to the multitrait definitions like those discussed above, it was recognized that these traits were present to different degrees and in different combinations. Collier and Collier suggested that this recognition helps to avoid "an excessively narrow conception of corporatism as a phenomenon that is either present or absent, and views it instead as a dimension (or, potentially, a set of dimensions ...) along which cases may be arrayed."[17]

The experience with corporatism was heterogeneous in other respects as well. For example, particular features of corporatism could be implemented in very different ways. In the sphere of labor unions, compulsory membership and monopoly of representation were sometimes established directly. But sometimes they were established indirectly, through complex provisions that provided partial approximations. Further, although these provisions were typically established by law, not surprisingly, major variations emerged in actual practice.[18] Finally, at an early point scholars observed that major differences in the corporative structuring of groups sometimes emerged in different geographic regions within a given country.[19]

A third element in the shared understanding was emphasized in Guillermo O'Donnell's analysis of the "segmentary" character of corporatism, involving its differing meaning and consequences for distinct social classes. He argued that in Latin America, the role of corporative structures in shaping worker organizations, as opposed to business organizations, is far more direct and coercive.[20] In addition, elaborating on an observation made earlier by Schmitter,[21] O'Donnell argued that business interests can often exercise informal power both inside and outside the state to such a degree that corporative structures may be far less constraining for them than for the working class.[22] Other authors in the Malloy volume, dealing with Mexico and Colombia, reached the same conclusion.[23] Concerning this distinction, it is important to note that the corporative structuring of worker organizations encompassed not only workers in the urban sector but also, in some important cases, peasants.[24]

Although the corporative structuring of business politics is very important in some time periods and in some countries, corporatism in Latin America has, in general, been less central to understanding business politics than worker politics. Indeed, labor law in most countries consists, in important measure, of a complex network of provisions for structuring, subsidizing, and controlling the labor movement. In that sense, state-labor relations in Latin America have been markedly corporative for many decades.[25] Consequently, a substantial part of research on corporatism has centered on the implications of corporatism for organized labor. It seems likely that corporatism would not have been viewed as such an important phenomenon were it not for the obvious importance of corporative provisions for the functioning of the labor movement.

Finally, along with the recognition of the incomplete character of the corporative structuring of group politics, one finds the insistence that its incomplete character was to be expected. Linn Hammergren warned against confusing "the master plans of political organizers and would-be institution builders" with the reality of day-to-day politics, and she pointed to the long history in Latin America of noncompliance with the law and with mandates of the state.[26] Douglas Chalmers and Alberto Ciria likewise emphasized that major changes in regime, such as those associated with the implementation of corporatism, have far less impact than is sometimes believed. Features of the national political regime and the structure of political groups, which may initially seem to be crucial attributes of a country's politics, are often soon eroded.[27]

Correspondingly, a significant degree of caution was reflected in many, though certainly not all, of the early analyses of corporatism. At the time of the rapid spread of scholarly interest in this topic, for example, perhaps the most dramatic new corporative policies in the region were those of the post-1968 military government in Peru. Yet, in an analysis initially written at the height of the military reforms, Malloy insisted that "there is no guarantee that the Peruvian military will continue in the corporatist direction or that it will be successful in imposing a new system of [corporative] political economy in Peru."[28]

At certain points, however, the warnings ran in the other direction, against the problem of *underestimating* the impact of corporatism. Schmitter referred to this when he observed that scholars who analyzed pluralism and democracy in Brazil between 1945 and 1964 were at times insufficiently attentive to the legacy of the corporatist experience of the 1930s and 1940s.[29] Whereas some scholars interpreted the post-1964 military regime in Brazil as a "fundamental restructuring of the polity,"[30]

Schmitter disagreed and saw the post-1964 experience as "restorationist," in that it was marked by attempts to further consolidate earlier corporative structures.[31]

Latin America has not experienced corporatism in its full-blown, classical form, yet corporatism has been a central feature of group politics in specific sectors, time periods, and countries. The shared scholarly recognition of this centrality accounts for the concept's ongoing importance in the literature. □

REFINEMENT AND DIFFERENTIATION
OF THE CONCEPT

Looking beyond this basic formulation, one finds a series of refinements and modifications that played an important role in the evolving literature on corporatism. To explore these innovations it is useful to employ the traditional notion of a hierarchy of concepts.[32] Such hierarchies play a powerful role in framing our thinking, and a self-conscious understanding of how conceptual innovations occur at different levels in these hierarchies can provide valuable insights into the way concepts evolve. In the initial phase of this literature, for example, the concept of corporatism was viewed as one type in relation to the overarching concept of systems of "interest representation"; and, in turn, "state corporatism" was seen as a subtype in relation to the concept of corporatism. The three levels in this hierarchy are examined in turn.

Refinements in the Overarching Concept

Some of the innovations that emerged in discussions of corporatism concerned the overarching concept, of which corporatism is a particular type. One of these refinements arose from a clearer recognition of what is entailed in a corporative, as opposed to pluralist, form of group politics. Schmitter had initially defined corporatism as a mode of *interest representation*. However, corporatively structured groups in Latin America do not simply represent actors in society. Rather, they often stand in an intermediate position between society and the state, since corporative structuring may cause them to become in part creatures of the state. Consequently, Schmitter suggested that the distinctive meaning of corporatism was better captured by broadening the overarching concept and referring to modes of *interest intermediation*.[33]

Another innovation at the level of the overarching concept derived from the increasing use in the 1980s of the term "concertation," which partially overlapped with the standard meaning of corporatism. A characteristic definition treated concertation as "a mechanism for establishing policy alternatives, encompassing the participation of labor and capital, based on sustained cooperation between these actors and the government."[34] Thus, concertation entailed the overarching process of forming social pacts and shaping public policy at the pinnacle of organized labor, organized business, and the state, which traditionally had been viewed as one major facet of corporatism, the other being the organization and structuring of the groups themselves. Schmitter suggested it might have been appropriate to label the structuring of groups as "corporatism$_1$," and this overarching process of mediation as "corporatism$_2$."[35]

Instead, Schmitter accommodated the new usage of concertation by proposing a narrower meaning of corporatism that excluded this overarching process of mediation.[36] In this more limited conception, corporatism remained a principal subtype of *interest intermediation*, another being pluralism. As shown in Figure 6.1, concertation was understood as a subtype of *policy formation*, another principal subtype being pressure politics. Here again, the concept of corporatism was refined by modifying the overarching concept of which it is a component. In this instance, the modification was accomplished by differentiating two separate hierarchies of concepts.

Situating Corporatism Vis-à-vis Related Concepts

Scholars who sought to elucidate the meaning of corporatism also clarified its meaning in relation to other concepts that are likewise concerned with alternative forms of exchange and accommodation. Differences among these concepts characteristically involved contrasts in the *institutional site* of the political relationships specified by the concept. This issue was central, for example, to the distinction between corporatism and clientelism. Robert R. Kaufman suggested that both concepts entail "rela-

FIGURE 6.1 Effort to Accommodate Discussion of "Concertation" Leads to Differentiation of Overarching Concept into Two Components

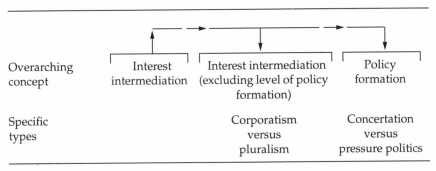

	Interest intermediation	Interest intermediation (excluding level of policy formation)	Policy formation
Overarching concept			
Specific types		Corporatism versus pluralism	Concertation versus pressure politics

tionships of domination and subordination," but with regard to the institutional site, corporatism is a mode of authority relations among groups, whereas clientelism is a mode of authority relations among individuals. This difference in institutional site is closely associated with a difference in form. Whereas corporatism tends to be more legalistic and bureaucratic, clientelism is personalistic and often more fluid.[37]

The issue of institutional site also arose in the comparison of corporatism and consociationalism. Jonathan Hartlyn argued that both are modes of conflict limitation that commonly emerge as an elite response to a perceived crisis, that both seek to establish a noncompetitive process of decisionmaking, and that "in both there is a tension between elite accords and the ability of these elites to carry along their mass following."[38] However, with corporatism these arrangements encompass interest groups, whereas with consociationalism they commonly encompass political parties.

Another important issue, given that corporatism is one type in relation to the overarching concept of interest intermediation, was the identification of other types. This issue was addressed in Schmitter's typology of group politics, which was organized around distinctions concerning the *degree of competitiveness* and the *locus of power*.[39] Building on his own definition of corporatism (characterized by a noncompetitive system of groups that are subject to substantial state control), Schmitter constructed parallel definitions of *pluralism* (characterized by the free and competitive formation of groups that are subject to little external control), *monism* (a noncompetitive mode in which groups are dominated by a single party),[40] and *syndicalism* (based on noncompetitive, unregulated, nonhierarchically organized groups characterized by autonomy and self governance). Schmitter thus situated the debate in a much larger comparative and historical framework of alternative types of group intermediation.

Subtypes and Dimensions of Corporatism

When a concept is first introduced, it may produce a sense of discovery as it gives scholars new analytic leverage. The initial enthusiasm can soon fade, however, and the generation of further insight often depends on the introduction of refinements in the concept. This refinement occurred as scholars delineated subtypes and dimensions of corporatism. Variations in the *locus of power* were crucial in this differentiation, just as they were in the discussion above of contrasting types of interest intermediation.

Differences in the locus of power were central, for example, in Schmitter's distinction between "state" and "societal" corporatism (Table 6.1).[41] Both are forms of group politics that tend to be monopolistic, and they are

TABLE 6.1   Subtypes and Dimensions: Differentiating in Terms
of the Locus of Power

Subtypes	Political Relationships
State versus societal	Noncompetitive political relationships are created and often imposed by the state versus noncompetitive relationships created by the groups.
Privatizing versus statizing	Groups penetrate and privatize a sector of the state versus state penetrates and controls groups.
Inclusionary versus exclusionary	State elite are more dependent on support or acquiescence of corporatized groups versus lesser or no dependence on their support or acquiescence.
Inducements versus constraints	Inducements are used by the state to win cooperation of groups versus direct control over groups.

structurally similar in many ways. Yet the former is created and often imposed by the state, and, in important respects, it reflects the control of the state over the corporatized groups. By contrast, societal corporatism emerges as the groups themselves construct monopolistic, hierarchically structured channels of representation. Through this process, some groups defeat or absorb other groups with little or no interference from the state. The subtypes of state and societal corporatism emerged as a fundamental distinction in the literature, and in the field of West European studies they were paralleled by Gerhard Lehmbruch's distinction between authoritarian and liberal corporatism.[42]

A somewhat different contrast was underscored in Guillermo O'Donnell's subtypes of statizing and privatizing corporatism. Statizing corporatism entails the penetration of groups by the state, whereas in the case of privatizing corporatism the groups penetrate the state, thereby placing certain arenas of the state and of policymaking under private control. The difference between O'Donnell's conception of privatizing corporatism and Schmitter's conception of societal corporatism can be seen in the fact that a given group that functioned in the framework of societal corporatism could fail to privatize an area of the state in which it had a special interest. Thus, O'Donnell's privatizing corporatism involves the penetration of selected areas of policy and of state bureaucracy by groups that function in the framework of Schmitter's version of societal corporatism. Given the dramatically different power relationships involved in statizing and privatizing corporatism, O'Donnell described corporatism as "bifrontal."[43]

A further distinction concerning the locus of power pointed to variability in the significance of corporatism for the working class. O'Donnell had earlier defined as "inclusionary" those political systems in which policymakers use the resources of the state to mobilize the working class and deliberately enhance its political power, or in which policymakers at least accommodate themselves to preexisting levels of worker mobilization and political power. This pattern contrasted with "exclusionary" systems, in which state policy is used to demobilize the working class and its organizations and to reduce its power.[44] Stepan used this distinction to generate subtypes of corporatism. On the one hand, the more prolabor variant of inclusionary corporatism, associated with mobilization of workers, granting of major benefits, and increased political leverage for labor, was found, for example, in Argentina under Perón in the 1940s. On the other hand, the more antilabor variant of exclusionary corporatism, associated with the demobilization of labor and the deliberate curtailment of its political leverage, occurred under the post-1964 military government in Brazil.[45] Thus, again, what appeared to be similar structures could have decidedly different political consequences.

The analysis of underlying dimensions of inducements and constraints, noted briefly above, pushed the differentiation of corporatism still further. Collier and Collier suggested that in these different contexts, corporative *structures* themselves are not necessarily the same. It is evident that all the traits identified in standard definitions of corporatism are not always present and that in different contexts they are present in different combinations. Depending on the goals and power resources of both the policymakers who initiate corporatism and the groups toward which their policies are directed, different patterns of inducements and constraints emerge. These patterns shift over time within the framework of an ongoing exchange, shaped by the changing goals and power capabilities of the relevant actors. This perspective underlined the interactive and changing character of corporatism. With regard to the contrast between inclusionary and exclusionary corporatism, Collier and Collier found that the more prolabor variant of corporatism provides substantial inducements and more limited constraints; whereas the more antilabor variant links the inducements to more extensive constraints. Thus, corporatism takes different forms in different contexts.[46]

A Further Look at the Subtypes

To gain insight into the meaning of these subtypes in relation to the overarching concept of corporatism, it is useful to discuss briefly the alternative ways in which subtypes of concepts may be formed. It turns out that the generic predicament that underlies corporatism has an important influence on the kind of subtypes it generates.

In what may be called the "classical" mode of forming subtypes, the subtype is identified by the attributes of the overarching concept, *plus* additional attributes.[47] This involves the traditional idea of defining concepts by "genus and difference" *(genus et differentia)*.[48] Thus one identifies an initial category and then establishes additional differentiating characteristics that distinguish the subtype. In set-theoretic terms, the subtype is nested within the overarching category. As Figure 6.2 shows, for example, bureaucratic authoritarianism is conventionally understood as a specific form of authoritarianism that has additional attributes that define the subtype, prominent among which is a bureaucratic, technocratic style of policymaking.[49]

A contrasting mode of forming subtypes may be called "radial."[50] Here the attributes that define a subtype are not introduced *in addition to* those of the overarching concept, but are *extracted from among them*. Thus, from the set of attributes associated with the overarching concept, one or more are isolated in the process of defining the subtype. To the extent that different subtypes isolate distinctive subsets of attributes, one can understand them as forming "radial" extensions. Because subtypes created in this way "leave behind" other attributes in the overarching concept, an interesting tension arises: Although they *are* subtypes of the overarching concept, they may lack key characteristics of that concept, so that some observers might argue that they are no longer really "instances" of it.

An example of a radial subtype is found in O'Donnell's recent discussion of "delegative democracy."[51] Although this form of regime maintains fully competitive elections, it exhibits a high degree of presidential dominance that overrides traditional checks and balances and "horizontal accountability" within the state. Such a subtype, rather than unambiguously being a case of democracy (as bureaucratic authoritarianism is unambiguously a case of authoritarianism), lacks what are often understood to be key features of democracy. As shown in Figure 6.2, delegative democracy therefore follows the radial pattern of being potentially less democratic than the overarching category of democracy.

The subtypes of corporatism exhibit a similar radial pattern, because in each of them one major facet of corporatism is accentuated and the other is attenuated, reflecting the generic predicament discussed above. Under societal corporatism, the component of state control is attenuated and the autonomy of groups increases, whereas under state corporatism, and especially exclusionary state corporatism, power shifts strongly toward the side of the state. In addition, with reference to organized

FIGURE 6.2   Classical Versus Radial Subtypes

☐   Box identifies the attribute that differentiates the subtype.
[ ]   Brackets identify the attribute that is substantially or severely attenuated
in the subtype.

CLASSICAL SUBTYPE: BUREAUCRATIC AUTHORITARIANISM

	Concept	Attributes	
Root Concept	Authoritarianism	L D	Differentiating
Subtype	Bureaucratic Authoritarianism	L D ☐T	attribute of the subtype is **in addition** to those of the root concept.

L = Underline{L}imited pluralism and mobilization[a]
D = Underline{D}istinctive mentalities, not guiding ideology[a]
T = Underline{T}echnocratic style of policymaking[b]

RADIAL SUBTYPE: DELEGATIVE DEMOCRACY

	Concept	Attributes	
Root Concept	Democracy	V H	Differentiating
Subtype	Delegative Democracy	☐V [H]	attribute of the subtype is **contained within** the root concept

V = Underline{V}ertical accountability[c]
H = Underline{H}orizontal accountability[c]

RADIAL SUBTYPES: STATE AND SOCIETAL CORPORATISM

	Concept	Attributes	
Root Concept	Corporatism	S C	Differentiating
Subtype	State Corporatism	☐S [C]	attributes of the subtypes are **contained within**
	Societal Corporatism	[S] ☐C	the root concept

S = Underline{S}tructuring and subsidy   Corporatism understood as entailing a
C = Underline{C}ontrol   balance between S and C[b]

[a] These two elements are from Juan J. Linz, "An Authoritarian Regime: Spain," in Erik Allradt and Yrjö Littunen, eds. *Cleavages, Ideologies, and Party Systems* (Helsinki: Academic Bookstore, 1975).

[b] See discussion in text.

[c] Guillermo O'Donnell, "Delegative Democracy," *Journal of Democracy* 5, no. 1 (January 1994): 55–69.

labor, those benefits that are provided may to a greater degree be extended to union leaders who cooperate with the state. Hence the crucial idea that corporatism entails policy toward interest groups *as organizations* may become less important. A parallel pattern appears in the case of O'Donnell's statizing and privatizing corporatism. With regard to privatizing corporatism, he emphasized that the state still seeks to exercise control, but its control is unquestionably attenuated.[52] In the interaction between inducements and constraints, the same pattern emerges: Accentuating one of these dimensions necessarily shifts the balance between them.

A concomitant of this radial pattern is that the subtypes of corporatism may at times be seen as having less in common with the overarching concept than they do with a neighboring concept. For example, exclusionary state corporatism might, as described above, more accurately be seen as a system for the *co-optation* of labor leaders. Similarly, O'Donnell's privatizing corporatism may have more in common with Theodore J. Lowi's concept of *interest group liberalism* than it does with the overall notion of corporatism.[53] To the extent that corporatism evolves to become a system of pure constraints and virtually no inducements, it might be viewed as a system of *repression*.[54] Finally, a parallel issue arose in the literature on European corporatism, where it has been claimed that societal corporatism is more similar to *pluralism* than it is to other forms of corporatism.[55]

What difference does it make that the subtypes of corporatism follow a radial pattern? One important implication concerns the long-standing problem of "conceptual stretching" identified more than two decades ago by Giovanni Sartori. In some phases of the literature on corporatism, scholars became concerned that the concept was applied too broadly. Yet interestingly, the solution to this problem was not to "climb a ladder of abstraction" and move toward more general, overarching concepts, as would have been suggested by Sartori's classical framework,[56] but rather to generate subtypes of corporatism. This was an appropriate response because radial subtypes can potentially be applied to cases to which the fit of the overarching concept is questionable. Thus, forming radial subtypes can serve as a means of avoiding conceptual stretching.[57]

At the same time, this very flexibility sometimes led to the problems just discussed: The subtypes of corporatism occasionally seemed conceptually closer to other concepts such as co-optation, repression, interest group liberalism, or pluralism than they were to corporatism. Though conceptual stretching was often avoided through the use of a radial subtype, it must be asked whether scholars were still really making use of this larger framework of understanding surrounding the concept of corporatism or whether this larger framework became less relevant to some of the subtypes.

This concern suggests the need to distinguish between *conceptual* stretching and *theoretical* stretching. Conceptual stretching is a mismatch between the concept and the case to which it is applied, in the sense that attributes associated with the concept are not present in the case. For example, if a scholar classifies a regime as bureaucratic authoritarian, even though it lacks a technocratic policymaking style, then conceptual stretching has occurred.

With theoretical stretching, the issue is not that the specific attributes associated with the concept do not *match* the case, but rather that the larger set of insights associated with the concept may not *illuminate* the case. Thus, in the choice between using the label "privatizing corporatism," as opposed to "interest group liberalism," the issue is whether one wishes to evoke the overall insights associated with the concept of corporatism, or with the concept of liberalism. To the extent that the insights associated with corporatism are less relevant to understanding the cases under consideration, then theoretical stretching may have occurred.

A final resolution of these issues of conceptual and theoretical stretching can be difficult to achieve, depending as they do on the analytical tastes of the authors who address any given topic. Yet, short of a definitive resolution, it is invaluable when examining the evolution of radial concepts such as corporatism to be alert to the problem of these two kinds of stretching. □

A CULTURAL PERSPECTIVE ON CORPORATISM

Along with this focus on group politics, the literature on corporatism in Latin America also included a debate over cultural approaches. This debate posed both the descriptive question of how broadly the term should be applied and the explanatory question of why corporatism emerged and persisted in Latin America. These questions were raised very centrally by Wiarda, and this perspective has also been explored, in different ways, by Newton, Erickson, Schwartzman, and Stepan, as well as by Morse and Anderson.[58]

Although Wiarda applied the concept of corporatism to the analysis of group politics, he also argued that the concept should be used more broadly in a general framework for the study of Latin America. He suggested that "the 'corporative framework' … refers to a system in which the political culture and institutions reflect a historic hierarchical, authoritarian, and organic view of man, society, and polity." In this system, "the government directs and controls all associations … and it is the 'general will' and the power of the state that prevail over particular interests." These traits are seen as so deeply ingrained that the region is "virtually inherently corporative."[59] Thus the concept of corporatism became, at the same time, a description of these political and cultural patterns and an explanation for them.

Wiarda maintained that the durability of these patterns of authority derive from the fact that "the Iberic-Latin nations were largely bypassed by the great revolutions associated with the making of the modern world." As a consequence, at least as of the early 1970s, "one still finds powerful echoes and manifestations of the earlier corporative-organic framework in virtually all contemporary regimes and institutions in Latin American and in their underlying political-cultural foundations." In describing these patterns, Wiarda evoked Charles Anderson's metaphor of Latin American politics as a "living museum" in which older institutions and traditions persist alongside newer political forms.[60]

The hypothesis that a strong historical tradition of state-centric, hierarchical authority relations is an important force in shaping Latin American politics reflects a well-established approach to the study of the region. Yet Wiarda's analysis of this tradition in relation to the concept of corporatism raised concern among other scholars who wrote about this concept. Schmitter sharply criticized this type of cultural approach. He questioned the plausibility of the claim that the cultural version of corporatism, as an underlying proclivity in Latin American politics, periodically reasserts itself to reshape state-group relations, thereby counteracting the influence of other political traditions, such as liberalism. He suggested that this account would seem to imply that "political culture is a sort of 'spigot variable' which gets turned on every once in a while to produce a different system of functional representation. ..."[61]

Schmitter also maintained that if one uses "corporatism" to refer to ideology, the phenomena thereby encompassed are so heterogeneous that it is not helpful to employ the label. Schmitter noted the "extraordinary variety of theorists, ideologues and activists that have advocated it [i.e., corporatism] for widely divergent motives, interests and reasons," and argued that "there is simply too much normative variety and behavioral hypocrisy in the use of the corporatist *ideological* label to make it a useful operational instrument for comparative analysis."[62]

O'Donnell likewise expressed concern about Wiarda's approach, arguing that the problem of achieving adequate theory in the field of development cannot be addressed by "elevating concepts that refer to authentic and important problems (e.g., corporatism ...) to the category of smuggled substitutes for a general theory, in the sense that they could by themselves describe and explain the fundamental characteristics and trends of the case being analyzed." He suggested that "the problem is the result of an unwarranted jump in the level of analysis, which has ... the important consequence of freezing perception around what the exaggerated central concept postulates as the society's alpha and omega."[63] In this sense, O'Donnell might be seen as raising the objection that Wiarda had engaged in conceptual stretching.

It may well be the case that in this part of the literature, the label of corporatism was applied too broadly, and carrying out causal analysis based on cultural factors is difficult. Yet three points of caution are in order with reference to these critiques.

First, it is no easy matter to assess a mode of explanation in which the influence of an underlying factor, such as a cultural proclivity, is hypothesized to be periodically deflected by other forces, only to be reasserted at a later point. Yet such a pattern can occur. What is called for is not the dismissal of such a pattern of causation as involving a spigot variable but rather an effort to find a mode of analysis that can plausibly evaluate hypotheses about such patterns; in particular, one that can yield insight into the mechanisms through which such patterns are "reproduced." Long-term cultural explanations seem perennially to get caught between appearing to account for too much and appearing to account for too little, and neither the Latin American field, nor perhaps any other field, has made much progress in systematically evaluating them.[64]

Second, in response to Schmitter's complaint that using corporatism to refer to ideology places under one label phenomena that are extremely heterogeneous, one could argue that this same charge can be leveled against the use of the label to refer to group politics. As argued above, corporative forms of group politics are likewise heterogeneous in terms of the power relationships they entail. Such heterogeneity does not obviate the value of the concept; it simply points to the need for refinement, of precisely the kind that was illustrated above in the discussion of subtypes.

Finally, Stepan suggested a constructive alternative to simply dismissing this approach. Any confusion that derives from applying the concept to culture and ideology can be addressed by a shift in terminology. He proposed the use of separate labels for (1) the corporative structuring of groups, which is an outcome that analysts often wish to explain, as opposed to (2) the normative, ideological tradition, which may be part of the explanation of this corporative structuring. Stepan thus distinguished between corporatism and "organic statism." Like many authors, he treated corporatism as "a particular set of policies and institutional arrangements for structuring interest representation." By contrast, he viewed "organic statism" as a normative and ideological approach to politics that favors a statist, hierarchical mode of political organization.[65] Stepan thereby incorporated an ideological/culturalist perspective in his analysis, yet he avoided applying the label of corporatism so broadly.

Notwithstanding the critiques of O'Donnell and Schmitter and this modification proposed by Stepan, the label "corporatism" continues to be employed in the Latin American field to refer to longer-term political, cultural, and ideological patterns. Further, it merits emphasis that this usage seems to generate little confusion. One still finds references to corporatism as the basis for a "political philosophy," as a "tradition," and as a set of "ideals" upon which policy may be based.[66] Employing the concept to refer to this longer tradition remains a comprehensible usage, and it hardly seems appropriate to ban it from the field. At the same time, for a great many scholars this does not remain the principal usage, and the final section of this chapter focuses on the application of the concept to interest group politics. □

CONCLUDING OBSERVATIONS: NORMALIZATION OF THE CONCEPT AND PARTIAL EROSION OF CORPORATISM

In recent years, the Latin American field has seen a significant decline in scholarly interest in corporatism, due to a "normalization" of the concept, a changing assessment of its importance, and a partial erosion of the phenomenon itself. With regard to normalization, it has been observed that, after an initial phase of intellectual excitement sometimes generated by a new concept, it commonly becomes "part of our general stock of theoretical concepts."[67] This process has occurred in the case of corporatism, which, as Wiarda has emphasized, now sparks less scholarly excitement due in part to the very familiarity of the concept and of the phenomena to which it refers.[68] Thus in the second half of the 1980s and in the 1990s the concept has commanded less attention in the Latin American field. In a few studies, the issues it raises remain a major theme.[69] In many other instances, the term is used with little or no elaboration to refer to the patterns of group politics discussed above.[70] Corporatism is treated as a familiar topic, not as a subject of special analytical interest.

The concept may also receive less attention because, as noted above, attempts to establish structured political mediation at the pinnacle of labor, business, and the state, which had previously been labeled as corporative, more recently came to be called concertation, or sometimes "social pacts." These attempts remain an important feature of Latin American politics; they are simply given a different label.

The concept of corporatism is also less prominent in the literature because the phenomena to which it refers are, in significant respects, perceived as less important. For example, in the 1980s scholars were confronted with dramatic episodes of democratization. Although some interest groups played a key role in the early phase of democratic openings, it has been argued that beyond this early phase political parties became a far more important force in the effort to organize new forms of democratic politics. Hence the sectors that had been among the most central in debates on corporatism have been seen as playing a less critical political role.[71]

Another aspect of the perceived decline in the importance of corporatism concerns the recent experience of the South American countries that had earlier generated some of the most extensive discussions of this topic. In the 1980s and early 1990s these countries experienced a greater degree of political stability that might earlier have been hypothesized to be a potential outcome of corporatism.[72] In fact, this stability has derived from other sources, including the deflation of developmental expectations that resulted from the economic crises of this period, particularly the debt crisis; the collapse of socialist models of development in other parts of the world; and the related erosion or reorientation of the political left. Further, in the countries that experienced bureaucratic authoritarianism (Argentina, Brazil, Chile, and Uruguay), an increased appreciation of democracy that grew out of the experience with authoritarian rule also played a critical role. For scholars concerned with the study of these patterns of stability and instability, these new forces, rather than corporatism, became the salient focus in the search for explanations.

Finally, basic changes have been occurring in public policies vis-à-vis interest group politics. Whereas in the 1960s and early 1970s some of the most important initiatives of national states in Latin America were conspicuously corporative, some of the most interesting subsequent initiatives have been conspicuously noncorporative. One example is found in the second half of the 1980s in Peru. An important consequence of the policies of the post-1968 Velasco government had been to accelerate the erosion of traditional ties between organized labor and the Peruvian APRA Party. Subsequently, when APRA won the presidency in 1985, one of its political options was to employ new corporative initiatives in an attempt to regain influence in the labor movement. Yet President Alan García's efforts at support mobilization took a different direction, focusing, to an important degree, on the informal sector. This may in part have been a political response to the erosion of the formal sector within the economy and hence to the diminished political payoff of creating or renewing corporative links within the formal sector.

Another example is found in Chile, which prior to 1973 had a highly corporative system of industrial relations. The post-1973 military government, after first dealing with the labor movement through severe repression, later pursued policies that combined less extensive repression with a more pluralistic framework for trade unions that abandoned many corporative provisions familiar from earlier Chilean labor law. In 1990, the new civilian government in Chile restored some of these provisions, but a return to the traditional Chilean system of highly corporative labor law seemed unlikely.

More broadly, Hector E. Schamis, in his examination of the experiences with bureaucratic authoritarianism, has observed that whereas the cases in the 1960s (Brazil and Argentina) saw an important use of corporative structuring of labor, those of the 1970s (Chile, Argentina after 1976, and Uruguay) did not.[73] It appears that traditional corporative structures were seen by military rulers as inadequate for containing the far higher levels of popular mobilization in the 1970s, and hence labor policies were based on repression rather than on corporatism. In addition, Schamis argues that corporatism, even exclusionary state corporatism, is incompatible with the new market-oriented economic policies that call for a reduced state role in regulating the economy and social groups. Relatedly, for some proponents of the market-oriented growth strategies, state initiatives that defend the classic notion of the "right of combination" of workers are seen as interfering with the free market. Strong labor movements are viewed as introducing distortions in labor costs, which can adversely affect economic growth;[74] hence, various forms of state protection for unions have been modified and weakened.

Taking these trends all together, it might be argued that Latin America's experience with corporatism in the twentieth century will prove to have been a delimited historical episode.[75] This episode began with major periods of reform, state-building, and expansion of the state's role in the economy, which were launched, with varying timing among countries, during the first five decades of this century. Recent processes of liberalization and marketization are, and are intended to be, a profound break with this earlier statist tradition, and to a significant degree they are also a break with the corporative elements of this tradition.

Yet, just as the emergence of corporatism occurred with divergent timing and at a variegated pace in these countries, so its displacement by alternative patterns of state-group relations will occur in an uneven and variegated manner. Historical shifts of this magnitude rarely take place uniformly across countries, and the politics of the end of the twentieth century revolves in part around how, and how quickly, this shift is occurring. Corporative provisions remain central features of the legal structure and informal practice of group politics in Latin America. For example, despite important changes, in many countries substantial continuity is found in labor law, in the functioning of labor ministries, and in the actions of other state agencies involved in industrial relations. The most striking case of the persistence of corporative relationships is certainly Mexico. In the face of repeated crises and challenges since the late 1960s, and notwithstanding important shifts in the relation between the party and the labor movement, the traditional corporative features of the Mexican system remained, at least until the end of 1994, a fundamental feature of national politics.

Further, Schmitter has argued that although interest groups may in some respects have been eclipsed during critical phases of the transition to democracy, they play a central role in influencing what *kind* of democracy is established. Schmitter conceptualizes democracy as being made up of five "partial regimes," three of which—the "concertation regime," the "pressure regime," and the "representation regime"—are hypothesized to be critically influenced by the character of interest groups and their interaction with one another and with the state. If this hypothesis is correct, a detailed knowledge of the structure of interest intermediation, with its various corporative, noncorporative, or postcorporative features, remains critical to the larger understanding of national political regimes.[76]

Finally, even if specific corporative provisions have been eroded in many contexts, concepts from the literature on corporatism continue to be relevant to the perennial issue of how new social groups and social movements relate to the state. Whether one is concerned with workplace organizations, neighborhood associations, women's groups, or other dimensions of associability, the interaction of these groups with the state remains crucial. The interplay between state initiatives that constitute inducements and those that impose constraints on groups is crucial to this interaction. Likewise, the strategic choices made by the leaders of old and new groups in the face of these inducements and constraints— through which they establish varying degrees and forms of involvement with, or independence from, the state—are still a central feature of group politics.

Apart from these substantive conclusions, a methodological observation may also be made. It is a common lament that conceptual debates in the social sciences are confused and unproductive. In the face of this problem, the systematic application of ideas about hierarchies of concepts, generic predicaments, classical versus radial subtypes, and the contrast between conceptual stretching and theoretical stretching can make a valuable contribution. Given the continuing need to understand the different forms and variants of corporatism found in Latin America, this effort to reduce confusion and build productive insight remains an important task. □

NOTES

I would like to thank Alfred Diamant for initially encouraging me to work on this chapter, and Elizabeth Busbee and, especially, Carol A. Medlin for their research assistance. Insightful comments were provided by other contributors to this volume, by students in the fall 1993 and spring 1994 political science/comparative methodology seminars at Berkeley, and by Ruth Berins Collier, Ernst Haas, Peter Houtzager, Peter Kingstone, Deborah L. Norden, Guillermo O'Donnell, and Mina Silberberg.

1. In the literature on corporatism in Europe, the term neocorporatism has been adopted to avoid the negative connotation that can derive from the identification of corporatism with fascism. This issue also has arisen in the Latin American field, but it has not been a major concern; consequently, "neocorporatism" has not been widely used and is not employed in this chapter. For valuable discussions of the relation of corporatism to fascism as well as the role of the concept of corporatism in the broader literature on comparative politics, see Douglas A. Chalmers, "Corporatism and Comparative Politics," in Howard J. Wiarda, ed., *New Directions in Comparative Politics* (Boulder: Westview Press, 1985); and Philippe Schmitter, "Corporatism," in Joel Krieger, ed., *Oxford Companion to Politics of the World* (New York: Oxford University Press, 1993).

2. For a summary of the scope of interest in the Latin American field and elsewhere, see Howard J. Wiarda, *Corporatism and National Development in Latin America* (Boulder: Westview Press, 1981), pp. xi–xii.

3. Robert J. Alexander, *Labor Relations in Argentina, Brazil, and Chile* (New York: McGraw Hill, 1962), p. 59; and Charles W. Anderson, *Politics and Economic Change in Latin America: The Governing of Restless Nations* (Princeton: D. Van Nostrand, 1967), p. 55.

4. Richard M. Morse, "The Heritage of Latin America," in Louis Hartz, ed., *The Founding of New Societies* (New York: Harcourt, Brace and World, 1964), p. 176.

5. Philippe C. Schmitter, *Interest Conflict and Political Change in Brazil* (Stanford: Stanford University Press, 1971), p. 127.

6. Important statements included those by Julio Cotler, "Bases del corporativismo en el Perú," *Sociedad y Política* 1, no. 2 (October 1972): 312; Howard J. Wiarda, "Toward a Framework for the Study of Political Change in the Iberic-Latin Tradition: The Corporative Model," *World Politics* 25, no. 2 (January 1973): 206–235; Philippe C. Schmitter, "The 'Portugalization' of Brazil?" in Alfred Stepan, ed., *Authoritarian Brazil: Origins, Policies, and Future* (New Haven: Yale University Press, 1973); a special issue of *The Review of Politics* 36, no. 1 (1974), edited by Frederick B. Pike, devoted to "The New Corporatism: Social and Political Structures in the Iberian World"; James M. Malloy, ed., *Authoritarianism and Corporatism in Latin America* (Pittsburgh: University of Pittsburgh Press, 1977); Kenneth Erickson, *The Brazilian Corporative State and Working Class Politics* (Berkeley: University of California Press, 1977); Alfred Stepan, *The State and Society: Peru in Comparative Perspective* (Princeton: Princeton University Press, 1978); Ruth Berins Collier and David Collier, "Inducements Versus Constraints: Disaggregating 'Corporatism,'" *American Political Science Review* 73, no. 4 (December 1979): 967–987; and Howard J. Wiarda, *Corporatism and National Development*. Although Wiarda was centrally concerned with a longer historical and cultural tradition of hierarchical authority relations in Latin America, he also analyzed corporative patterns of interest group politics. For example, see Wiarda, "Corporative Origins of the Iberian and Latin

American Labor Relations Systems," in Wiarda, *Corporatism and National Development*.

7. This pluralist framework was certainly more familiar to Latin Americanists within the U.S. academic community; consequently, the concept of corporatism probably commanded more attention and was seen as a more important innovation within that community. At the same time, Latin American scholars also made important contributions to the debate on corporatism.

8. Philippe C. Schmitter, "Still the Century of Corporatism?" *The Review of Politics* 36, no. 1 (January 1974): 93–94.

9. See, for example, James M. Malloy, "Authoritarianism and Corporatism in Latin America: The Modal Pattern," p. 4; Guillermo O'Donnell, "Corporatism and the Question of the State," p. 49; Robert R. Kaufman, "Corporatism, Clientelism, and Partisan Conflict: A Study of Seven Latin American Countries," p. 111; David Collier and Ruth Berins Collier, "Who Does What, To Whom, and How: Toward a Comparative Analysis of Latin American Corporatism," p. 493; all in Malloy, *Authoritarianism and Corporatism*. See also Stepan, *The State and Society*, p. 46.

10. Adapted from Collier and Collier, "Who Does What, To Whom, and How," p. 493.

11. For Schmitter, see the definition quoted above. Stepan used the expression "in return for" (*The State and Society*, p. 46).

12. Collier and Collier, "Inducements Versus Constraints."

13. On pages 296 and 301–316 in *The State and Society*, Stepan uses the label "generic predicament." On page 43 he refers to "inherent predicament."

14. See Evelyne P. Stevens, "Mexico's PRI: The Institutionalization of Corporatism?" in Malloy, *Authoritarianism and Corporatism*, p. 253.

15. Erickson, *The Brazilian Corporative State*, p. 42. See also Kenneth S. Mericle, "Corporatist Control of the Working Class: Authoritarian Brazil Since 1964," in Malloy, *Authoritarianism and Corporatism*, p. 307. It may be added that overarching confederations did emerge in the early 1960s and also beginning in the late 1970s.

16. David Chaplin, "The Revolutionary Challenge and Peruvian Militarism," in David Chaplin, ed., *Peruvian Nationalism: A Corporative Revolution* (New Brunswick, NJ: Transaction Books, 1976), pp. 19 and 22.

17. Collier and Collier, "Who Does What, to Whom, and How," p. 493.

18. Collier and Collier, "Who Does What, to Whom, and How," pp. 495 and 502.

19. George I. Oclander, "Córdoba, May 1969: Modernization, Grass-Roots Demands, and Political Stability," in Alberto Ciria et al., *New Perspectives on Modern Argentina* (Latin American Studies Working Papers, Center for Latin American Studies, Indiana University, Bloomington, Indiana, 1972).

20. O'Donnell, "Corporatism and the Question of the State," p. 49.

21. Schmitter, *Interest Conflict and Political Change*, 162.

22. O'Donnell, "Corporatism and the Question of the State," pp. 71 and 73.

23. John F. H. Purcell and Susan Kaufman Purcell, "Mexican Business and Public Policy," p. 194, and John J. Bailey, "Pluralist and Corporatist Dimensions of Interest Representation in Colombia," pp. 282–283, both in Malloy, *Authoritarianism and Corporatism*. The comparative literature on business associations is, unfortunately, far more limited than that on labor unions, and a full comparative

documentation of this contrast is lacking. A highly promising collaborative project, "Business Peak Associations and Social Change in Latin America," directed by Francisco Durand, promises to shed new light on these issues.

24. The relevance of corporatism for peasant organizations was discussed in two chapters in the Malloy volume: Kenneth E. Sharpe, "Corporative Strategies in the Dominican Republic: The Politics of Peasant Movements"; and Stevens, "Mexico's PRI," pp. 232–233. At least in Peru, corporatism was relevant to workers not only through its role in relation to organized labor, but also in relation to squatter settlements. See David Collier, *Squatters and Oligarchs: Authoritarian Rule and Policy Change in Peru* (Baltimore: Johns Hopkins University Press, 1976), p. 120, and Henry A. Dietz, "Bureaucratic Demand-Making and Clientelistic Participation in Peru," in Malloy, *Authoritarianism and Corporatism*.

25. Collier and Collier, "Who Does What, to Whom, and How," pp. 494–495. The major exception to this pattern is Uruguay, where the organization of labor unions remained highly pluralistic. For an extended analysis of this case, see Ruth Berins Collier and David Collier, *Shaping the Political Arena: Critical Junctures, the Labor Movement, and Regime Dynamics in Latin America* (Princeton: Princeton University Press, 1991), esp. chaps. 5 and 6.

26. Linn A. Hammergren, "Corporatism in Latin American Politics: A Reexamination of the 'Unique' Tradition," *Comparative Politics* 9, no. 4 (July 1977): 444, 449.

27. Douglas A. Chalmers, "The Politicized State in Latin America," in Malloy, *Authoritarianism and Corporatism*, pp. 28–29; and Alberto Ciria, "Old Wine in New Bottles? Corporatism in Latin America," *Latin American Research Review* 13, no. 3 (1978): 210.

28. James M. Malloy, "Authoritarianism, Corporatism, and Mobilization in Peru," *The Review of Politics* 36, no. 1 (January 1974): 84.

29. Schmitter, *Interest Conflict and Political Change*, pp. 127–128.

30. Fernando Henrique Cardoso, "Associated-Dependent Development: Theoretical and Practical Implications," in Stepan, *Authoritarian Brazil*, p. 142.

31. Schmitter, "The 'Portugalization' of Brazil?" pp. 185–186.

32. For discussions of the different forms such hierarchies can take, see George Lakoff, *Women, Fire, and Dangerous Things: What Categories Reveal About the Mind* (Chicago: University of Chicago Press, 1987), chaps. 1 and 6; and David Collier and James M. Mahon, Jr., "Conceptual 'Stretching' Revisited: Adapting Categories in Comparative Analysis," *American Political Science Review* 87, no. 4 (December 1993): 845–855.

33. Philippe C. Schmitter, "Modes of Interest Intermediation," in Philippe Schmitter and Gerhard Lehmbruch, eds., *Trends Toward Corporatist Intermediation* (Beverly Hills: Sage Publications, 1979), pp. 35–36, note 1.

34. Liliana De Riz, Marcelo Cavarozzi, and Jorge Feldman, *Concertación, estado, y sindicatos en la Argentina contemporánea* (Centro de Estudios de Estado y Sociedad, Estudios CEDES, 1987), p. 7 (translation by the author).

35. Philippe C. Schmitter, "Reflections on Where the Theory of Neo-Corporatism Has Gone and Where the Praxis of Neo-Corporatism May be Going," in Gerhard Lehmbruch and Philippe C. Schmitter, eds., *Patterns of Corporatist Policy-Making* (Beverly Hills: Sage Publications, 1982), pp. 262–263.

36. It merits note that this change has an important implication for the issue of the pejorative identification of corporatism with fascism, raised above in note 1. In these revised definitions, the elements of corporatism most conspicuously identified with the fascist state, that is, overarching mechanisms of mediation, are explicitly excluded.

37. Kaufman, "Corporatism, Clientelism, and Partisan Conflict," p. 113.

38. Jonathan Hartlyn, *The Politics of Coalition Rule in Colombia* (Cambridge: Cambridge University Press, 1988), p. 244; see also p. 3.

39. Schmitter, "Still the Century of Corporatism?" pp. 96–98. The following discussion adopts Schmitter's revised usage in which he refers to systems of interest intermediation rather than interest representation ("Modes of Interest Intermediation," p. 64, note 1, and pp. 65–66).

40. Given this definition, the Mexican system might be characterized as monist. However, in the literature on Mexico and in comparative writing that includes the Mexican case, it is generally referred to as corporatist.

41. Schmitter, "Still the Century of Corporatism?" pp. 102–105.

42. See Gerhard Lehmbruch, "Consociational Democracy, Class Conflict, and the New Corporatism" (paper presented at the International Political Science Association Round Table on Political Integration, Jerusalem, 1974 [subsequently published in Schmitter and Lehmbruch, *Trends Toward Corporatist Intermediation*]), and Gerhard Lehmbruch, "Liberal Corporatism and Party Government," *Comparative Political Studies* 10, no. 1 (April 1977): 91–126.

43. O'Donnell, "Corporatism and the Question of the State," p. 48 and pp. 64–77. O'Donnell actually refers to the "privatist" element of corporatism (p. 74), or to the "privatization" of some institutional arenas of the state (p. 64). For the sake of clarity, the term privatizing is used here.

44. Guillermo O'Donnell, *Modernization and Bureaucratic-Authoritarianism: Studies in South American Politics*, Politics of Modernization Series, no. 9 (Berkeley: University of California, Berkeley, Institute of International Studies, 1973), chap. 2.

45. Stepan, *The State and Society*, chap. 3.

46. Collier and Collier, "Inducements Versus Constraints."

47. See again, Lakoff, *Women, Fire, and Dangerous Things*, chap. 6, and Collier and Mahon, "Conceptual 'Stretching' Revisited," p. 846.

48. See Morris R. Cohen and Ernest Nagel, *An Introduction to Logic and Scientific Method* (New York: Harcourt Brace, 1934), pp. 235–236, and Irving M. Copi and Carl Cohen, *Introduction to Logic*, 9th ed. (New York: Macmillan, 1994), pp. 189–191.

49. David Collier, ed., *The New Authoritarianism in Latin America* (Princeton: Princeton University Press, 1979), p. 4. For a standard baseline in discussions of authoritarianism and its subtypes, see Juan J. Linz, "An Authoritarian Regime: Spain," in Erik Allardt and Yrjö Littunen, eds., *Cleavages, Ideologies, and Party Systems* (Helsinki: Academic Bookstore, 1975).

50. Lakoff, *Women, Fire, and Dangerous Things*, chap. 6; and Collier and Mahon, "Conceptual 'Stretching' Revisited," pp. 848–852. The question of *why* particular concepts generate radial as opposed to classical subtypes remains to be addressed.

51. Guillermo O'Donnell, "Delegative Democracy," *Journal of Democracy* 5, no. 1 (January 1994): 55–69.

52. O'Donnell, "Corporatism and the Question of the State," p. 49.

53. Theodore J. Lowi, *The End of Liberalism: Ideology, Policy, and the Crisis of Public Authority* (New York: Norton, 1969), pp. 68–85.

54. Collier and Collier, "Inducements Versus Constraints," pp. 974 and 979.

55. See Ross M. Martin, "Pluralism and the New Corporatism," *Political Studies* 41 (1983): 86–102 (see esp. pp. 98–102). Martin, like most writers on Europe, uses the term "liberal corporatism" instead of "societal corporatism."

56. Giovanni Sartori, "Concept Misformation in Comparative Politics," *American Political Science Review* 64, no. 4 (December 1970): 1034.

57. See Collier and Mahon, "Conceptual 'Stretching' Revisited," pp. 848–852.

58. Although Morse and Anderson were part of this larger discussion, they did not directly center their analysis around the concept of corporatism. See Ronald C. Newton, "Natural Corporatism and the Passing of Populism in South America," *Review of Politics* 36, no. 1 (January 1974): 34–51; Erickson, *The Brazilian Corporative State*; Simon Schwartzman, "Back to Weber: Corporatism and Patrimonialism in the Seventies," in Malloy, *Authoritarianism and Corporatism*; Stepan, *The State and Society*; Morse, "The Heritage of Latin America"; and Anderson, *Politics and Economic Change*. Louis Hartz's bold analysis in *The Founding of New Societies* (New York: Harcourt, Brace and World, 1964) places these studies of Latin America in a larger comparative perspective.

59. Wiarda, "Toward a Framework for the Study of Political Change," pp. 222–223. See also his "Corporative Origins of the Iberian and Latin American Labor Relations Systems," in Wiarda, *Corporatism and National Development*.

60. Wiarda, "Toward a Framework for the Study of Political Change," pp. 209, 213, and 214.

61. Schmitter, "Still the Century of Corporatism?" p. 90.

62. Schmitter, "Still the Century of Corporatism?" pp. 87 and 89.

63. Guillermo O'Donnell, "Reflections on the Patterns of Change in the Bureaucratic Authoritarian State," *Latin American Research Review* 13, no. 1 (1978): 4.

64. For an innovative effort to evaluate such explanations in another context, see Robert D. Putnam (with Robert Leonardi and Raffaella Y. Nanetti), *Making Democracy Work: Civic Traditions in Modern Italy* (Princeton: Princeton University Press, 1993). On the other hand, see Robert W. Jackman and Ross Miller, "A Renaissance of Political Culture?" (unpublished paper, Department of Political Science, University of California, Davis).

65. Stepan, *The State and Society*, p. 46; see also chap. 1.

66. Brian H. Smith, *The Church and Politics in Chile: Challenges to Modern Catholicism* (Princeton: Princeton University Press, 1982), p. 82, David Rock, *Argentina 1516–1982: From Spanish Colonization to the Falklands War* (Berkeley: University of California Press, 1985), p. 185, and Joel Horowitz, *Argentine Unions, the State and the Rise of Perón, 1930–1945* (Berkeley: Institute of International Studies, 1990), p. 69.

67. Clifford Geertz, *The Interpretation of Cultures* (New York: Basic Books, 1973), p. 3.

68. Howard J. Wiarda, "Concepts and Models in Comparative Politics: Political Development Reconsidered and Its Alternatives," in Dankwart A. Rustow and Kenneth Paul Erickson, eds., *Comparative Political Dynamics: Global Research Perspectives* (New York: Harper Collins, 1991), p. 41.

69. Corporatism remains a major theme in Paul G. Buchanan, "State Corporatism in Argentina: Labor Administration Under Perón and Onganía," *Latin American Research Review* 20, no. 1 (1985): 61–95; Carlos H. Waisman, *Reversal of Development in Argentina* (Princeton: Princeton University Press, 1987); Neil Harvey, "Peasant Strategies and Corporatism in Chiapas," in Joe Foweraker and Ann L. Craig, eds., *Popular Movements and Political Change in Mexico* (Boulder: Lynne Rienner Publishers, 1990); Jeffrey W. Rubin, "Popular Mobilization and the Myth of State Corporatism," in Foweraker and Craig, *Popular Movements*. Sharon Phillips Collazos, *Labor and Politics in Panama: The Torrijos Years* (Boulder: Westview Press, 1991), focuses very centrally on themes raised in the literature on corporatism but without emphasizing the label.

70. See, for example, David Rock, *Argentina 1516–1982*; Ben Ross Schneider, *Politics Within the State: Elite Bureaucrats and Industrial Policy in Authoritarian Brazil* (Pittsburgh: University of Pittsburgh Press, 1991), pp. 245–257; Ann L. Craig, "Institutional Contexts and Popular Strategies," in Foweraker and Craig, *Popular Movements*, pp. 276–277; and the chapters by Ellner, Carr, and Moreira Alves, all in Barry Carr and Steve Ellner, eds., *The Latin American Left: From the Fall of Allende to Perestroika* (Boulder: Westview Press, 1993).

71. Guillermo O'Donnell and Philippe C. Schmitter, *Transitions from Authoritarian Rule: Tentative Conclusions About Uncertain Democracies* (Baltimore: Johns Hopkins University Press, 1986), pp. 57–59; and Philippe C. Schmitter, "Interest Systems and the Consolidation of Democracies," in Gary Marks and Larry Diamond, eds., *Reexamining Democracy: Essays in Honor of Seymour Martin Lipset* (Newbury Park: Sage Publications, 1992), pp. 163–166.

72. Compared to the period prior to the coups and military regimes that extended from the 1960s into the 1980s, the scope of opposition movements and political crises in the postmilitary period in much of South America has been far more limited. Interestingly, the greatest instability—in Peru and Colombia—has occurred outside the domain of labor-business-state relations in the modern formal sector, on which discussions of corporatism have generally focused.

73. Hector E. Schamis, "Reconceptualizing Latin American Authoritarianism in the 1970s: From Bureaucratic-Authoritarianism to Neoconservatism," *Comparative Politics* 23, no. 2 (January 1991): 201–220.

74. Alejandro Foxley, *Latin American Experiments in Neo-Conservative Economics* (Berkeley: University of California Press, 1983), pp. 193–194.

75. These themes are discussed in Collier and Collier, *Shaping the Political Arena*, chap. 8; and Marcelo Cavarozzi, "Beyond Transitions to Democracy in Latin America," *Journal of Latin American Studies* 24, pt. 3 (October 1992): 665–684.

76. Schmitter, "Interest Systems," pp. 166–175.

■

CHAPTER SEVEN

Assessments of State Strength

Evelyne Huber

AFTER FIVE DECADES AT THE CENTER of developmental and distributive efforts, in the 1980s the Latin American state came under severe attack for being the root cause of failures in precisely these areas. Neoliberal antistatism pushed by international financial institutions and core countries became near-hegemonic in the hemisphere and induced governments to launch resolute shrinking of their states. By greatly reducing state intervention in the economy, space would be made for the unhindered play of market forces. Simultaneously, austerity policies imposed in the wake of the debt crisis greatly weakened the functioning of most Latin American states. The early 1990s saw a tremendous concentration of wealth and economic control in private hands and a rapid escalation of poverty and lawlessness. These pitfalls of indiscriminate and rapid shrinking of the state led politicians and technocrats to rediscover the importance of the state. Issues of governability and development of human resources, along with the institutional underpinnings of markets returned to the forefront.

The challenge of consolidating newly (re)established democratic regimes added urgency to these issues. The rule of law is one of the pillars of a democratic order, and increasing crime and corruption directly challenged democratic consolidation in Latin America. Uneven application of the law across territories and social classes and the privatization of power in many areas gave rise to what Guillermo O'Donnell calls "low intensity citizenship."[1] Moreover, democratic political leaders must take into consideration their electorates, which forces a recognition of the importance of the state's welfare function, if only to undermine political competitors. In the present context of extreme scarcity of resources, efficient and politically beneficial use of resources for social expenditures becomes crucial. Accordingly, this moves to the center of political attention the question of state capacity to enforce the rule of law and to allocate resources efficiently. Parallel to these political dynamics, one can identify a surge of interest within the community of Latin Americanist social scientists to understand the determinants of state strength or state capacity.

Though the role of the state has long been recognized as crucial for Latin American development, there is a relative scarcity of theoretical and methodological reflections on the subject. The treatment of the state in the study of Latin American politics mirrors, to some extent, that in the disciplines of political science and sociology as a whole, prior to work by the Social Science Research Council Committee on States and Social Structures.[2] Until then, the dominant approach in the Latin American literature had been Marxist or neo-Marxist, starting with the premise that the state is an instrument of domination or the expression of a pact of domination. Accordingly, the relevant subject has been power and domination in society and the economy, not the structural characteristics of the state and its potentially autonomous impact on policy outcomes.[3]

In mainstream North American political science and sociology, the dominant views were pluralist and structural-functionalist; state policy was seen as the result of competing interest groups or as a response to societal needs. This view ignored the independent impact of the state apparatus.[4] The Marxist approach uncovered systematic power imbalances in the supposedly competitive political market of interest group activity and revealed systematic neglect of some societal needs, but it did not direct attention to the role of the state apparatus.[5] Since the 1980s, though, the work of the Committee on States and Social Structures has refocused the discussion in political science and sociology to make the role and the independent contribution of the state apparatus an integral part of theoretical perspectives on political, social, and economic change. To bring the study of Latin American politics into the mainstream of social science, we need to follow the lead of such authors as Alfred Stepan, Peter Evans, Dietrich Rueschemeyer, Theda Skocpol, and Joel Migdal and refocus our attention on the nature of the state apparatus and on its relationship to society and the economy.[6]

The state plays an important role in the newer literature on structural adjustment.[7] Key points of study are the presence of a team of technocrats insulated from pressures by economic interest groups and protected by the chief executive, the technical/administrative capacities of the state apparatus, the skill of the chief executive in coalition formation and timing of adjustment policies, and regime characteristics.[8] However, there has been little spillover to more general analyses of political dynamics. There is still a relative scarcity of explicit theorizing about the role of the state and of systematic comparative analyses of state characteristics and capacities. In *Capitalist Development and Democracy*, my coauthors and I attempted to include the state as one of three crucial factors explaining the relationship between economic development and political democratization in Latin America and the Caribbean and the advanced industrial nations.[9] In this chapter I propose a conceptualization of state strength that identifies determinants of strength appropriate for comparative analyses of a range of questions regarding political, social, and economic change both within the region and across regions. □

CONCEPTUALIZATIONS OF STATE STRENGTH

Before one develops conceptualizations of state strength, one has to clarify the conceptualization of the state itself. Given the theoretical acceptance of the state's independent impact on socioeconomic dynamics, a Weberian approach is most useful. The Weberian tradition sees the state as a set of institutions that claims control over territories and people based on a monopoly of organized force and that performs administrative, legal, coercive, and extractive functions. Adopting this conceptualization does not preclude the recognition that the state is also an arena for class struggle, or that in some situations it may act as the executive committee of the bourgeoisie, just as in other situations it may enjoy great relative autonomy. These views can all be accommodated within a basically Weberian conception; their accuracy in any given case is an empirical question.

Political analysis often lumps together three different dimensions under the generic label of the "state": a set of institutions, the nature of the regime, and the character of incumbents in the government's chief executive positions. A differentiation of these dimensions is particularly important for an explanation of state strength. The nature of the regime consists of the rules that govern access to power and its exercise and the rights of the ruled vis-à-vis the rulers; the most basic distinction here is that between democratic and authoritarian regimes. The character of incumbents refers to their social base and general policy orientation; a basic distinction rests on the orientation toward distribution of resources in the society, that is, the level of commitment to a redistribution of material and nonmaterial resources in favor of popular classes. Both the nature of the regime and the character of incumbents influence state strength in significant ways by mediating the relationship between the state and different groups in civil society and thus the ability of the state to exercise power over the economy and civil society.

In its most basic sense, state strength is the capacity of the state to preserve itself and the territory and people over which it claims control. This means that a strong state is capable of ensuring security from external attacks and from internal challenges to its monopoly of organized force. Extractive capacity is a fundamental prerequisite for self-preservation, that is, the ability of the state to mobilize resources to counter the application of physical force from internal and external challengers. Extractive capacity is also a prerequisite for the performance of other state functions.

In its widest sense, state strength is the capacity to achieve the goals set by incumbents in chief executive positions. This conceptualization departs in one respect from the pathbreaking work by Evans, Rueschemeyer, and Skocpol.[10] It follows their lead in discarding the search for general qualities of strong states (or global categorizations of strong versus weak states) and by disaggregating the notion of state strength into discrete capacities. Nevertheless, this approach locates goal-setting functions in the hands of elected, appointed, or self-appointed presidents, prime ministers, and cabinets; and when incumbents are elected officials, one assumes that their goals significantly reflect demands and interests of civil society. By contrast, the primary theoretical aim of Evans, Rueschemeyer, and Skocpol was to demonstrate the autonomous nature of the state. Their focus was on autonomy in goal-setting and on autonomy and capacity in implementing those goals:

> States ... may formulate and pursue goals that are not simply reflective of the demands or interests of social groups, classes, or society. This is what is usually meant by "state autonomy." Unless such independent goal formulation occurs, there is little need to talk about states as important actors. Especially in times of crisis that call for state-initiated reforms or repression, the crucial goal-setting actors are organizationally coherent collectivities of state officials, especially collectivities of career officials relatively insulated from ties to currently dominant socioeconomic interests.[11]

This concern with the state's potential goal-setting autonomy was understandable and necessary in the context of current theoretical debate, which was dominated by structural-functionalist, pluralist, and Marxist perspectives that denied that the state had an independent impact on economic and social processes. Since the 1980s, however, there has been wide acceptance of the need to include the state as an actor that shapes socioeconomic conditions. Even where goals set by incumbents largely reflect demands and pressures from powerful economic and social actors, the capacities of the state apparatus shape the degree to which these goals can be met. These capacities, in turn, are shaped by the nature of civil society and by the relationships of the state apparatus to civil society, to the domestic economy, and to the international economy and system of states.

Empirically, the focus on autonomous goal-setting by collectivities of state officials is relevant during major reconstructions of the state apparatus and of the economy and society. Such reconstructions are mainly undertaken by governments coming to power in nonconstitutional ways. This focus was appropriate for Latin American countries such as Cuba, the bureaucratic-authoritarian governments in Argentina, Brazil, Chile, and Uruguay, or the reformist military government in Peru. Today, constitutional forms of rule with elected chief executives and representative institutions are the norm in Latin America, as in advanced industrial nations, and thus the focus on the capacities of states to pursue the goals and policies formulated by chief executives is now important.

The extent and ways in which economic and social actors influence goal-setting remains a significant determinant of state capacity. Democratic systems vary in the degree of autonomy with which executives set goals in response to societal interests. Responding to interests of class factions restricts the ability to achieve more encompassing and fundamental goals; in contrast, responding to collective demands of capital and labor, or balancing demands against each other, enhances the capability to realize collectively rational goals. Notably, however, relative goal-setting autonomy is not necessarily superior to responsiveness to collective interests in enhancing state capacity for the implementation of goals. My discussion of determinants of state strength below substantiates this point. The relative autonomy of incumbents, and whether they are likely to respond to particularistic versus universalistic demands, depends on the structure of civil society and its relationship to the state apparatus.

What are the encompassing, fundamental, collectively rational goals sought by states? Conceptualizing state strength very broadly as the ability to meet goals set by incumbents in executive positions makes systematic assessment and comparison exceedingly difficult, since there is great variation in the patterns of goals set, and some goals are clearly easier to meet than are others. Often executives initiate preemptive scaling down of goals due to the anticipated inadequacy of state strength. Most importantly, one misses the essential difference between the pursuit of short-term particularistic versus long-term universalistic goals. To establish a yardstick for comparison, it is more useful to narrow the focus to an achievement of four basic goals: (1) enforcement of the rule of law throughout the state's entire territory and population (legal order); (2) promotion of economic growth (accumulation); (3) elicitation of voluntary compliance from the population over which the state claims control (legitimation); and (4) shaping of the allocation of societal resources (distribution). Incumbents are presumably committed to the rule of law, to accumulation, and to legitimation, but there is significant variation with regard to the desirable shape of distribution of material and nonmaterial resources in society.[12]

Ability to meet these four goals varies among states, and a capacity in one area does not necessarily translate into capacity in another. For instance, some states attain universal law enforcement but fail to promote accumulation. Nevertheless, the four goals stand in a systematic relationship to each other, insofar as achievement of the first goal greatly facilitates achievement of the second, both of them facilitate achievement of the third, and all three of them make possible the achievement of the fourth. Over the long term, it is arguable that achievement of the first goal is a necessary but not sufficient condition for achievement of the second, and the first two for the third. For successful redistribution, only the first goal is a necessary condition, given that coercion can be used to effect redistribution at least temporarily. However, accumulation is a necessary condition to sustain a viable social order and to protect the effects of redistribution. Combining redistribution with the achievement of the other three goals is very difficult, especially when redistribution is directed toward lower-ranking social groups. Egalitarian redistribution entails an interference in market processes and confrontation with the interests of economically dominant groups, which restricts accumulation and which, in turn, is detrimental for the achievement of legitimacy.

The prototype of a strong state, then, is a developmental state, that is, a state capable of stimulating industrial transformation as a basis for sustained accumulation in a developing economy, which is at the same time capable of shaping distribution in a less-inegalitarian direction.[13] This is an empirically rare case. The states most successful in combining accumulation with distribution have been advanced industrial nations, where the growth imperative is lower than in developing countries. Even strictly developmental states are a rare breed. Their emergence requires the simultaneous presence of particular characteristics of the state apparatus and its environment. It is to the specification of the structural conditions of the state itself, its environment, and its relationships to that environment that I now turn. □

DETERMINANTS OF STATE STRENGTH

The achievement of the four aspects of state strength—legal order, accumulation, legitimation, and distribution—requires the state to enlist cooperation of other actors. Coercion may be an effective strategy for enforcing the legal order and for short- and medium-term redistribution of resources, but neither aspect promotes accumulation or attains legitimacy. Over time, purely coercive regimes lacking cooperation from civil society are susceptible to internal conflicts and disintegration. Consequently, state strength is determined by two sets of factors: (1) the structural characteristics of the state apparatus itself, and (2) the state's relationship to other relevant actors—civil society, foreign controllers of capital (both public and private), and other states. Thus, state strength is relational and contingent and not an inherent and immutable quality.

To avoid circular reasoning or post hoc explanations, one must conceptualize a strong state as exhibiting structural characteristics and certain relations to domestic and foreign actors typical of states that have previously achieved the four basic goals. Based on the theoretical literature and on studies of determinants of state performance in the four areas, one can construct an ideal type of a strong state, which exhibits specific structural characteristics and specific relationships to civil society, foreign controllers of capital, and other states. Strictly speaking, one should construct four ideal types, one for each goal, since determinants of capacity in one area are not necessarily the same as in the others. To assess the strength of a particular state in a given area, and thus to predict its ability to realize that goal, one should know to what extent its structural characteristics and relationship to other actors approximate the ideal type.

Structural Characteristics

To specify the determinants of state strength, one can begin with the structural characteristics of the set of institutions that constitute the state. Both the structural characteristics of the individual institutions and the way in which these institutions interrelate are important. For a model of individual institutions, one can take the Weberian ideal type of a bureaucracy. A strong state needs an administrative apparatus that functions according to the principles of a Weberian bureaucracy, that is, fixed jurisdictional areas, distribution of authority in a stable and hierarchical manner, generally regulated qualifications as conditions of employment, management based on written documents or files, and strict separation of the public from the private sphere.[14] In other words, the key to the efficient functioning of state institutions is the quality of personnel, the clarity of definitions of tasks and domains of authority, and the quality of infrastructure and equipment. Weber further emphasized the career nature of state employment, the distinct social esteem accorded officials, and the principle that holding office not be exploited for the extraction of rents. To draw out some of the most basic implications of this Weberian view, an efficient bureaucracy requires application of merit criteria for appointment and promotion (as opposed to personal or political clientelistic criteria).

If one turns attention to the set of institutions that constitute the state, it is immediately clear that different constituent institutions may have different characteristics and differential strength. This is partly due to the clienteles, that is, groups in civil society with which these institutions interact, and it is partly due to structural characteristics of these institutions. Examples of weak, inefficient institutions are ministries of agriculture: sprawling bureaucracies, with overlapping responsibilities of different agencies, insufficiently controlled field offices, clientelistic entanglements of bureaucrats, lack of accountability for funds spent, rampant corruption, and so forth. In contrast, gems of state agencies also exist, operating efficiently, with relatively few but highly qualified employees, engaging in innovative activities, incorruptible, and commanding the respect of incumbents and civil society alike. Some agencies in charge of dealing with transnational corporations (TNCs) offer an example. Cases in point are the Jamaica Bauxite Institute[15] and the National Bank for Economic and Social Development in Brazil.[16] Typically, newer institutions created for a specific purpose tend to be staffed with highly educated and specialized personnel and to have exclusive authority over their area of responsibility. In contrast, older institutions with broader mandates often have diffuse areas of responsibility, and personnel with fewer special qualifications. These institutions have frequently undergone redefinitions of their areas of responsibility with the result that there may be overlaps with other institutions. The Peruvian and Jamaican Ministries of Agriculture provide examples.[17]

The structural characteristics that make a set of institutions strong as a whole are internal coherence, clear lines of authority, and commitment by bureaucratic elites to pursuing the goals and strategies formulated by incumbents. This commitment can be a result of corporate identification and constitutionality (that is, of the self-perception of leading bureaucrats as the promoters of the goals formulated through constitutional procedures), or it can be a result of a more substantive commitment of leading bureaucrats to the political project of incumbents.[18] Internal coherence presupposes that these different institutions ultimately respond to a single authority, the chief executive. Only then does the strength of constituent units contribute to the strength of the state as a whole. Enforcement of this authority is particularly problematic with regard to state security forces; it is the state's only constituent institution over which the chief executive has only de jure but not de facto sanctioning power based on the application of physical force.

The compliance of the security forces with the chief executive's authority rests primarily on the commanders' internalization of norms of obedience to constitutional authority. This is favored by a long tradition of constitutional rule, and it presupposes professionalization of the police and military. Clearly, the countries where these conditions exist are largely confined to advanced industrial nations. In most developing countries, other factors affect the degree of executive control over the security forces. Corporate identification and internal unity of the forces is of great importance not only for civilian but also for military incumbents.

For instance, under the bureaucratic-authoritarian regimes, control of the secret services was problematic since agencies in charge of surveillance and repression engaged in unauthorized acts.[19] Another example is Guatemala's military regime, in which factions pursued their own interests to gain power and wealth. Where a professional military exists, with acceptance of lines of command, a civilian chief executive's ability to control the security forces largely depends on the state's relationship to civil society and to external factors. Strong opposition to the political project of incumbents from major groups in civil society increases the likelihood of security-force action. Availability of external support may also afford security forces a degree of autonomy from the rest of the state apparatus and thus reduce incentives for compliance with executive directives.

Constitutional structure also shapes the state's capacity to pursue the four goals. Enforcing the legal order in a uniform way, promoting accumulation, and shaping distribution are facilitated by a centralization of power. In contrast, federalism facilitates differential enforcement of the law. It reduces executive control over the state apparatus. Threats can arise from local security forces that are not controlled from the national level. Moreover, power distributions at the level of the constituent units of the federal state may favor those opposing major legislation emanating from the central state and thus block implementation. On one hand, enforcement of civil rights for blacks in the U.S. South offers a case in point, as does the enforcement of legislation for rural labor in the Brazilian states of the interior and the Northeast. On the other hand, federalism enhances the capacity of the state to attain legitimacy, particularly in multiethnic societies, which is precisely why state builders choose this constitutional option. With regard to accumulation and distribution, federalism provides for multiple points of access for veto groups, which may undermine coherence of legislation. Not only do the constituent units have direct authority over some areas of legislation, such as taxation and incentives for corporations, but federal states exhibit strong bicameralism, making passage of coherent legislation more difficult.[20]

In a fashion parallel to federalism, presidentialism disperses power and thus can provide more points of access for opponents of legislation than does parliamentarism. This statement appears to contradict recent discussions about the relative merits of presidentialism and parliamentarism for the consolidation of democracy, in which power concentration in the presidency is a major point of concern.[21] However, the intervening variable here is the nature of political parties. Parliamentary systems favor party discipline, and where political parties are disciplined and programmatic, a prime minister in a parliamentary system is in a stronger position to pass coherent legislation than is a president in a system without such parties (e.g., compare Britain to the United States). If there are no disciplined parties capable of forming a parliamentary majority, however, a president is arguably in a stronger position to implement a coherent legislative program (e.g., compare Italy to the United States).

The size of the state apparatus itself is not necessarily a positive determinant of strength. The bloated, inefficient, rent-seeking state apparatuses celebrated in the neoliberal and rational choice literatures do exist. Yet, in order for a state to intervene effectively in the economy and society, it needs state agencies and enterprises with technical, informational, and managerial resources. If a state lacks these instruments, its capacities to promote accumulation and effect distribution are greatly limited.[22]

The effective strength of a state varies according to the strength of other actors. Actors in civil society and on the international system of states can influence the ability to enforce the legal order, promote accumulation, legitimate itself, and shape the distribution of resources. In turn, state actions have an impact on civil society, the economy, and the international system of states by favoring certain groups over others, selecting certain patterns of economic activity, and constructing international alliances. This feeds back into the state's ability to pursue the four basic goals. Thus state strength is shaped in interaction with civil society, the economy, and the international system of states.[23]

State Strength and Civil Society

Authors have conceptualized civil society in a variety of ways. The meaning given to the term here is inspired by Gramsci: Civil society is the totality of social institutions and associations, both formal and informal, that are not strictly production-related nor governmental or familial in character.[24] Political parties in democracies are part of civil society; they provide the political articulation of the interests of other social institutions and associations. In authoritarian systems, in contrast, political parties identified with the regime have to be conceptualized as part of the state (e.g., the Partido Revolucionario Institucional [PRI] in Mexico or the Partido Comunista de Cuba [PCC] in Cuba), whereas opposition parties are part of civil society.

A dense civil society is one that is rich in such institutions and associations. What is crucial for the balance of power between dominant and subordinate classes within civil society is the extent and degree of autonomy in the organization of subordinate classes. Dominant classes are less dependent on organization as a source of power, since they can exercise power through control over capital, land, and information. Moreover, they can often coordinate their actions without recourse to formal organization. For subordinate classes, organization is their only source of power. Where they have few organizations, civil society remains weak; where the state or dominant classes sponsors such organizations, civil society becomes a conduit for the dominant ideology and is subject to manipulation by incumbents. In contrast, where autonomous organizations include large sectors of the subordinate classes, they can become the carriers of a counterhegemony and they can acquire significant mobilization skills, which endows them with power to support or oppose state policies. Crucial among organizations of subordinate classes are unions and allied political parties.

Civil society shapes state power by enhancing or constraining the state's capacity to enforce the rule of law, promote accumulation, affect distribution, and attain legitimacy. A minimal requirement for effective state action, in addition to the structural characteristics outlined above, is a degree of state autonomy from the economically dominant classes. Theoretically, when the state operates as the "executive committee of the bourgeoisie," that boosts the capacity for accumulation. However, such situations are extremely rare; if the economically dominant classes are not threatened by demands from subordinate classes, they rarely attain a great degree of unity; if they are threatened from below and close ranks, then these same pressures also affect the state and make it difficult for incumbents to act as sole representatives of the economically dominant classes. When factions of these classes capture parts of the state apparatus, their private interests are likely to prevail and interfere with more coherent societal strategies. Divisions in the dominant classes and pressures from subordinate classes facilitate the relative autonomy of the state.

Relative autonomy, however, is not to be equated with aloofness of the state apparatus from civil society or the absence of channels of access. In order to be successful in accumulation, distribution, and legitimation, the state apparatus has to be connected to civil society. It has to be in a position of "embedded autonomy," or, where its autonomy is low, it has to be embedded in "tripartism." It needs institutional channels to generate support for accumulation strategies from capitalists and labor (where labor is organized) and for distributive policies from the intended beneficiaries. "Embedded autonomy" refers to a combination of internal bureaucratic coherence with dense institutionalized interactions between the state and leading private sector executives. "Tripartism" refers to institutionalized interaction in policymaking between the state and peak associations of capital and labor. Preconditions for the emergence of tripartism are the presence of encompassing, centralized unions and business associations that can represent labor and capital as a whole and the presence of strong political parties associated with the unions.[25] It is critical to emphasize the need for encompassing and centralized organizations, because only such organizations are capable of supporting universalistic policies.[26] Strong but fragmented organizations of labor and capital result in pressures on the state for particularistic, clientelistic policies that in the long run are detrimental to the promotion of accumulation and societywide redistribution. Successful examples of embedded autonomy are provided by the linkages of state agencies to leading business executives in South Korea and Japan, or by the policy networks that link the public and the private sector in Switzerland.[27] Successful examples of tripartism are the state-party-union-employer linkages in Sweden and Austria.[28]

The influence of civil society on state power is mediated by the nature of both the regime and the incumbents. The weight of civil society, or its relative power vis-à-vis the state, is enhanced under democratic rules of the political game. First of all, civil society itself grows stronger under democracy, because the right of organization is protected. Conversely, the existence of a dense civil society with autonomous organizations of subordinate classes increases the chances that democracy will be installed and consolidated. Second, if elections are an important political currency, public opinion becomes a battlefield where incumbents compete with opponents. This competition constrains incumbents who wish to pursue policies of accumulation or distribution that run counter to the interests of powerful groups in civil society. Under democratic as well as authoritarian regimes, the ability to meet the four goals is strengthened by the extent to which policies conform to the perceived interests of powerful groups, and, conversely, capacity is reduced when policies run counter to those interests. This is particularly true for democratic regimes. Before developing the discussion of the interaction between civil society, nature of incumbents, and state capacity further, one needs to look at the ways in which the state can influence civil society.

Just as civil society can reduce or enhance state capacity, the state can significantly shape civil society. It can do so in an instrumental or deliberate way or in an indirect way, insofar as specific state characteristics and policies provide incentives for groups in civil society to organize.[29] In terms of deliberate actions, the state can simply tolerate autonomous organization of subordinate groups; it can actively support such organization; it can sponsor, incorporate, and control organization of subordinate classes; or it can repress organizing attempts and already existing organizations of subordinate classes. Simply tolerating the self-organization of subordinate classes does not imply an entirely passive attitude by the state. Rather, it requires the universalistic enforcement of civil rights. Labor rights especially need to be protected against employer attempts to prevent the formation of unions.

Such state action was seen in the policy of the British colonial state following a wave of labor unrest that swept the Caribbean in the 1930s. The British allowed unions and political parties to organize, and these nationalist movements formed and began to press for internal democratization and independence. By the time of independence in the 1960s, civil society was comparatively strong and the subordinate classes had acquired a degree of organizational strength and autonomy that constituted a counterweight to the dominant classes. The Caribbean states thus had a better ability to shape the allocation of resources in a less-inegalitarian direction and to legitimate themselves.

This situation contrasts sharply with the actions and effects of Central American states in the same period, particularly in El Salvador, Guatemala, and Nicaragua.[30] These Caribbean and Central American societies had similar plantation economies and structures of social domination, but the role of the state differed sharply. The state in Central America was controlled by the economically dominant classes in collaboration with the military. The British Caribbean was controlled by the British state, which by the 1930s pursued more tolerant policies toward subordinate classes than the local economically dominant classes would have wanted. Thus Central American labor unrest of the 1930s met an intensification of state repression of popular organizations and the political left. The middle-class reformist parties that were formed in the post–World War II period met with a similar fate. Accordingly, civil society remained comparatively weak, and challenges to the dominant classes and the state assumed a revolutionary character. This constellation negatively affected state power in these Central American societies in the 1970s and 1980s.

The state also can promote popular organization, either to support the formation of strong popular movements that are autonomous from the state apparatus or to create movements dependent on the state apparatus and thus susceptible to control. The former is typical of state action under left-wing, social democratic or democratic socialist incumbents who attempt to foster strong popular movements linked to socialist parties, such as Salvador Allende in Chile and Michael Manley in Jamaica. In the developed world, examples of social democratic incumbents passing legislation that, for instance, facilitated labor organization are to be found in virtually every country in which such parties came to power.[31] The creation of popular movements dependent on the state apparatus is typical of state action under populist incumbents who attempt to create a personalistic power base, such as Juan Perón in Argentina, or who are concerned with preempting the emergence of any type of class struggle, such as Getúlio Vargas in Brazil or Juan José Velasco in Peru. Their political projects and the resulting systems of interest representation have been conceptualized in the literature as state corporatist.[32]

Dependence on the state apparatus consists of reliance on the state for organizational resources and incentives for members, which can include, for example, membership dues channeled through the state apparatus or access to state-financed health care and pensions tied to union membership. Dependence on the state apparatus is to be distinguished analytically from representation and participation in decisionmaking bodies in state agencies, which occurs frequently as well in the presence of strong and autonomous lower-class organizations in advanced industrial nations characterized by societal corporatism.

One can conceptualize four basic forms of civil society. First, civil society may be weak, or not dense; there are relatively few social institutions and associations, and they encompass only limited sectors of the population, such as in Central America in the 1950s or in Chile under Augusto Pinochet. These examples illustrate the two different origins of such a civil society. One is a low level of economic development, particularly low urbanization and industrialization, which reduces everyday opportunities for the formation of associations. The other one is a high degree of repression, which destroys existing institutions and associations. In the latter case, the economically dominant class, the bourgeoisie, may be quite influential, despite a low degree of formal organization. The second form is one in which civil society as a whole is relatively dense, but the majority of organizations of subordinate classes lack coherence and autonomy from dominant classes (e.g., early Imperial Germany, before the lapse of the anti-Socialist laws). In the third form, civil society is again relatively dense, but the majority of organizations of subordinate classes are dependent on the state for resources and subject to manipulation by incumbents (e.g., Argentina under Perón). In the fourth type, civil society is dense and organizations of subordinate classes are coherent and autonomous from both dominant classes and the state (e.g., Sweden, Norway, and Denmark).

Empirically, few cases can be put unambiguously into one of these four categories; most civil societies have intermediate levels of density and organizations of subordinate classes, with varying degrees of autonomy and coherence. Nevertheless, these forms are heuristically useful in an analysis of the ways in which civil society shapes state strength.

These types of civil society have different impacts on the capacity of the state to meet its goals, depending on the regime form and the political project of the incumbents, primarily their orientation toward redistribution. As noted above, the influence of civil society is stronger under democratic than authoritarian regimes. Authoritarian regimes generally are capable of repressing resistance from civil society, particularly if the internal consensus of incumbents to use repression is strong. However, authoritarian regimes also need cooperation from the economically dominant classes for accumulation, and, in the longer run, they cannot escape the problem of legitimacy. The need for cooperation means that the policymaking process has to be opened up to some extent to allow for consultation with members of these classes. Lack of legitimacy among major organized groups creates or aggravates internal tensions among the incumbents and adds another constraint on state action. Thus one could argue that the difference in the impact of civil society on state capacity under authoritarian and democratic regimes is one of degree rather than of a qualitative nature.[33]

The influence exercised by civil society can be direct and indirect. Cooperation of organizations in civil society with state agencies directly increases the state's ability to meet its goals; resistance of these organizations to state directives diminishes this ability. Cooperation or resistance of social groups can also modify the relationship of incumbents in executive positions to the rest of the personnel in the state apparatus and can thus indirectly modify their success in policy implementation. Cooperation from civil society is likely to increase commitment of the personnel to the goals set by incumbents, whereas active resistance may create opposition, or at least foot-dragging, by those charged with the execution of state policies. A dramatic example of this indirect effect of civil society on state capacity is the situation in Jamaica before the 1980 elections. The People's National Party government under Michael Manley had lost much of its popular support due to three years of economic hardship under successive International Monetary Fund (IMF) programs. The polls indicated quite clearly that the party was going to lose the elections that had been announced several months in advance. Producer organizations and the opposition Jamaica Labour Party had relentlessly opposed any policy initiatives taken by the government for more than two years. In this situation, the state bureaucracy noticeably lost interest in pursuing the government's policies in many areas, and the security forces turned against the government. As a result, the government appeared inept and out of control; most obviously, it lost ability to enforce the rule of law (some five hundred people were killed in political violence) and to maintain legitimacy.

A weak civil society appears, on the face of it, to have a positive impact on state capacity, because it affords high state autonomy. However, it cannot offer any significant support for state actions either. This is most clearly the case for legitimation. There is little or no active questioning of the state, but insofar as legitimacy denotes the quality of being accepted as right and proper, it presupposes the dissemination of values and norms through social institutions. Therefore, where social institutions are weak, large sectors of the population are not socialized into these norms and values. For these sectors, the state lacks legitimacy but the sectors do not have sufficient power to challenge it actively. This was the case, for instance, in the British Caribbean before the growth of the labor and nationalist movements beginning in the 1940s.[34]

One can argue that a weak civil society enhances the state's capacity to promote accumulation. There is little resistance to maximum allocation of resources for growth purposes and reduction of consumption of the population at large. Two examples are South Korea and Central America in the 1950s and 1960s. The two regions experienced comparatively high growth rates in this period, encouraged by state policies and unencumbered by consumption pressures from popular forces. Over time, however, they had very different degrees of success in promoting accumulation. The difference can be explained by structural characteristics of the state apparatus and its relationship to the international system.

The state in South Korea revived the traditional pattern of selecting only the most qualified personnel, which brought them significant prestige and encouraged coherence, commitment, and relative autonomy from the economically dominant class.[35] In Central American countries, in contrast, state bureaucrats were recruited on the basis of political or personal connections, which encouraged clientelism, fragmentation, and commitment to the promotion of particularistic interests rather than a coherent overall plan of accumulation. The state's relative autonomy from the economically dominant class in South Korea was greatly improved by its position in the international system, as recipient of enormous amounts of resources in the form of U.S. aid.[36] These resources put the state in a position virtually to create the private sector and to build permanent channels of interaction, which sustained its ability to influence the private sector to engage in activities conducive to national accumulation. The South Korean state developed a high degree of embedded autonomy and became a very effective developmental state.[37] In Central American countries, in contrast, the state remained dependent on resources generated by the private sector and was unable to direct private sector activity to any significant extent.

As noted earlier, a weak civil society means above all that subordinate classes lack an organizational power base. Thus the leverage of the economically dominant classes is strengthened by default. This implies that the state's ability to redistribute resources upward is amplified, but its ability to redistribute resources downward is restricted. Rarely do political leaders committed to downward redistribution come to power in countries with weak civil societies, simply because such leaders lack a strong social base. The most likely path to this outcome is a revolutionary one (as in Nicaragua in 1979), but an upheaval followed by elections can also lead there (as in Guatemala from 1944 to 1954). Political leaders in these situations tend to place high priority on strengthening civil society by encouraging the formation of popular organizations. Such popular organizations temporarily improved the state's redistributive capacities in Guatemala and Nicaragua, but in both countries the state's relationship to the international system was decisive in putting an end to redistribution.

The constellation with a dense civil society but weak autonomy in popular organizations is rare. Where subordinate classes lack autonomy, it is mostly autonomy from the state apparatus. In the absence of state sponsorship and incorporation, working-class organizations particularly have been developed by left-wing, laborite, socialist, or Communist forces, clearly opposed to dominant-class interests. The only way in which a dense civil society under the hegemony of the dominant classes could develop was in the context of an economically relatively advanced society, with high levels of urbanization and education but with repression or de facto restriction of the labor movement, such that the labor movement was deprived of significant influence in civil society.

This was the case in early Imperial Germany, when enforcement of anti-Socialist laws kept the labor movement and the Socialist party from developing strength. Even after the lapse of these laws, middle-class organizations remained under the hegemony of the economically dominant classes.[38] Thus civil society enhanced state capacity in all areas. Dissemination of norms of law and order facilitated enforcement of the legal order, such associations as the Naval League and the Agrarian League generated support for industrialization and legitimacy for the Empire, and selective redistribution downward could be used by the state for co-optative purposes.[39]

The constellation of dense civil societies with organizations of subordinate classes sponsored by the state is empirically more frequent than the previous one, but it is, for the most part, an unstable constellation. State controls are subject to erosion under competitive politics and a declining resource base because they depend heavily on a combination of representational monopoly and material incentives. The country with the most enduring history of stability is Mexico; other, more temporary cases of this constellation are that of Argentina under Perón, Brazil under Vargas's *estado nôvo*, and Grenada under Eric Gairy. As the failed attempt by Velasco in Peru to construct such a system underlines, the building of this kind of arrangement is only possible under special circumstances, particularly in the very early phases of labor mobilization or in a postrevolutionary situation. Where the state does manage to sponsor and control organizations of subordinate classes, state capacity is theoretically enhanced in all areas, since the state can enlist mass compliance with the legal order and mass support for its accumulation and distribution policies. During the construction phase, though, redistributive policies must be directed downward, because material incentives are critical to successful incorporation strategies. Once incorporation is accomplished, the system may encourage the state's capacity to pursue distributive policies that amplify income concentration.

In practice, however, accumulation tends to be the Achilles' heel of these systems, and failure in the task of accumulation eventually hurts legitimacy. This is particularly true for the many cases where changing political dynamics, such as a transition to competitive politics, eroded the state's control mechanisms and enabled popular organizations to acquire a considerable degree of autonomy from the state. Typically, the creation phase entailed significant popular mobilization and material concessions, which provoked noncooperation among the economically dominant classes and growing consumption pressures from subordinate classes. In some cases, most notably in Argentina, mass consumption pressures remained an enduring legacy and greatly constrained state capacity in accumulation and distribution, until extreme repression critically weakened popular organizations. In other cases, such as in Mexico, creation was followed by a long period in which control mechanisms could be used to restrict popular consumption and promote accumulation and concentration of wealth and income. By the late 1960s, however, even Mexico experienced considerable difficulties with accumulation and legitimation. In sum, then, this constellation does bolster state strength, but it is generally a short-lived constellation, and in the long run it may have the opposite effect and weaken state capacity.

In the final of the four constellations of civil society, a dense civil society with subordinate organizations that possess high autonomy from both dominant classes and the state apparatus, state capacity is increased in all four areas if centralization of labor organizations and tripartism are present and if the orientation of incumbents is compatible with the perceived interests of subordinate classes. In contrast, if centralization and tripartism are absent, and particularly if the political project of the incumbents runs visibly counter to the interests of subordinate classes, state capacity in all areas can be hampered. Prime examples of the former constellation are that of the smaller European countries, particularly the Scandinavian countries and Austria. Many of the larger West European countries also have comparatively strong and autonomous civil societies, but they lack centralization and tripartism. In the Latin American/Caribbean context, Venezuela, pre-1973 Chile, Jamaica, and Trinidad and Tobago come closest to the latter constellation. Both types of constellations are, for the most part, the result of long periods of stable constitutional rule, which means that the norms and values disseminated through civil society include respect for the law, and this improves the state's ability to protect the legal order.[40] However, if incumbents attempt to change legislation specifically affecting interests of subordinate-class organizations, their capacity to pass and enforce such legislation may be limited by mobilization of mass opposition. Telling examples are the strike wave to block the attempt of the Conservative British government to curb the rights of unions in the early 1970s, or the mass protests against austerity policies in Venezuela and Jamaica.

A similar argument, with a different twist, can be made with regard to legitimation. A strong and autonomous civil society can erode the legitimacy of incumbents who pursue a political project that affects subordinate-class interests negatively. However, such situations do not necessarily lead to crises of state legitimacy, because in these societies constitutional norms tend to have become internalized by dominant and subordinate classes alike, and constitutional procedures hold the promise of replacement of illegitimate incumbents. Examples are the unpopular Edward Seaga government in Jamaica in the 1989 elections, or the impeachment of Carlos Andrés Pérez in Venezuela in 1993. However, where external constraints limit the latitude of incumbents to deviate from policies that negatively affect popular groups, the legitimacy deficit may extend to regime form and to the state itself. Signs of this are visible in Venezuela, Jamaica, and Trinidad and Tobago, in the wake of the prolonged austerity policies imposed by the debt crisis.

A dense and autonomous civil society can similarly enhance or restrict the state's capacity to promote accumulation, depending on the presence of tripartism and the perceived distributional consequences of the accumulation project. The European countries with the strongest and most centralized labor movements are characterized by corporatist patterns of interest representation, that is, patterns in which peak organizations of labor and employers, together with the state, are engaged in tripartite negotiations over labor relations and economic and social policies, and they also have frequent incumbency of left parties. Incumbents in these societies were able to impose some degree of wage restraint in the entire postwar period and thus to produce better growth rates than other Organization for Economic Cooperation and Development (OECD) countries in the 1970s, while maintaining stronger welfare states and less inegalitarian distributions of resources.[41] In the 1980s, other factors intervened, particularly the increasing internationalization of capital. These factors eroded the advantage of these societies based on their domestic policymaking patterns.[42] In Britain, in contrast, where civil society is also dense but corporatist institutions are lacking, the role of unions has primarily been a negative, defensive one, blocking policy initiatives for accumulation that would have required sacrifices from the working class. Argentina from the mid-1950s to the mid-1970s is the prime Latin American example of a dense civil society without tripartism and with a predominantly confrontational and defensive union role.

The discussion of state capacity to promote accumulation has already extended to the issue of distribution. Strong civil societies with autonomous popular organizations encourage a more egalitarian distribution of resources. Strong labor movements significantly raise the probability of incumbency of parties committed to a reduction of inequality. Incumbency of social democratic/democratic socialist parties leads to redistributive welfare state policies and less inequality in income distribution.[43] In the face of conservative incumbents, strong labor and popular movements act as a constraining force. For instance, despite the significant appeal of conservative supply-side economics for the Conservative-led Swedish government that came to power in 1991, this government managed to implement only very mild tax reforms and spending cuts, compared, for instance, to the tax reforms and spending cuts implemented in the United States under Ronald Reagan.

Civil societies, of course, change over time, and thereby modify their relationship to the state. Though there is no one-to-one relationship, economic development strengthens civil society. Urbanization and industrialization increase the frequency of human interactions and provide opportunities and incentives for the creation of formal organizations. Consequently, states that are successful in promoting accumulation may undermine their own capacities to continue to do so and to pursue distributive policies that concentrate income and wealth. An example is the South Korean state. First, its successful industrialization policies greatly strengthened the private sector and reduced the relative autonomy of the state bureaucracy from the economically dominant class in implementing economic policies. Then, the growth of heavy industries favored unionization and reduced state autonomy from subordinate classes. Urbanization and the spread of education had also strengthened middle-class organizations. Despite a very repressive response from the state, civil society continued to assert itself and eventually wrested concessions from the incumbents for a change in regime form. Whereas the transition to democracy by no means signifies the demise of state strength, it does necessitate a redefinition of the relationship between state and civil society and greater concern of incumbents with the distributional consequences of their accumulation policies.

The State and the International System

The aspect that privileges the state over civil society in many respects is the state's position as interlocutor between the domestic economy and population on the one hand and the world economy and other states on the other hand. Recognition by other states and participation with other states in international bodies provides legitimacy to the state and the incumbents in executive positions. External aid is typically received and allocated domestically by the state, which bolsters the state's accumulation and distribution capacities. Where such aid is substantial, as it was in South Korea in the 1950s and 1960s, the state can be put in an extremely strong position to foster accumulation and shape distribution. Finally, most states can count on some international support in their efforts to protect the legal order, at least as far as the sharing of intelligence about violators is concerned. In these ways, then, the state is strengthened by its relationships to the international system of states.

In many other ways, however, the international system can weaken individual states. An extreme case is that of military aggression from other states, which can threaten the very survival of a state. Short of outright physical destruction, military pressure can divert so many resources to self-preservation that it critically weakens the state's capacities for accumulation, distribution, and legitimation. External economic pressures further aggravate these problems. A recent example is that of Nicaragua. The prerevolutionary situations in France, Russia, and China provide examples of countries where military and economic competition with more advanced states ultimately led to a breakdown of capacity in all areas.[44] External influences can also fragment a state apparatus. Where support is channeled primarily to the security forces, these forces can acquire considerable autonomy and act independently of constitutional authority. A case in point is the effect of U.S. military aid on the security forces in El Salvador.

The international economy can also strengthen or weaken individual states. In a paradoxical relationship, penetration by foreign capital provides an impetus for state expansion and for the buildup of new state capacities, but, at the same time, it reduces the areas of potential economic control by the state and thus the state's overall promotion of accumulation.[45] An example mentioned before is the Jamaica Bauxite Institute; it was created by the Manley government in response to the total ownership of the Jamaican bauxite industry by a handful of foreign companies. The institute was put in charge of managing all aspects of the government's bauxite policy and became a highly capable actor, bypassing or replacing the foreign companies in the search for markets. Nevertheless, the Jamaican economy's heavy reliance on foreign investment in bauxite and tourism restricted the state's accumulation capacity. When new investment in, and revenues from, these sectors declined, Jamaica was faced with a severe structural balance-of-payments deficit, which ultimately led to a balance-of-payments crisis and subjection to IMF policy prescriptions.[46]

Private and public actors—transnational corporations, banks, and international financial institutions—can provide essential support to states for accumulation if their goals and strategies coincide with those of incumbents. A prime example is the "triple alliance" in Brazil under the post-1964 bureaucratic-authoritarian regime.[47] These actors can also withhold resources from states whose incumbents pursue policies that run counter to the interests of international controllers of capital. Generally, the key disagreement between incumbents and international controllers of capital concerns the issue of distribution, which is intimately linked to popular consumption.

In addition to withholding new resources, corporations can withdraw resources from these economies and thus contribute to actual deaccumulation. Such actions have a direct impact on state strength by depriving incumbents of resources to deal with the problems of accumulation and distribution, and they have an indirect impact by strengthening popular opposition to policies affecting downward redistribution. Jamaica in the late 1970s provides a clear example of the direct and indirect weakening of the state's accumulation and distribution capacities and the legitimacy of incumbents by pressures from public and private international economic actors. In contrast, in the early 1980s, international financial institutions bolstered Jamaica's accumulation capacity and legitimacy by providing more resources on more lenient terms in response to the ideologically more congruent project of current leaders.[48]

Implications

To draw out the implications of the preceding discussion of determinants of state strength, it is clear that state strength is not only a relational, contingent quality, but that, in addition to structural characteristics of the state apparatus itself, a complex set of relations has to be considered in an attempt to assess the capacity of a particular state to perform effectively in the four basic tasks. First, the state's relationship to civil society has to be considered, both with regard to the state's relative autonomy from members of the economically dominant classes and with regard to the balance of power in civil society and the resulting potential support for, or opposition to, state initiatives for accumulation and distribution. Second, the location of the state in the international economy and its relationship to international controllers of capital and to other states has an impact on its capacities.

This also implies that a global assessment such as "the Brazilian state is stronger than the Peruvian state" is problematic. At least two kinds of specification should be made; one referring to a particular time period (with a particular regime, set of incumbents, constellation in civil society, and international economic and political context) and the other one referring to a particular capacity or capacities. For instance, it is reasonable to say that the Brazilian state under the bureaucratic-authoritarian regime from 1964 to roughly 1980 was strong with regard to enforcement of the legal order, accumulation, and (upward) distribution, but not legitimation, beyond a small bourgeois sector. One could also safely assert that the South Korean state under the military regimes in the 1960s and 1970s was even stronger than the Brazilian one with regard to law and order and accumulation.

Comparing the strength of these two states in these periods with regard to distribution is complicated by the fact that they started from very different initial distributions and thus faced very different tasks. In Brazil, labor militancy and popular consumption demands were perceived as a major problem. Accordingly, policies were pursued to reduce the consumption by the working and lower classes. This increased income-distribution inequality. In South Korea, in contrast, the labor movement was weak, and the main task was to keep wages from rising. Thus there was no need to redistribute income.

This comparison confirms that the conceptualization developed here avoids *ex post* explanations. If one were to infer state strength simply from results—in this case from the change in income distribution—one would conclude that the Brazilian state in this period had a greater capacity to redistribute income than did the South Korean state. However, if one takes civil society as one determinant of state strength, in addition to structural characteristics of the state apparatus, it then appears that South Korea had a greater capacity for shaping income distribution. This assessment squares with differences in state capacity in the other three areas.

The final implication is that state strength, by virtue of being a relational and contingent quality, is also conjunctural. Several conditions must occur together to strengthen state capacities. To use the South Korean example again, accumulation in the 1960s and 1970s was so successful because the state had the necessary structural characteristics. It had a weak civil society, a strategic location in the international system (it received massive amounts of U.S. aid), and it manufactured exports in a period of world economic expansion.[49] In the Philippines, where similar attempts were made at a similar time, at least two of these conditions were absent: The structural characteristics and the U.S. economic aid. Consequently, the Philippine state failed to promote accumulation.[50] □

MEASUREMENT OF STATE STRENGTH

If one accepts this conceptualization of state strength and the arguments about their determinants, then the most reasonable methodology to measure state strength is qualitative comparative analysis. The linear and additive assumptions of quantitative analysis, and its inability to deal with conjunctural causation, make it an inappropriate approach to the problem.[51] Qualitative comparative analysis cannot be a pretext for imprecision; rather, it can be approached with the same rigor as quantitative analysis by identifying constellations of determinants that result in state capacity to enforce the legal order, promote accumulation, shape the distribution of resources, and attain legitimacy.

For aspects of individual determinants, one can construct quantitative measures. The key, though, is to have a clear concept and straightforward operationalization. Much of the quantitative literature that seeks to measure effects of state structures on policy outcomes suffers from weaknesses in conceptualization and operationalization. Attempts to measure state effects on welfare state expenditure have tended to show weak and inconsistent results, for instance, in part because the measurements were only tenuously connected to the actual hypotheses and concepts.

One of the hypotheses in the welfare state literature is that bureaucratic capacity and state centralization affect welfare state expansion. However, in practice, only state centralization has been measured, and studies with pooled data using a single or a series of single indicators of centralization yielded few significant results.[52] An alternative approach has been to factor analyze a variety of indicators of state centralization.[53] However, the validity of the resulting measures is weak, because they include plausible indicators of centralization, such as revenue centralization and absence of federalism, along with more questionable measures such as government employee share of total employment. To begin with state structure, one needs to specify clearly the structural characteristics that are expected to have a given impact. For instance, to use the welfare state literature for illustrating how certain structural characteristics affect the state's distributive capacity, one can hypothesize that constitutional structures that facilitate the taking and implementation of majority decisions favor the establishment of broad, coherent, and generous welfare state programs and constitutional structures that disperse political power and provide multiple points of access for interest groups hinder it. One can then construct an index made up of five such structural characteristics: federalism, presidentialism, strong bicameralism, single-member district electoral systems, and provisions for referenda. This index allows one to classify countries into categories for systematic comparison, such as high, medium, and low dispersion of political power.[54] These characteristics, though, should be put into context. They have a stronger impact in the presence of incumbency of political parties committed to welfare-state expansion.

In a similar fashion, one can certainly construct measures for the quality and coherence of the state apparatus. For instance, reasonable indicators of this are the proportion of jobs in the state bureaucracy that are filled by political appointments; the proportion of jobs with formally specified qualifications or access through competitive examinations; remuneration levels in the public compared to the private sector; or prestige rankings (in surveys) of bureaucratic jobs compared to other professional jobs. Yet, just these few examples already highlight a serious problem: Most of these data are not routinely collected in a comparable manner across countries. Moreover, rules for recruitment to bureaucratic jobs may be customary rather than formally specified. For instance, in France a very large proportion of top public officials are graduates of one of two schools with very competitive entrance examinations, though having graduated from these schools is not a formal requirement for recruitment to the job. Thus there are simply no quantitative indicators that could substitute for the analyst's knowledge of the cases she or he is dealing with and for a qualitative analysis putting these indicators into the larger context. Again, though, it bears reiterating that it is useful to construct such hypothetical measures and to use qualitative and contextually grounded rankings of countries on these measures in systematic comparisons.

Similarly, one can construct indicators of the constellation of civil society. Density of affiliation to voluntary associations in different social classes is one indicator; financing of these associations from dues as opposed to donations from corporations or wealthy individuals is another, indicating the relative autonomy of associations of subordinate classes. Autonomy from the state apparatus is more difficult to measure. Receipt of public funds by voluntary associations may or may not be an indicator of control by the state apparatus. If the rules for disbursement of public funds are clearly legislated and made independent of political loyalties, and, consequently, the room for discretion of state bureaucrats is close to nil, then the receipt of public funds does not entail any loss of autonomy vis-à-vis the state apparatus. For instance, in many European countries political parties receive public funds, and no reasonable political analyst would claim that their autonomy is curtailed because of this. If, in contrast, public funds are awarded with a heavy dose of discretionary power for bureaucrats, or if private funds are controlled in this manner, then the autonomy of recipient organizations is clearly very limited. Again, no international agency is likely to obtain and collect data on the finer points of the awarding of public funds, and the researcher is forced to rely on her or his qualitative assessment of this aspect.

Some indicators for the relationship of a state to international controllers of capital are comparatively easy to construct. One can begin with a classification of a country's position in the world economy, that is, core, semiperiphery, or periphery. Next, one can look at current inflows of external aid (bilateral or multilateral grants and loans), commercial loans, and direct foreign investment. Equally important, of course, is an operationalization of the legacy of past loans, in other words, of accumulated debt and the associated indicators of debt service burden. However, to get at the nature of the relationship between the state and these actors, and at the impact of this relationship on the quality of these capital inflows (e.g., the types of investments they finance and their potential for increasing domestic accumulation), one needs to look at interaction patterns and the quality and standing of negotiators for both sides. Such information again requires in-depth knowledge of one's cases.

Constructing measures for a country's relationship to the international system of states is more difficult. Take, for instance, the presence of a military threat. In the extreme case, such as that of U.S. support for the *contras* in Nicaragua, it is possible to state unambiguously that such a threat was present. But in the absence of actual acts of aggression, it is difficult to assess perceived military threats even in a qualitative manner. To take another example, assurances of mutual assistance in the case of aggression from a third party are also difficult to assess. How reliable are such assurances, and to what extent do they take the pressure off a given state to divert resources from accumulation to defense? Again, only careful study of individual cases can provide tentative answers to such questions; the quest for "hard" data would be illusory.

In summary, whereas it is possible to operationalize individual determinants of different state capacities, coming to an assessment of the overall relative capacities of individual states in the different areas and of different states in the same areas calls for qualitative comparative analysis, grounded in a thorough historical knowledge of the cases. The reason to strive for operationalization and the use of quantitative measures of aspects of state strength is to facilitate replication in other countries, to stimulate critical evaluation of one's analysis by other researchers, and to enable systematic comparisons across cases. The reason such measures need to be integrated into holistic, contextualized comparative analyses is to capture the relational nature and causal complexity of the shaping of state capacities. Given the contingent nature of different types of state capacities, this qualitative comparative analysis must have a historical component. In other words, it should be part of an analytical comparative historical analysis.[55] □

NOTES

I would like to thank John D. Stephens and the participants in the 1993 Quito meeting, particularly David Collier and Peter H. Smith, for comments on an earlier draft of this chapter.

1. Guillermo O'Donnell, "On the State, Democratization, and Some Conceptual Problems (A Latin American View with Glances at Some Post-Communist Countries)," *World Development* 21, no. 8 (August 1993): 1355–1369.

2. The first programmatic volume produced by the Social Science Research Council Committee was that of Peter Evans, Dietrich Rueschemeyer, and Theda Skocpol, eds., *Bringing the State Back In* (Cambridge: Cambridge University Press, 1985).

3. There are important exceptions in the literature; Alfred Stepan, *The State and Society: Peru in Comparative Perspective* (Princeton: Princeton University Press, 1978), deliberately set out to correct this omission. See also Peter S. Cleaves and Martin J. Scurrah, *Agriculture, Bureaucracy, and Military Government in Peru* (Ithaca, NY: Cornell University Press, 1980), and Evelyne Huber Stephens and John D. Stephens, *Democratic Socialism in Jamaica: The Political Movement and Social Transformation in Dependent Capitalism* (Princeton: Princeton University Press, 1986). In the literature on bureaucratic-authoritarian regimes, of course, the state is in the center of the analysis, but the main focus is on the nature of the regime (that is, the rules governing access to power and the rights of the ruled), the support coalition for the government, the major policies, and socioeconomic and political conditions giving rise to bureaucratic-authoritarianism. See David Collier, ed., *The New Authoritarianism in Latin America* (Princeton: Princeton University Press, 1979).

4. On the similarities between pluralist and structural-functionalist views, see Robert Alford and Roger Friedland, *Powers of Theory: Capitalism, State, and Democracy* (Cambridge: Cambridge University Press, 1985).

5. Important works in the Marxist tradition are Nicos Poulantzas, *Political Power and Social Classes* (London: New Left Books, 1973), and Ralph Miliband, *The State in Capitalist Society* (New York: Basic Books, 1969).

6. Stepan, *The State and Society*; Evans, Rueschemeyer, and Skocpol, *Bringing the State Back In*; and Joel S. Migdal, *Strong Societies and Weak States: State-Society Relations and State Capabilities in the Third World* (Princeton: Princeton University Press, 1988).

7. See Joan M. Nelson, "The Politics of Pro-Poor Adjustment," in Joan M. Nelson, ed., *Fragile Coalitions: The Politics of Economic Adjustment* (New Brunswick, NJ: Transaction Books, 1989), and Stephan Haggard and Robert R. Kaufman, *The Politics of Economic Adjustment* (Princeton: Princeton University Press, 1993).

8. See Thomas Callaghy, "Toward State Capability and Embedded Liberalism in the Third World: Lessons for Adjustment"; Stephan Haggard and Robert R. Kaufman, "Economic Adjustment in New Democracies"; and John Waterbury,

"The Political Management of Economic Adjustment and Reform," in Nelson, *Fragile Coalitions*.

9. See Dietrich Rueschemeyer, Evelyne Huber Stephens, and John Stephens, *Capitalist Development and Democracy* (Chicago: University of Chicago Press, 1992).

10. Evans et al., *Bringing the State Back In*.

11. Theda Skocpol, "Bringing the State Back In: Strategies of Analysis in Current Research," in Evans et al., *Bringing the State Back In*, p. 9.

12. Even incumbents subscribing to neoliberal ideologies recognize that the state has the obligation to facilitate accumulation, though in their view this precludes a directly productive role for the state and extensive regulation of economic activity. For them, the state needs to perform the essential functions of providing infrastructure and an appropriate legal environment and preventing union interference with a competitive labor market.

13. See Chalmers Johnson, *MITI and the Japanese Miracle: The Growth of Industrial Policy, 1925–1975* (Stanford: Stanford University Press, 1982), and Peter Evans, "Predatory, Developmental, and Other Apparatuses: A Comparative Political Economy Perspective on the Third World State," *Sociological Forum* 4, no. 4 (December 1989): 562–563.

14. See Max Weber, *Economy and Society* (New York: Bedminster, 1968). Excerpts reprinted in H. H. Gerth and C. Wright Mills, *From Max Weber: Essays in Sociology* (New York: Oxford University Press, 1958).

15. See Stephens and Stephens, *Democratic Socialism in Jamaica*.

16. See Ben Ross Schneider, "Partly for Sale: Privatization and State Strength in Brazil and Mexico," *Journal of Interamerican Studies and World Affairs* 30, no. 4 (winter 1988–1989): 99.

17. See Stephens and Stephens, *Democratic Socialism in Jamaica*, and Cleaves and Scurrah, *Agriculture, Bureaucracy, and Military Government in Peru*.

18. Rueschemeyer and Evans emphasized the importance of inculcating among core participants "shared assumptions and expectations on which a common rationality can be based" as a precondition for effective state intervention in the pursuit of economic transformation. Dietrich Rueschemeyer and Peter B. Evans, "The State and Economic Transformation: Toward an Analysis of the Conditions Underlying Effective Intervention," in Evans et al., *Bringing The State Back In*, p. 51. They further argued that the formation of an esprit de corps is an essential part of such an institution-building process and that this process takes a long time, maybe generations.

19. For an example, see Alfred Stepan, *Rethinking Military Politics: Brazil and the Southern Cone* (Princeton: Princeton University Press, 1988).

20. See Arend Lijphart, *Democracies: Patterns of Majoritarian and Consensus Government in Twenty-One Countries* (New Haven: Yale University Press, 1984).

21. See Juan Linz, "Perils of Presidentialism," *Journal of Democracy* 1, no. 1 (1990): 51–69.

22. See Rueschemeyer and Evans, "The State and Economic Transformation."

23. For a similar interactive conception of state strength, see Migdal, *Strong States and Weak Societies*, p. xvii.

24. See Rueschemeyer et al., *Capitalist Development*, pp. 49–51, for this conceptualization of civil society and a discussion of the importance of civil society for democracy.

25. See John D. Stephens, *The Transition from Capitalism to Socialism* (Urbana: University of Illinois Press, 1979), and Bruce Western, "A Comparative Study of Corporatist Development," *American Sociological Review* 56 (June 1991): 283–294.

26. See Mancur Olson, *The Rise and Decline of Nations* (New Haven: Yale University Press, 1982).

27. On South Korea and Japan, see Evans, "Predatory, Developmental, and Other Apparatuses," and Peter Evans, "The State as Problem and Solution: Predation, Embedded Autonomy, and Structural Change," in Stephan Haggard and Robert R. Kaufman, eds., *The Politics of Adjustment* (Princeton: Princeton University Press, 1992). On Switzerland and Austria, see Peter Katzenstein, "Small Nations in an Open International Economy: The Converging Balance of State and Society in Switzerland and Austria," in Evans et al., *Bringing the State Back In*.

28. See Jonas Pontusson, *The Limits of Social Democracy: Investment Politics in Sweden* (Ithaca, NY: Cornell University Press, 1992), and Peter Katzenstein, *Small States in World Markets: Industrial Policy in Europe* (Ithaca, NY: Cornell University Press, 1985).

29. Skocpol calls this latter case a Tocquevillian effect ("Bringing the State Back In," p. 21).

30. The contrast between state action, the development of civil society, and political regimes in Central America and the English-speaking Caribbean is analyzed in chapter 6 of Rueschemeyer et al., *Capitalist Development and Democracy*. In Costa Rica, state action resembled that in the British Caribbean, insofar as popular organization was tolerated.

31. State action can also have unintended negative (for state capacity) effects on civil society. For instance, the housing policy of the Danish Social Democrats divided beneficiaries into homeowners and renters and thus introduced divisions into the social democratic movement and reduced the capacity of the Social Democratic incumbents to further pursue redistributive policies. See Gösta Esping-Andersen, *Politics Against Markets* (Princeton: Princeton University Press, 1985).

32. See Philippe Schmitter, "Still the Century of Corporatism," Review of Politics 36, no. 1 (January 1974): 85–131, and David Collier and Ruth Berins Collier, "Who Does What, to Whom, and How: Toward a Comparative Analysis of Latin American Corporatism," in James M. Malloy, ed., *Authoritarianism and Corporatism in Latin America* (Pittsburgh, PA: University of Pittsburgh Press, 1977).

33. My analysis, then, is in agreement with Stepan's conclusions that under authoritarian regimes (1) the power of the state cannot be analyzed in isolation from the nature of cleavages in civil society and the horizontal ties that bring different sectors of civil society together, and (2) the evolution of opposition to the state within civil society is shaped by the way in which the state defines its project and by conflicts inside the state apparatus. See Alfred Stepan, "State Power and the Strength of Civil Society in the Southern Cone of Latin America," in Evans et al., *Bringing the State Back In*, p. 340. However, my conceptualization of state

strength is different from his, insofar as it refers to the capacity to achieve four different goals, whereas his refers to the capacity of both the state and civil society to define and promote primarily a political project. In his conceptualization, the key dimensions of state strength are the ability to maintain internal coherence (referring mostly to relations between the military as an institution and the military as the government) and support of allies in civil society for the state's project, and a key dimension of the strength of civil society is associational life as a base of the ability to formulate an oppositional political project.

34. See Stephens and Stephens, *Democratic Socialism in Jamaica*, pp. 52–56.

35. See Byoung-Doo Lee, "The Development of the Textile Industry in South Korea and the Philippines" (Ph.D. diss., Northwestern University, 1992).

36. See Jung-En Woo, *Race to the Swift: State and Finance in Korean Industrialization* (New York: Columbia University Press, 1991).

37. See Evans, "The State as Problem and Solution."

38. Catholic organizations are a partial exception because they formed a subculture insulating their members, to some extent, from the dominant norms and values.

39. See Rueschemeyer et al., *Capitalist Development and Democracy*, pp. 106–115, and Hans Ulrich Wehler, *The German Empire 1871–1918* (Dover, NH: Berg Publishers, 1985).

40. This sounds somewhat odd if one considers the high crime rate in Jamaica. However, crime is concentrated among ghetto gangs of unemployed youths—those not integrated into any organizations in civil society—and citizen support for law and order is very high, as is citizen solidarity in fighting crime.

41. See Peter Lange and Geoffrey Garrett, "The Politics of Growth," *Journal of Politics* 47 (1985): 792–827, and "The Politics of Growth Reconsidered," *Journal of Politics* 48 (1986): 257–274, and Evelyne Huber, Charles Ragin, and John D. Stephens, "Social Democracy, Christian Democracy, Constitutional Structure, and the Welfare State," *American Journal of Sociology* 99, no. 3 (1993): 711–749.

42. These societies are particularly vulnerable to the internationalization of capital because they are the smaller European countries with highly open economies. See Stephens, *The Transition from Capitalism to Socialism*, and Roland Czada, "Bestimmungsfaktoren und Genese politischer Gewerkschaftseinbindung," in Manfred G. Schmidt, ed., *Staatstätigkeit: International und historisch vergleichende Analysen* (Opladen, Germany: Westdeutscher Verlag, 1988).

43. See Stephens, *The Transition from Capitalism to Socialism*, Walter Korpi, *The Democratic Class Struggle* (London: Routledge and Kegan Paul, 1983), and Gösta Esping-Andersen, *The Three Worlds of Welfare Capitalism* (Princeton: Princeton University Press, 1990).

44. See Theda Skocpol, *States and Social Revolutions* (New York: Cambridge University Press, 1979).

45. See Peter Evans, "Transnational Linkages and the Economic Role of the State: An Analysis of Developing and Industrialized Nations in the Post–World War II Period," in Evans et al., *Bringing the State Back In*, pp. 194–207.

46. See Evelyne Huber Stephens and John D. Stephens, "Bauxite and Democratic Socialism in Jamaica," in Peter Evans, Dietrich Rueschemeyer, and Evelyne Huber Stephens, eds., *States Versus Markets in the World-System* (Beverly Hills:

Sage Publications, 1985). Also see Stephens and Stephens, *Democratic Socialism in Jamaica*, and Evelyne Huber Stephens, "Minerals Strategies and Development: International Political Economy, State, Class, and the Role of the Bauxite/Aluminum and Copper Industries in Jamaica and Peru," *Studies in Comparative International Development* 22, no. 3 (fall 1987): 60–102.

47. See Peter Evans, *Dependent Development: The Alliance of Multinational, State, and Local Capital in Brazil* (Princeton: Princeton University Press, 1979).

48. See Evelyne Huber and John D. Stephens, "Changing Development Models in Small Economies: The Case of Jamaica from the 1950s to the 1990s," *Studies in Comparative International Development* 27, no. 3 (fall 1992): 57–92.

49. Peter Smith makes a similar argument when he states that the main differences between East Asian and Latin American states, which kept the latter from being successful in promoting accumulation, were the world historical timing of their integration into the global economy, the weakness of the domestic capitalist class, and the lack of autonomy of the state from both elite and mass pressures. See Peter H. Smith, "The State and Development in Historical Perspective," in Alfred Stepan, ed., *Americas: New Interpretive Essays* (New York: Oxford University Press, 1992).

50. See Lee, "The Development of the Textile Industry."

51. For a compelling discussion of quantitative versus qualitative comparative analysis, and for suggestions regarding a more systematic use of the latter, see Charles Ragin, *The Comparative Method: Moving Beyond Qualitative and Quantitative Strategies* (Berkeley: University of California Press, 1987).

52. See Fred C. Pampel and John B. Williamson, *Age, Class, Politics, and the Welfare State* (New York: Cambridge University Press, 1989), and Walter Korpi, "Power, Politics, and State Autonomy in the Development of Social Citizenship," *American Sociological Review* 54 (1989): 309–329.

53. See Fred C. Pampel and Robin Stryker, "State Context and Welfare Development in Advanced Industrial Democracies, 1959–1980" (paper prepared for the Workshop on Comparative Research on Social Policy, Labor Markets, Inequality, and Distributive Conflict, International Sociological Association, Research Committee 19, Stockholm [August 1988]). Also see Alexander Hicks and Duane Swank, "Politics, Institutions, and Welfare Spending in Industrialized Democracies, 1960–1982," *American Political Science Review* 86 (1992): 658–674.

54. Indeed, even in quantitative analyses this index shows consistent and significant effects on welfare state expansion; the presence of these characteristics has a clearly negative effect on welfare state expenditures. See Huber et al., "Social Democracy."

55. For an insightful discussion of this type of analysis, see Theda Skocpol, "Emerging Agendas and Recurrent Strategies in Historical Sociology," in Theda Skocpol, ed., *Vision and Method in Historical Sociology* (New York: Cambridge University Press, 1984).

■

CHAPTER EIGHT

Reassessing Political Culture

Frederick C. Turner

THE CONCEPT OF POLITICAL CULTURE has been a staple of the literature in comparative politics since the 1960s, yet, as a paradigm for research in Latin America, it remains fresh and alluring. Writers have referred repeatedly to the concept, sometimes defining or utilizing it in creative ways. By and large, however, they have failed to analyze it in relation to the masses of quantitative data that have accumulated on Latin America in recent years. Whereas some social scientists view political culture as essentially a national phenomenon, encompassing the distinctive values of each national community, shaped by that community's distinctive history and environment, others feel that there is a "Latin" culture that defines the region as a whole. At the very least, survey and electoral data should be able to point to one of these approaches as more fruitful than the other.

What else can one expect of studies in political culture in the decade ahead? How else can they work to establish a firmer understanding of political realities in Latin America and the best theoretical approaches to those realities? On one hand, one can test fundamental assumptions of the general theories of recent decades, including the most prestigious theories, using the better quality data and the more sophisticated analytical techniques and understandings that have more recently become available. More broadly, one can also investigate particular dimensions of political change in each nation, relating them to the culture of that nation as a whole, linking, for example, the new literatures on institutional development, democratization, or corruption to underlying patterns of values. Finally, of course, one can compare the results for various nations, both within Latin America and between Latin America and other parts of the world. These approaches by no means exhaust the investigations that can and should be done in a region as varied as Latin America and on a concept as rich and as centrally significant as political culture, but they do provide far more work than can be done in one decade. □

ASSUMPTIONS OF THE LITERATURE

Before one considers new roads to travel, it is necessary to examine what maps already have been created. First, one must arrive at an operational definition of political culture. This search sparked a series of useful studies by Archie Brown and his colleagues in Eastern Europe in the 1970s. They concluded that political culture can be understood "as the subjective perception of history and politics, the fundamental beliefs and values, the foci of identification and loyalty, and the political knowledge and expectations which are the product of the specific historical experience of nations and groups."[1] This definition stresses the methodological importance of survey research, especially survey data on values, which endure over long periods of time, rather than attitudes, which shift with times and circumstance. Substantively, political culture in this sense shapes the context within which people construct and reconstruct their political institutions, or, as Aaron Wildavsky has put it, "cultures constitute one's political selves."[2] If these orientations establish our operational view of what political culture is, then one may usefully employ it to investigate more broadly assumptions in the literature of political science and the social sciences.

In the 1990s, political culture must be interpreted in a far broader context than did Gabriel Almond and Sidney Verba in *The Civic Culture*, published in the 1960s. As Carole Pateman has thoughtfully noted, Almond and Verba advocated citizen participation in politics, with their characterizations of "participant," "subject," and "parochial" cultures, yet they failed to appreciate that the functioning of the system depended upon its limitations of the participation of some citizens, such as women and people in the lower socioeconomic strata.[3] Furthermore, all parts of the world have their own cultures and their own cultural values, so it is not appropriate to take a model drawn from some countries (such as Great Britain and the United States, as in *The Civic Culture*) and assume that it should or will come to supplant other cultures. Nevertheless, within this broader conceptualization, it remains highly interesting to approach elements of political culture (or political *cultures*) in terms of the comparative survey data for different nations that formed the empirical backbone of Almond and Verba's work.

One of the most exciting developments since the 1960s has been the proliferation of survey research around the world, which now allows scholars to test and retest the empirical foundations for theorizing in regard to culture and politics in Latin America. For example, how reliable are the survey data on which some of the most influential theories of recent decades have been based? One argument, which comes from an initial reading of some of the data from the 1960s, is that the middle class came to support military coups in such nations as Argentina. This assumption led to widely admired interpretations, such as José Nun's classic article about the middle-class military coup and Guillermo O'Donnell's influential thesis concerning bureaucratic-authoritarianism.[4] The postulation of middle-class support for the Argentine coup of 1966 is only one dimension of these interpretations. This facet is significant, however, and past scholars, in their best and most thorough critiques, have not questioned it.[5] More detailed and recent work on Argentine public opinion from 1964 to 1966 seriously questions these interpretations, however, suggesting that the coup had only shallow public support, even though the *golpistas* tried to make it seem otherwise.[6] If this is true for the 1966 Argentine coup, then surely one needs to investigate the full context of public attitudes toward political events in other nations and periods as well.

An even more fundamental issue in the literature is whether Latin America essentially has *one* political culture, an overriding "Latin" culture, or whether the key elements of political culture differ substantially among Latin American nations. The first viewpoint goes back to historical interpretations of the Iberian heritage and to scholarly assumptions like those of Kalman Silvert, Gino Germani, and Kenneth Organski in the 1970s. They assumed that the political culture of Southern Europe (Spain, Portugal, and Italy) were essentially those of Brazil and the nations of the Southern Cone in South America. These notions have raised questions by social scientists, but they have remained empirically untested in any rigorous way.[7] Nevertheless, they have been expanded geographically in two challenging books by Glen Caudill Dealy, *The Public Man* (1977) and *The Latin Americans* (1992).[8]

Roland Ebel, Raymond Taras, and James Cochrane similarly envisioned a single political culture for Spanish America, one that they defined as "monism" and one that they suggested may be "tested" through "description."[9] Like Dealy's approach to Latin culture, their view of monism starkly contrasts with that of Almond and Verba. The latter have assumed that political culture varies greatly among nations, because it is shaped by the overriding experiences that each nation's people go through together, such as the American Revolution of 1775 or the Mexican Revolution of 1910.[10] Whereas for his interpretations Dealy depended upon wide reading and personal experience in Latin America, Almond and Verba and their followers relied instead upon comparative survey data.

The approach of Almond and Verba throws into question the conclusions the other scholars. For example, Dealy wrote that "the crucial variable in the Catholic ethos is friendship," but in fact the best comparative data on values in the Latin American nations demonstrate that their peoples vary enormously in the degree to which they find friendship to be particularly important in their lives.[11] As the figures in Table 8.1 reveal, using data from the World Values Survey in the early 1990s, Chileans are among the people who find religion to be important in their lives. On the whole, they are the most "Catholic" in this sense. Yet only 20 percent of the Chileans said that their friends were very important to them, as compared with 69 percent of the Swedes, 63 percent of the respondents from the Netherlands, 53 percent of the Nigerians and the citizens of the United States, and 52 percent of the South Koreans. The 20 percent in Chile also contrasts rather dramatically with the 45 percent figure for Spain, suggesting that Chilean values—at least in regard to the value assigned to friendship—are far from merely being "Hispanic," and far from those of the colonial *madre patria*, far from representing just one more example of a "Latin" or "Catholic" ethos that some writers reify for the Hispanic world.

Both Mexico and Chile rate low on the "importance of friends" scale, whereas Argentina ranks high, pointing again to a striking absence of uniformity among the Latin American nations. Of course, one would obtain different results from other questions about friendship, say, a question about reserving a job for a friend.[12] Nevertheless, the self-reported importance of friendship, as measured in the World Values Study, turns out to vary almost as much *within* Latin America as it does within other world regions.

In regard to the family, similarly Dealy wrote that "the stormy and passionate extended Latin family exudes warmth and shelters its members from the outside world to a degree unmatchable by capitalist countries."[13] This is certainly the stereotype, but what is the empirical evidence? Table 8.1 demonstrates that the importance of family is indeed high in Argentina, Chile, and Mexico. But it is equally high or higher in such "capitalist" nations as the United States, South Korea, and Nigeria.[14] Furthermore, Dealy's approach is also flawed in that he tends to speak in the same voice about all groups—as well as all nations—in Latin America. For instance, even for those of us who personally know the impressive warmth of certain Latin American families, a warmth that has led many to give credence to Dealy's observation, the familial orientation that he describes is limited in terms of social class. As Federico Reyes Heroles has observed, on the basis of careful study of Mexican values as revealed in the two waves of the World Values Study done in Mexico, such warmth and protection are largely limited to families of the

TABLE 8.1 What People in Different Countries Find To Be
Very Important, 1990–1991

Regions and Countries	Percentage of Respondents Saying that Each of the Following Items Was "Very Important"				
	Friends	Religion	Family	Politics	Work
Latin America					
Argentina	51	40	91	15	75
Mexico	25	34	85	12	67
Chile	20	51	86	14	75
British North America					
United States	53	53	93	16	62
Canada	51	31	92	15	59
Europe					
Sweden	69	10	87	11	67
Netherlands	63	19	82	11	49
Britain	48	16	88	10	51
Spain	45	23	83	6	65
France	41	14	82	8	61
Italy	39	33	86	7	61
West Germany	37	13	71	9	35
Portugal	20	17	65	3	35
Asia and Africa					
Nigeria	53	85	94	21	94
South Korea	52	26	93	31	69
Japan	34	6	78	14	41
India	30	49	77	13	86
China	22	1	62	29	64

Question: "Please say, for each of the following, how imporatant it is in your life." The items were: work, family, friends and acquaintances, leisure time, politics, and religion. The response categories were: very important, quite important, not very important, and not at all important.

Source: The data came from the World Values Study. The surveys cited above were conducted in 1990, with the exception of that for Argentina, which was conducted in 1991. The data set for the World Values Study is available from the Inter-University Consortium for Political and Social Research, University of Michigan, P.O. Box 1248, Ann Arbor, Michigan 48106.

Mexican middle and upper classes, whereas poor families are far more frequently rent by strife and desertion,[15] as are the poor families in both Mexico and the United States described by anthropologist Oscar Lewis in his observations of "the culture of poverty."[16]

Dealy's studies illustrate the limitations of a normative or purely descriptive approach to political values and culture in Latin America. His books make for easy and enjoyable reading, his erudition is evident, and his examples are seductively intriguing. Some of the data from the World Values Study may be interpreted to support his central theses on religion, family, and friendship.[17] Nevertheless, he may also be wrong on a number of points, and the only way to know whether his generalizations hold up across national borders or over time is to look at empirical survey data among nations in various periods. His approach appeals, somewhat dangerously, perhaps, to many Anglo-Americans, particularly to Protestants, because it appears to justify the superiority of their public institutions. In doing so, however, Dealy's conceptualization may distort the distinctiveness as well as the uniformity of the Latin American experience and underestimate the flexibility of political institutions in Latin America. For instance, the move toward privatization, so evident in the 1980s and the 1990s, demonstrates a flexibility in public policy decisionmaking that Dealy's thesis denied to the Latin Americans. He wrote that, in Latin America, "frugality with government funds ... seem[s] to be largely missing," failing to appreciate the privatization that has come to Carlos Salinas's Mexico and Carlos Menem's Argentina, just as it came to Margaret Thatcher's Britain and Ronald Reagan's United States.[18] The United States, whose allegedly Protestant ethos Dealy continually contrasts with that of Latin America, has become such a monumental debtor nation since 1980 that it would be ludicrous to see the United States as more "frugal with government funds" than its Latin American neighbors.

In debates over matters like this, the most important issue is how scholars approach values and political culture in Latin America, and this issue goes well beyond the writing of any one person or one school of thought. One needs to test empirically assumptions in the literature through analysis of the best available data on Latin American values. When people do so, they naturally come to question many of the assumptions in the literature. The data in Table 8.1 challenge a number of such generalizations; better said, perhaps, they suggest that the generalizations are not so much mistaken as superficial, in need of clarification in depth. Thus most observers would agree with Alan Riding, who said that the Catholic Church "remains a powerful force" in Mexico. The data in Table 8.1, however, demonstrate that only one Mexican in three finds religion to be very important in his or her life.[19] Alternatively, though many would agree with Carlos Rangel that Latin Americans, like the

Spanish *conquistadores*, find "regular work [to be] singularly unattractive," the data in Table 8.1 contrastingly emphasize that between two-thirds and three-quarters of Mexicans, Chileans, and Argentines find work to be personally important.[20]

The way to deal with such apparent contradictions is *not* simply to conclude that one position or the other is correct or that "the data prove" to be invalid certain generalizations in the literature. Rather, Latin Americanists need to analyze fundamental dimensions of survey literature in depth, to draw out data from large numbers of surveys over time, and to use measures of association to tease out of the raw data the relationships and interconnections that are not evident from simple percentages and the marginal values. When this is done in regard to dimensions of political culture, or family values, or religious sociology, deeper understandings will be reached of the dimensions of the issues studied. When these findings contradict generalizations in the more popular literature on Latin America, those generalizations can be reworked, with a process of hypothesis testing and reformulation in the social sciences that is not fundamentally unlike the testing and reformulations of the natural sciences. □

THE BEST WAY TO STUDY POLITICAL CULTURE

One strategy for approaching political culture is to work from the simple to the complex and to do this systematically in terms of two profoundly different levels of analysis: first, data analysis by social groups within a nation and, then, for the nation as a whole, and, second, comparisons of patterns of political culture among nations, to see where continuities exist and where they may, or may not, suggest the existence of similar cultures or even "civilizations." This should be done for various dimensions of "culture," including those that relate to religion, the family, and work, as well as to politics. Fortunately, the World Values Study provides the vehicle for several of these steps on a cross-national basis, and it has the thus far unprecedented virtue of building up a longitudinal database for international comparisons over time.

Before scholars think about issues of international comparison, however, they need to address those of consistency within the nation-state. When researchers talk to experts on the politics of individual countries about patterns of values that may reflect dimensions of a national political culture, one frequent reaction is that the experts claim that distinctive groups have their own political cultures—that there is one for the elite and one for the mass, one for the highly educated and another for the uneducated citizens of the country.[21] This is one of two fundamental reasons that Ann Craig and Wayne Cornelius cited to explain

TABLE 8.2   Practices and Attitudes Relating to the Transition Toward
Democracy by Social Class: Mexico, 1990 (in percentages)

Actions and Beliefs of Respondents	Upper Class	Middle Class	Skilled Working Class	Unskilled Working Class
Has signed a petition	48	38	33	28
Has taken part in a lawful demonstration	22	24	24	18
Agrees that "the way that our society is organized should change radically through revolutionary action"	12	15	15	22
Agrees that "the way that our society is organized should change little-by-little through reform"	76	74	70	65
Agrees that most people can be trusted	35	34	30	34
Expresses much confidence in the legal system of our country	22	13	18	14
Is very proud to be a Mexican	66	54	55	56

Source: The data came from the World Values Study. The data set for the World
Values Study is available from the Inter-University Consortium for Political and
Social Research, University of Michigan, P.O. Box 1248, Ann Arbor, Michigan
48106.

why more research has not been carried out on political culture in Latin
America.[22] Instead of limiting the research agenda, however, such reactions among academics should extend the agenda, encouraging them to
go on to investigate systematically and to compare the attitudes and
values of political elites, social classes, and regional populations. When
this is done empirically for political attitudes in Mexico by social class,
the differences sometimes turn out to be slight.

The data in Table 8.2 reveal that, in relation to central actions and to
attitudes related to political culture in Mexico, there is surprising com-
monalty in practice and attitudes across classes. The higher the social
class, the more likely respondents are to have signed a petition and to
prefer reformist as opposed to revolutionary strategies of change. This
relationship does not hold true, however, for taking part in a lawful demonstration or for agreement with the statement that most people can be
trusted. Given the gulf that separates the upper class and the unskilled
working class in Mexico, one might expect these differences to be much

TABLE 8.3 The Assignment of Responsibility for Political, Economic, and Social Change by Social Class: Urban Residents in Mexico, 1961 (in percentages)

Agency to Which Responsibility Was Assigned	Total	Upper and Upper-Middle Class	Middle Class	Lower Class
The government	74	71	70	78
Other group	2	1	3	1
Citizen him- or herself	23	27	27	21
Total	100	100	100	100
Number of cases	(1,224)	(157)	(407)	(660)

Question: "Who, does it seem to you, should have the primary responsibility for seeing that these changes come about—the government, some other group or the citizen himself?" The question was asked only of those respondents who said that they wanted specific economic, political, or social changes in Mexico.

Note: The figures above have been recalculated from those in the United States Information Agency (USIA) report. The original table included 1 percent of the respondents who had no opinion. It also showed that 18 percent of the sample were not asked this question because in the previous open question these respondents had not indicated at least one change they wanted in Mexico.

Source: The Research and Reference Service, United States Information Agency, *Mexican Aspirations and Expectations: Indications from a Survey of National Urban Opinion,* research report R–78–62 (R) (Washington, DC, August 1962), p. 4.

greater. The fact that they are not points to similarities in underlying attitudinal perspectives. It also tends to confirm the finding in other contexts that the political impact of social class has declined in a number of countries.[23]

The 1961 data in Table 8.3 similarly demonstrate considerable class consistency in attitudes toward the role of government and the role of the citizen in bringing about changes that urban Mexicans said they wanted.[24] For all classes identified, at least seven out of ten respondents who said that they wanted some social or economic change identified the government as the appropriate agent of that change; whereas, overall, only two to three out of ten said that the individual citizen should be the agent of change. Interestingly, this latter response, which saw citizen participation as more important, was favored by 27 percent of the upper, upper-middle, and middle classes, as opposed to only 21 percent of the lower class. But all classes remained consistent in their view that the Mexican government should be the primary engine of change. The data reported by class for 1961 and 1990 in Tables 8.2 and 8.3 do not allow one to speak of consistencies in Mexican political culture, but they do provide two of the myriad building blocks that might support such generalizations.

Omnibus surveys such as the World Values Study still remain limited with regard to the number of groups within the nation-state that they can compare, because their samples of such groups as political elites or ethnic or religious minorities are too small to allow valid comparisons with the general population. Specialized surveys of distinct population groups are necessary, when possible, using the same survey questions at roughly the same time as more general national and international survey instruments are being administered. In the absence of this, one can often find the same questions asked of specialized populations at different points in time, and this at least allows some significant distinctions among the perspectives of groups.

As analysis moves to detailed investigation of national public opinion surveys, it naturally becomes more complex. The mass of the reading public better understands percentages and ratios rather than cross-tabulations and correlations, so the former simplistic statistics formed the basis of the many books written in each nation using the initial World Values Study data of the 1980s. Underlying patterns and relationships within the data can be discussed, however, only by going beyond simple percentage calculations and by the comparison of individual question responses for different countries. The next step, again a simple one, is using cross-tabulation in order to seek out relationships between the attitudes, then moving on to multivariate techniques in order to uncover patterns among the variables. More sophisticated analysis undertaken in Ann Arbor, Budapest, and Moscow has revealed not only new patterns but also a realization that what had appeared true from examining the marginals was unsubstantiated.[25] Regression and path analysis have proven especially helpful in studying dimensions of political culture in Latin America. More innovative techniques of analysis may do so in the future, even though Daniel Levine is right in reminding us that it is not methodological innovation per se that will "save us," but rather using the techniques of analysis to address the right sorts of questions.[26]

When analysis has been completed at the national level, the results can be compared internationally. Once again, the analysis can move from the simple to the complex. Single questions can be compared; patterns of questions can be compared; and so can the interpretations of the operational dimensions of political culture in various nations. This raises an intriguing question of whether values in certain countries are converging, and, if so, why. Such convergence has profound political implications for economic integration and for possible political integration in such areas as Europe and North America, and it has already been studied in detail on the basis of the World Values data.[27]

The ideal way to study political culture longitudinally is to have large national populations respond to the same survey questions over many decades. As Ronald Inglehart has recently said, "There is no substitute for time series data if one hopes to draw firm conclusions about social change."[28] But, in the real world, numerous problems intrude: In some countries, only enough funds can be raised to pay for sample populations that are so small that the values of component groups cannot be analyzed by multivariate techniques; in other countries, surveys are done but are not shared promptly or fully with colleagues internationally; problems of language and question wording need to be carefully considered at the analytical and comparative stages, because, even for the same language, particular words sometimes hold meanings or implications that vary significantly in different regions of the world.

Despite these and other problems of coordinating survey research among dozens of nation-states, the World Values Study is becoming the best single archive for analyzing political culture over time, with the possibility of built-in international comparisons. At a meeting of the steering committee of the World Values Study in Madrid in September 1993, it was decided to repeat the survey worldwide again in 1995, and thereafter every five years, rather than to wait a decade, as was done between 1981 and 1990. Although there will always be heated controversy among those who design the questionnaires as to which questions to retain and which new questions to add, those questions deemed most important for trend analysis will be retained, because this sort of analysis has already proven highly useful in the United States and other nations.[29] For 1995, it is hoped some sixty or more nations will participate in the World Values Survey, which would double the number that participated in the original wave of the survey in the early 1980s. Within the expanded number of countries, Latin Americanists can reasonably expect that survey researchers in more Latin American countries will gather data as time goes on.

In addition to the longitudinal and the expanded geographic coverage of the World Values Study, there are several other ways that political culture in Latin America can also be strategically approached in the 1990s. Dozens of other surveys from Latin America either focus directly on political culture or contain key questions relevant to it. These surveys can be obtained from the Roper Center or from national data banks in Brazil, Mexico, and Venezuela. Moreover, some coordinated surveys were done decades ago in several Latin American countries, and their results can be compared with those of the World Values Study in the 1980s and the 1990s. For example, the three waves of the World Survey sponsored by the United States Information Agency in the 1960s contained important questions touching upon political culture, and the same issues are treated with different question wordings in the World Values Study.[30] The questions asked in the 1990s differ in the sense that they provide for more response categories and cover more dimensions of the issues than did the simpler questions of the 1960s. But those seeking to study political culture over time will find rich treasures in the survey archives by comparing results from the best surveys done today with those done three decades ago.

Even more broadly, of course, survey data need to be compared with other sorts of data as new interpretations of political culture are formulated. In order to understand what is happening politically over time within a nation, one cannot look only at survey data, especially summary statistics taken out of a national context and placed in a framework with similar statistics from other nations. Instead, one needs to compare economic data, electoral data, and survey data, doing so within frameworks that vary from a few months to many decades. To understand the political system of a nation and the ways in which political culture influences that system, one must be as "data rich" as possible, gathering, analyzing, comparing, and reinterpreting data from many sources, to finally compare across nations both interpretation schemes and specific databases. Since this is the research context that promises the best results for intellectual understanding and for the potential contribution that social scientists can make to ongoing political debates and practices, there is clearly room for more data-based research.

Ultimately, what may Latin Americanists expect from this enterprise? At the very least, they should be able to speak more precisely to the challenging issues raised in the traditional literature and in the literature of the early 1990s. In his important reconceptualizations of political culture, for example, Richard Wilson envisioned a future for nation-states in which societal institutions more fully allow people to realize their potential. If one analyzes political culture over decades with quantitative measures, one may be able to judge whether the underlying assumptions of his interpretation are in fact proving true. Wilson assumes that political culture changes slowly, generationally; for example, the economic and technological advances of the twentieth century make citizens more equal within nations. As the educational, career, and earnings opportunities for many citizens become at least somewhat more equal, new generations come to think it proper for them to enjoy more equality before the law and more equal access to influence in politics than was true in the past. Wilson argues with special relevance to the end of the twentieth century that "as law becomes more fully committed to equity and toleration, ... the differences between morality and law begin to recede. ... The letter of the law and the spirit of the law coincide. ... For the first time, institutions become vehicles for the genuine realization of the full potential of all individuals."[31]

Alternatively, and even more controversially, Samuel Huntington has written that "civilizations" are what will matter most in the years ahead, that warfare will be primarily among civilizations, and that Latin America constitutes what he views as a civilization.[32] Detailed comparisons, like those of Table 8.1 above, may seriously challenge the interpretation that values are either consistent or distinctive within Huntington's "civilizations," and the grounds for either defending or attacking his position will certainly change as scholars come to understand political culture better, first within nations and then among nations. Before that time comes, however, studies of political culture will more immediately focus upon what since the late 1980s has become the most important single area of political science research on Latin America: the transition to democracy and the consolidation of democratic regimes. □

CONTINUITY OF POLITICAL CULTURE AND CONSOLIDATION OF DEMOCRACY

Has the inheritance of the Iberian tradition, or the influence of the long periods of military and authoritarian rule, created political culture(s) in Latin America that prevent or greatly impede the contemporary transition to democracy? Answers to this question vary greatly, and therein lies some of the fascination of the study of political culture in the 1990s. One school sees the political cultures of Latin America as essentially authoritarian, unbending, and impeding, but others note contrasting dimensions that can support democratic norms and institutions. Political culture encompasses values that citizens hold most deeply, and, by definition, these values change only very slowly. Now that longitudinal analysis of attitudes and values in Latin America is possible, however, it is also feasible to investigate the shift in value patterns. In the 1980s and the early 1990s, Latin American social scientists uncovered changes in directions that support wider political participation, gradual changes in underlying values that bode well for the consolidation of democracy, at least in some nations.

There are those who, without reference to these recent data, contend that an authoritarian political culture impedes democratization in Latin America. These scholars have a large, traditionalistic literature on their side. One of the strongest proponents of this view is Howard Wiarda, who wrote in 1992 that Latin America remains "hierarchical, authoritarian, paternalistic, Catholic ... elitist, corporatist, and patrimonialist to its core."[33] Wiarda concludes that Latin America possesses "a dominant Iberian-Catholic political culture that remains quite different from that of the Anglo-American nations," one that seriously impedes change, creating a situation in which "corporative, centralized, authoritarian institutions, reinforced by a political culture strongly grounded on hierarchy, status considerations, paternalism, and patronage, are what enable the prevailing systems to hang on so tenaciously."[34]

Some writers are even more dogmatic than Wiarda. According to Lawrence Harrison, for example, "It is culture that principally explains ... why some countries develop more rapidly and equitably than others." He added, "in the case of Latin America, one see a cultural pattern, derivative of traditional Hispanic culture, that is anti-democratic, anti-social, anti-progress, anti-entrepreneurial, and, at least among the elite, anti-work."[35] Some Latin American writers agree with Harrison, finding culture to be determinative of development. To take a recent example, José Ignacio García Hamilton declared that "the ultimate causes of the recurrence of authoritarianism and economic deterioration lie in the realm of culture," that the "authoritarian predisposition" and the "authoritarian relationships of the Catholic tradition of the Latin American people" come from the "cultural base" of the region.[36]

A very different outlook is found among social scientists such as Juan Linz, Seymour Martin Lipset, and Larry Diamond. They assume that political culture conditions the system within which democratic institutions arise, that in Latin America elite decisions in favor of democracy have preceded the widespread acceptance of democratic values, and that democratic values have grown (and continue to grow) once democratic institutions were in place. Following Lipset's early contention that democratic legitimacy grew in the United States as a result of the economic success of the system in the first decades after independence,[37] Diamond and Linz contend that "intellectual and mass public commitment to democracy is deepened by a generally successful performance of democratic systems." In a sense, these writers look at values that are the reverse of those on which Wiarda, Harrison, or García Hamilton concentrate. Diamond and Linz conclude that "the development and maintenance of democracy is greatly facilitated by values and behavioral dispositions (particularly at the elite level) of compromise, flexibility, tolerance, conciliation, moderation, and restraint."[38]

Yet another approach to links between "culture" and regime type is the perspective of John Booth and Mitchell Seligson, who demonstrate that Mexicans espouse democratic orientations, at least at an abstract level, even though they continue to live under an authoritarian political system.[39] Similarly, Susan Tiano has demonstrated with 1965 survey data that workers' attitudes in both Argentina and Chile "show no evidence of an authoritarian political culture."[40] This statement contradicted much of the traditional literature, which assumed that the political culture of

Argentina was notably more authoritarian than that of Chile. Intriguingly, Peter H. Smith has laid out three possible explanations for this apparent inconsistency: (1) that the surveys in question explored only superficial adherence to democratic principles and may have missed underlying dimensions of authoritarianism, (2) that the imposition of authoritarian regimes may result from conflicts and decisions at the elite level, regardless of popular preferences for democracy, or (3) that political culture may be more relevant to the consolidation and continuation of democratic regimes than to the imposition of authoritarian regimes.[41]

Each of these explanations may contain part of the answer, yet they need to be supplemented by two further interpretations, one that conforms with conclusions from Booth and Seligson and the other that derives from Tiano's data.[42] Distinguished Mexican anthropologists sometimes argue that underlying values of contemporary Mexicans *are* fundamentally authoritarian in the sense that Mexican children learn in their families to accept the authority of their fathers and they later transfer this acceptance of authority to political leaders, including the president of Mexico.[43] From this standpoint, one may contend that anthropologists, through participant observation, learn more about citizen's deepest values than do survey researchers, whose questions— including many of those questions used to inform us about political culture—really measure attitudes more than values.

The survey research profession can also contribute to this line of analysis. One of the most familiar pitfalls of survey research is that respondents say what they feel it is socially acceptable to say and keep hidden attitudes, values, or voting intentions about which it is deemed socially prudent to keep silent.[44] The Mexican Constitution details social goals as rights that everyone admires and yet that no one expects to be immediately enforced. Similarly, surveys in Mexico reveal attitudinal support for democratic norms in which people genuinely believe (partly because they are *supposed* to believe in them). Yet these attitudes do not lead most people to rebel against the authoritarianism of the one-party system in which they grew up. The attitudes that the survey responses pick up are not "untrue"; they simply do not prevent a grudging acceptance of the daily norms under which Mexican authoritarianism continues to operate.

The careful analytical techniques that Tiano used to interpret the 1965 data point to another dimension of the lack of links between attitudes and contemporary political structures in Chile and Argentina—the importance of formal education in reducing support for authoritarianism: "The finding that education reduces authoritarianism among workers from Argentina as well as Chile suggests that this association is stable across different types of political regimes. Education appears to inhibit authoritarianism even in the absence of a long-standing democratic political heritage. ... Democratic norms and values might be part of a society's cultural traditions even though its political leaders are not able to achieve and sustain a stable democratic government."[45] Certainly historical events can impose authoritarian regimes in nations that lack authoritarian political cultures, as they did in Argentina in 1966 and in Chile in 1973. But where the level of formal education in a nation increases, and where the nature of that education challenges rather than reinforces support for authoritarianism, it can help to lay the foundation for more open regimes that replace the rule of military autocrats and reject their orientations, as did the regimes of Raúl Alfonsín in Argentina and Patricio Aylwin in Chile.

The apparent inconsistency between democratic attitudes and authoritarian regimes may thus have explanations that depend partially upon what are considered "acceptable" attitudes in particular political cultures, and it may reflect a growth in the level of formal education in a society that tends to undercut authoritarianism in the long run. If so, then which of the two foregoing interpretations of political culture comes generally closest to the truth? Did, or does, political culture impede the transition to democracy of the 1980s and the 1990s, or, in each nation, is political culture a conditioning element of that transition?

On one hand, since 1980 people have witnessed the widespread departure of military regimes in Latin America, the insertion of formally democratic institutions everywhere except Cuba, Haiti, and Peru, and notable tendencies toward more widespread political participation at the local and the municipal levels, and nothing in the authoritarian traditions of Latin America prevented these events from taking place.[46] On the other hand, people must also agree with the pragmatic view of Peter H. Smith: that the concept of "redemocratization" is historically inaccurate for Latin America, that systemic change has, so far, not involved serious challenges to the underlying roles of the armed forces, and that the contemporary euphoria over democratization must not prevent scholars from asking in very specific terms just how far this process has actually gone in each nation.[47] As even Linz and Diamond have noted, the development of democratic values may also be reversed, and, even if the present generation learns norms that broadly favor democracy, crises in the political system may lead a future generation to accept norms that differ profoundly.[48]

These issues lead naturally into a central concern of those who study political culture in Latin America: What *are* the elements, and the directions of change, within the political cultures of the Latin American nations? Venezuela provides an especially interesting test case of the continuity and the adaptation of political culture in the region. Although much press attention has focused upon the attempted military coups against the government of Carlos Andrés Pérez, raising the old fear that Latin Americans would back military regimes in times of crisis, the underlying, but most important, shift in Venezuelan politics may be the shift in the political culture of its citizens.[49] As Friedrich Welsch has emphasized, this change is slow but perceptible. On the basis of extensive survey data collected by his firm and also other data collected in the data bank of the Universidad Simón Bolívar in Caracas, Welsch characterizes the shift in political culture as one from formal to more broadly participant democracy. That is, during the past three and a half decades of democratic government in Venezuela, citizens have seen their roles primarily in electoral and partisan terms, assuming that it is enough to vote in national elections and to register as a member of a political party. Increasingly, however, especially with the political cynicism associated with the charges of corruption against President Pérez and earlier leaders at the national level and a precipitate decline in 1991 and early 1992 in the level of confidence in the fundamental institutions of the society, people see that they must become much more involved in politics, particularly at the local and the municipal levels. Ironically, but clearly, this cynicism is fueling a broadening of political participation and the norms of participation that must underlie democratic government.[50]

And what of other nations? In Argentina, the careful survey work of the late Edgardo Catterberg has, for the first five years of the democratic transition from 1984 to 1989, pointed to an initial pattern of political stability, buttressed by the decisions of both Radical and Peronist leaders to prevent the success of military coups, working to strengthen democratic legitimacy.[51] In these years, citizens became more disposed to the effective competition of political parties, although attitudes favoring democracy continued to coexist with orientations that remained populist.[52] Although the wide acceptance of the privatization policies of President Carlos Menem tends to lead to a questioning of Catterberg's assumption that the "fundamental core for Argentina political culture" is both "individualistic and statist," his basic interpretation that the presence of political stability and economic prosperity promote democratic legitimacy has been supported by events during the Menem administration.[53] Others who know Argentine values and opinion well, such as Mariano Grondona and Manuel Mora y Araujo, tend to agree with the broad outlines of Catterberg's interpretation.[54] As Mora wrote, "Absolutist and intolerant values have not disappeared from the scene," but Argentines have changed "their expectations, their *mentality*" during the past decade, moving toward the values of private achievement and productivity.[55]

Over time, Argentina and the other nations of Latin America may well be going through a process that Oscar Mejía Quintana and Arlene B. Tickner have recently described as the movement from formal democracy, to representative democracy, to participant democracy, a process that, they rightly note, differs in each nation according to the "singularities and particularities" of that nation.[56] The process ultimately must be one of social incorporation, one in which, as Gustavo Lagos wrote, "the masses, the people, are integrated into the system, not only through the vote and through formal participation, but also when they receive the benefits of the system."[57] If so, what is required is economic and institutional analysis as well as survey research.

Nevertheless, survey research from the early 1980s and the 1990s may be able to capture some dimensions of these changes. An especially interesting vehicle for comparative analysis is the World Values Study, which includes data on Argentina, Chile, and Mexico. The data in Tables 8.4, 8.5, and 8.6 confirm much of what Latin Americanists know about value change and the transition to democracy in Latin America. Between the 1981 and 1991 World Values Surveys, values in Argentina and Mexico— the two Latin American nations for which scholars have the most comparative data—did not change dramatically.[58] But there is some evidence of movement toward more participant practices, especially in Mexico, where a significant increase appeared in the percentages of citizens who said that they had signed a petition or participated in a lawful demonstration. About three-fourths of the populations in Argentina, Chile, and Mexico favored incremental change as opposed to radicalism or revolution, even though in Argentina and Mexico the confidence of citizens in their legal system was low and, for a number of citizens, became even lower during this period. These data confirm that shifts in political culture are very gradual, with changes over generations rather than in a period of eight or ten years, and the data also mark dimensions of underlying values relating to democratic values, attitudes, and practices for the three nations.

Moreover, one can see in these tables something of the particularities of each nation, demonstrating once again that survey data must be interpreted in the context of the values and the meanings of words and concepts within specific national communities. In Mexico, for example, the 17 percent of the national population that agreed in 1990 that change should come radically through "revolutionary action" (Table 8.5) did not mean that nearly one-fifth of the Mexicans were ready to take up arms against the government. Instead, the words "revolutionary action" in Mexico recall the myriad references in Mexican history and civics courses to the Revolution of 1910; the 17 percent reflects a substantial number of people dissatisfied with the economic situation of recent years in Mexico, but it must be interpreted contextually rather than literally. Similarly, in Argentina, when the percentage of adults who had signed a petition or participated in a lawful demonstration dropped between 1983 and 1991

TABLE 8.4   Practices Relating to the Transition Toward Democracy: Mexico, Argentina, and Chile, 1981–1991 (in percentages)

Practices About Which	Argentina		Chile		Mexico	
People Were Asked	1984	1991	1983	1990	1981–1982	1990
Respondent has signed a petition	29	21	–	23	10	35
Respondent has taken part in a lawful demonstration	19	15	–	30	9	22

Question: "Now I'd like you to look at this card. I'm going to read out some different forms of political action that people can take, and I'd like you to tell me, for each one, whether you have actually done any of these things, whether you might do it or would never, under any circumstances, do it." The forms of participation were (A) signing a petition, (B) joining in boycotts, (C) attending lawful demonstrations, (D) joining unofficial strikes, and (E) occupying buildings or factories.

Source: The data came from the World Values Study. The data set for the World Values Study is available from the Inter-University Consortium for Political and Social Research, University of Michigan, P.O. Box 1248, Ann Arbor, Michigan 48106.

(Table 8.4), does this reflect a decline in support for democratic participation? The answer almost certainly is "no." Instead, in the sweep of Argentine politics, it may reflect the heightened political activism following Argentina's defeat in the Malvinas War of 1982. Therefore, these data reveal more than the outlines of political culture in these nations; they also demonstrate that care must be taken in analyzing political cultures in a comparative framework. □

CONCLUSION

To carry out research outlined in this chapter, scholars require access to reliable survey data, collected over decades, for most, if not all, Latin American nations. Such data already exist, especially for Brazil, Mexico, Venezuela, and Chile, with historically important data from Argentina limited to the 1960s and early 1970s. Some of these surveys deal directly with political culture, and, even when books have been written on the basis of them, the books may well take up other issues. Thus, in Jeane Kirkpatrick's classic study of Argentina, her focus was to determine who the Peronists really were, rather than to follow up the numerous questions in the questionnaire that came from The Civic Culture.[59] Creative

TABLE 8.5   Views of Whether Change Should Come Through Reform or Through Revolutionary Action: Mexico, Argentina, and Chile, 1981–1991 (in percentages)

Statements About Which People Were Asked	Argentina		Chile		Mexico	
	1984	1991	1983	1990	1981–1982	1990
"The entire way our society is organized must be radically changed by revolutionary action."	11	7	–	5	12	17
"Our society must be gradually improved by reforms."	67	74	–	72	77	71

Question: "On this card are three basic kinds of attitudes concerning the society we live in. Please choose the one which best describes your own opinion." The statements on the card were: (A) The entire way our society is organized must be radically changed by revolutionary action. (B) Our society must be gradually improved by reforms. (C) Our society must be valiantly defended against all subversive forces.

Source: The data came from the World Values Study. The data set for the World Values Study is available from the Inter-University Consortium for Political and Social Research, University of Michigan, P.O. Box 1248, Ann Arbor, Michigan 48106.

social scientists can find in such surveys important material on political culture as well. Indeed, some of the most innovative Latin Americanist graduate students have made important contributions to the literature by turning to specific survey instruments in order to study issues that the designers of those instruments did not have in mind.[60] Moreover, even in surveys conducted for commercial purposes, politically significant information may be found, as Carmen Zayuelas discovered after the military government banned political polling in Argentina in 1976.[61] Tragically, the original data from some important Latin American surveys have been lost, such as the elite study in Venezuela conducted by José Silva Michelena, Frank Bonilla, and their colleagues, but such instances are not the norm.[62]

In order to minimize such losses in the future, hundreds of Latin American surveys have recently been archived at the Latin American Survey Data Bank (LASDB) of the Roper Center at the University of Connecticut and the data archives of the Universidade do Campinas in Brazil and the Universidad Simón Bolívar in Venezuela.[63] These data banks

TABLE 8.6   Attitudes Toward Citizen Participation, Interpersonal Trust, Confidence in the Legal System, and Patriotism: Mexico, Argentina, and Chile, 1981–1991 (in percentages)

Issues About Which People Were Asked	Argentina		Chile		Mexico	
	1984	1991	1983	1990	1981–1982	1990
Respondent advocates increasing the participation of citizens in important government decisions	21	25	26	19	25	24
Respondent agrees that most people can be trusted	24	22	25	23	18	34
Respondent expresses much confidence in the legal system of his or her country	13	7	20	22	24	16
Respondent says that he or she is very proud to be an Argentine, a Chilean, or a Mexican	46	53	54	53	65	56

Questions: The questions read: (1) There is a lot of talk these days about what the aims of this country should be for the next ten years. On this card are listed some of the goals which different people would give top priority. Would you please say which of these you, yourself, consider the most important? And which would be the next most important? The statements on the card were: (A) maintaining a high level of economic growth, (B) making sure this country has strong defensive forces, (C) seeing that people have more to say about how things are done at their jobs and in their communities, (D) trying to make our cities and countryside more beautiful. (2) Generally speaking, would you say that most people can be trusted or that you can't be too careful in dealing with people? (3) Please look at the card and tell me, for each item listed, how much confidence you have in them. Is it a great deal, quite a lot, not very much, or none at all? The items were: (A) the church, (B) the armed forces, (C) the education system, (D) the press, (E) the legal system, (F) trade unions, (G) the police, (H) parliament, (I) civil service, (J) major companies, (K) the social security system, (L) the European Community, (M) NATO, (N) the Mexican political system. (4) How proud are you to be Mexican? (an Argentine?; a Chilean?) The response categories were: (A) very proud, (B) quite proud, (C) not very proud, (D) not at all proud.

Source: The data came from the World Values Study. The data set for the World Values Study is available from the Inter-University Consortium for Political and Social Research, University of Michigan, P.O. Box 1248, Ann Arbor, Michigan 48106.

form a vast repository, much of it of very good quality. It is important to bring the best new survey research into these archives, to create others so that social scientists in such countries as Mexico, Argentina, and Chile have easier access to the large numbers of surveys done there, and to establish an exchange network among data centers, so that data sets on particular topics can be shared among them.

Another need is to train students in the quantitative techniques necessary to analyze these data most effectively and efficiently. This takes time, but once graduate students come to appreciate the importance of the data, the need for thorough methodological training to make sense of them, and the inherent intrigue of understanding the competing claims of the advocates of different multivariate techniques, graduate students of this generation will emerge from their doctoral programs far more prepared than those of the past to exploit the vast survey resources that have recently become available. For those involved in doctoral studies, and also for professors and other researchers who want to turn seriously to this area of analysis, courses in the summer program of the University of Michigan provide especially appropriate training.

What can be expected from the significant investment of human talent and financial resources that such studies will require? In broad terms, the answer is a clearer understanding of Latin America, its political processes, and the institutionalization of democratic norms within it. Political culture touches far more than the study of values, depending as well upon national history and political socialization, raising questions of differences among social classes and the influence of other nations, pointing to the links between value change, widened political participation, and the appropriate functioning of democratic institutions.[64] The approach of political culture is not narrow, sectarian, or behavioralistic. Rather than excluding the humanities, it depends upon them. Analyzing *Martín Fierro* is necessary to understand the political culture of Argentina, just as watching *Memorias de un mexicano* or looking through family albums of the brutal postcards of the 1910 Revolution help us to understand the political culture of Mexico. Work on political culture through survey research needs to be integrated with other approaches to Latin American realities; it must test out assumptions derived from those approaches; and in the end it must be integrated with the information sources and the interpretive schemes of those approaches, rather than stand apart from them. In the process, a number of specific questions need to be answered for as many nations as possible. For example, do older citizens tend to be more authoritarian in outlook, as recent research on political culture in Australia has demonstrated, or can groups of people ordered according to their core values and their partisan preferences that have been carefully researched in Sweden be usefully compared with similar groups and similar partisanship in other parts of the world?[65] Over time, the emerging literature on political culture in Latin America, or significant parts of it, can be compared in detail with experiences in other regions, especially Asia, Eastern Europe, and the constituent republics of the former Soviet Union. Support for privatization, widened participation, local initiatives, and the creation of more effective bureaucracies and legislatures will significantly impact political processes in these parts of the world, and it is up to social scientists to provide the literatures and the deeper understanding that will help political decisionmakers and informed publics to make the wisest choices possible. In the 1980s and the 1990s, dramatic political and economic change in the nations of Latin America, Asia, and Eastern Europe has demonstrated that authoritarian norms held no vicelike grip there on political processes and that the political cultures of nations in these regions did not prohibit movements toward far more broadly participant political systems. Now it is the turn of social scientists to analyze the processes involved, as deeply and as thoroughly as possible, including the dimension of political culture and its gradual but highly significant evolution. □

NOTES

This chapter benefited from the detailed and constructive criticism of Miguel Basáñez, Carlos Elordi, Fabián Echegaray, and Peter H. Smith. As critic more than editor, Smith asked the right questions, which remains the most difficult task in both survey research and political science.

1. Archie Brown, Introduction to Archie Brown and Jack Gray, eds., *Political Culture and Political Change in Communist States* (New York: Holmes and Meier, 1977), p. 1.

2. Aaron Wildavsky, "Choosing Preferences by Constructing Institutions: A Cultural Theory of Preference Formation," in Arthur Asa Berger, ed., *Political Culture and Public Opinion* (New Brunswick: Transaction Publishers, 1989), p. 40.

3. See Carole Pateman, "The Civic Culture: A Philosophic Critique," in Gabriel A. Almond and Sidney Verba, eds. *The Civic Culture Revisited* (Boston: Little, Brown and Company, 1980), esp. pp. 75–79.

4. See José Nun, "A Latin American Phenomenon: The Middle Class Military Coup," in James Petras and Maurice Zeitlin, eds., *Latin America: Reform or Revolution?* (New York: Fawcett, 1968); Guillermo O'Donnell, *Modernization and Bureaucratic-Authoritarianism: Studies in South American Politics* (Berkeley: Institute of International Studies, University of California, Berkeley, 1973); and Guillermo O'Donnell, *Bureaucratic-Authoritarianism: Argentina, 1966–1973, in Comparative Perspective* (Berkeley: University of California Press, 1988). For an excellent summary of the concept and its implications, see David Collier, "Bureaucratic Authoritari-

anism," in Joel Krieger et al., eds., *The Oxford Companion to Politics of the World* (New York: Oxford University Press, 1993), pp. 96–98.

5. See David Collier, ed., *The New Authoritarianism in Latin America* (Princeton: Princeton University Press, 1979).

6. See Carlos Elordi, "Political Attitudes and the Coup d'Etat of 1966 in Argentina" (unpublished paper, 1993).

7. According to Susan Calvert and Peter Calvert (*Argentina: Political Culture and Instability* [Pittsburgh: University of Pittsburgh Press, 1989], p. 165) "Despite similar value systems, Mediterranean countries, for example, have fared better in terms of development than many of the nations of Latin America. Indeed Italy and Spain today [1989] exhibit very striking economic growth, indicating that it is not a Mediterranean heritage alone which resists development."

8. Glen Caudill Dealy, *The Public Man: An Interpretation of Latin American and Other Catholic Countries* (Amherst: University of Massachusetts Press, 1977), and *The Latin Americans: Spirit and Ethos* (Boulder: Westview Press, 1992).

9. It is the view of Ebel, Taras, and Cochrane that "the dominant value system of Latin America has been, and continues to be, what has been called political monism—a constant search for a harmonious, non-competitive social blueprint that can be imposed from the top." Roland H. Ebel, Raymond Taras, and James D. Cochrane, *Political Culture and Foreign Policy in Latin America: Case Studies from the Circum-Caribbean* (Albany: State University of New York Press, 1991), p. 35. They define five propositions in relation to monism: "We test these propositions empirically by describing the general features of international behavior in Latin America since World War II" (p. 49). In social science that is even more self-consciously empirical, however, one cannot test through description. Instead, empiricism should focus on sources of data through which comparisons of values can be made among nations and among specific groups within nations. These sources include survey data, electoral data, and the systematic comparisons of historical sociology.

10. On the basis of comparisons in the survey data among the five nations that they studied, Almond and Verba concur that "the Mexican pattern of more widespread political than administrative competence is paralleled only in the United States, the other nation whose political formation has represented, as has the Mexican Revolution, a rejection of traditional authority." Gabriel A. Almond and Sidney Verba, *The Civic Culture: Political Attitudes and Democracy in Five Nations* (Princeton: Princeton University Press, 1963), p. 229.

11. Dealy, *The Latin Americans*, p. 48.

12. Tapping other dimensions of the meaning of friendship, another useful question is, "If you had a job to give to someone, would you be more likely to give it to a friend whom you could trust or to another candidate who was said to have better qualifications?"

13. Dealy, *The Latin Americans*, p. 5.

14. In fact, the South Koreans may have even more family solidarity tied into their collective work ethic than do most Latin Americans. The results of this solidarity may appear not only in the impressive economic growth of South Korea since the 1960s but also in their success within Latin America itself, as in their

takeover of the garment trade in the Plaza Once of Buenos Aires, which they captured from the previously entrenched Jewish community. For data and interpretations of South Korea in comparative perspective, see Frederick C. Turner, "Worldwide Social Inequalities and Their Political Implications at the End of the Cold War," in Hiroshi Mannari, Harry K. Nishio, Joji Watanuki, and Koya Azumi, eds., *Power Shifts and Value Changes in the Post Cold War World* (Kurashiki, Japan: Kibi International University Press, 1992), esp. pp. 153–159.

15. Comments of Federico Reyes Heroles at the Segundo Seminario en México de la Asociación Mundial de Estudios de la Opinión Pública, Mexico City, October 9, 1992. For data supporting the interpretation of Reyes Heroles, see Enrique Alduncín Abitia, *Los valores de los mexicanos. México: Entre la tradición y la modernidad* (México, DF: Fomento Cultural Banamex, 1989), pp. 185–238.

16. Oscar Lewis, *Five Families: Mexican Case Studies in the Culture of Poverty* (New York: Random House, 1959), *The Children of Sánchez: Autobiography of a Mexican Family* (New York: Random House, 1961), and *La Vida: A Puerto Rican Family in the Culture of Poverty* (New York: Random House, 1966).

17. Commenting upon an earlier version of this chapter, Miguel Basáñez noted that some evidence in the World Values Study supports contentions that Dealy makes. For example, the data demonstrate a low level of interpersonal confidence among citizens in Catholic countries; Dr. Basáñez suggested that because they do not trust others, people place a high value on their trust of family members and of close friends.

18. Dealy, *The Latin Americans*, p. 11.

19. Alan Riding, *Distant Neighbors: A Portrait of the Mexicans* (New York: Alfred A. Knopf, 1985), p. 89.

20. Carlos Rangel, *The Latin Americans: Their Love-Hate Relationship with the United States*, rev. ed. (New Brunswick: Transaction Books, 1987), p. 192. Of the Spanish heritage, according to Rangel, "The Castilian considered fighting, or saying or hearing Mass, as masculine activities par excellence; rejecting labor as we conceive it, men lived on bounty extracted from Moorish territory—or, later, from the Americas. Such an approach could only confirm the view that it is better to live freely and adventurously by one's wits and personal daring, than to eke out a mediocre living in a stable and organized society."

21. This point of view was upheld by Denise Dresser's articulate commentary on "Repensando la cultura política mexicana" (a presentation by Frederick C. Turner at the Instituto Tecnológico Autónomo de México, October 7, 1993).

22. Craig and Cornelius wrote, "Many Latin Americanists deliberately chose to avoid broad national studies of political culture, generally for one of two reasons: (1) that internal diversities based on class, ethnicity, region, rural-urban differences, or differences of participation opportunities militated against the possibilities of arriving at meaningful, national generalizations about political culture; and (2) that the basic terms defining the context and outcomes of political activity were determined more by political structures and economic relations than by values and attitudinal orientations." Ann L. Craig and Wayne A. Cornelius, "Political Culture in Mexico: Continuities and Revisionist Interpretations," in Almond and Verba, *The Civic Culture Revisited*, p. 340.

23. Terry Nichols Clark, Seymour Martin Lipset, and Michael Rempel, "The Declining Political Significance of Social Class," *International Sociology* 8, no. 3 (September 1993): 259–292.

24. The question for the data in Table 8.3 was preceded by an open question: "Now, speaking of things in general, the economic, political and social aspects, let us suppose that you could change things here and all over Mexico the way you liked. Which are some of the changes you would like to make?" The responses revealed far more economic concerns than political concerns; the highest three classification areas for responses to the open question were economic. The percentages of the top five response categories were: 29 percent for "give people more material advantages at economical prices," 28 percent for "provide more sources of work," 10 percent for "increase workers' salaries, give more fringe benefits," 10 percent for "put honest, responsible people in government," and 8 percent for "get rid of centers of vice." See the Research and Reference Service, United States Information Agency, *Mexican Aspirations and Expectations: Indications from a Survey of National Urban Opinion*, research report R-78–62 (R) (Washington, DC, August 1962), p. 3.

25. Elena Bashkirova, the general director of the Russian Public Opinion and Market Research (ROMIR) in Moscow, has commented that, on the basis of her twenty-three years in survey research, she is convinced that merely using the marginals and cross-tabulations can lead to mistaken conclusions. She strongly urged members of the Quito conference to use multiple methods, including surveys, in-depth personal interviews, focus groups, and economic data. (See Chapter 11 of this volume, "Public Opinion Research in Russia and Eastern Europe").

26. Levine wrote, "Methodological innovation is critical, but not because new techniques will save us. They will not, and in any case … much of the most fruitful recent work has less to do with new techniques than with efforts to use existing tools to answer new kinds of questions." Daniel H. Levine, "Constructing Culture and Power," in Daniel H. Levine, ed., *Constructing Culture and Power in Latin America* (Ann Arbor: University of Michigan Press, 1993), p. 24.

27. See, in particular, Ronald Inglehart, Miguel Basáñez, and Neil Nevitte, *Convergencia en Norteamérica: Comercio, política y cultura*, trans. Lucila Christen de Remond (Mexico, DF: Siglo Veintiuno Editores, 1994).

28. Inglehart, "Modernization and Postmodernization: The Changing Relationship Between Economic Development, Cultural Change and Political Change" (unpublished paper, 1993), p. 4.

29. On the importance of question continuity, see Tom W. Smith, "America's Most Important Problem—A Trend Analysis, 1946–1976," *Public Opinion Quarterly* 44, no. 2 (Summer 1980): 164–180.

30. Question seven from World Survey II, for example, asked "Now, which one of these do you think our country needs most?" The response categories were: "an honest government without corruption," "a government that gets things done," "a fair distribution of wealth," "national unity," and "individual freedom." This survey was carried out in 1964 in Argentina, Brazil, Mexico, and Venezuela, as well as in countries in other parts of the world. Relating to a number of issues in that World Survey II question, the 1990 World Values Survey

asked: "I am going to read out some statements about the government and the economy. For each one, could you tell me how much you agree or disagree? Please use the responses on this card." The response categories were: "agree completely," "agree somewhat," "neither agree nor disagree," "disagree somewhat," and "disagree completely." The specific statements were: (a) This country's economic system needs fundamental changes; (b) our government should be much more open to the public; (c) we are more likely to have a healthy economy if the government allows more freedom for individuals to do as they wish; (d) if an unjust law were passed by the government I could do nothing at all about it; and (e) political reform in this country is moving too rapidly. The questionnaire for the World Values study is available from the Inter-university Consortium for Political and Social Research at the University of Michigan, Ann Arbor, and that for World Survey II is available from the Roper Center at the University of Connecticut, Storrs.

31. Richard W. Wilson, *Compliance Ideologies: Rethinking Political Culture* (New York: Cambridge University Press, 1992), pp. 74–75. For related views of equality and political culture, see Frederick C. Turner and Marita Carballo de Cilley, "Equality and Democracy," *International Social Science Journal*, no. 136 (May 1993): 271–283.

32. Samuel P. Huntington, "The Clash of Civilizations?" *Foreign Affairs* 72, no. 3 (summer 1993): 22–49. Huntington identifies the seven or eight major civilizations as "Western, Confucian, Japanese, Islamic, Hindu, Slavic-Orthodox, Latin American, and possibly African," p. 25.

33. Howard J. Wiarda, "Introduction: Social Change, Political Development, and the Latin American Tradition," in Howard J. Wiarda, ed., *Politics and Social Change in Latin America: Still a Distinct Tradition?* (Boulder: Westview Press, 1992), p. 20. See also chap. 3, "The Political Culture(s) of Latin America," in Howard J. Wiarda, *The Democratic Revolution in Latin America: History, Politics, and U. S. Policy* (New York: Holmes and Meier, 1990).

34. Howard J. Wiarda, "Conclusion: Toward a Model of Social Change and Political Development in Latin America—Summary, Implications, Frontiers," in Wiarda, ed., *Politics and Social Change in Latin America*, pp. 316–317, 327.

35. Lawrence E. Harrison, *Underdevelopment Is a State of Mind: The Latin American Case* (Lanham, Maryland: University Press of America, 1985), pp. xvi, 165. Harrison also noted, "By 'culture' I mean the values and attitudes a society inculcates in its people." In terms of prescriptions, Harrison's "hope is that the need for cultural change will be taken seriously by political and intellectual leaders," p. 176.

36. José Ignacio García Hamilton, *Los origenes de nuestra cultura autoritaria (e improductiva)* (Buenos Aires: Calbino y Asociados, Editores, 1990), pp. 16, 216, 225.

37. Seymour Martin Lipset, *The First New Nation: The United States in Historical and Comparative Perspective* (New York: Basic Books, 1963).

38. Larry Diamond and Juan J. Linz, "Introduction: Politics, Society, and Democracy in Latin America," in Larry Diamond, Juan J. Linz, and Seymour Martin Lipset, eds., *Latin America*, vol. 4 of *Democracy in Developing Countries* (Boulder: Lynne Rienner, 1989), pp. 10–11 and pp. 12–13.

39. John A. Booth and Mitchell A. Seligson, "The Political Culture of Authoritarianism in Mexico: A Reexamination," *Latin American Research Review* 19, no. 1 (1984): esp. p. 81.

40. Susan Tiano, "Authoritarianism and Political Culture in Argentina and Chile in the Mid-1960s," *Latin American Research Review* 21, no. 1 (1986), 81.

41. Letter from Peter H. Smith to Frederick C. Turner, August 5, 1993.

42. Booth and Seligson wrote that "the public participation and demand-making that do occur (which are carefully managed by the PRI), plus official propaganda and socialization efforts all combine to promote popular support for civil liberties, even though much of what actually transpires under such auspices is highly managed. The corporatist-populist elite of Mexico may in essence delude Mexicans into support for democratic values that simultaneously reinforce the system." Booth and Seligson, "The Political Culture of Authoritarianism in Mexico," pp. 119–120.

43. Discussion with Lourdes Arizpe, Palma de Mallorca, Spain, November 28, 1990. On the political socialization of Mexican children, see Rafael Segovia, *La politización del niño mexicano* (México, DF: El Colegio de México, 1975).

44. See Elisabeth Noelle-Neumann, *The Spiral of Silence: Public Opinion, Our Social Skin* (Chicago: University of Chicago Press, 1984).

45. Tiano, "Authoritarianism and Political Culture in Argentina and Chile in the Mid-1960s," p. 89.

46. On the tendencies for wider political participation, see Lawrence S. Graham, "Rethinking the Relationship Between the Strength of Local Institutions and the Consolidation of Democracy: The Case of Brazil," and Frederick C. Turner, "Municipal Government in Argentina and Chile: Democratization Processes and Their Causation," *Establishing Democratic Rule: The Reemergence of Local Government in Post-Authoritarian Systems*, a special issue of *In Depth* 3, no. 1 (winter 1993): 151–193. On the causal links between civic culture and democracy more broadly, see Edward N. Muller and Mitchell A. Seligson, "Civic Culture and Democracy: The Question of Causal Relationships," *American Political Science Review* 88, no. 3 (September 1994): 635–652.

47. Peter H. Smith, "On Democracy and Democratization," in Wiarda, ed., *Politics and Social Change in Latin America*, pp. 297–300.

48. Diamond and Linz, "Introduction: Politics, Society, and Democracy in Latin America," p. 14. See also Juan J. Linz, *The Breakdown of Democratic Regimes: Crisis, Breakdown, and Reequilibration* (Baltimore: Johns Hopkins University Press, 1978).

49. On the very extensive support in public opinion for the objectives of Colonel Hugo Chávez and the other leaders of the coup attempts, see José Vicente Carrasquero and Marco Cupolo, "The Venezuelan Democratic System and the Failed Coup Attempt" (paper presented at the annual conference of the World Association for Public Opinion Research, Saint Petersburg, Florida, May 16, 1992). In 1973, Robert Scott articulated this interpretation, which seemed particularly appropriate in the year that Augusto Pinochet Ugarte toppled the regime of Salvador Allende in Chile. The view was that ordinary citizens would support military coups and regimes, because they brought stability, because people could not support the psychological strains and economic uncertainties associated with

democratic experiments, and because, as Scott put it, "a military-style administration may be welcome as a surcease from 'future shock.'" Robert E. Scott, "National Integration Problems and Military Regimes in Latin America," in Robert E. Scott, ed., *Latin American Modernization Problems: Case Studies in the Crises of Change* (Urbana: University of Illinois Press, 1973), p. 330.

50. Between July 1991 and April 1992 the proportion of Venezuelans who said that they had little or no confidence in Venezuelan institutions rose sharply: from 44 percent to 85 percent for Congress, from 69 percent to 84 percent for the government, from 71 percent to 91 percent for the Confederación de Trabajadores, and from 90 percent to 91 percent for political parties. See table 7 in Friedrich Welsch, "Venezuela: Transformación de la cultura política," *Revista Nueva Sociedad*, no. 121 (August 1992), p. 20. Discussion with Friedrich Welsch, Storrs, Connecticut, June 28, 1993. Along with Gustavo Méndez, Welsch directs DOXA, one of the leading survey research firms in Venezuela and one of only three firms worldwide that successfully predicted the Sandinista defeat in Nicaragua. Welsch is also professor of political science at the Universidad Simón Bolívar and the Venezuelan national representative of the World Association for Public Opinion Research.

51. Edgardo Catterberg, *Argentina Confronts Politics: Political Culture and Public Opinion in the Argentine Transition to Democracy* (Boulder: Lynne Rienner, 1991), pp. 108–109.

52. Ibid., pp. 47, 57.

53. Ibid., p. 18. A fundamental reason that Argentines have accepted widespread privatization, despite the strong statist attitudes that once prevailed there, is the dramatic hyperinflation that the nation underwent in the 1980s. For a strong, data-based argument to this effect, see Fabián Echegaray, "Understanding Support for Free-Market Policies in Argentina," *International Journal of Public Opinion Research* 5, no. 4 (winter 1993): 369–375.

54. In 1981, Grondona wrote that Argentines wanted a rhythm for their public life that was "Lineal. Gradual. Constant," and, in essays that he wrote during the next decade he described political processes in Argentina as moving closer to these dimensions that he had advocated in 1981. See "¿Esta cambiando el humor político de los argentinos?" an article originally published in May 1981, and republished in Mariano Grondona, *La construcción de la democracia* (Buenos Aires: Editorial Universitaria de Buenos Aires, 1983), pp. 379–381.

55. Manuel Mora y Araujo, *Ensayo y error* (Buenos Aires: Planeta, 1991), pp. 59–60, 185. Italics in the original. In a Spanish that is difficult to render literally into English, Mora wrote that "Los nuevos valores fueron, efectivamente, privatistas, liberales, universalistas y productivistas," p. 60.

56. Oscar Mejía Quintana and Arlene B. Tickner, *Cultura y democracia en América Latina: Elementos para una reinterpretación de la cultura y la historia latinoamericanas* (Bogotá: M&T Editores, 1992), pp. 239–258.

57. Gustavo Lagos, "Humanismo y consenso para una estabilidad democrática," in Augusto Varas, ed., *Transición a la democracia: América Latina y Chile* (Santiago: Asociación Chilena de Investigaciones para la Paz, 1984), pp. 167–168.

58. Political questions could not be asked in Chile in 1983 under the Pinochet dictatorship.

59. Jeane Kirkpatrick, *Leader and Vanguard in Mass Society: A Study of Peronist Argentina* (Cambridge: MIT Press, 1971).

60. Wayne Cornelius investigated the original Civic Culture data in terms of issues of urbanization in Mexico, and Roberto Guimarães analyzed a survey dealing with leadership and political legitimacy in Argentina to study support for terrorism and political violence, issues that did not figure prominently in the original survey design. See Wayne Cornelius, "Urbanization as an Agent in Latin American Political Instability: The Case of Mexico," *American Political Science Review* 63, no. 3 (September 1969): 833–857, and Roberto P. Guimarães, "Understanding Support for Terrorism Through Survey Data: The Case of Argentina, 1973," in Frederick C. Turner and José Enrique Miguens, eds., *Juan Perón and the Reshaping of Argentina* (Pittsburgh: University of Pittsburgh Press, 1983).

61. While doing market research, Carmen Zayuelas discovered that Argentine housewives were giving up readymade products, going back to baking and making their own pasta at home, and, since this trend contradicted trends in other nations, she set out in her survey firm, IPSA S. A., to discover why. The answer was that the military governments of the *proceso* had engineered major advertising campaigns to convince Argentine women that they were the hearts of their families, that they needed to prevent political subversion by their children, and that, therefore, they should devote more time to their domestic duties and supervision of their teenagers. Interview with Carmen Zayuelas, Buenos Aires, August 25, 1990.

62. See especially José Agustín Silva Michelena, *The Illusion of Democracy in Dependent Nations* (Cambridge: M.I.T. Press, 1971).

63. A catalog of the holdings of the LASDB may be obtained by writing to the Director, Latin American Survey Data Bank, the Roper Center, P. O. Box 440, Storrs, Connecticut 06268. These data banks were created through a major grant from the Tinker Foundation and through matching funds raised in Brazil and Venezuela.

64. For an example of how the norms of national culture are defined, and redefined, partially in relation to other nations, see Frederick C. Turner and Marita Carballo de Cilley, "Argentine Attitudes toward the United States," *International Journal of Public Opinion Research* 1, no. 4 (December 1989): 279–293.

65. Clive Bean, "Conservative Cynicism: Political Culture in Australia," *International Journal of Public Opinion Research* 5, no. 1 (spring 1993), 70. Bean also found that religious affiliation and lower levels of education also tend to predict authoritarian attitudes in Australia. Karin Busch and Hans L. Zetterberg, "The Study of Values: Some Methodological Aspects" (paper presented at the Regional Conference of the World Association for Public Opinion Research, Tallinn, Estonia, June 11, 1993).

PART THREE

Political Roles of Social Science

One underlying theme throughout this volume concerns the way that social and political change affects social science. But there also exists a reciprocal effect, and thus the chapters in this section deal with the *uses* and *impacts* of social science research in processes of political transition.

In a case study of Peru, Catherine M. Conaghan shows how public opinion polling was used to legitimate the authoritarian *autogolpe* by Alberto Fujimori in April 1992. Acknowledging the orthodox wisdom that polls have a positive impact on democracy by giving voice to citizens, Conaghan examines alternative judgments—mostly by European analysts—to the effect that surveys can serve to "pacify" or "domesticate" public opinion. So it seems to have been in Peru. This presents a fundamental challenge: "If there is a positive side to the Fuji-golpe," Conaghan concludes, "it is that it forces Peruvian democrats back to the drawing board—to evaluate what went wrong and to think about how to construct a democracy that is meaningful to people. Public opinion research could be used to inform and animate the process of rethinking and restrategizing democratization in Peru."

A leading practitioner of public opinion research in Mexico, Miguel Basáñez examines the promise, and the difficulty, of conducting surveys in an undemocratic setting. The presidential campaign of 1988 triggered an explosion in political polling, he recounts, and governmental attempts at censorship had the unintended effect of skyrocketing interest within the general public. Over the years, the Mexican regime has taken a number of steps to curtail independent public opinion research—from economic sanctions to defamation of investigators to legal impediments—while building up its own in-house research capacity. And revealingly enough, intense political debates have often revolved around apparently obscure methodological questions (such as the classification of "undecided" voters). There will continue to be obstacles in the

225

short run, Basáñez concludes, but the long-run prospects for survey research are encouraging.

In the concluding chapter, Elena Bashkirova explores the nature and role of public opinion research in Eastern Europe and the former Soviet Union. In Russia, especially, the complexity and fragility of the political situation add considerable importance to popular surveys. Of course, survey research can provide an instrument for social control, as it did from the 1950s through the mid-1980s. But in the current context, polling results can expand the range of ideological tolerance, shape party platforms, and provide a mirror of social reality. It can also serve to disseminate information, combat apathy, and stimulate popular participation.

Taken together, these chapters provide empirical material for analytical approaches espoused through the course of this book: intraregional comparison, between Peru and Mexico (or between Eastern Europe, Russia, and other former republics of the Soviet Union), and cross-regional comparison, between Latin America (or Mexico or Peru) and Eastern Europe or the former USSR. The authors also raise fundamental questions: Under what circumstances does public opinion research promote democracy? And when does it serve authoritarian ends? More broadly, this query applies to the social sciences in general: What are the political and social functions of scholarship?

CHAPTER NINE

■

Polls, Political Discourse, and the Public Sphere: The Spin on Peru's Fuji-golpe

Catherine M. Conaghan

ON THE EVENING OF APRIL 5, 1992, TANKS ROLLED through the streets of Lima as President Alberto Fujimori announced his decision to disband the national Congress, dismiss the judiciary, and suspend the Constitution. Fujimori's creation of a "government of emergency and national reconstruction" constituted the first definitive breach in Peru's constitutional order since its political transition from military rule in 1980; it also counted as the first outright deviation from Latin America's most recent wave of political democratization.

Within hours of the "Fuji-golpe," a different kind of army—one composed of dozens of interviewers hired by commercial polling firms—fanned out across Lima to gather public reaction to the event. By any standards, the results of the initial "flash" polls and the ones that followed in the ensuing weeks were extraordinary. All the polls showed overwhelming public approval of Fujimori's actions. The approval ratings registered in the 70 to 80 percent range.

The polls became Fujimori's most powerful tool in his campaign to legitimate the new regime in the eyes of both domestic and international audiences. In declarations to the press immediately after the coup, Fujimori flatly stated his understanding of the new political equation: "The measures taken last Sunday have popular approval of the majority and this gives them [the measures] legitimacy."[1] Meanwhile, opposition deputies of the disbanded Congress floundered in their initial attempts to mobilize against the de facto government, disheartened by the public's apparent disinterest in their efforts.

227

In this chapter I examine the role that polls played in the recent regime change in Peru. The Peruvian experience is important because it raises serious questions about the impact of public opinion research on political development, particularly its repercussions in countries still struggling through early stages of democratization and institution-building. Debate about the impact of polls on democracy is not new. Starting with George Gallup, U.S. pollsters have argued that polls have a positive impact on democracy because they "give voice" to the opinions of citizens who might otherwise be ignored by politicians in the interims between elections.[2]

In contrast with this populist interpretation of polls is a diverse body of critical work pointing to the perverse effects of polls on democracy.[3] Work by C. Wright Mills and the Frankfurt School, produced following the end of World War II, raised profound questions about the authenticity of the views expressed by "mass" publics.[4] More recently, Benjamin Ginsberg argued that polls are used by elites to "pacify or domesticate opinion" in a variety of ways; polls reduce citizens to passive respondents who voice opinions in reference to an elite-determined range of choices.[5] The ideas of Michel Foucault have inspired an approach to polls as yet another modern "disciplinary mechanism" of surveillance and social control.[6] Pierre Bourdieu can also be found among the ranks of poll critics. He argued that much of what is depicted as public opinion is an artifact of polls themselves, that is, polls create the impression of a formed public opinion, which, in many instances, does not exist. According to Bourdieu, "The fundamental effect of polls is to create the idea that a unanimous public opinion exists in order to legitimate policy."[7]

The work of Jürgen Habermas also provides a rich point of departure for critical reflections on public opinion and the impact of polling on democracy. In his early work on the subject, Habermas was concerned with the ways in which opinion research was used for the purposes of manipulation and domination.[8] In Habermas's view, authentic public opinion can only be formed through a process of rational-critical debate among citizens. Such debates take place within a public sphere, which is an autonomous terrain between state and society where citizens are free to become informed and exchange views without interference by state institutions. In seventeenth- and eighteenth-century Europe, salons, coffeehouses, and clubs were the sites of the public sphere, and citizens gathered there to confer and form opinions about public affairs. James Curran summarized Habermas's model of the public sphere: "a neutral zone where access to relevant information affecting the public good is widely available, where discussion is free of domination by the state and where all those participating in public debate do so on an equal basis. Within this public sphere, people collectively determine through the processes of rational argument the way in which they want to see society develop, and this shapes in turn the conduct of government policy. The media facilitates this process by providing an arena of public debate, and by reconstituting private citizens as a public body in the form of public opinion."[9]

According to Habermas, this "bourgeois public sphere" collapsed and was replaced by a different kind of public sphere with the onset of the welfare state and mass democracy. The mass media and mass-based organizations constituted the new channels of a public sphere, but ones that were highly susceptible to manipulation by the state.[10] Habermas concluded that much of what is portrayed as "public opinion" (as expressed in elections, plebiscites, or polls) is in fact "nonpublic opinion," an aggregate of shifting moods that does not represent an informed and autonomous judgment by a "reasoning public."

Drawing heavily on the work of Habermas, Susan Herbst pointed to how polls undermine the prospects for such rational-critical debate— namely the capacity of polls to *shut down* rather than stimulate reasoned public discussion. As Herbst put it, "In a way, polls make many public discussions superfluous, since they give the illusion that the public has already spoken in a definitive manner. When the polls are published, and presidents and policymakers claim that they will heed these polls, what more is there to say?"[11]

So far, the impact of polling on late-democratizing countries such as those in Latin America or Eastern Europe has not received much attention. Nor have scholars systematically attempted to describe the problematical nature of the public sphere in these evolving polities. Yet, if the arguments about the detrimental effects of polls on the quality of democracy have any validity, the topic should be regarded as an important new issue in the research agenda of comparative politics. The effects of polls and their relationship to the public sphere may be especially germane to our current discussions regarding the evolution of regime types.[12] Among the many questions that might be posed are the following: How does the availability and legitimacy of such quantified measures of public opinion affect the discourses and behavior of political elites in situations in which the "regime rules" are still fluid? Does the availability of such information (which is projected as scientific knowledge) enhance or diminish the public sphere in the sense of opening up or closing down civic discussions? If polling does indeed contribute to the debasement of the public sphere, what kinds of democracies are being constituted? Alternatively, can public opinion research be designed and used in ways that would help stimulate inclusive public debates, especially in countries where highly inegalitarian class structures have traditionally created obstacles to popular participation in national political life?

Because the polls relayed genuine popular frustrations about the malfunctioning of Peruvian democracy, they provided Fujimori with a rationale for breaking with the Constitution. With evidence of public support for his actions in hand, Fujimori was able to present his breach of the Constitution as a democratic exercise. Fujimori used polls to legitimate his assault on institutions and to steamroll ahead with political reforms that accelerated the disorganization of the party system, weakened the legislature, and concentrated even more power in an already near-imperial presidency.[13]

Yet polls have not worked unequivocally in favor of an authoritarian remaking of the political system. In the wake of the coup, its opponents tried to fashion an alternative discourse based on polls, an action that emphasizes the contingent nature of popular support for Fujimori and the "limits" posed by public opinion. Polls continue to confirm the presence of widespread support for basic democratic values in Peru (e.g., respect for human rights, commitment to elections); as such, polls are being used to promote the idea that such norms cannot be transgressed by the government without incurring significant political costs. This poll-based portrayal of a domestic consensus about basic democratic values coincided with the international lobby to restore "democratic institutionality" in Peru. In response to those pressures, Fujimori was forced to call an election for a constituent assembly in November 1992, to go forward with postponed municipal elections in January 1993, and to hold a referendum on the new Constitution in October 1993.

In the remainder of this chapter, I focus on the rhetorical and symbolic uses of poll results in the unfolding of recent events in Peru—the ways in which polls were interpreted and reinterpreted by political elites and the news media in Peru. The "spin" on the polls by elites has been an important factor in defining options and political strategies in the ongoing process of regime change.[14] □

WHERE THE NUMBERS COME FROM: AN ASCENDANT OPINION INDUSTRY

As in most of Latin America, the Peruvian public opinion industry is a relatively new business, one that emerged with the reinstatement of elections and civilian rule during the 1980s. Peru's first major political poll was done by a commercial firm, Indices U., in conjunction with the 1963 presidential election that brought Fernando Belaúnde to power. But the military coup of 1968 and the ensuing dictatorship interrupted further development of commercial political polling until 1978.

As in the United States, news organizations generated much of the initial demand for public opinion polling in Peru. Compañía Peruana de

Investigación (CPI), a market research firm, was commissioned by the newspaper *El Comercio* to conduct preelection polls for the 1978 constituent assembly election. Manuel Torrado, trained in the Gallup organization in Spain, left CPI in 1980 to form his own firm, Datum S.A. Datum was subsequently commissioned by the leading newsmagazine, *Caretas*, to provide its political polling in the early 1980s. *Caretas* became a regular publisher of polls, featuring the first presidential approval rating during the Belaúnde government. The media continue to rely on commercial firms for public opinion data; unlike in the United States, in Peru there is no in-house polling by news organizations themselves, other than the nonrandom "person-in-the-street" interviews sometimes used by television.

Thus far, the academic community has not played a leading role in the development of opinion research in Peru. Political polling developed as an extension of commercial market research.[15] Along with Datum, Imasen, and CPI, Apoyo S.A., founded in 1984 and headed by Alfredo Torres Guzmán, became a high-profile player in political polling as well as in market research. In addition to traditional types of survey research, the firms also use election simulations and the "focus group" technique to probe the public's reactions to products and political candidates.[16]

Like people in any new profession, Peruvian pollsters have struggled to establish their claims to legitimacy as practitioners of a neutral "science" and to counter the frequent criticisms of polls as biased public relations gimmicks made-to-order for their political clients.[17] Errors in election predictions periodically trigger charges of political manipulation or methodological incompetence. In the 1990 presidential campaign, for example, leaders of the Alianza Popular Revolucionaria Americana (APRA) party accused Apoyo of systematically overestimating voter support for the rightist candidate, Mario Vargas Llosa.[18] As part of an effort to set common standards of practice, the majority of polling firms have joined the professional association, the Asociación Peruana de Empresas de Investigación de Mercados (APEIM). APEIM vigorously defended the practices of their member firms during the APRA attack of 1990.[19]

Swift population increases in Lima and the inadequate physical infrastructure of Peru create a variety of problems for pollsters. Since only a small fraction of the population has telephones, polling must be done through personal interviewing. Because of inadequacies in national census data, pollsters have had to improvise methods to ensure an adequate sampling in new neighborhoods, particularly in the poor *pueblos jóvenes* that cover the landscape around Lima. Given the transportation difficulties and cost considerations, most polls completely ignore the rural population of the interior and are confined to Lima. The "national" polls are based on samples exclusively from urban areas. Along with the problems of potential sampling error, political conditions in Peru sometimes heighten the likelihood of nonsampling errors. For example, some of the errors in the 1990 preelection polls have been attributed to the nightly curfew in Lima. The curfew, enacted as part of the security measures against Sendero Luminoso, forced more interviewing during the daytime hours; this is thought to have overrepresented conservative voters and inflated support of Mario Vargas Llosa in the polls.[20] According to one pollster, the surge in Sendero violence also made people more suspicious of unknown interviewers and contributed to heightened refusal rates in surveys.[21]

These problems notwithstanding, the growth of commercial polling has rendered urban Peru a "surveyed society"—one in which mass preferences on everything from shampoo to television shows to politics are constantly probed and scrutinized. Some of this information is recycled to the public through the news media. Private consumption of polling data by elites also takes place through confidential reports and newsletters, which are circulated by the commercial firms to their customers.[22] □

OMENS AND IMAGES:
THE PRECOUP POLLS

When viewed against the backdrop of previous poll results, the actions of President Fujimori on April 5, 1992, appear far less audacious than they might have originally seemed to outside observers. Polls documented a steady decline of public confidence in government institutions and political parties, and they thus served up the raw materials for the coup; they provided the ideological justification for it (i.e., the actions could be depicted as the "will of the people") and could be taken as evidence of the political feasibility of such a measure. The collapse of trust in government, especially in political parties, became a touchstone in Peruvian political discourse in conjunction with the 1990 presidential election. In his 1989 profile of the Peruvian electorate, Alfredo Torres of Apoyo noted that only 17 percent of those surveyed expressed confidence in political parties; this finding corresponded with the low ratings of other government institutions.[23] The early popularity of the presidential candidacy of Mario Vargas Llosa was widely interpreted as a function of his image as a nontraditional, independent candidate—an image that was progressively lost during the last months leading to the first round.[24]

Fujimori's surprising victory in the 1990 race was attributed, at least in part, to his ability to capitalize on the negative public sentiment toward parties and traditional politicians. Once in power, Fujimori persisted with nonstop attacks on the party system; he blamed politicians in

Congress for creating obstacles to his economic program and the military campaign against the guerrilla movement, Sendero Luminoso. In September 1991, an Apoyo poll reported a steep decline in public confidence in the Congress; only 19 percent of the public surveyed expressed confidence, in comparison with the 45 percent confidence rating they had registered in their poll of September 1990. In the same poll, the confidence rating for political parties slipped to a mere 13 percent (see Table 9.1).

In December 1991, Fujimori used the occasion of his address to an annual conference of business executives to make a blistering attack on parties and other governmental institutions. Fujimori declared that it was time *hacer y luego hablar* ("to act now and to talk later") and floated the idea of major institutional restructuring. His proposals included plans for midterm congressional elections and the reorganization of the judiciary and national comptroller's office.

Fujimori's aggressive posturing found a favorable response in the polls. Apoyo reported from 70 percent to 80 percent approval for Fujimori's specific proposals of institutional reorganization; the approval rating of Fujimori's governing philosophy of "act now and talk later" was 60 percent. In a report submitted to Congress in December 1991, Datum also pointed to the extreme deterioration of the image of all gov-

TABLE 9.1 Confidence in National Institutions: Peru, 1990–1992 (percentages)

	Sept. 1990	March 1991	Sept. 1991	March 1992	Sept. 1992
Central Bank	44	35	27	40	39
Cabinet	52	25	24	27	37
Public schools	38	33	–	30	5
Armed forces	58	53	47	54	57
Public hospital	23	23	–	21	38
Church	81	83	85	80	81
Social security	23	23	32	30	37
Mass media	60	48	55	57	58
Parties	21	13	13	12	13
Courts	23	16	22	14	28
Police	47	31	33	20	48
Presidency	57	29	26	42	54
Congress	45	19	19	17	–

Source: Data courtesy of Apoyo S.A., September 1992.

ernment institutions, with the exception of the presidency. On the basis of their findings, Datum urged congressional leaders to initiate reforms to streamline the legislature and to improve its public image.[25]

Congressional leaders did not act on the recommendations of the Datum report. Instead, the first three months of 1992 were dominated by clashes between the Congress and Fujimori over budgetary matters and new antisubversion laws. A controversial Supreme Court decision only added to the mix of intense intergovernmental conflict. In February, the Supreme Court ruled that there was insufficient evidence to pursue corruption charges against former President Alan García and dismissed the case. García, despite his enormous unpopularity, continued with his high-profile attacks on the Fujimori government.

Fujimori also proceeded with his rhetorical attacks on Congress and the judiciary, and he again received a positive response in polls to the attacks. As the data in Table 9.2 show, Fujimori's presidential approval rating stood at 64 percent in February 1992; this represented a substantial improvement over his 35 percent approval rating of a year earlier.[26]

By March 1992, the confidence rating for Congress fell to an all-time low of 17 percent, but confidence in the presidency recouped to 42 percent, after having fallen to a low of 26 percent in mid-1991 (Table 9.1). Moreover, the Supreme Court decision on the García case proved to be wildly unpopular; Apoyo reported that 60 percent of the public disagreed with the Supreme Court determination about the lack of evidence and that 72 percent of those surveyed said they did not trust the judiciary.

According to Alfredo Torres, the polls clearly indicated that "conditions were extant for the institutional coup" of April 5, 1992.[27] Yet it is important to note that the polls did not unilaterally demonstrate that the public supported a breach of the Constitution and a movement toward authoritarian government. The newspaper *Expreso* commissioned a Datum poll to explore the character of the support for Fujimori. The poll results were published in January 1992, along with a commentary by sociologist Julio Cotler, an outspoken critic of Fujimori's governing style. Cotler argued that the Datum results showed strong support for the notion of checks and balances among governmental branches; 85 percent of those surveyed agreed that Congress should have oversight functions vis-à-vis the executive branch. Moreover, 68 percent of the respondents rejected the notion that the "president should be able to govern without interference." A large majority, 83 percent of those sampled, agreed that it would be best to have a government that made policies on the basis of agreements among a broad array of political and social forces. On the basis of the results, Cotler challenged what he saw as the reigning notion in the presidential palace—that is, that the public favored a *mano dura* ("heavy hand"). Cotler cautioned, "A broad majority favors democratic

TABLE 9.2   Approval Rating of Alberto Fujimori as President, 1990–1993 (percentage of respondents expressing approval in answering the following question: "In general, do you approve or disapprove of Alberto Fujimori as president?")

	1990	1991	1992	1993
January	–	43	65	60
February	–	35	64	62
March	–	38	53	61
April	–	49	81[a]	63
May	–	45	76	59
June	–	35	76	66
July	–	31	65	61
August	46	39	62	n.a.
September	51	32	74[b]	n.a.
October	53	54	68	n.a.
November	59	58	65	n.a.
December	61	60	64	n.a.

[a] Rating after the April 5, 1992, coup.
[b] Rating after the capture of Sendero Luminoso leader, Abimael Guzmán.
n.a.: Data not available at time of publication.

Source: Data courtesy of Apoyo S.A., September 1992.

forms of government: they want a president controlled by parliamentary representatives and not an emperor. ... These results should re-educate the president as to the need to abandon authoritarian measures and expressions and come together with different forces in the citizenry to strengthen the precarious democratic institutionality."[28]

Thus, even prior to the coup, there was an alternative interpretation of public opinion that emphasized the public's desire to see more consensus and cooperation. Clearly, that was not the interpretation that Fujimori and his advisers favored. Starting on April 6, Fujimori's campaign to assert a uniform interpretation of Peruvian public opinion began in earnest. □

LA HISTORIA OFICIAL:
LEGITIMATING THE COUP

In the televised speech delivered at 10:30 P.M. on April 5, Fujimori laid out his initial justification for closing Congress and suspending the Constitution. Fujimori argued that Peru's democratic institutions were a deceptive formality—a facade used by self-serving interest groups and party elites that was hindering Peru's struggle against subversion, narcotrafficking, and chronic economic crisis. In contrast to the immorality and obstructionism of other public officials, Fujimori portrayed himself and his administration as the only agency capable of bringing about the profound socioeconomic transformations that Peru needed. From the start, Fujimori framed the coup as a democratic exercise. He concluded the speech by reiterating that the coup was "not a negation of real democracy, but on the contrary, it is the initiation of a search for an authentic transformation to assure a legitimate and effective democracy."[29]

By the next day, every commercial polling firm had a survey under way. On the morning of April 7, the official government newspaper, *El Peruano*, cited a poll by Peruana de Opinión Pública (POP) reporting that 73 percent of the public supported the president's actions. Although the rapidity with which POP produced its survey provoked questions by some as to the integrity of the results, data collected by Apoyo, Datum, and CPI over the next week confirmed the popularity of the measures. Apoyo, Datum, and CPI reported approval of the closure of Congress at 71 percent, 84 percent, and 87.2 percent, respectively. The approval ratings of Fujimori's presidential performance after the coup also showed marked upward swing from his precoup rating. Datum reported a jump from a precoup rating of 63 percent to 79 percent after April 5. As seen in Table 9.2, Apoyo noted a similar climb, moving from 53 percent in March 1992 to 81 percent after the April 5 coup.

The poll results were immediately incorporated into the official discourse defending the coup. In his first postcoup speech, delivered at the Association of Exporters (Asociación de Exportadores, ADEX) on April 9, Fujimori reminded journalists of the high level of public support for the measures and asserted that the Peruvian people should have the right to determine their own political future. Fujimori challenged the journalists to conduct their own polls if they had any doubts as to the accuracy of the statistics.[30] In a subsequent television appearance, Fujimori repeated references to the approval ratings of the polls.[31] In a statement to the Mexican press, Fujimori reiterated the argument that Peruvian democracy had been a "shell without content" and that the coup had simply broken through a "chain of corruption." Once again, he underscored the extent of popular support for the coup and expressed the hope that the world would understand that what had happened in Peru was "a popular uprising within order."[32]

Fujimori's plea for world understanding of the *autogolpe* as a "popular uprising" expressed in polls came in reply to a crescendo of international condemnation. The Organization of American States (OAS) convened to discuss possible sanctions against Peru and individual Latin American countries, and it expressed varying levels of dismay over the rupture of democratic institutions. President Carlos Andrés Pérez of Venezuela suspended diplomatic relations with Peru.[33] In the United States, the Bush administration decried the coup as "unjustified" and "unacceptable."[34] The *New York Times* editorialized against the coup and joined in the calls for economic sanctions.[35]

It was immediately evident that Fujimori had seriously misjudged how the coup would be received in international circles. The external backlash threatened to undo the efforts to "reinsert" Peru into the international financial community, after the isolation induced by President García's militant position on debt issues. Heavy-handed government tactics at the outset—the house arrest of congressional leaders, the detention of journalist Gustavo Gorriti, the street beatings of protesting congressional representatives, and the occupation of newspaper and magazine offices—conjured up images of a traditional military-style seizure of power.[36] To international observers watching the televised images on the Cable News Network (CNN), the first few days of the "emergency government" appeared ominous.

Foreign Minister Augusto Blacker Miller was dispatched to the OAS in Washington to ward off the movement to impose sanctions on Peru, favored by Canada and the United States. His speech to the OAS on April 13 played heavily on the notion that the coup was legitimated by virtue of the 90 percent approval ratings expressed in polls. Blacker Miller repeated Fujimori's argument about inefficiency and corruption of Peruvian institutions; the official view was that the coup replaced the "formal legality" represented by these institutions with a "real legality" based on "the will of the people in their broad and complete acceptance." At the end of the speech, Blacker Miller reiterated the equation of poll results and governmental legitimacy, noting that "the popular support on which we rely and that is made clear in the results of polls carried out on a near daily basis confers on us [the Fujimori government] the status of being the legitimate bearers of the sovereign will [of the people]." Blacker Miller concluded by characterizing himself "only as the intermediary for the immense majority of the Peruvian people."[37]

The Peruvian diplomatic mission was successful insofar as the OAS postponed imposing any concrete sanctions, but intense diplomatic pressures on the Fujimori government continued. The OAS and the U.S. government demanded to see a concrete plan and timetable for returning the country to "democratic institutionality." By mid-May, Fujimori was forced to jettison his initial idea of holding a mid-July plebiscite to ratify the coup and mandate constitutional reform. It was replaced by a proposal to elect a constituent assembly, a formula more likely to find support in the OAS, which was insisting on a return to "representative" democracy.

Fujimori presented the new transition recipe to an OAS gathering in the Bahamas on May 19. The occasion also presented an opportunity for Fujimori to put forth a more elaborate justification of his actions based on a lengthy analysis of Peru as a *partidocracia* ("party-ocracy"). Fujimori portrayed precoup Peru as a pseudodemocracy, a disguised dictatorship run by self-serving and incompetent party elites. These elites, according to Fujimori, did not function as legitimate representatives because they did not enjoy popular support; he pointed to poll results reporting that only 9 percent of the public belonged to a political party. In contrast, Fujimori pointed to his own origins as an "independent" candidate whose electoral victory was based on a groundswell of popular support.[38]

The poll-based claims to legitimacy of the Fujimori government were rehearsed by much of the domestic news media. Influential newspaper columnists Manuel D'Ornellas and Patricio Ricketts regularly contemplated poll findings and attested to their veracity. Television and newspapers produced a steady diet of poll results as evidence of the popularity of the *autogolpe*. □

REPLACING DEMOCRACY WITH POLLS: THE CRITIQUES

The government-defined discourse on polls did not go completely unchallenged. Domestic opponents of the coup raised a variety of questions regarding the results and the desirability of using polling data as a justification for the installation of a de facto government. In addition, Fujimori's critics reasserted the earlier argument by Cotler that support for the government was conditional and that public opinion demarcated clear limits on Fujimori's ability to restructure the rules of the political game.

One initial and obvious response to the official discourse was to challenge the accuracy of the polls themselves. Mario Vargas Llosa, the novelist and presidential candidate who was defeated by Fujimori in 1990, vigorously condemned the *autogolpe* and intimated that the results had been manipulated in some way.[39] But the vague suggestion that the results had been tampered with to favor the government did not seem likely, even to fellow opponents of the coup. The polling firms reported similar findings across the board; moreover, some of the firms were associated with political opponents of the coup and would have been delighted to produce results to undercut Fujimori's claims. Apoyo S.A., the firm headed by Alfredo Torres Guzmán, issued its procoup poll results, with a terse statement of opposition to the coup noting that "professional responsibility obliges us to furnish information which is both timely and true. Because of this, we make these results public."[40]

An editorial in the opposition newspaper *La República* heated up the polemic on polls and contested the government's use of them along a number of lines.[41] The editorial raised questions as to the accuracy of polling data, citing previous mistakes by the polling firms in preelection projections. In addition, the newspaper pointed to the fickleness of public opinion and to the ethical and political problems associated with policymaking via polls. Finally, the editorial suggested that something of a "bandwagon" effect was taking place—that the polls themselves, by showing a large margin in favor of Fujimori, were artificially inflating the level of support for him. On the following day, *La República* published a column by leftist politician and intellectual Henry Pease García, who pointed to the passive and atomized character of the opinions expressed in polls. Pease contrasted this disembodied style of opinion with that which is forged out of an active process of discussion in parties, the media, and organizations of civil society.[42]

Attacks on the polls also emanated from the leading newsmagazine opposed to the Fuji-golpe, *Caretas*. The first volley came in April with a reprint of the Datum poll of January 1992, which showed support for congressional oversight of the presidency. When it referred to public opinion circa January, *Caretas* emphasized the volatility of polls and suggested that Fujimori's support could evaporate quickly.[43] In the same edition of the magazine, Aprista columnist Luís Alberto Sánchez ridiculed the polls, suggesting that they were simply tapping popular ignorance and a desire for conformity. "The illiterate is the primary object of the survey. A young woman or man stops an ordinary guy on the street and asks him what he thinks of the government, the regional system, the economic model—and the poor guy, so as not to be stumped, answers anything or answers what the pollsters have hinted at."[44]

In a subsequent piece entitled "Strange Surveys," *Caretas* underscored the difficulties of tapping genuine opinions in the political climate of Lima, citing a refusal rate in surveys of at least 50 percent. "It's one thing to knock on the door and ask about preferences in soap or radio stations, it's another thing to inquire about opinion concerning a de facto government," noted the magazine. The article went on to mention previous cases in Peru in which polls erred in their electoral forecasts, and it cited the most notorious Latin American experience with polling errors—that of the 1990 Nicaraguan presidential elections.[45] *Caretas* then made brief reference to Elisabeth Noelle-Neumann's controversial "spiral of silence" thesis, which asserts that people express opinions in surveys so as to conform with what they believe is the dominant, socially acceptable opinion.[46]

But the attempt to cast doubts on the methodology of the polls did not resonate, either domestically or among international observers. The intellectual counterattack on the polls was scattershot. Even though the newspaper *La República* and the newsmagazine *Caretas* had challenged the method and substance of polls (the possibility of a bandwagon effect, the "framing" effect of media coverage, a "spiral of silence" syndrome, the meaning of high refusal rates, the possibility of "interviewer" effect on respondents, and so forth), there was no concerted effort by parties, the press, or the social science community to systematically appraise the limitations of public opinion polling in a political atmosphere as volatile as that which prevailed in Peru.[47]

Several factors account for this uneven and ineffective response to Fujimori's discourse. As a major disseminator of polling data, the press as a whole had neither the skill nor the interest in spearheading national soul-searching about the uses and abuses of polls.[48] Although some of the news media (especially *La República* and *Caretas*) opposed the coup, other news sources did not—most notably the government newspaper, *El Peruano*, another newspaper, *Expreso*, and television stations. Procoup editorial positions of these organizations ruled out any effort to question the methods and content of polls.

Like the press, political parties did not have the in-house expertise to launch a studied attack on the polls. Moreover, as long-time consumers of polls themselves, many politicians had become accustomed to taking the numbers at face value. At the same time, attacks on the polls fell flat because they smacked of "sour grapes"—as the objects of vilification in polls, it seemed only natural that politicians would attempt to reject the findings.

The press and political parties had themselves been active participants in a process that turned polls into a critical instrument in Peruvian public life, but knowledge and control over the instrument was left in the hands of a small number of private commercial firms. This monopolization of public opinion expertise by those firms meant that there was no "critical mass" of experts outside the industry who were capable of mounting an intelligible and credible counteroffensive in the aftermath of the coup. Fujimori's capacity to exploit the polls to such a degree was yet another manifestation of the weaknesses in Peruvian parties and civil society.

Predictably, the polling community vigorously defended its methods; and the sheer continuity in popular support for Fujimori in the months following the coup ran counter to the argument that the initial findings were aberrant in some way—a reflection of fear, misunderstanding, or blatant manipulation.[49] Although he defended the integrity of the polls themselves, pollster Alfredo Torres Guzmán challenged the wisdom of tying government legitimacy to presidential approval ratings. In a column published in the newspaper *Expreso*, Torres characterized public opinion as expressed in polls as "volatile, emotional, ill-informed, [possessing] a fragile memory" and illustrated his point with a reference to the precipitous plunge in George Bush's approval ratings after they had previously climbed to an astronomical high during the Gulf War.[50] Torres cautioned that governments too closely attuned to poll findings were likely to fall into demagoguery and populism. He urged the opposition not to dismiss the findings of the polls as irrelevant, but to reflect on their message. Although Torres acknowledged that a majority of Peruvians were willing to concede some dictatorial powers to Fujimori, he emphasized the poll findings, indicating that the concession was conceived as a partial and transitory one by most of the public.

When people were queried about the prospect of Fujimori failing to return the country to constitutional rule, 69 percent of the public voiced disapproval. When respondents were asked if they would approve of the Fujimori government if the military were to be accorded greater influence, 64 percent said they would disapprove. An overwhelming majority of those polled, 87 percent, said they would not approve of the Fujimori government in the event that it restricted freedom of the press. In addition, majorities favored the holding of scheduled municipal elections in 1993 and presidential elections in 1995, with new parliamentary elections prior to 1995. When they were queried in general terms about democracy, most Peruvians responded affirmatively; 57 percent of those questioned in an Apoyo poll in June 1992 said they favored democracy and freedom of speech to a government of law and order. In fact, public approval of the coup was linked to the public's perception that it did not constitute a rupture of Peruvian democracy; 54 percent of those polled after April 5 characterized the government as "democratic" rather than "dictatorial." When they were asked to identify the defining characteristics of democracy, most respondents identified an "elected president" and "civil liberties" as the most important; the presence of other institutions (such as Congress) was not deemed as important by the public—thus the continuing identification of the Fujimori government as "democratic."

The contradictory mix in the polls after April 5 did not indicate that Peruvians were ready to accept a blatant slide into authoritarianism. Instead, Torres and other analysts characterized the support for Fujimori as conditional and performance-based. The data in Table 9.3 show the extent to which approval for Fujimori was linked to the restoration of elections and effective policy performance.

Torres concluded that "out of every four Peruvians who support the government, only one does so unconditionally. The other three support the government only under the condition that it returns to constitutional rule." □

DOMESTIC DISCOURSE
AND INTERNATIONAL PRESSURES

It is not unusual for coups to be made in the name of the "the people." What was novel about Peru's Fuji-golpe was that the assertion could be tied to a body of "scientific" data. The immediate availability of quantified measures of public approval lent a credibility to Fujimori's political discourse that it might otherwise have lacked. At the same time, the data that showed low levels of trust in political parties and the Congress helped to strip away the opposition's claims to legitimacy based on their functions as "representatives" of the people.

The anticoup forces were left to struggle with the question of how to interpret the polls—or, more precisely, how to renegotiate the meaning of the poll results in public discussion so as to establish some role for themselves in defining the ongoing process of regime change. As noted earlier, an initial response was to deny either the accuracy or the significance of the numbers. But one of the serious problems with denial as a discursive strategy was that it seemed to play right into Fujimori's hand—to deny meaning to the polls seemed like the stereotypical act of an arrogant political elite, completely out of touch with popular sentiments.

Rather than denying the polls, some opponents of the Fuji-golpe suggested that the results be taken seriously and be used to spark a process of self-criticism and renewal in the party system. The strategy of taking the numbers seriously also meant that the opposition could use the poll results credibly for ideological containment, that is, to restrain attempts by Fujimori or his allies in the military to move the regime in an even more authoritarian direction.

This "conditional" support interpretation of public opinion dovetailed with U.S. and OAS pressure on Fujimori to return the country to "democratic institutionality." These mutually reinforcing democratic discourses emanating both from abroad and from within Peru were an important element in shaping the parameters of the regime transition after April 5. Fujimori's original proposal for postcoup political restructuring involved an immediate plebiscite to affirm public support, to be followed by a government-directed constitutional reform, subsequent legislative elections, and a reopening of Congress on April 5, 1993. But the OAS pushed for a quicker reinstatement of "representative democracy," insisting on the importance of reestablishing the electoral connections of government to the public.

The OAS push for a reestablishment of representative mechanisms and a reentry of opposition political forces into the political arena had an important referent in public opinion data. Questions posed in various

TABLE 9.3   Conditions of Continued Approval/Disapproval of
Fujimori Presidency, 1992 (Percentages of responses when the following
question was posed to respondents who indicated approval of Fujimori's
performance as president: "Would you continue approving of the president's
performance if ...?")

	Continued Approval	Disapprove	No Response
Unemployment increases	19.8	38.0	7.8
Constituent assembly elections are not held	19.3	37.5	8.8
Inflation increases	16.8	39.5	9.3
Indefinite postponement of municipal elections	13.0	42.5	9.0
Terrorism increases	8.5	47.8	9.3
Corruption increases	1.5	54.8	9.3
Total number of interviews	400		

Source: IMASEN, June 1992. Data cited by Marcial Rubio, "El espejismo de la
fuerza," Quehacer 77 (May–June 1992), 7.

surveys produced findings showing that the public did not want to completely cede policymaking initiatives or deliberative powers to the executive. For example, Caretas published a June Datum poll, reporting that 55
percent of the public believed that a constituent assembly, not the executive, should design a new political parties law. In the same article,
another poll indicated that 54 percent of the public was in favor of a dialogue between Fujimori and political party leaders.[51] In an Apoyo poll,
an overwhelming 85 percent of the public wanted the 1992 municipal
elections to proceed as scheduled.

The obvious interpretation of these findings was that most Peruvians
did not view the coup as a carte blanche to suspend the electoral process
or to unilaterally dictate the course of political reform. As Fujimori and
his advisers vacillated over the timetable and sequencing of the transition mechanisms, Caretas exhorted Fujimori to heed the message of the
polls that he "defended so much and praised."[52]

Thus diverse types of poll data could be marshaled as part of an
oppositional discourse reasserting principles of representative democracy. The confluence of the domestic oppositional discourse and international pressures were important to the dynamics of the transition process
and forced a readjustment in Fujimori's approach to the mechanics of
restoring "democratic institutionality." □

POLLS AND THE MISSING PUBLIC

The Peruvian case is a fascinating and troubling example of how polls can become powerful rhetorical tools in the hands of elites. In democratic systems, regime legitimacy is tied to notions of popular sovereignty. With polls in hand, political elites can represent their opinions and actions as expressions of the public's will. The potency of polls in the elaboration of such elite discourses stems from survey research's claim to "scientific" status and the attendant appeal of numeracy.[53]

It would be a gross oversimplification to conclude on the basis of this case study that polls exert a wholly negative effect on developing democratic systems. The Peruvian case amply demonstrates the malleability of public opinion research, however. Clearly, the effect of polling on political systems has to do with how elites understand and represent the meaning of poll results. Polls can be wielded for democratic or antidemocratic ends.

To conclude, I would like to return to the broader concern of the role that polls may play in the construction or disintegration of the public sphere in incipient democracies, because I think that Habermas's notion of the public sphere may be particularly useful in scholarly efforts to understand what kinds of regimes are being constituted in countries where some liberal democratic practices are in place (e.g., elections, civil liberties) but where the quality of democracy persistently appears to be compromised. Habermas's notion of the public sphere as a normative ideal draws attention to the importance of access to information and discussion as part of the experience of the democracy. Without opportunities for such informed conversation among citizens, democracy is reduced to what Habermas views as periodic "stagings" of a public sphere—the creation of appearances of public discussions, stripped of any real content or prospect of dialogue.

The use of polls by the Fujimori government certainly has not facilitated a process of rational-critical debate in Peru. Polls were one of the devices it used to shut down debate on issues connected to the *autogolpe*. With an overwhelming majority of Peruvians expressing support in the polls for Fujimori, the opposition's arguments concerning the unconstitutionality of the government's April 5 initiatives were easily portrayed as arcane and irrelevant. Fujimori incorporated a derision for legality into his discourse on the coup, frequently drawing the distinction between "legal" Peru and the "real" Peru. Legal Peru was identified as the world of corrupt party elites, who occupied positions in the institutional structures of the state, but the real Peru was defined as the "people," whose will Fujimori embodied.[54] This rhetorical assault on legality was effective;

even OAS officials were disinterested in sticking to legal niceties in reference to the structuring of a transition. The OAS regarded the congressional opposition's proposal to restore "democratic institutionality" by removing Fujimori and replacing him with his rightful constitutional successor, Vice President Máximo San Roman, as excessively legalistic and politically inappropriate, particularly in light of the poll results.

Poll results were neatly worked into Fujimori's anti-institutional discourse, which revolved around discrediting all contending political entities (e.g., Congress, parties, the judiciary) and centralizing power in the presidency. This anti-institutionalist and power-concentrating political project interlocks with the neoliberal economic project aimed at restructuring and shrinking the public sector.[55] Fujimori and his economic team came to view contending institutions as impediments to the pursuit of the draconian neoliberal economic reforms that they were committed to undertaking; the *autogolpe* conveniently removed the remaining institutional obstacles to neoliberal economic reforms.[56]

For the near term, Fujimori's political and economic projects imply at least a reproduction, if not a worsening, of the problematic conditions that have hindered the emergence of a citizenry-as-public in Peru.[57] According to C. Wright Mills, at least four minimal conditions must be met for individuals to become constituted as a "public" in a democratic political system. First, many citizens must be involved in expressing as well as receiving opinion. Second, citizens must have access to channels of communication that allow them to "answer back" the state. Third, people must have outlets for political participation that give them opportunities to act on their opinions. Fourth, the formation of public opinion must not be dominated by the state.[58]

Clearly, the vast socioeconomic inequalities and the racial divisions in Peruvian society have been a chronic obstacle to the constitution of the citizenry as a public, or as a community of publics. Peru's grinding poverty and highly skewed distribution of income are not the creation of the Fujimori government; but there is little evidence that the draconian neoliberal program now under way will provide any relief in regard to those basic problems. Enormous economic stress has been a critical factor underlying the disintegration of the social fabric; the signs of this disintegration range from the political violence practiced by Sendero Luminoso to the physical "exit" of Peruvians from the country itself to the abandoning of school by hundreds of thousands of children who are compelled to work in order to supplement family income. In the absence of a minimum of material welfare, basic education, and physical security, large segments of the Peruvian population are automatically deprived of the potential to be meaningful participants in public life. Severe economic conditions also undermine the organizational capacities of grass-roots groups, which provide one of the bases for participation in a public life by the lower class.[59]

Economic conditions and economic policies in Peru are creating "physical" limitations on the extent to which citizens have the opportunity to act as a public. Fujimori's project has also led to a series of ideological and political barriers to public debate. For example, the unilateral imposition of the neoliberal economic program and its management by technocrats effectively closed the range of policy options that are open to public discussion. Major components of the program have been enacted with virtually no debate. Even business interest groups, who have strongly supported Fujimori and the *autogolpe*, find themselves frustrated by their lack of voice on economic issues.

The shutdown of debate on economic issues has its counterpart in the political realm. The government-controlled constituent assembly endorsed the Fujimori package of constitutional reforms (which includes a provisions for immediate presidential reelection and allows for the dismissal of Congress by the president) with almost no debate. Attempts by opposition members of Congress to fully investigate charges of human rights abuses by the armed forces have also consistently been stymied by the government-controlled majority in the constituent assembly and the military.[60]

The elimination of institutional sites for debate within the state apparatus has also furthered the ideological control that the administration has been able to exert so far. The state-owned media (press and television) play an important part in this process of ideological control, as do the privately owned stations and newspapers, which engage in a certain amount of self-censorship for fear of possible retributions by the government. (Such retributions can assume a variety of forms, including tax audits, the withdrawal of advertising by state agencies, and so forth.)[61] □

POLLS AND A NEW POLITICS:
FROM PUBLIC OPINION TO PUBLIC JUDGMENT?

The Fuji-golpe won popular support as a critique of the extant democracy; Fujimori could successfully portray Peruvian democracy as "false" because of the inadequacy of its institutions (particularly parties) in providing effective channels for the articulation and representation of the diverse interests in Peruvian society. In short, Fujimori aptly recognized the widespread disillusion with what most people already regarded as a debased and distorted public sphere. He was able to exploit that disenchantment (distilled in the polls) to legitimate an autocratic restructuring of the political system, which in all likelihood will pivot around an imperial presidency and in which there may be scant opportunity for citizens to "answer back" the state.

The challenges facing the opposition to Fujimori are daunting. Thus far, the opposition has had to grapple with a number of strategic decisions regarding how to deal with the Fujimori government in the short term.[62] But the long-term question of how to root democracy more firmly in Peruvian society remains.

One of the most urgent tasks facing the opposition is that of turning parties and intermediary associations into vehicles that are regarded as legitimate voices of Peruvian society. To do this, parties and organizations must be reorganized as internally democratic associations that encourage democratic practices and debates among their members. Such a "bottom-up" approach to democratization would create microcosmic public spheres within groups. This intraorganizational infrastructure of participation would serve to valorize democracy as an end in itself and would lay the groundwork for transposing these micropractices onto macropolitics.[63]

How might polls be employed constructively in this rethinking and remaking of Peruvian democracy? One model that might be useful to contemplate is that proposed by American pollster Daniel Yankelovich in his work *Coming to Public Judgment*. Yankelovich argued that the quality of U.S. democracy could be greatly improved by using polls as part of a broader effort of civic education and public discussion, which would produce "public judgment." According to Yankelovich, much of the data that are generated by polling reflects "mass public opinion"—poor quality public opinion that can be identified by its internal inconsistencies, volatility, and the failure of people to take into account the consequences of their views. In contrast to mass opinion, Yankelovich identified "public judgment" as opinion that is consistent, stable, and cognizant of consequences. In Yankelovich's model, arriving at public judgment is the culmination of a process in which citizens first undergo a consciousness-raising in regard to issues, which is followed by "working through"—deliberations on concrete proposals to deal with the particular problems under discussion.[64]

In such a process in Peru, survey research (along with other techniques such as focus groups and in-depth interviewing) could prove extremely useful in delineating the key concerns of citizens and in uncovering inconsistencies and contradictions in the views of the mass public. This information could then be utilized to open up public discussion. In short, in this model, polls are a starting point, not an end.

Using polls as catalysts for serious discussion within a broader effort at reviving civil society requires that surveys attempt to explore the complexity of people's views. The "horse race/beauty contest" questions that are the standard fare produced by commercial firms and the typical grist for public consumption do not provide the raw materials for fruitful civic discussions. A "coming-to-public judgment" approach demands a textured and more adventurous survey research that is explicitly concerned with uncovering popular concerns and understandings of problems. Surveys structured exclusively around close-ended questions and an elite-defined agenda of issues do not offer much opportunity for people to speak out through the polls.

It is unrealistic to expect commercial polling firms to undertake an ambitious agenda of new research on their own; the participation of the academic community in Peru is indispensable. A few Peruvian scholars are already engaged in such textured attitude research. One of the best examples of such work can be found in a recent study of the urban poor by Centro de Estudios de la Democracia y la Sociedad (CEDYS), led by Jorge Parodi.[65] The mass survey of six hundred low-income residents in Lima, done with the technical assistance of Apoyo S.A., was combined with selective in-depth interviewing, which allowed the research team to explore the logic and meaning underlying individuals' responses to the survey questions. The study produced illuminating and provocative findings. For example, one of the most interesting findings concerns how the urban poor's abstract commitment to democracy coexists with their support for strong, effective, but not necessarily democratic leadership. The authors concluded that a largely plebiscitary conception rather than representative conception of democracy dominates the thinking of the lower classes. Although in and of itself the finding is extremely useful in understanding popular reaction to Fujimori, it is an example of a "mass opinion" that deserves to be the subject of a serious discussion across Peruvian society, since it raises profound questions about political culture and conceptions of leadership. Many groups and associations in Peru (parties, unions, neighborhood associations, universities, and others) would benefit from such a discussion. These groups might also benefit from conducting their own polls on issues of interest to their members. Such "advocacy" polling would break up the oligopolistic position of the public opinion firms and would create a more diverse picture of the state of public opinion.[66]

Clearly, the mass media have played and will continue to play a primary role in the diffusion of poll results. If polling is to be incorporated into a broader effort to improve the quality of public debate, the press needs to develop its capacity to report poll results in ways that inform, educate, and place the results in perspective, and in ways that invigorate debate. Apart from the scattershot criticisms of the polls raised by the magazine *Caretas*, the Peruvian press has tended to report results without much of a critical perspective. As a first step to developing a more critical approach, the Peruvian press should consider the adoption of standard reporting procedures for poll results, which would provide readers with more information on poll taking and which would sensitize them to the limitations of polls.[67] A critical journalistic approach to polls necessarily entails the development of in-house expertise on public opinion, so that editors could make better judgments as to when and how poll results should be reported. With such in-house expertise in place, the Peruvian media would be in a position to make creative use of poll results as a means to further public discussion on critical issues.

Political polls are now an entrenched part of the conduct of Peruvian politics, as they are elsewhere across the globe. No amount of detraction or disdain will prevent people from employing them. As my analysis suggests, polls can be marshaled to serve a variety of elite discourses. Although Fujimori has thus far dominated the battle to define the meaning and the mandate of the polls, their volatility may open up opportunities for the opposition to reinterpret the results and to recast the range of political choices.

Nevertheless the prospective contributions of polls to Peruvian democratization go well beyond the immediate question of how the democratic opposition might "spin" them to shape a transition away from presidential authoritarianism. Polls could be employed creatively as part of a more ambitious effort to promote the development of a public sphere by invigorating "conversations among citizens," both inside societal organizations and the polity at large.

The Fuji-golpe and ensuing events in Peru distressingly demonstrate the continuing vulnerability of democracy in Latin America. If there is a positive side to the Fuji-golpe, it is that it has forced Peruvian democrats back to the drawing board—to evaluate what went wrong and to think about how to construct a democracy that is meaningful to people. Public opinion research could be used to inform and animate the process of rethinking and restrategizing democratization in Peru. □

NOTES

I gratefully acknowledge the help provided by Harold Mah, Alfredo Torres, Manuel Torrado, C.D.D. Walker Cohen, Guillermo Loli, Julio Carrión, Humberto Campodónico, and the Banco de Datos of the Centro de Estudios y Promoción del Desarrollo (DESCO) at various stages in the research of this chapter. Field work in Peru in April 1993 was supported by the Social Sciences and Humanities Research Council of Canada.

1. *El Peruano*, April 12, 1992.

2. For the classic defense of polls, see George Gallup and Saul Rae, *The Pulse of Democracy: The Public Opinion Poll and How It Works* (New York: Harcourt, Brace

1940). For further discussion of the contributions of commercial pollsters in the United States, see David W. Moore, *The Superpollsters: How They Measure and Manipulate Public Opinion* (New York: Four Walls Eight Windows, 1992).

3. For a review of the populist literature on polls and its critics, see Irving Crespi, *Public Opinion, Polls, and Democracy* (Boulder: Westview Press, 1989), pp. 1–13.

4. See C. Wright Mills's discussion of "mass society" in *The Power Elite* (New York: Oxford University Press, 1956), pp. 298–324. For a discussion of how opinions are fabricated in modern society by authors in the Frankfurt School, see Max Horkheimer and Theodor Adorno, *Dialectic of Enlightenment*, trans. John Cumming (New York: Continuum, 1987). Another early and influential critique of public opinion polling is that of Herbert Blumer, "Public Opinion and Public Opinion Polling," *American Sociological Review* 13, no. 5 (1948): 542–554.

5. Benjamin Ginsberg, *The Captive Mind: How Mass Opinion Promotes State Power* (New York: Basic Books, 1986).

6. For an analysis of polls in this vein, see Limor Peer, "The Practice of Opinion Polling as a Disciplinary Mechanism: A Foucauldian Perspective," *International Journal of Public Opinion Research* 4, no. 3 (autumn 1992): 230–242. The application of Foucault to the study of polling is also discussed in Susan Herbst, *Numbered Voices: How Opinion Polling Has Shaped American Politics* (Chicago: University of Chicago Press, 1993).

7. Pierre Bourdieu, "Public Opinion Does Not Exist," in Armand Mattelart and Seth Siegelaub, eds., *Communication and Class Struggle*, vol. 1 (New York: International General, 1979), p. 125.

8. The original German version of Habermas's work was published in 1962. The English translation was only published recently. See Jürgen Habermas, *The Structural Transformation of the Public Sphere: An Inquiry into a Category of Bourgeois Society*, trans. Thomas Burger (Cambridge: M.I.T. Press, 1989).

9. See James Curran, "Mass Media and Democracy: A Reappraisal," in James Curran and Michael Gurevitch, eds., *Mass Media and Society* (London: Edward Arnold, 1991), p. 83.

10. For a summary version of Habermas's arguments on the "public sphere," see "The Public Sphere," in Mattelart and Sieglaub, eds., *Communication and Class Struggle*, pp. 198–201. Habermas's concept of the public sphere has provoked a number of interesting criticisms by historians and political theorists. See the collection in Craig Calhoun, ed., *Habermas and the Public Sphere* (Cambridge: M.I.T. Press, 1992).

11. Herbst, *Numbered Voices*, p. 166.

12. In recent work, Guillermo O'Donnell has been especially concerned with the question of how to characterize the polyarchies in Latin America and has put forth the notion of "delegative democracy" as a new regime type. See, for example, "On the State, Democratization and Some Conceptual Problems (A Latin American View with Glances at Some Post-Communist Countries)," *World Development* 21, no. 8 (August 1993):1355–1369. The question of evolving regime types is considered in Catherine M. Conaghan and James M. Malloy, *Unsettling Statecraft: Democracy and Neoliberalism in the Central Andes* (Pittsburgh: University of Pittsburgh Press, 1994). The work points to the potential usefulness of Tocque-

ville's notion of "democratic despotism" as a way to describe the type of hybrid regime emergent in Latin America.

13. For a detailed analysis of the political dynamics of the Fujimori government, see Henry Pease García, "La democracia colapsada: Perú 1990–1992" (paper delivered to the XVII International Congress of the Latin American Studies Association, September 24–27, 1992, Los Angeles, California).

14. In American politics, "spin" is the slang used to denote efforts by elites to set and maintain control over the public agenda by defining the meaning of news events. For a discussion of the process in reference to the presidency, see John A. Maltese, *Spin Control: The White House Office of Communications and the Management of Presidential News* (Chapel Hill: University of North Carolina Press, 1992).

15. For a discussion of how commercial and academic research on public opinion intersected in the United States, see Jean M. Converse, *Survey Research in the United States: Roots and Emergence 1890–1960* (Berkeley: University of California Press, 1987). Other political polling firms in Peru include: Analistas & Consultores, SAMIMP, and Mercadeo de Opinión. A number of other marketing and consulting firms also do occasional political polling and focus group work.

16. A focus group is composed of ten to fifteen individuals who are nonrandomly chosen to probe the attitudes of subsets within a population (e.g., women, low-income groups, and others). They meet under the direction of a trained discussion-group leader, who prompts them to react to a series of open-ended questions about political candidates, issues, and so forth. The discussions are usually videotaped and observed by analysts via two-way mirrors. The advantage of the focus group is that it allows analysts to probe attitudes at some depth and it is much cheaper than survey research. Focus groups are frequently used in the development of media campaigns for political candidates. For a discussion of the use of focus groups in U.S. politics, see Larry J. Sabato, *The Rise of Political Consultants: New Ways of Winning Elections* (New York: Basic Books, 1981).

17. For an overview of the history of professionalization and a discussion of how professions struggle to assert their control over discourse in their field, see Magali Sarfatti Larson, "In the Matter of Experts and Professionals, or How Impossible It Is to Leave Nothing Unsaid," in Rolf Torstendahl and Michael Burrage, eds., *The Formation of Professions: Knowledge, State, Strategy* (London: Sage, 1990), pp. 24–50.

18. *Diario La Tribuna*, April 22, 1990.

19. *La Semana*, March 12, 1990.

20. Interview, Manuel Torrado, Lima, April 6, 1993.

21. Interview, *Medio de Marketing*, Lima, April 29, 1993.

22. For examples of the work that is distributed to subscribing clients, see *Medio de Marketing*, a monthly magazine dealing with marketing trends and issues published by the Medio de Cambio, headed by Guido Pennano. Apoyo S.A. circulates *Awareness Publicitario*, which tracks the public's level of product recognition and popularity; it also publishes *Estadística poblacional*, which provides data on demographics.

23. Alfredo Torres Guzmán, *Perfil del elector* (Lima: Editorial Apoyo, 1989), p. 58.

24. For further discussion of the 1990 presidential campaign, see Carlos Iván Degregori and Romero Grompone, *Demonios y redentores en el nuevo Perú: Una tragedia en dos vueltas* (Lima: Instituto de Estudios Peruanos, 1991). For recollections of the campaign by the candidate, see Mario Vargas Llosa, *El pez en el agua* (Madrid: Seix Barral, Biblioteca Breve, 1993); an earlier English version appeared as "Fish Out of Water," *Granta* 36 (summer 1991): 17–75.

25. Interview, Manuel Torrado.

26. For a discussion of the evolution of presidential approval ratings in Peru and their relationship to the problem of inflation, see Julio Carrión, "Presidential Popularity in Peru, 1980–1990" (paper delivered at the XVII International Congress of the Latin American Studies Association, September 24–27, Los Angeles, California).

27. Alfredo Torres Guzmán, "The Coup in Peru and its Popular Support," photocopy (Lima: Apoyo S.A., 1993).

28. *Expreso*, January 5, 1992.

29. The entire text of the speech can be found in Eduardo Ferrero Costa, ed., *Proceso de retorno a la institucionalidad democrática en el Perú* (Lima: Centro de Estudios Internacionales, 1992), pp. 129–135.

30. *El Peruano*, April 9, 1992.

31. *El Peruano*, April 11, 1992.

32. *Resumen Semanal*, April 10–14, 1992.

33. *New York Times*, April 16, 1992.

34. *New York Times*, April 7, 1992; April 11, 1992.

35. *New York Times*, April 7, 1992. Mario Vargas Llosa's condemnation of the coup was published as an op-ed, *New York Times*, April 12, 1992.

36. For Gorriti's description of his arrest and his analysis of the coup, see the interview with Sarah Kerr, "Fujimori's Plot: An Interview with Gustavo Gorriti," *New York Review of Books*, June 25, 1992, pp. 18–22.

37. The text of the speech is reproduced in Blacker Miller's memoirs of his tenure as foreign minister, see *La propuesta inconclusa* (Lima: Consorcio La Moneda, 1993), pp. 225–248.

38. The speech is reproduced in Ferrero Costa, *Proceso de retorno*, pp. 191–202.

39. See the reference to Vargas Llosa's suggestion of manipulation by columnist Manuel D'Ornellas in *Expreso*, April 15, 1992. D'Ornellas ridiculed the idea and suggested that Vargas Llosa return from his self-imposed European exile in order to get a real reading of public opinion.

40. Press release from Apoyo, photocopy (Lima: Apoyo S.A., 1992).

41. See "Porcentajes en vez de democracia: El reino de las encuestas," *La República*, April 18, 1992.

42. *La República*, April 19, 1992.

43. See "Encuestas: Pompas de jabón," *Caretas*, April 27, 1992.

44. Luís Alberto Sánchez, "Ahora hay que elegir por encuestas," *Caretas*, April 27, 1992. The quotation illustrates one of the problems in arguing against polls—the tendency to sound elitist.

45. For a review of the debate over preelection polling errors in this case, see Peter V. Miller, "Which Side Are You On? The 1990 Nicaraguan Poll Debacle," *Public Opinion Quarterly* 55, no. 2 (summer 1991): 281–302.

46. For the complete argument, see Elisabeth Noelle-Neumann, *The Spiral of Silence: Public Opinion—Our Social Skin* (Chicago: University of Chicago Press, 1984). For a discussion of the research spawned by the "spiral of silence argument," see Charles T. Salmon and Chi-Yung Moh, "The Spiral of Silence: Linking Individual and Society Through Communication," in J. David Kennamer, ed., *Public Opinion, the Press, and Public Policy* (Westport: Praeger, 1992), pp. 145–162.

47. All of the methodological concerns raised by opponents are important topics of debate within the public opinion community in the United States. One only need look through journals such as *Public Opinion Quarterly* to see how salient these issues are.

48. In an interview with the author, one noted television reporter speculated that the television stations were afraid to challenge the pollsters' findings because the stations depend on the same firms for their own television ratings. Thus any methodological questioning of polling would throw into question their own ratings, especially in the minds of potential sponsors. Although there is no way to confirm this observation, it does raise an interesting question as to how economic considerations might affect the interpretation of polls by actors in civil society. Interview, August 5, 1993, Lima.

49. For a response to the criticisms raised in *Caretas*, see the letter to the editor by Alfredo Torres Guzmán in *Caretas*, October 29, 1992.

50. Alfredo Torres Guzmán, "Cuidado con las encuestas," *Expreso*, April 29, 1992.

51. *Caretas*, June 8, 1992.

52. *Caretas*, June 8, 1992.

53. For a discussion of the popularity of quantification and the way in which it was used to confer "objectivity" to the political positions staked out by reform movements in the United States, see Patricia Cline Cohen, *A Calculating People: The Spread of Numeracy in Early America* (Chicago: University of Chicago Press, 1982).

54. This juxtaposition of legal versus real Peru was picked up by various defenders of the coup. Blacker Miller, for example, repeated the formulation in his previously cited speech to the OAS. The newspaper columnist and coup defender, Patricio Ricketts, is cited as the originator of the expression (for example, see his columns in *Expreso*, April 15, 1992; *Expreso*, November 19, 1992).

55. As Richard Webb correctly points out, a good deal of "state shrinking" in Peru had already taken place prior to Fujimori's tenure due to the profound economic crisis and the collapse of public finances. See Richard Webb, "Prologue," in Carlos E. Paredes and Jeffrey Sachs, eds., *Peru's Path to Recovery: A Plan for Economic Stabilization and Growth* (Washington: The Brookings Institution, 1991), pp. 1–12.

56. Fujimori's economic minister, Carlos Boloña, believed that former president Alan García was ordering APRA party members in the judiciary, the comptroller's office, and the Congress to act to derail the neoliberal economic program. See "Entrevista a Carlos Boloña," *Debate* 15, no. 70 (September–October 1992): 8–14. He repeated that interpretation of events in a personal interview with the author, although he denies that he was consulted by Fujimori prior to the coup. Interview, Lima, April 27, 1993.

57. Legitimate questions may be raised concerning the extent to which Peruvians are completely constituted as a "citizenry," much less a "public." Guillermo O'Donnell has suggested that in countries like Peru a low-intensity type of citizenship prevails, given the ineffective operation of the legal system. See his "On the State, Various Crises and Problematic Democratizations," p. 1361. Moreover, questions can also be raised as to what extent "publics" exist even in the advanced capitalist democracies. For a discussion of the "missing public" in the United States, see Todd Gitlin, "The Politics of Communication and the Communication of Politics," in Curran and Gurevitch, *Mass Media and Society*, pp. 329–341.

58. These criteria are taken from Mills, *The Power Elite* (New York: Oxford University Press, 1956), pp. 302–304.

59. In addition to the problems caused by a lack of economic resources, there are other difficulties involved in transforming grassroots organizations into channels of a public sphere. Recent studies of such organizations suggest that authoritarian leadership styles are prevalent. See the concluding chapter by Luis Pásara and Alonso Zarzar, "Ambigüedades, contradicciones e incertidumbres," in Luis Pásara et al., *La otra cara de la luna: Nuevos actores sociales en el Perú* (Lima: Centro de Estudios de Democracia y Sociedad, 1991), pp. 174–203.

60. In April 1993, opposition congressional representatives attempted an investigation into the 1992 disappearance of ten people from La Cantuta University outside Lima; the military had been implicated in the disappearances. The army responded with harsh language and a parade of tanks through Lima. The U.S. government reacted negatively to what it saw as an open threat by the military. In an effort to placate the international community and to avoid an extension of the investigation into the upper ranks of the armed forces, the government-majority of the Congreso Constituyente Democrático (CCD) directed a study that concluded that soldiers, acting on their own without orders from superiors, killed the ten suspects. The finding of the commission was reported by Reuters Information Service, June 17, 1993. For further discussion of civil-military relations and the obstacles to democracy in Peru, see Fernando Rospigliosi, "Las débiles perspectivas de la democracia en el Perú" (paper delivered to the Conference on Peru in Crisis, The Woodrow Wilson Center, June 1–2, 1993, Washington, DC).

61. The major media's financial dependence on the state has been a chronic problem affecting the independence of the press. For an analysis of the problems in the Peruvian press, see Cynthia McClintock, "The Media and Re-Democratization in Peru," *Studies in Latin American Popular Culture* 6 (1987): 115–133.

62. Opposition groups decided to participate actively in the campaign to defeat the new Constitution designed by the pro-Fujimori majority in the constituent assembly. A referendum on the Constitution was held on October 31, 1993. The new Constitution was narrowly approved by voters, winning with just 52.3 percent of the total valid vote. The opposition did surprisingly well in its "No" campaign despite a well-heeled government effort to secure an overwhelming majority. The narrow government victory raised serious questions about the possibility of fraud in some areas, particularly in regions of the country still governed by the military under "state of emergency" provisions. The government delayed in announcing the official results of the referendum until December 18, 1993.

63. Henry Pease García has suggested "radicalizing democracy" by extending democratic principles throughout society. See Pease García, "La democracia collapsada," p. 14. In a recent study, Robert Putnam also emphasized the importance of societal factors in creating conditions for the development of effective public institutions, noting especially the role of horizontal networks of "civic engagement." See Robert D. Putnam, *Making Democracy Work: Civic Traditions in Modern Italy* (Princeton: Princeton University Press, 1993). This suggests that discussions of problems of governance in Peru should not be disconnected from the broader problem of democratization. For a discussion of Peru's problems as a "crisis of governance," see Francisco Sagasti and Max Hernández, "The Crisis of Democratic Governance in Peru" (paper delivered to the Conference on Peru in Crisis, The Woodrow Wilson Center for International Scholars, June 1–2, 1993, Washington, DC).

64. Daniel Yankelovich, *Coming to Public Judgment: Making Democracy Work in a Complex World* (Syracuse: Syracuse University Press, 1991).

65. Jorge Parodi, ed., *Los pobres, la ciudad y la política* (Lima: Centro de Estudios de Democracia y Sociedad, 1993). For another insightful work on the attitudes of youth, see Gonzálo Portocarrero and Patricia Oliart, *El Perú desde la escuela* (Lima: Instituto de Apoyo Agrario, 1989). Another important attitude study currently under way is a comparative work on Lima and Guayaquil, under the direction of Abelardo Sánchez León at DESCO.

66. For a practical guide to "advocacy" polling, see Celinda Lake, *Public Opinion Polling: A Handbook for Public Interest and Citizen Advocacy Groups* (Washington, DC: Island Press, 1987).

67. The rules put forward by the American Association for Public Opinion Research and the World Association for Public Opinion Research provide useful guidelines regarding the type of information that should accompany polls. The disclosure should include data as to: (1) source and client of survey, (2) methods of sample selection, (3) organization of field interviewing, (4) success of field work including rates of nonresponse, (5) interview questionnaire, and so forth. For further discussion of reporting on polls in the United States, see Peter V. Miller, Daniel M. Merkle, and Paul Wang, "Journalism with Footnotes: Reporting the 'Technical Details' of Polls," and Jack K. Holley, "The Press and Political Polling," in Paul J. Lavrakas and Jack K. Holley, eds., *Polling and Presidential Election Coverage* (Newbury Park, CA: Sage Publications, 1991), pp. 200–214 and 215–237, respectively.

CHAPTER TEN

■

Public Opinion Research in Mexico

Miguel Basáñez

WHEN LA JORNADA IN JULY 1988 commissioned a poll on the upcoming presidential election, publication of electoral opinion polls was finally launched in Mexico—fifty-three years after it had formally begun in the United States.[1] This lengthy delay was mainly due to problems inherent in three traditions: political, economic, and educational. In regard to the first, Mario Vargas Llosa, the well-known Peruvian novelist (and former presidential candidate), labeled the Mexican political system "the perfect dictatorship"—a quality that made the development of election surveys irrelevant for many years. Second, Mexico's economic protectionism produced little demand for the kind of market research that is characteristic of market economies. Third, an antiempirical and antiquantitative academic tradition retarded the teaching and use of survey methods in the social sciences. During the 1970s, moreover, the teaching of mathematics was attacked as reactionary and was eliminated from many political and social science departments in Mexican universities.

This picture changed rapidly in 1988. An increase in electoral competitiveness made public opinion polling attractive for both researchers and the press. North American Free Trade Agreement (NAFTA) negotiations made market research not only possible but indeed crucial for many firms. New currents of thought entering universities, coupled with the demand for survey research, led to a burgeoning attention to quantitative methods.

In regard to the impact of polling on processes of democratization, however, Mexican outlooks have been closer to European interpretations than to optimistic prodemocracy views held by U.S. scholars. Skeptical analyses by Jürgen Habermas, Pierre Bourdieu, and Benjamin Ginsberg are in line with most Mexican views on the subject. Dominant critiques

257

of survey research in Mexico have focused on the absence of informed debate and on the use of polls as "tools of manipulation by the elite" aimed at "domesticating the masses." Certainly, in the Latin American context, there are good reasons for suspicion, as illustrated by political exploitation of polls about the U.S. invasion of Panama or Alberto Fujimori's *autogolpe* in Peru. One question I address in this chapter is whether such susceptibility to manipulation lies in the nature of polling itself or in the culture and practice of Latin American politics. □

POLLING IN MEXICO

Before 1988 only a few Mexican studies were based on public opinion research. Curiously enough, the world's first journal of public opinion research was published by the Instituto Mexicano de Opinión Pública, under the leadership of Hungarian professor Lazlo Radvanyi.[2] In 1942 Radvanyi also encouraged the magazine *Tiempo* to briefly go into survey research.[3] In 1954 Rogelio Díaz Guerrero published his psychological study of social values, and in 1963 Gabriel Almond and Sidney Verba published their classic comparative study, *The Civic Culture*.[4]

During the 1970s there were books by Eric Fromm, Kenneth Coleman, Rafael Segovia, Wayne Cornelius, and Jorge Montaño, as well as articles about the 1968 student movement. The *Los Angeles Times* conducted one national survey.[5] During the 1980s there appeared only two books on public opinion research, both dealing with cultural values in Mexico, in addition to four articles: one about the nationalization of banks, another on the first attempt at an election forecast, a third that compared that forecast with postelectoral results, and the fourth about a survey of political values among younger Mexicans.[6] The *New York Times* conducted a nationwide poll in 1986. In the 1990s books, articles, and dissertations based on survey research are becoming increasingly common.[7]

Since 1988 the government and the Partido Revolucionario Institucional (PRI) have become key promoters of survey research, especially in the electoral arena. The other Mexican political parties, and the Mexican media, have made little use of polls.[8] In September 1988 *Nexos* launched "Encuestalia," a section on polls, and *Este País*, a magazine specializing in public opinion, appeared in 1991. A second magazine, *Voz y Voto*, appeared a little later. In 1992 contested elections in Chihuahua, Michoacán, and Sinaloa attracted the attention of pollsters, and during 1993 the North American Free Trade Agreement (NAFTA) did so as well. The Mexican presidential campaign heated up by the end of 1993, and several surveys focused on the process of presidential succession.[9] As interest in these issues increased, discussion and conferences flushed out related themes and ideas.

Today the leading groups in Mexican survey research are the Centro de Estudios de Opinión Pública (CEOP), founded in 1988 to work for newspapers; Pulso Mercadológico (PM), started in 1989 with a marketing orientation; Investigaciones Sobre Opinión (ISOP), established in 1990 to serve as the polling arm of the PRI; Opinión Profesional (OP), founded in 1990 to work for the president's office; Gabinete de Estudios de Opinión (GEO), formed in 1990 to serve the government newspaper, *El Nacional*. Recently added to this group are the Centro de Estudios de Opinión (CEO) of the University of Guadalajara and the Centro de Estudios de Opinión (CEO) of the University of Colima. In addition, the Centro de Estudios Económicos y Sociales of the Banco Nacional de México and the United States Information Agency (USIA) have also been polling regularly. Market research is dominated by a handful of firms, which from time to time conduct social surveys as well.[10]

To gain access to international-level conferences on public opinion research, Mexican researchers took part in the 1988 meeting of the World Association for Public Opinion Research (WAPOR), which developed a code of professional ethics. In October 1989 WAPOR opened a regional office for Mexico and Central America.[11] The first meeting of Latin American members of WAPOR took place in Venezuela in January 1990, prompting extensive discussion about the possibility of establishing a regional database and creating a continental "barometer" (analogous to the well-known EuroBarometer studies). Today the University of Michigan, the University of Connecticut, the University of North Carolina, and Tulane University all house collections of Mexican poll data. In February 1990 Mexico was invited to join the Inter-University Consortium on Political and Social Research (ICPSR) at the University of Michigan and to participate in the second World Values Survey, and in October 1993 a representative from Mexico received a seat on the steering committee of the Third World Values Survey Council.

WAPOR has organized three international seminars in Mexico, which has the second largest WAPOR membership in the world. In February 1993 a group of marketing researchers formed the Asociación Mexicana de Agencias de Investigación (AMAI) with the support of the European Society for Opinion and Marketing Research (ESOMAR).[12] The AMAI organized a Latin American meeting in July 1993 and WAPOR welcomed this association.[13] □

POLITICAL IMPACT AND GOVERNMENT REACTION TO POLLS

Two significant elements combined in 1988 to break down ignorance and skepticism surrounding opinion research in Mexico: Many researchers sought to use polls to study the presidential election, and government attempts at censorship led to skyrocketing interest in the election among the general public. More than twenty polls were taken in 1988.[14] The majority of surveys were organized with scant financial resources, using techniques acquired in elementary sociology courses. In some cases, researchers were attempting quantitative methods for the very first time. These efforts, however deficient, nonetheless contributed to the breakdown of antiempirical and antiquantitative traditions in Mexico. They also served to challenge the government monopoly on political truth.

In March 1988, after three failed attempts, the newspaper La Jornada sponsored a national poll about the presidential election. La Jornada asked Prospectiva Estratégica (PEAC), a private firm, to conduct a trial poll in Mexico City for immediate release.[15] Largely as a result of that poll, leftist opposition to the government decided to form a united electoral front against the PRI.[16] Public reaction to the poll also encouraged La Jornada to undertake a full-scale national survey, which the government tried to prevent. Among other contrivances, the PRI threatened to default on a $2 million debt to the paper. Subsequently, La Jornada officials told PEAC to discontinue the study because of "internal financial problems." Given the importance of the presidential elections, PEAC asked La Jornada to seek alternate funding for the national poll, and PEAC itself launched a fund-raising campaign. As donations arrived, La Jornada representatives informed PEAC that it would not publish the results of the poll in view of "internal disagreements." PEAC countered by threatening to publish the findings in a U.S. newspaper. In response, La Jornada "solved" its internal disagreements and eventually published the poll in July and August 1988.[17]

The problems did not end there. In an attempt to discredit the survey, the Secretaría de Gobernación attacked the results in an editorial, denouncing the poll as "unprofessional, reflecting clear electoral and partisan purposes, with notorious bias and from a dubious source."[18] The PRI then materialized its earlier threat by refusing to honor its $2 million debt to La Jornada. In addition, the government published imaginary polls—attributed to Mexican universities—that reported a fairly strong lead by the PRI presidential candidate, Carlos Salinas de Gortari.[19] The regime also made arrangements for a poll to be conducted jointly by U.S. Gallup and Televisa, Mexico's leading television network. Though interviewing ended nearly eight weeks prior to the election, the results of the joint poll were disseminated profusely by television, radio stations, and newspapers during the final three weeks of the campaign.[20]

Despite its negative features, the public attention proved beneficial to survey research. It sparked much discussion and observation about polling, the very thing that the government had sought to avoid. In turn, the dialogue made glaringly visible the complete ignorance and naiveté of the Mexican press in the field of polling and public opinion studies. As an editor of one of the most important newspapers in the country inquired in June 1988: "What's Gallup?"

The capacity of polls to disclose the electorate's preference took the regime by surprise. The government's hostile reaction was due largely to its lack of preparation for coping with survey results. In 1988 the PRI and government officials approached PEAC in an attempt to stop the surveys, or at least to convince the pollsters that any reliable poll would reveal a minimum of 65 percent in favor of the PRI presidential candidate. Having failed in that attempt, they then set out to persuade PEAC to raise the PRI share of the voters' preference from 50 percent to 58 percent.

During 1989 the political impact of polls became even more apparent. In competitive, closely scrutinized local-level elections in Baja California and Michoacán, the PRI share dropped to 42 percent. To counteract independent polling results (and to guide PRI strategies) the government hastily built up its own public opinion research capability. The strategy was first applied to a local election in Uruapan, Michoacán, in March 1990. Through intensive polling, the PRI was able to map in detail party preferences throughout the *municipio*. With these results in hand, the government then thoroughly purged the electoral registry. Careful regression analysis on previous elections had shown that the lower the turnout, the better the chance for a PRI success; higher turnout meant more votes for opposition parties. The PRI's electoral tactic in Uruapan was clear: It succeeded in reducing voter turnout (only 18 percent on election day), and this guaranteed a two-thirds share of the vote for the PRI.

Implications of the pilot test in Uruapan were applied in November 1990 to a much larger arena, the State of Mexico. According to a CEOP poll for *La Jornada*, the left-wing Partido Revolucionario Democrático (PRD) was likely to receive 42 percent of the vote, the PRI 38 percent, and the right-wing Partido Acción Nacional (PAN) 17 percent.[21] (In 1988 the parties had received 52 percent, 30 percent, and 17 percent respectively.) By contrast, the PRI and government pollsters claimed that the PRD would receive only 15 percent, the PRI 61 percent, and the PAN 18 percent.[22] In fact, the raw data yielded nearly identical results; the debate concentrated on how to deal with the 35 percent of respondents who were apparently undecided. The government analysts simply eliminated the undeclared vote from their percentage calculations. Using more sophisticated techniques, the independent CEOP pollsters examined social profiles of the undecided voters in order to identify their preferences on the basis of statistical probabilities. Seeking to avoid a technical debate, the government orchestrated a political attack against the CEOP. The PRI-controlled newspaper, *El Nacional*, hired columnists and cartoonists to uphold the *oficialista* poll results and to discredit the CEOP. In the end, the reported results of the election coincided with the government's forecasts.

Mexico's brief interlude of political opening had come to an end. The PRI was gradually returning to its traditional goal of winning two-thirds of the vote. In the March 1991 Morelos local election and in the August 1991 midterm federal congressional election, the new technical strategies—tested in Uruapan and confirmed in the State of Mexico—were put on full display. Electoral chemistry had developed into electoral engineering. The PRI's return to old-time practices was not painless; many electoral conflicts took place. Popular opposition sometimes made it impossible for officially elected PRI candidates to assume their offices.[23] From 1991 to 1993, public interest in electoral polls practically vanished. Citizens of Mexico concluded that the vote was not respected, that parties and the government were corrupt, and that there was little to be done. Thereafter, public interest in opinion polls surged once again, especially as they began to reveal the genuine possibility of a defeat for the PRI in the presidential elections of August 1994.

Interference in Professional Associations

In 1990 the Mexican government attempted to interfere in professional associations as well as to create legal barriers to the practice of polling. The world's leading associations of public opinion research—WAPOR, the American Association for Public Opinion Research (AAPOR), and ESOMAR—soon found themselves embroiled in the regime's maneuvers to control polling.

Establishment of the Sociedad Mexicana de Estudios de Opinión Pública (SMEOP) in March 1988 was the first attempt to organize an independent pollster's association in Mexico. Members of the U.S.-based Latin American Studies Association (LASA) took part in the founding of SMEOP, which later became the Mexican chapter of WAPOR. In February 1991 a group primarily employed by the Mexican government took steps to form a rival association.[24] It was led by Ricardo de la Peña, the pollster from the government-owned newspaper, *El Nacional*. WAPOR refused to recognize the new association because its unofficial purpose was to discredit and remove the head of the WAPOR chapter in Mexico.

This affair started in May 1990 at the WAPOR meeting in Paris. Two Mexicans approached the WAPOR president, Frederick C. Turner, to express a poor opinion of their national representative. About this time, Turner coincidentally received an invitation to visit Mexico, with a generous expense account; he promptly declined the offer. In December 1990 the PRI and government pollsters sent a formal letter of protest to the new WAPOR president, Elizabeth Nelson of Britain. They enclosed press clippings from the State of Mexico election poll debate and accused Mexico's WAPOR representative of being politically motivated and of "questioning their professional prestige." They claimed that this behavior discredited both WAPOR and public opinion research in general. The letter concluded with a threat to "reconsider our membership" in WAPOR if its representative were not sanctioned for his behavior.

In January 1991 Nelson replied, saying that she could not pass judgment on the case without substantial evidence. Nelson added that "the issues which you are raising must be dealt with by the appropriate professional association in Mexico." She simultaneously sent a copy of the complete case file to Miguel Basáñez, who was still serving as Mexico's WAPOR representative.

Only two weeks later, there suddenly appeared in Mexico a new and "independent" pollsters association, with by-laws, officers, members, and supporters. It showed little concern for technical, statistical, or methodological standards. The organization's most important committee was for "justice and honor." And almost immediately, all government agencies that had been so slow and reluctant to attend AAPOR and WAPOR meetings in the United States promptly agreed to join the new organization. In February 1991, as Mexico's WAPOR representative, Miguel Basáñez responded to the accusations of the government pollsters. He also invited them to debate the issues they raised in a panel at the AAPOR meeting to be held in May 1991, but they never replied.

Legal Barriers

In July 1990 the Mexican Congress passed a law making it illegal to publish poll results within five days prior to an election.[25] Until then, no Mexican legislation on polling had existed. The initiative for this new statute came from the PRI pollster, María de las Heras.[26] WAPOR fought against the passage of the law. Lawyers ultimately concluded that a legal loophole meant that the law was applicable only to political parties, not to the media or to independent firms. Because of that interpretation, polls were published during the forbidden period (without apparent effect on voter preferences) in the 1992 state elections in Michoacán and Chihuahua.

In June 1993 the PRI attempted to rectify its mistake by submitting a second, more restrictive proposal to Congress. The proposal demanded that all pollsters register with electoral authorities and submit their methods to governmental scrutiny. Disobedience could lead to prison sentences. (This is the law that was in effect for the 1994 presidential election.) Inadvertently, however, the rule was written in such a way as to apply to the media that commissions polls or to anyone who contracts for the undertaking of polls, but not to the pollsters themselves. □

SURVEY RESULTS

In this section I present selective findings from public opinion polls in Mexico on party preference, presidential popularity, economic performance, and respect for the vote.

The importance of measuring party preference via polling (instead of with electoral results) is that it allows one to identify the percentage of the electorate that does not express party preference. The data in Figure 10.1 show the proportions of those who consider themselves to be "independents." From 1982 to 1987, this group ("None" in Figure 10.1) increased from fewer than 25 percent to almost 50 percent, plunging briefly in 1988 but surging up back to 50 percent by 1990. Clearly, presidential elections tend to sharpen definitions of party preference and to reduce the proportion of independents. In 1988, especially, the opposition increased its support, but the PRI experienced a sharp reduction.

In contrast to the U.S. tradition, Mexico has kept minimal information on presidential popularity. Figure 10.2 shows data for the last decade; only since 1993 has the magazine *Este País* begun weekly reporting on the subject. Nonetheless, the results are suggestive. In 1979, according to a poll taken by the *Los Angeles Times*, José López Portillo enjoyed great popularity at the midpoint of his *sexenio* (1976–1982). His prestige plummeted, however, and by 1982 only one-third of the public approved of his performance. President Miguel de la Madrid started 1983 with a low approval profile, which decayed even further in 1984 and bottomed out in 1985, to recover only slightly in the final years of his administration. Even though Carlos Salinas started out at a middling range of popularity, after winning just over 50 percent of the vote, his approval rating rose to almost 80 percent within a few months. Afterward it declined slightly but never dropped below 60 percent.

Figure 10.3 displays data on popular estimates of economic conditions. From 1987 to 1990 the general perception was slightly negative: about 33 percent reported their personal situation to be worse than the previous year and 31 percent to 32 percent reported it to be better. This relationship held fairly steady until 1991, when the negative response dropped below the positive response. In 1992 the percentage of those with a negative outlook returned to its previous level. Since 1992 *Este País* has carried out weekly measurements of this indicator, which has begun to show a cyclical pattern.

FIGURE 10.1 Party Preferences in Mexico, 1982–1993

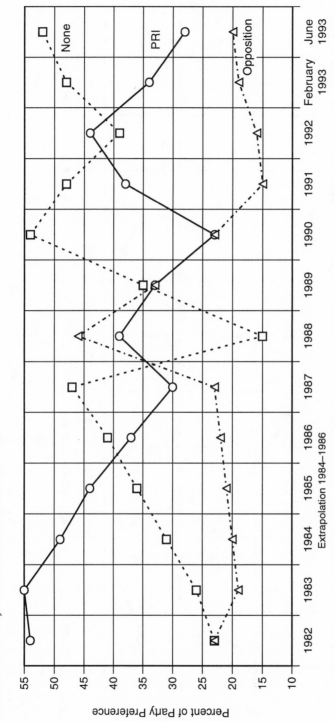

Extrapolation 1984–1986

Sample sizes: 1982–4,928; 1983–7,051; 1987–9,032; 1988–4,414; 1989–1,835; 1990–3,587; 1991–1,228; 1992–1,480; 1993/Feb.–1,471; and 1993/June–1,516.

Source: Miguel Basáñez, "Eucuesta Electoral 1991," *Este Pais,* no. 5, August 1991, p. 3; 1992: "Eucuesta Nacional," *Este Pais,* April 1992, n = 1,475; 1993 – February: "Eucuesta Nacional," *Este Pais,* February 1993, n = 1,471; 1993 – June: "Eucuesta Nacional," *Este Pais,* June 1993, n = 1,513.

FIGURE 10.2 Do You Approve or Disapprove of the Way the President is Handling His Job? Mexico 1982–1983

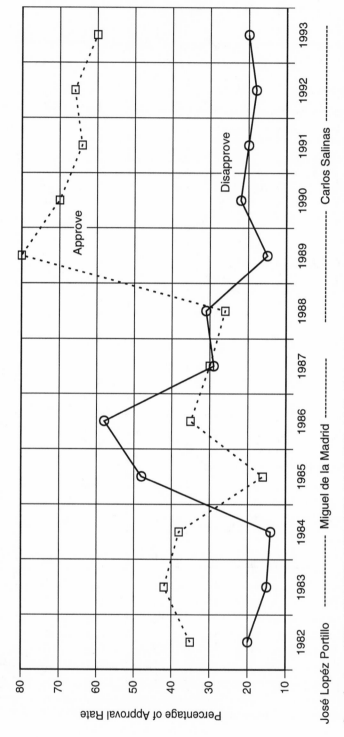

Sample sizes: 1982–4,928; 1983–7,051; 1984–2,216; 1985–1,039; 1986–1,999; 1987–9,032; 1988–4,414; 1989–1,835; 1990–1,531; 1991–1,228; 1992–1,214; 1993–1,234.
Source: Miguel Basáñez, "Elecciones Popularidad y Reelección," Este País, no. 6, September 1991, p. 11; 1992: "Eucuesta Nacional," Este País, April 1992, n = 1,475; 1993: "Pulsóme tro," Este País, no. 33, December 1993, p. 39.

FIGURE 10.3   Would You Say Your Personal Situation Is Better Today, the Same, or Worse Than It Was A Year Ago? Mexico, 1987–1993

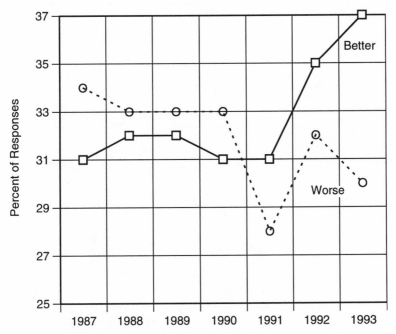

Sample sizes: 1987–9,032; 1988–4,414; 1989–extrapolation; 1990–3,587; 1991–1,228; 1992–1,214; 1993–1,234.

Source: National Basáñez's Surveys.

Polls also report on people's perceptions of the integrity of elections. From 1988 to 1991, as can be seen in Figure 10.4, there was an improvement in perceived levels of respect for voter preferences. In 1988, 53 percent declared that the vote was not respected, and only 23 percent believed that it was. By 1991 almost half of the Mexican population believed that their vote would be respected, and only one-third felt that it would not be respected.

Public opinion research can also produce cross-national and cross-regional comparisons. Using data from the World Values Survey, Ronald Inglehart found a clear and positive correlation between interregional trust and gross national product (GNP) per capita: The greater the prosperity, the greater the trust.[27] Mexico occupies its expected position, scoring low on both trust and GNP per capita (whereas Norway, for

FIGURE 10.4   Do You Think Elections Will Be Respected? Mexico, 1988–1991

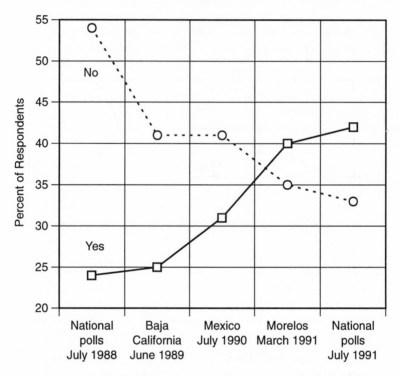

Sample sizes: 1988–4,414; Baja California–999; Mexico–6,886; Morelos–963; 1991–1,228.

instance, scores high on both measures). The data for Mexico thus not only confirm a broad cross-regional hypothesis but they also shed light on the structure and dynamics of Mexican society.

Such findings, partial and preliminary, illustrate both the utility and the potential for survey research in Mexico. Before polling came into general use, it was literally impossible to carry out empirical research on popular beliefs and attitudes. Now it is technically feasible; it is also socially and politically urgent. □

PRINCIPAL ISSUES

Discussions, critiques, and debates about polling in Mexico have focused on six major themes: sample size; methods (quotas versus random sampling); application of statewide polling results to local elections; influence of polls over electoral outcomes; assignment of the undecided vote;[28] and in-home versus on-the-street interviews. The first two issues refer to sampling techniques. Some analysts, revealing total ignorance of statistical probability, have expressed doubt that a two-thousand-person sample could accurately represent the 46 million adult citizens of Mexico. Critics of the second concern, showing somewhat more sophistication, assessed the relative merits of random methods or quotas. (Professional consensus has rapidly developed in favor of random samples.)

A third preoccupation concerned the application of statewide samples to local elections. A member of Congress, Leonel Godoy, criticized a poll that focused on the entire state of Michoacán, rather than on each of the eighteen separate electoral districts for local deputies.[29] Representing *La Jornada*, Miguel Angel Granados Chapa replied that polling at each district level was beyond the newspaper's financial reach. The poll was not in error; the paper had simply sought to achieve a general image of public opinion at the state level.

This debate lacked technical significance, but electoral results showed that it had political meaning. According to the poll, the PRD and the PRI both stood at 41 percent. The official result was 45 percent for the PRI and 40 percent the PRD. This should have meant that each party would have nine of the eighteen local deputies; in fact, the distribution was twelve for the PRI and six for the PRD. Upon a review of the official results, the situation became clear by subtracting the districts most sharply challenged by the PRD.[30] Excluding the four questionable districts, for example, the overall vote for the PRI went down to 43 percent and for the PRD it went up to 43 percent. Excluding the next three most debated districts—thus taking into account only eleven districts—the PRI vote went down to 40 percent and the PRD tally went up to 44 percent. And excluding the last two districts under debate, the PRI result fell to 38 percent and the PRD share rose to 47 percent. In the absence of a district-by-district poll, in other words, electoral authorities were able not only to recognize the overall results as predicted by the statewide poll but also to turn those results upside down dramatically in the composition of the local Assembly. Representative Godoy's preoccupation was correct. It was not a technical problem; it was an utterly political maneuver.

Another issue referred to the influence of polling on the electorate. At a meeting called by the PRI in November 1989, the party pollster, María de las Heras, argued that it was inappropriate to publish polls before the elections because they had a negative influence over the population. She suggested the idea of legislation to prohibit the publication of preelection polls. A few weeks later, Congress picked up this proposal and approved legislation banning the publication of poll results five days before the elections.

One of the most intense debates involved methods for assigning or eliminating undecided respondents in preelectoral polls—those who do not declare their probable vote. Some analysts insisted that undeclared respondents should be excluded from estimations of party preferences (which is equivalent to treating them as though they were the same as declared voters). My own view, buttressed by findings from Nicaragua as well as Mexico, is that this is a mistake. Survey respondents often withhold true beliefs, giving pollsters what they take to be the most "socially acceptable" opinion—which, in the Mexican context, means support for the PRI. Elimination of the "undecideds" thus tends to inflate the estimation of *oficialista* sentiment among the populace. Empirical data confirm that "second-guessing" of undeclared voters—on the basis of demographic characteristics or responses to attitudinal items in surveys—has substantially improved the accuracy of poll results.[31]

A final discussion concerned differences between interviews at home and on the street. This debate began in reference to the State of Mexico in November 1990, when Iván Zavala proclaimed:

> I hope that in CEOP they know that no serious survey institution in the world makes interviews on the streets. The meaning of questioning at home is not only, like those who make surveys in CEOP pretend, to be able to get random samples, but in a very important way, so that the interviewee feels confidence. That he is in front of an identified interviewer, whose name he knows, as well as the address and telephone numbers of the firm from which they were sent. So that he doesn't suffer the pressure of saying his most intimate convictions in front of immediate pedestrians, and so that he has a minimum atmosphere of concentration. The anonymity of the interviewer is what motivates lack of confidence of the interviewee, more than the anonymity of the interviewee. Besides, interviews on the streets can be done to the people who are on the streets and at the time of the interview, excluding by this, those who are not in any of these conditions. If the fundamental rule of the random samples is that the whole population to be studied has the same probability of appearing in the sample, the interviews on the street are the typical example of non-random samples.[32]

CEOP firmly replied: "In the first aspect, 'that the interviewee feels more insecure on the street than at home and suffers the pressure of saying his most intimate convictions in front of pedestrians,' in CEOP we depart from the exact opposite hypothesis. We do not sustain that street polls are in general better than home polls, but only for electoral aspects. We have insisted that to obtain truer answers about party sympathies, it is preferable that the interviewed doesn't feel any risk of his anonymity. The case of Nicaragua seems to sustain this argument."[33]

According to Leslie Kish, perhaps the world's foremost authority on sampling, research should be done in a way that guarantees the measurement of probability; in the meantime, there is no reason for uncritical dismissal of street interviews, as long as they follow all the rules of a random survey.[34] □

REFLECTIONS ON THE ROLES
OF PUBLIC OPINION RESEARCH

Polling and public opinion research have contributed to Mexican democracy, although the struggle has been characterized by retreats as well as by advances. Despite its short history, the first contribution of polling showed the general public that they could actually "see," in print, what they thought. This demonstrated to people that they, too, have a voice in politics and the political process. Polling has also made it much harder for the government to "modify" electoral results.

In the past, electoral debates took place almost solely among rival candidates within the ruling party; consequently, public opinion was not at all important. Beginning in 1988, and through the end of 1989, however, the Mexican government paid great attention to all of the polling that was taking place. Poll results reflected a propensity toward political openness and democracy in Mexico, and this view was evident even within the inner levels of the Cabinet. (And the PRI, for the first time ever, lost a state governorship, in Baja California, and half of the mayorships in Michoacán.

The second contribution of public opinion research is somewhat ambiguous. The creation of government polling agencies was certainly a positive step. It permitted politicians and government officials to become more sensitive to the needs and feelings of the Mexican people. However, the formation of these government agencies also constituted a danger for independent pollsters, since official pollsters attempted to discredit other researchers. By 1990, as electoral tension mounted, the PRI abandoned its short-lived tolerance of competition and regressed to triumphalist proclamations of overwhelming victories.

The third contribution of opinion polling is also somewhat mixed: Polls produced a "modernization" of electoral fraud. The practice of robbing the ballot box or changing results has been replaced by an elaborate electoral apparatus that can better control the electorate and its decisions. The ruling party now maintains profiles and locations of potential problem regions. This has enabled them to carry out campaigns of selective vote promotion in areas already favorably disposed to the PRI and simultaneous inhibition of voter turnout in high-risk areas. This maneuvering is difficult to detect by the opposition, given the high cost of public opinion research. Only the ruling party can command the necessary resources. (For the 1991 congressional elections, for example, the PRI commissioned one poll of 125,000 interviews.) For the 1994 presidential election they spent, together with the government, over US$100 million on polling.

Apart from these problems, which may be quite normal in the evolution of polling, the final balance seems positive for Mexico. Public opinion research has opened a window on quantitative and empirical approaches that have been quite foreign to epistemological traditions in the social sciences. Prospects for the future are encouraging. □

NOTES

I want to express special thanks to Peter H. Smith for comments, suggestions, and editorial assistance.

1. Norman M. Bradburn and Seymour Sudman, *Polls and Surveys* (San Francisco: Jossey-Bass, 1988), p. 12.

2. Lazlo Radvanyi lived in Mexico from the late 1930s to the early 1940s and published the *International Journal of Public Opinion Research*, antecedent of the current journal published by the World Association for Public Opinion Research. Interview with Elisabeth Noelle-Neumann, Montreal, Quebec, Canada, February 1993.

3. *Tiempo* started a survey to find out what the typical Mexican thought of Mexico's involvement in World War II, but this project was suspended before it was finished. *Tiempo*, no. 4 (May 1942).

4. Rogelio Díaz Guerrero, *Psicología del Mexicano* (Mexico City: Trillas, 1954); Gabriel Almond and Sidney Verba, *The Civic Culture: Political Attitudes and Democracy in Five Nations* (Princeton: Princeton University Press, 1963).

5. Eric Fromm and Michael Maccoby, *Socio-psicoanálisis del campesino mexicano* (Mexico City: Fondo de Cultura Económica, 1970); Kenneth M. Coleman, *Public Opinion and Elections in One Party Systems: The Case of Mexico* (Chapel Hill: University of North Carolina Press, 1970), and *Public Opinion in Mexico City About the Electoral System* (Chapel Hill: University of North Carolina Press, 1972); Rafael Segovia, *La politización del niño mexicano* (Mexico City: El Colegio de México, 1975); Wayne Cornelius, *Politics and the Migrant Poor in Mexico City* (Stanford: Stanford University Press, 1975); Jorge Montaño, *Los pobres de la ciudad en los asentamientos espontáneos* (Mexico City: Siglo XXI, 1976); Juan Manuel Cañibe, "El movimiento estudiantil y la opinión pública," *Revista Mexicana de Ciencia Política* 59 (March 1970): 1–21; and Cecilia Imaz, "El apoyo popular al movimiento estudiantil y la opinión pública," *Revista Mexicana de Sociologia* 37, no. 2 (July 1975): 363–392.

6. Enrique Alduncín, *Los valores de los mexicanos, México: Entre la tradición y la modernidad* (Mexico City: BANAMEX, 1986). The sequel to this was published in 1992, comparing the results of the 1981 study with those of a second study con-

ducted in 1987. Alberto Hernández and Luis Narro, eds., *Cómo somos los mexicanos* (Mexico City: CEE-CREA, 1987). It seems that the collection of articles contained in this work are analyses of the first World Values study. Miguel Basáñez and Roderic Camp, "La nacionalización de la banca y la opinión pública en México," *Foro Internacional* 98 (December 1984): 202–217; Miguel Basáñez, "México 85: Un pronóstico electoral," *Nexos* 91 (July 1985); Miguel Basáñez, "Elections and Political Culture in Mexico," in Judith Gentleman, ed., *Mexican Politics in Transition* (Boulder: Westview Press, 1993); Iván Zavala, "Todos heterodoxos: Cómo piensan los jóvenes mexicanos," *Nexos* 95 (November 1985): 37–43.

7. Miguel Basáñez, *El pulso de los sexenios: Veinte años de crisis en México* (Mexico City: Siglo XXI, 1990); Miguel Basáñez, "Las encuestas en México," in Soledad Loaeza, ed., *México: Auge, crisis y ajuste* (Mexico City: Fondo de Cultura Económica, 1992); Miguel Basáñez, "Is Mexico Heading Towards a Fifth Crisis?" in Riordan Roett, ed., *Political Consequences of Economic Reform* (Boulder: Westview Press, 1993); Ronald Inglehart, Neil Nevitte, and Miguel Basáñez, *Convergence in North America: Trade, Politics and Values* (Princeton: Princeton University Press, forthcoming); also translated as *Convergencia en Norteamérica: Comerico, política y cultura* (Mexico: Siglo XXI, 1994); Alejandro Moreno, "Participación política y confianza partidistas en México: 1982–1992" (thesis, Instituto Tecnológico Autónomo de México [ITAM], 1991); Ana Vásquez and Mónica de la Torre, "Las simpatías partidistas en Mexico: 1982–1992" (thesis, Instituto Tecnológico Autónomo de México [ITAM], 1993).

8. Two exceptions are *El Norte* and *El Financiero*, which are polling on a regular basis. *La Jornada, Excelsior, El Economista, El Sol de México*, and *El Día* occasionally conduct polls. On radio, *MORI-Para Empezar* reports on surveys conducted.

9. Vega y Asociados sent out a mail questionnaire in 1970 to determine electoral preferences. Sánchez Aguilar (1976) and Raul Cremoux (1982) carried out similar exercises. The results of those polls were not published.

10. European Society for Opinion and Marketing Research (ESOMAR) Newsbrief (April 1993).

11. WAPOR, "Código de ética," *Perfil de la Jornada* (July 5, 1988).

12. The firms that initially made up AMAI were A. C. Nielsen, Asesoría e Investigaciones Gamma, Buró de Investigación de Mercados (BIMSA), Centro de Análysis Motivacional (CAM), Estudios Psicoindustriales (EPSI), Factum Mercadotécnico, IBOPE/México, and Investigación de Mercados Profesionales Direccionales (IMPRODIR).

13. WAPOR published in its monthly page in *Este País* an invitation to attend the meeting that AMAI had organized with ESOMAR. *Este País* (May 1993): 63

14. Rosario Martínez, "Las Encuestas Electorales," *El Cotidiano* 25 (October 1988).

15. "Encuesta Electoral: El Distrito Federal," *La Jornada* May 23, 1988.

16. On Heberto Castillo's withdrawal from the presidential race in favor of Cuauhtémoc Cárdenas, see *Proceso* 605 (June 6, 1988), 11.

17. Miguel Basáñez, "Encuesta electoral: El país y el Distrito Federal," *La Jornada*, July 5, 1988; and Miguel Basáñez, "Las encuestas y los resultados oficiales," *La Jornada*, August 8, 1988.

18. *Excelsior*, July 6, 1988, p. 6.

19. *Excelsior,* May 13, 1988, 1; *Uno Más Uno,* May 15, 1988, 1; and *Proceso* 608 (June 27, 1988).

20. *La Jornada,* June 21, 1988.

21. *La Jornada,* December 9, 1990, p. 17.

22. *La Jornada,* November 9, 1990, p. 21.

23. Popular opposition concerning the governorships of Guanajuato, San Luis Potosí, and Michoacán are the notable cases.

24. Asociación Mexicana de Opinión Pública.

25. Article 130, Subsection III (*Código Federal de Instituciones y Procedimientos Electorales,* 1990).

26. An explanation for this statement about the statute can be found in María de las Heras, "Encuestas: Controlar a los autoerigidos controladores," *El Nacional,* December 8, 1989.

27. Ronald Inglehart, *Culture Shift in Advanced Industrial Society* (Princeton: Princeton University Press, 1990), p. 37.

28. Liga de Economistas Revolucionarios, "¿A quién favorecen las encuestas en el Estado de México?" *La Jornada,* November 9, 1990; Miguel Basáñez, "La guerra de las encuestas," *La Jornada,* December 7–9, 1990; María de las Heras, "A la guerra sin fusil," *La Jornada,* December 11–13, 1990; Enrique Alduncín, "Mi cuarto de espadas," *La Jornada,* December 14, 1990; Liga de Economistas Revolucionarios, "¿Guerra de encuestas o monólogo de mentiras?" *La Jornada,* December 19, 1990.

29. Letter from Leonel Godoy to *La Jornada,* June 28, 1989, p. 1.

30. Miguel Basáñez, *La Jornada,* July 16, 1989, p. 1.

31. Miguel Basáñez, "The Art of 'Second-Guessing' the Undeclared Voters: Preliminary Ideas from Cases in Mexico and Nicaragua" (paper prepared for the Annual Meeting of WAPOR, St. Petersburg, Florida [May, 1992]).

32. Iván Zavala, "La brújula loca," *La Jornada,* March 5, 1991.

33. Miguel Basáñez and Enrique Alduncín, "Respuesta a Zavala," *La Jornada,* March 16, 1991.

34. Personal communication, July 1993.

■

CHAPTER ELEVEN

Public Opinion Research in Russia and Eastern Europe

Elena Bashkirova

ECONOMIC AND POLITICAL REFORMS IN RUSSIA and other countries of the former Soviet Union—as well as global changes in all spheres of life— have given public opinion important influence over trends of political, economic, and social development. Democracy brings public opinion to a new stage. Referenda and free elections involving competition among political parties and other organizations have turned public opinion into a decisive instrument of power and the expression of popular will.

At the same time, there are practical aims in polling. Survey research shapes the attitudes of people and provides information to the state and public organizations. People experience the influence of the new infor- mation because results of surveys are regularly reported by the media. Thus accuracy of information becomes critically important and depends on the ability of public opinion researchers to provide competent and reliable survey results and to employ the best methods when evaluating views and opinions. □

IMPACTS OF PUBLIC OPINION RESEARCH

Among current hypotheses about the influence of sociological surveys on political and social life in Russia and Eastern Europe, one stands out above all others: The complexity of Russia's situation dramatically increases the influence of polls, because instability and confrontation in society make public opinion a powerful source of ideological pressure.

Public opinion polling has other impacts as well. First, it can assist public organizations and political parties in strengthening their platforms and correcting practical activity. As political parties and movements launch preelection campaigns, they need to be aware of the opinions and preferences of the voters if they wish to receive the majority of the votes. A new parliamentary election procedure makes this especially important, since half of all seats in the new Parliament must now be given to representatives of contending political parties. Second, public opinion surveys indicate the general direction of societal development and serve as a mirror of social reality. They can reveal the correlation of social forces, the readiness for major transformation, and the strength of civil society.

Third, public opinion polls may significantly influence the future of Russia by providing "stimulation." That is, they can influence politically neutral and apathetic members of society as they begin to form political sympathies and preferences. In Russia, as in most societies, the politically apathetic compose the majority—which potentially endows them with great importance. Survey research reveals that the most politically active parts of the population live in the big cities, although the events of August 1991 and October 1993 prove that even in urban settings political activists remain in the minority. Surveys provide information on public opinion and, more importantly, shape the attitudes of people toward the major problems of Russia's development and engage popular participation in referenda, elections, and other critical political activity.

Fourth, because the media regularly report on the rising or falling fortunes of leaders, polls can influence the attitudes of politically neutral citizens about political leadership. Finally, surveys provide a "feedback phenomenon": Public forecasts may provoke specific action by public organizations and political parties and groups, and they can lead to conceptual changes that accelerate, create, deflect, delay, or modify projected public phenomena and processes.

Although the influence of public opinion polls is very great, their positive role should not be overestimated. Even though surveys contribute to the development and strengthening of democratic processes, in Russia they may also be used for other purposes. Independent sociological services remain very rare. When it is controlled by the state or other political institutions, public opinion research is often shaped and manipulated in favor of prevailing powers. It can become an instrument of social control, rather than an opportunity for popular expression. □

DEVELOPMENT OF SURVEY RESEARCH

During Stalin's tenure, public opinion was completely ignored. This seriously affected the social climate and severely limited the creative potential of the Soviet people, who suffered destructive political, social, and economic mistakes as a result of deliberate neglect of public opinion. Sociological research had been carried out in the prerevolutionary and civil war periods, but Stalin equated such studies with bourgeois influences and declared them "hostile to Marxist ideology." The situation changed dramatically after his death. In 1956, when Stalinism was strongly criticized by Nikita Khrushchev at the Twentieth Congress of the Communist Party of the Soviet Union (CPSU), modern empirical sociology arrived in the USSR.

Yet this was not a time of complete freedom. As in other countries, the dominant political ideology and policies pursued by state authorities had an impact on the choice of survey topics and the rigor of research. There were no surveys funded by private sources, and the state exercised direct control over the topics chosen for study. Successful development of the country's command socialist economy required accurate and reliable information about the implementation and effectiveness of government programs. Yet Communist authorities failed to reveal the true and complete results of surveys, for fear that they might highlight the serious mistakes and weaknesses of socialist planning. These leaders were primarily interested in strengthening their own power, which depended upon repression and other mechanisms of totalitarian rule, but they simultaneously had to estimate the degree of popular support for the Communist Party and for other major institutions of the state. Outcomes were predetermined, however, because the Soviet people had no opportunity to express their opinions without fear of state repression. The main goal of the surveys of this period was to create the impression of unanimous support for the policies and plans of the Communist Party.

Early years of the post-Stalin period saw only a few books published on the results of surveys conducted under the strict control of party and state officials. Research did not touch such "forbidden areas" as politics and ideology, and surveys dealt with practical problems of the "successful" socialist economy. Only during the 1960s did sociological and public opinion survey research receive a powerful stimulus. Investigation began to penetrate political and ideological issues as Soviet sociologists received the long-awaited opportunity to host seminars and conferences on methodological questions, to travel abroad, and to exchange views with foreign social scientists. Since then, public opinion surveys have been carried out regularly, and the theory and methodology of public opinion research has developed quickly. Party control of sociological studies tightened and retarded development of the field after the events of 1968 in Czechoslovakia, but some research still occurred and allowed for exploration of areas such as labor turnover and rural sociology.

The situation did not change much in the 1970s, when the results of public opinion polls were seldom announced by the media. Party and state officials occasionally used data to demonstrate the "advantages of the socialist way of life." The country's leadership nonetheless remained hostile to authentic sociology.

Perestroika and *glasnost* under Mikhail Gorbachev introduced a new phase in the 1980s in the development of sociological and public opinion research. Many local, large-scale, or countrywide public opinion surveys were carried out to reveal Soviet citizens' attitudes toward various aspects of domestic life, international relations, and other topics.[1] Numerous institutions, agencies, departments, and private firms conducted survey research in the USSR, and the network of sociological services expanded throughout the country.[2] The All-Union Center for Public Opinion Studies of Social and Economic Problems was established, together with many other survey research institutions.

After the events of August 1991, the control on the field of sociology exerted by state bodies and public structures was practically eliminated. Sociologists received unlimited opportunities to conduct research on any subject, to cooperate freely with sociological organizations and institutions, and to participate actively in international projects. This was a time for reorganization and restructuring of formerly unwieldy institutions and for the establishment of new firms specializing in public opinion polls and market research.

Among these new institutions is the Russian Public Opinion and Market Research (ROMIR). It is an independent research institute that conducts various types of surveys, from small-scale qualitative surveys (group discussions, in-depth interviews) to large-scale quantitative surveys based on representative samples. Forty-eight field managers and over five hundred specially trained interviewers take part in surveys conducted by the ROMIR within the territory of the Russian Federation. This large-scale research work involves up to 3,000 respondents from all eleven economic-geographic regions of Russia. Because it is in continuous contact with international organizations, such as the European Union, Gallup International, and others, the ROMIR participates in major international projects. Surveys are carried out within the territory of Russia and in the former republics of the USSR. Recent ROMIR surveys have been held in the Russian Federation, Ukraine, Belarus, Armenia, and Uzbekistan. Joint research has also been conducted with U.S. organizations and universities, including the Times Mirror Organization, the Gallup Organization, and the University of Michigan. Close contacts are maintained with mass media organizations, and with state and scientific institutions in the United States, Great Britain, France, Germany, Sweden, Finland, Japan, and elsewhere. □

METHODOLOGY AND ORGANIZATION

When they conduct sociological surveys, Russian scholars inevitably face methodological questions. The peculiarity of these problems depends on the type of study. First, I examine problems related to the most frequently used method, the quantitative one. I then discuss the mass and elite polls that are currently being conducted in Russia.

Quantitative Research

Sampling is crucial to surveys. The ROMIR now applies a new approach to form a nationwide sample in Russia. The primary stage of forming the sample is analogous to that used in the United States national sample, designed at the Institute for Social Research at the University of Michigan.

In the former USSR, administrative divisions including oblasts, krays, and republics were the primary sampling units (PSUs) for national samples. The use of such large units made it impossible to comply with standards of statistical probability. At the same time, a lack of local institutes with qualified professional field managers and interviewers made it difficult to employ smaller units.

The Research Institute of Goskomstat attempted a different approach, proposing the use of town and village Soviets as PSUs. Sample size (number of interviews) was allocated proportionally to population size of economic and geographic regions and selected PSUs in regions. The pattern was suitable for government statistical institutions having a widespread network of local offices that cover the whole country. For research institutes, however, this design is unacceptable because of its high cost. Modern approaches to sample construction at the primary stage require the formation of strata of equal size and, therefore, the assignment of equal number of interviews in all PSUs.

The ROMIR sample represents the adult population of the Russian Federation. The sample design is a five-stage plan, where sampling units are: (1) administrative districts (rayons) and separate cities equivalent to administrative districts at the primary stage; (2) towns and village Soviets (aggregating several villages) at the second stage; (3) voting districts in towns and separate settlements in village Soviets at the third stage; (4) households (apartments) at the fourth stage; and (5) randomly selected respondents at the fifth stage. Sampling units at the first three stages are selected with a probability proportional to unit size (PPS). Households are drawn systematically from a list of addresses and Kish grids are used for random selection of respondents in the household.

Russian researchers lack access to a sufficient number of trained inter-viewers. Networks of qualified interviewers exist in some urban areas—including capitals of republics, big cities, and university towns—where sociological institutes, laboratories, centers, departments, and self-financed companies operate. A national network of interviewers was never in place, although significant progress has been made in this respect by the All-Russian Center of Public Opinion (VCIOM) and other sociological centers.

The low refusal rate evident in the former Soviet Union was linked to a perception among respondents that they had no choice but to partici-pate in government-sanctioned surveys. One way to avoid fear associ-ated with giving frank answers to sensitive questions is to ensure the anonymity of the respondents. A guarantee of anonymity, if accepted by the respondent as genuine, reduces fear that providing truthful answers could ultimately prove to be personally damaging.

Side by side with mass polls there exist surveys of Russian elite groups, including prominent public and political figures and policymak-ers. One special feature of this type of survey comes from the difficulty of creating a representative sample of respondents, which is due to the ab-sence of data banks on elite structures of Russian society. There are no ref-erence books of the "Who's Who" type; and simple information (addresses or telephone numbers) about those people who might com-pose this general universe is also unavailable. In the preparatory stages of respondent selection, researchers compiled inventories of five key institu-tions—government agencies (both legislative and executive branches), mass media, business, the military, and academics. A principal criterion for selection of individuals was rank: high- and middle-ranking officials took part in the survey. Random selection was used at the next stage of re-spondent selection. Different approaches were applied to different elite sectors because of the absence of systematic information.

Conducted primarily among the representatives of the political elite, these surveys focused on problems of economic and political reform as well as on foreign policy. A matter of special interest was to compare the opinions of the two segments of the Russian population—the mass public and the political elite. In general, results revealed that the political elite stands more to the radical "left" than does the rest of Russian society. Among the general population, when compared with the politi-cal elite, there is a higher percentage who: adhere to the tendencies of isolationism; consider military force a primary tool of international rela-tions; support a high level of military expenditures; feel anxious about the "American threat"; and believe that policies of the United States and the West threaten Russia's national security. The data further show that foreign policy hard-liners usually take clear-cut conservative and anti–democratic positions on matters of domestic policy. In particular, they support the idea of reestablishing state control of the economy and the imposition of restrictions on political democracy.

Qualitative Research

The ROMIR has also conducted qualitative surveys. Group discussion has proven particularly useful. This form is usually used to carry out market and pilot surveys in which complicated problems arise in preparation of survey questionnaires. Focus groups have helped, for instance, to evaluate radio programs and to explore preferences for specific groups of listeners (e.g., young, old, businesspeople, etc.).

In addition, in-depth interviews have examined Russian attitudes toward the economic reform and business activity. Since in-depth interviewing demands special skills, on-the-job training is usually required for prospective interviewers. Upon the completion of the training course, candidates conduct test interviews. Only those who succeed at this stage actually take part in the survey. The ROMIR has also gained substantial experience in conducting mixed-type research, the so-called qualitative-quantitative surveys (e.g., in which the questionnaire for the formal interview includes in-depth questions probing respondents' motivations). □

RESULTS FROM RECENT SURVEYS

The year 1992 began with a historic event—the departure of the old Soviet Union and its replacement with the Commonwealth of Independent States (CIS). (The Baltic States and Georgia emphasized their new-found independence by refusing to join the CIS.) Thus the number of countries being polled has substantially increased: Armenia, Belarus, Georgia, Moldova, and the Ukraine from the former USSR; Slovenia and Macedonia from the former Yugoslavia; and the Czech Republic and Slovakia, which were split in the anticipation of the dissolution of Czechoslovakia.

In the wake of these events, the ROMIR carried out a European Economic Commission survey to assess public support for political and economic changes in eighteen Central and East European countries.[3] The study covered countries of the former socialist community and former member states of the Soviet Union. In this connection, the results can be compared in two ways: (1) between Russia and former socialist countries of Eastern Europe, and (2) between Russia and former member states of the Soviet Union.

Central and Eastern Europe

Because the overwhelming majority of former socialist countries initiated democratic reforms earlier than did the former Soviet Union, the result of policy reforms influenced people's attitudes. According to a survey, compared with the Russians, people living in the former socialist countries have a much more positive attitude toward development and economic reform. They oppose the revival of former policies and dictatorships. They are quite optimistic about the future of their nations' economies and of their own well-being.

Within this context, the majority of people in the European part of Russia believe that the development of the country has taken a wrong direction (50 percent); less than one-third (27 percent) consider the new direction to be the right one. In nearly all former socialist countries, more people support the new policies. Absolute majorities of Albanians, Slovenians, and Czechs, as well as a relative majority of Estonians, Bulgarians, and Macedonians, say things are going in the right direction. Recently separated Slovaks are divided on the issue.

Hungary and Poland were the only countries in which the percentage of respondents who considered that the things had taken a wrong turn was higher than in the Russian Federation (67 and 56 percent, respectively). Compare these figures to results obtained in former republics of the USSR: Ukraine (52 percent), Lithuania (64 percent), Armenia (63 percent), and Moldova (73 percent).

In comparison with the former socialist countries of Eastern Europe, Russia has many more people considering that within the last twelve months the economic situation in their country has worsened (76 percent). Yet former Soviet republics showed even higher figures: Armenia (92 percent), Lithuania (87 percent), Latvia (84 percent), Ukraine (81 percent), and Belarus (79 percent). Georgia and Moldova each scored 75 percent on this item.

Household income also diminished from 1992 to 1993. Georgians and Russians have fared only slightly better financially than have the people of the other former republics of the USSR. Compared to other former socialist countries, the plight of people in Russia is much more serious; in Poland, Macedonia, and Hungary, however, the level of household finances declined even more sharply than it did in Russia (see Figure 11.1).

Compared to 1992, there is greater optimism about the prospects for 1993. As shown in Figure 11.2, a quarter of the regional population (25 percent) expects economic conditions to improve, but two out five (41 percent) predict further decline. One-fifth of those interviewed (18 percent) say the economic conditions in their country will remain largely unchanged. On balance, people in the region expect their household

FIGURE 11.1 Perception of Improvement in Household Finances in the Past Twelve Months, East European Countries (excluding Albania), 1992–1993

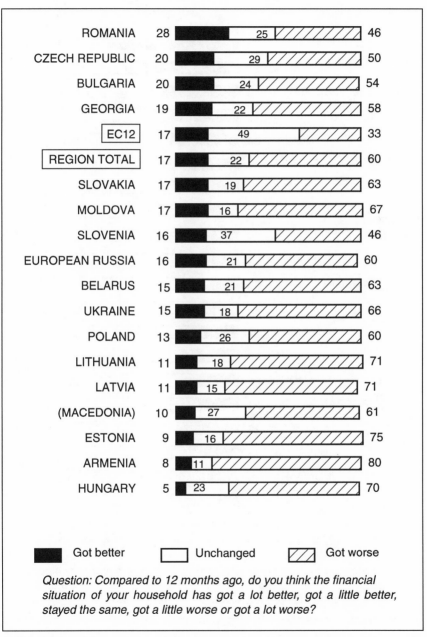

Question: Compared to 12 months ago, do you think the financial situation of your household has got a lot better, got a little better, stayed the same, got a little worse or got a lot worse?

Source: Central and Eastern Eurobarometer (Brussels: European Commission), annex Figure 1.

284

FIGURE 11.2   Perception of Outlook for General Economic Situation in the Next
Twelve Months: East European Countries, 1993

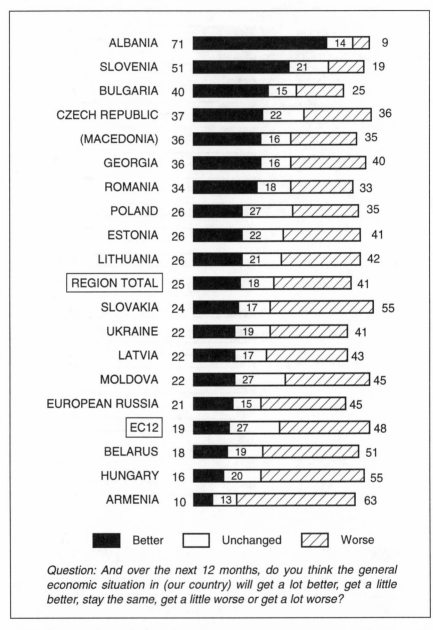

Question: And over the next 12 months, do you think the general
economic situation in (our country) will get a lot better, get a little
better, stay the same, get a little worse or get a lot worse?

Source: Central and Eastern Eurobarometer (Brussels: European Commission), annex
Figure 1.

finances to diminish in 1993 (22 percent "better," 24 percent "same," and 36 percent "worse"). By 1992, virtually all countries in the region had in place active economic reform programs reflecting varying degrees of commitment to market economies.

Early reforming countries—the new Czech Republic, Hungary, and Poland—had gone sufficiently far down that road to be considered by Western experts as being on the brink of economic growth in 1993. Many other economies—particularly those served by the European Union's Technical Assistance for Community of Independent States (TACIS) program (Armenia, Belarus, Moldova, Russia west of the Urals, Ukraine plus Georgia) and the Baltic states—are still in "free fall" as difficult political decisions are delayed while inflation erodes the purchasing power of citizens.

In all former socialist countries except Macedonia, more than half of the people think that the establishment of a free market economy is the right step to contribute to a better future (see Figure 11.3). In all former Soviet republics, less than half of the population believe the same (from 49 percent in Estonia to 31 percent in Armenia). In Russia, 37 percent of interviewees favor the development of market economy, and 44 percent oppose it. For the region as a whole, 6 percentage points separate those who believe in the free market (44 percent) and those who do not (38 percent).

Also for the region as a whole, as displayed in Figure 11.4, more than four out of ten (44 percent) say economic reforms are going "too slowly," one-tenth (11 percent) "at about the right speed," and one-sixth (16 percent) "too fast." One-eighth (12 percent) remark spontaneously that there are no economic reforms.

Similarly, almost half (45 percent) of the people in the region as a whole think the privatization of state enterprises is going "too slowly," one-eighth (12 percent) "at about the right speed," and one-seventh (15 percent) "too fast." People in the former Soviet republics are more likely to want the process to accelerate than are those in former socialist countries, where privatization is more advanced. Only in the former Yugoslav Republic of Macedonia and in Lithuania are people divided as to whether privatization should go faster rather than slower. In the Czech Republic, Slovakia, Hungary, and Poland, where economic reforms first started, more people are saying that privatization is going too slowly, but at least as many are now saying that the rate of change is acceptable or it is too fast. Clearly, despite disillusionment, and perhaps even the remains of old ideological distrust of the market economy, the majority of people from TACIS—as well as PHARE countries—still want economic reforms and the privatization of their state enterprises to succeed.[4] PHARE (originally Aid for the Economic Reconstruction of Poland and Hungary) is the European Union's assistance program to Albania, Bulgaria, the Czech

FIGURE 11.3 Is the Creation of a Market Economy Right or Wrong?
East European Countries, 1993

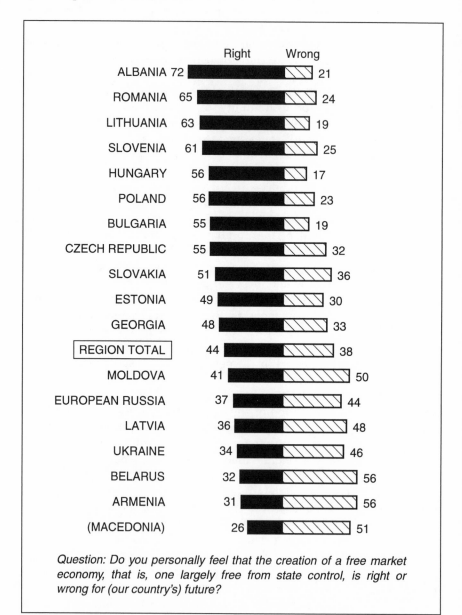

Question: *Do you personally feel that the creation of a free market economy, that is, one largely free from state control, is right or wrong for (our country's) future?*

Source: Central and Eastern Eurobarometer (Brussels: European Commission), annex Figure 1.

FIGURE 11.4   Are Economic Reforms Proceeding Too Fast or Too Slowly?
East European Countries, 1993

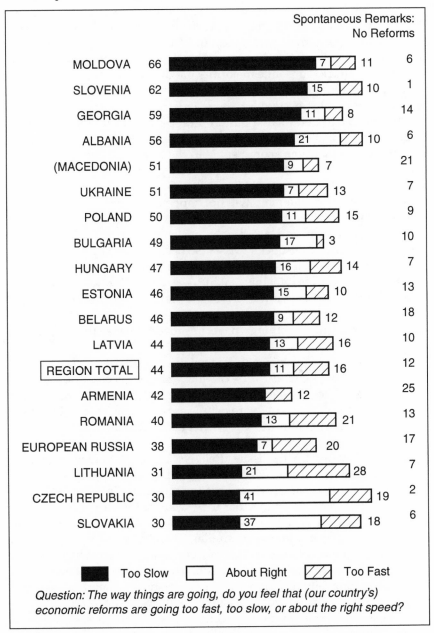

Source: Central and Eastern Eurobarometer (Brussels: European Commission), annex
Figure 1.

Republic, Estonia, Hungary, Latvia, Lithuania, Poland, Romania, Slovakia, and Slovenia.

Lithuania continues to be the only country in Central and Eastern Europe in which more citizens are satisfied rather than dissatisfied with the development of their democracy. In Macedonia, Georgia, and Slovenia, people are divided on the issue. Everywhere else, but especially in the TACIS countries, absolute majorities are dissatisfied.[5]

People were asked to speculate on the likelihood of a "nondemocratic" dictatorship existing in their country within the next twelve months. People in Central and Eastern Europe are two-to-one (52 percent to 26 percent) of the opinion that a dictatorship will not arise in their country within that time span. People in the former Soviet republics are less confident. Both Moldovans and Armenians are divided as to whether this will happen to their country. Georgians, two-to-one, are of the opinion that a dictatorship will not happen; however, 9 percent spontaneously say a dictatorship already exists. It is significant that these countries are at war and are highly unstable politically. One-third of people in Latvia and European Russia (33 percent and 34 percent, respectively) also expressed fears about the potential for dictatorship.

People were asked whether, taking everything into account, life is better for them now than it was under the previous political system. Half (50 percent) say that they were better off before and only just over one-quarter (27 percent) say things have improved. One-sixth (16 percent) say "neither."

There is, however, a major difference in attitudes between people in PHARE and TACIS countries. In the former socialist countries, on one hand, most perceive the current system to be better. In the former Soviet republics, on the other hand, more people are nostalgic for the old days.

Majorities in Albania, the Czech Republic, Romania, and Slovenia praise their current system. People in Slovakia, Lithuania, Bulgaria, and Poland are divided on the issue. Relative or absolute majorities elsewhere—including, surprisingly, many people in Hungary—say that things were better before. Russians are the most nostalgic and least optimistic, with 59 percent saying that they were better off previously and only 18 percent believing things are better for them now. Responses to the same questions in Ukraine are similar, 59 and 19 percent, respectively.

These results do not indicate that most people in these countries would prefer to see the return of communism. They simply find times much harder in the transition period from a command to a market economy. Before, shortages existed, but at least the goods were affordable.

Almost twice as many people feel there is no respect for individual human rights in their country as say there is respect (only 32 percent registered "respect," but 56 percent said "no respect"). In all former socialist countries, except Macedonia and Poland, the majority claim there is respect for human rights. In contrast, fewer than half the respondents in the former Soviet republics feel that way: Russia (67 percent) and Georgia (80 percent) being the worst cases. Absolute majorities in Slovakia, Hungary, Albania, Bulgaria, the Czech Republic, Slovenia, and Romania say human rights are respected in their countries. People are divided on the issue in Macedonia and Estonia, but everywhere else absolute majorities say there is no respect. Poland is the only country outside the Baltic states and TACIS countries to have a majority saying human rights are not respected.

Members of minority groups were asked whether they feel disadvantaged in their country because of their nationality or ethnic background. From over one-third to one-half of minorities in Macedonia (50 percent), Estonia (49 percent), Latvia (42 percent), and Moldova (37 percent) say they do feel disadvantaged. Nearly half (45 percent) of those in Georgia would not answer.

A crucial feature of human rights is the free flow of information. Especially when it comes to making a democratic choice, nothing is more important than having access to unbiased information from the media. Central and Eastern Europeans as a whole believe national radio, on balance, is the most trustworthy media source of news and current affairs (54 percent registered "trust," and 33 percent registered "no trust"), followed by national television (53 percent to 41 percent). They are divided as to whether they believe what is written in national newspapers (40 percent to 38 percent) and national magazines (27 percent to 24 percent). Too few give an opinion about Western television (16 percent to 14 percent) and Western radio (15 percent to 13 percent) except to say little more than it remains controversial (among the one-third who were willing to give an opinion).

Georgia is the only country in which a majority consistently expressed distrust toward its national media. The same is true for most Armenians; however, they are divided over the trustworthiness of national radio. Moldovans also lack trust in the national media, and they voice uncertainty over national television. Georgians and Moldovans also express the greatest distrust of Western media (along with people from Belarus, concerning Western radio). In Central and Eastern Europe, all media had been controlled by the state under the previous political system, and moves are under way to free them. Most countries now have a thriving independent national press. Throughout Central and Eastern Europe, most people are of the opinion that there should be "not very much/no" state control over television and radio (57 percent to 34 percent) as well as "not very much/no" state control over the press (57 percent to 35 percent).

Russia

In Russia, analysis of survey data reveals a consistent pattern. The situation there appears to be preferable to that in the former states of the USSR, which have met with serious difficulties. Under a well-established division of labor between the Soviet republics and various regions, Russia provided substantial economic assistance within the framework of the Soviet Union. When economic ties were cut, those republics suffered more damage than did the Russian Federation. Many republics lack the necessary resources for developing their own national economies. Today the newly born sovereign states must pay for Russian assistance at world-market prices. In many cases, they fail to do so. This is why the CIS countries are now eager to establish a new economic union and strengthen economic ties with other countries, especially with Russia. Continuous bloodshed between Armenia and Azerbaijan and between Georgia and Abkhazia, as well as the threat imposed by the Afghan Islamic fundamentalists to the former republics of Central Asia, put additional burdens on the former Soviet republics.

The most predictable supporters of reform in Russia are young, well-educated, urban males already economically active in the emerging private sector and relatively well paid. These individuals are also likely to be more optimistic, or at least less pessimistic, about the future. Women, in general, view reform less favorably than do men; and older people, those with less education, the unskilled and poorly paid (especially in agriculture), and pensioners tend to oppose reform and are more pessimistic about the future. Although those working on state and collective farms voice more than the average opposition to recent changes and further marketization, there is majority support in the rural community and the farm labor force for privatization of land. This shows a strengthening of rural support for land reform, compared with earlier survey findings.

Further analysis by occupation and workplace is interesting but needs to be treated with caution, in view of small numbers in some categories. With this reservation, it can be noted, for example, that military personnel appear to be divided between liberals and traditionalists. Alternatively, representatives of the security services, the militia, and the judiciary are markedly more traditionalist and opposed to change.

Responses by region show a tendency for traditionalist views to be stronger in the Central Black Earth, Volga-Vyatka, and North Caucasus regions, with the north, northwest, and central areas more in favor of change. Some of these differences can be explained by the urban/rural, educational, and occupational characteristics of the various regions—for instance, the more traditionalist regions tend to have larger rural populations. Other differences may be affected by local political issues; the marked pessimism about the near future revealed in the Volga and North Caucasus regions could reflect uncertainty caused by the regions' ethnic tensions.

The latest polls showed, in general, a stability of opinion. The main change was an increase in the numbers who answered "don't know" to a number of questions, reflecting perhaps a growing uncertainty or resignation. Otherwise, minor changes were mostly in a slightly encouraging direction. A majority still believed that the country was going in the wrong direction and that the economic situation had declined further and was likely to continue to worsen; but the preponderance of negative over positive thinking was somewhat reduced.

People were still highly dissatisfied with their standard of living and disapproving of economic changes, though disapproval was slightly less strong than in June 1993. And even though most people were still critical of the government's performance, they were slightly less critical than they were in June. The small majority in favor of efforts to establish a free market economy remained about the same, but the majority in favor of price liberalization was slightly reduced. There was a slight decline in the numbers of people interested in starting their own businesses, and a bigger decline in those contemplating financing a business from their own savings.

On the political side, the small majority disapproving of political changes (unspecified) actually increased. However, the degree of trust in the government marginally increased. The numbers approving of Boris Yeltsin's performance remained constant, but those who disapproved dropped below 50 percent—with a substantial reduction in the proportion "disapproving strongly."

In brief, the picture remains sombre, with a high level of dissatisfaction, pessimism, and lack of confidence in the Russian government. But the government might take some comfort from the fact that, over a six-month period of continuing severe difficulties, attitudes have not significantly worsened and, in some respects, have improved marginally. □

PROSPECTS AND CHALLENGES

The confrontation between legislative and executive branches of power in Russia led to crisis and bloodshed in October 1993. Uncertainty about the future, sky-rocketing prices, and decline of living standards have led to widespread pessimism. No doubt, events in October 1993 changed the attitudes of many Russians toward political, social, and economic matters. The task for researchers is to ascertain and evaluate these new opinions and attitudes. The current situation calls for regular and repeated surveys of public opinion.

Parliamentary elections and large-scale election campaigns by various political parties and movements call for the use of reliable opinion polls to guide political platforms and practical activity. In this connection, public opinion polls become very important, because they may seriously influence leaders through effective feedback mechanisms and thus contribute to the development and consolidation of democracy. □

NOTES

1. "Bolshinstvo odobryaet" (The majority approves), *Pravda* (December 17, 1987): 2; E. I. Bashkirova, "Dialogue SSSR-SShA: Chto dumayut o nyom sovetskiye lyudi" (Dialogue USSR-USA: What Soviet people think about it), *Agitator* 6 (1988): 14–18; and Elena Bashkirova, "Interes i ozhidaniya" (Interest and expectations), *New Times* 49 (1987).

2. "Erst lernen, eine eigene Meinung zu haben," "Vertrauen statt Raketen," *Der Spiegel* 24 (June 12, 1989): 34–54; Pentii Raittila, Elena Bashkirova, and Ludmila Semionova, *Perestroika and Changing Neighbour Images in Finland and the Soviet Union* (Tampere, Finland: University of Tampere, 1989); and M. Kent Jennings and Richard Niemi, *Generations and Politics* (Princeton: Princeton University Press, 1981).

3. From a survey conducted between November 1 and 15 in European Russia on a sample of 1,000 respondents (*Central and Eastern EuroBarometer*, no. 3 [February 1993]).

4. PHARE (originally "Aid for the Economic Reconstruction of Poland and Hungary") is the name of the European Union's assistance program to Albania, Bulgaria, the Czech Republic, Estonia, Hungary, Latvia, Lithuania, Poland, Romania, Slovakia, and Slovenia. For the purpose of this survey, "PHARE" demonstrates the average values of the views of the permanent residents of the above countries, weighted by the respective country's population size.

5. Technical Assistance for the Community of Independent States (TACIS) is the European Union's assistance program.

About the Book

This book, the inaugural publication in a multivolume series entitled *Latin America in Global Perspective*, highlights the necessity and feasibility of analyzing Latin American society and politics within broad comparative frameworks.

The rapidly changing agenda for social science research on the region calls for the rigorous application of new concepts and methodologies, especially in light of the apparent exhaustion of the "dependency" paradigm. The examination of broad themes, such as development strategies and processes of democratization, can be facilitated through systematic comparisons with other world regions, and the study of specific issues—such as electoral behavior or social inequality—requires the judicious use of quantitative measurement. The question, therefore, is not only *what* to investigate but also *how*.

This volume brings together original research by distinguished scholars from a variety of countries. Analytical chapters explore methodological strategies for cross-regional comparison, intraregional comparison, and the application of rational choice; topical chapters offer new approaches to the study of women, state power, corporatism, and political culture. A concluding section examines the political significance of public opinion research in Mexico, Peru, and the former Soviet Union.

About the Editor and Contributors

Miguel Basáñez is professor of public opinion and Mexican politics at the Autonomous Institute of Technology (ITAM) in Mexico City. He received his Ph.D. in political science from the London School of Economics. Basáñez is the author of three books and numerous articles on Mexico's current affairs. Since 1990 he has served as the Mexican representative to the World Association for Public Opinion Researchers (WAPOR); and he is also president of MORI de México (Market and Opinion Research International) and publisher of the monthly magazine *Este País*, which specializes in dissemination of public opinion polls in Mexico.

Elena Bashkirova has been director of ROMIR (Russian Public Opinion and Market Research) since 1991. She is a member of Gallup International and holds a Ph.D. in sociology. In 1990–1991, Dr. Bashkirova served as department head of the Institute of Sociology in the USSR Academy of Sciences in Moscow, and she has published major studies on public opinion in Russia. Since 1992, she has served as the Russian representative to the World Association for Public Opinion Researchers (WAPOR).

Fernando Bustamante is professor of political science and international politics at the Facultad Latinoamericana de Ciencias Sociales (FLACSO) in Quito, Ecuador. He has studied civil-military relations in Latin America and has published many articles and books on that topic and on the field of international security. He has concentrated on such topics as arms transfers, military expenditure, national security doctrines, threat perception, and drug traffic and violence.

David Collier is professor of political science at the University of California, Berkeley. He is editor and coauthor of *The New Authoritarianism in Latin America* (1979) and coauthor of *Shaping the Political Arena: Critical Junctures, the Labor Movement, and Regime Dynamics in Latin America* (1991). Collier has served as chair of both the Center for Latin American Studies and the Department of Political Science at Berkeley.

Catherine M. Conaghan is associate professor of political studies at Queen's University, Canada. She is the author of *Restructuring Domination: Industrialists and the State in Ecuador* (1988) and *Unsettling Statecraft: Democracy and Neoliberalism in the Central Andes* (with James Malloy). Conaghan has been a visiting fellow at the Kellogg Institute at the University of Notre Dame and the Center of International Studies at Princeton University.

Barbara Geddes is associate professor of political science at the University of California, Los Angeles, where she teaches courses on Latin American politics, revolution, and research design and methodology. Her publications include *Politician's Dilemma: Building State Capacity in Latin America* and articles on civil service reform, authoritarian regimes, corruption, and comparative methodology. During 1993–1994 she was a National Fellow at the Hoover Institution, Stanford University.

Gary Gereffi is a professor of sociology at Duke University. He received his Ph.D. from Yale University. Gereffi is author of *The Pharmaceutical Industry and Dependency in the Third World* (1983), *Manufacturing Miracles: Paths of Industrialization in Latin America and East Asia* (coedited with the late Donald Wyman, 1990), and *Commodity Chains and Global Capitalism* (coedited with Miguel Korzeniewicz, 1994). Gereffi's current research deals with business organizations, trade and production networks, and the social bases of international competitiveness.

Evelyne Huber is Morehead Alumni Distinguished Professor of Political Science at the University of North Carolina and director of the Institute of Latin American Studies. She is the author of *The Politics of Workers' Participation: The Peruvian Approach in Comparative Perspective* (1980), *Democratic Socialism in Jamaica: The Political Movement and Social Transformation in Dependent Capitalism* (with John D. Stephens, 1986), and *Capitalist Development and Democracy* (with Dietrich Rueschemeyer and John D. Stephens, 1992). Huber's research focuses on democracy and socioeconomic reform in Latin America and the Caribbean, with a comparative perspective on Western Europe.

Jane S. Jaquette is professor of politics at Occidental College in Los Angeles. She writes on comparative women's political participation, women in development, and feminist theory. Her most recent book is *The Women's Movement in Latin America: Participation and Democracy* (second edition, Westview, 1994), and she is coediting, with Sharon Wolchik, a book comparing women's roles in democratization in Latin America and Central and Eastern Europe.

Amparo Menéndez-Carrión is professor of comparative politics and international relations at the Facultad Latinoamericano de Ciencias Sociales (FLACSO) in Quito, Ecuador. She is director of FLACSO-Ecuador as well. Menéndez-Carrión is the author of *La conquista del voto* (1986), a study of urban politics and clientelism in Ecuador. Her studies on issues of voting behavior, political culture, and urban politics have been published in Europe, the United States, and Latin America. Her current research examines the question of citizenship and the public sphere in the Andean region.

Peter H. Smith is professor of political science, director of the Center for Iberian and Latin American Studies, and Simón Bolívar Professor of Latin American Studies at the University of California, San Diego. He is a specialist on political methodology, comparative politics, Latin American politics, and U.S.–Latin American relations. His publications include more than a dozen books and nearly fifty book chapters and journal articles. Smith is coauthor of *Modern Latin America* (1984), now in its third edition (1992). His forthcoming book is *Talons of the Eagle: Dynamics of U.S.–Latin American Relations*.

Frederick C. Turner is professor of political science at the University of Connecticut and past president of the World Association for Public Opinion Research. He received his Ph.D. from the Fletcher School of Law and Diplomacy. Turner is the editor of *Social Mobility and Political Attitudes: Comparative Perspectives* (1992) and *Juan Perón and the Reshaping of Argentina* (with José Enrique Miguens, 1982). He is also the author of *Catholicism and Political Development in Latin America* (1971) and *The Dynamic of Mexican Nationalism* (1968).

Index

AAPOR. *See* American Association for Public Opinion Research
Accumulation
  civil society and, 178, 180
  state strength and, 167–168, 190(n12)
Agenda control, defined, 93
Aggregation effects, 93–96
Aggregation levels, 71–72
Aid for the Economic Reconstruction of Poland and Hungary (PHARE), 285, 288, 292(n4)
Alberto Sánchez, Luís, 239
Alexander, Robert J., 136
Allende, Salvador, 175
All-Russian Center of Public Opinion (VCIOM), 280
All-Union Center for Public Opinion Studies of Social and Economic Problems, 278
Almond, Gabriel, 196, 197–198, 258
AMAI. *See* Mexican Association of Research Agencies
American Association for Public Opinion Research (AAPOR), 262, 263
Ames, Barry, 11, 97
Amsden, Alice, 40–41
Anderson, Charles W., 136, 151
Anthropology, public opinion research vs., 209
APEIM. *See* Peruvian Association of Market Research Companies
Apoyo S.A., 231, 233, 234, 238, 241, 243, 248
Area studies
  geography and, 66–68
  U.S. funding for, 21–22
  value of, 61
Arendt, Hannah, 115

Argentina
  academic research in, 21
  corporatism in, 146
  cultural surveys in, 197, 211–213, 213–215(tables), 224(n61)
  political culture in, 211–212, 223(nn 53, 54)
Argentine Chamber of Deputies, 11
Arrow, Kenneth, 93
Asia
  cross-regional comparison with Latin America, 16, 35–50, 193(n49)
  development strategies in, 35–43
Attitudes, values vs., 196, 209
Authoritarianism
  civil society and, 174, 176–177, 191(n33)
  corporatism and, 137, 145
  democracy and, 73, 207–210
  developmental strategies and, 41, 56(n25)
  education and, 209–210, 224(n65)
  intraregional comparison and, 64, 73
  political culture and, 207–210
  political parties in, 172
  public opinion polls and, 230, 241
  rational choice arguments and, 103(n1), 104(n8)
Authoritarianism and Corporatism in Latin America (Malloy), 139

Barry, Brian, 85
Basáñez, Miguel, 12, 225, 257, 263, 295
Bashkirova, Elena, 13, 226, 275, 295
Bates, Robert, 82, 97
Behavior
  beliefs vs., 14

See also Congressional behavior;
    Electoral behavior; Political behavior
Belaúnde, Fernando, 230
Beliefs, behavior vs., 14
Benería, Lourdes, 119
Bergquist, Charles, 15
*Between Power and Plenty: Foreign Economic
    Policies of Advanced Industrial States*
    (Katzenstein), 70
Blacker Miller, Augusto, 237
Bollen, Kenneth, 12
Boloña, Carlos, 253(n56)
Bonilla, Frank, 214
Booth, John, 208, 209
Boserup, Ester, 118, 119
Bourdieu, Pierre, 228, 257
Brazil
    academic research in, 21
    corporatism in, 139, 140, 141–142, 146
Brown, Archie, 196
Brunner, José Joaquín, 19
Buchanan, James, 97, 98
Bureaucracies
    intraregional comparison and, 64, 69–70
    state strength and, 187
Bureaucratic authoritarianism
    corporatism and, 155
    military regimes under, 171
    the state and, 189(n3)
    as subtype of authoritarianism, 147
Business organizations, corporatism and,
    140, 158(n23)
Bustamante, Fernando, 15, 21, 31–32, 59, 295
Buyer-driven commodity chains, 45

Cable News Network (CNN), 237
Calculating ability, rational choice
    arguments and, 87–90
Camp, Roderic A., 11
Cardoso, Fernando Henrique, 16
Caretas (newsmagazine), 231, 239, 240, 243,
    248
Caribbean Community and Common
    Market (CARICOM), 60
CARICOM. *See* Caribbean Community and
    Common Market
Carmen Feijoó, Maria del, 115
Catterberg, Edgardo, 13, 21, 211
CEDYS. *See* Center for the Study of
    Democracy and Society
Censorship, of public opinion research, 260
Center for Planning Research and Study
    (CIEPLAN), 20

Center for the Study of Democracy and
    Society (CEDYS), 248
Center for the Study of Public Opinion
    (CEOP), 259, 261–262, 270
Central America, comparison to South
    Korea, 178, 218(n14)
Central American Common Market, 60
Central and Eastern Europe. *See* Eastern
    Europe
CEOP. *See* Center for the Study of Public
    Opinion
Chalmers, Doug, 141
Cheng, Tun-jen, 42
Chile
    corporatism in, 154–155
    cultural surveys in, 198, 212, 213–
        215(tables)
    education expenditures in, 20
Chodorow, Nancy, 113
Chuchryk, Patricia, 122
Chungara, Domitila, 114
CIEPLAN. *See* Center for Planning
    Research and Study
Ciria, Alberto, 141
CIS. *See* Commonwealth of Independent
    States
Civic Culture, The (Almond & Verba), 196,
    213, 258
Civil society
    authoritarianism and, 174, 176–177,
        191(n33)
    democracy and, 174, 176–177
    four categories of, 176
    social class and, 172–173, 176, 178–179
    state action and, 174–175, 191(nn 30, 31)
    state strength and, 172–182, 187
CLACSO. *See* Latin American Council for
    Social Science
Class, social. *See* Social class
Classical subtype formation, 147,
    148(figure)
Clientelism
    corporatism and, 143–144
    intraregional comparison and, 68, 71
CNN. *See* Cable News Network
Coatsworth, John, 21
Cochrane, James, 197
Cohen, Jean, 121
Cohen, Monique, 125
Col, Jeanne Marie, 125
Collaborative research, 51
Collective action problems
    game theory and, 99–100
    rational choice arguments and, 94–96

Collier, David, 11, 15, 109, 135, 138, 140, 146, 295
Collier, Ruth Berins, 15, 138, 140, 146
Collor de Mello, Fernando, 73
Comercio, El (newspaper), 231
Coming to Public Judgment (Yankelovich), 247
Committee on States and Social Structures, 164
Commodity chains. *See* Global commodity chains
Commodity Chains and Global Capitalism (Gereffi & Korzeniewicz), 44, 51
Common Market of the South (MERCOSUR), 17, 59
Commonwealth of Independent States (CIS), 281, 290.
   See also Russia
Communism
   public opinion research after fall of, 282–291
   public opinion research under, 277–278
   See also Marxism
Communist Party of the Soviet Union (CPSU), 277
Comparative analysis
   redefining, 76–78
   research on Latin America through, 1–2, 14–18
   of state strength, 186–189
   statistical analysis vs., 2–3, 7
   types of, 3–6
   See also Cross-regional comparisons; Intraregional comparisons; Statistical analysis
Component-supply subcontracting, 48
CONACYT. *See* National Council on Science and Technology
Conaghan, Catherine M., 13, 225, 227, 295–296
Conceptual stretching, 149–150
Concertation, 142–143
Confucian traditions, 36, 37–38
Congressional behavior
   rational choice arguments and, 93–94, 97
   statistical research and, 11–12, 13
   See also Political behavior
Conservativism, 83
Consociationalism, 144
Constitutional structure, 171
Context, rational choice arguments and, 90–91, 92
Cooperation
   in civil society, 177

game theory and, 99–100
Co-optation, 149
Corcoran-Nantes, Yvonne, 122
Cornelius, Wayne, 201
Corporatism
   civil society and, 176
   concepts related to, 143–144
   conceptualization of, 138–139
   cultural perspective on, 150–153
   defined, 138
   described, 109, 135
   emergence of, 136–137
   erosion of, 153–156
   labor organizations and, 140–141, 146, 155, 158(n23), 159(nn 24, 25), 181–182
   normalization of concept of, 153, 156
   refinements in concept of, 142–143
   shared empirical understanding of, 139–142
   subtype formation and, 146–150
   subtypes and dimensions of, 144–146
Cotler, Julio, 234
Country-level mapping, 47–48
CPI. *See* Peruvian Research Company
CPSU. *See* Communist Party of the Soviet Union
Craig, Ann, 201
Cross-regional comparisons
   data gathering in, 50–53
   development strategies and, 35–43
   export roles and, 48–50
   global commodity chains and, 43–50
   individualizing comparisons and, 42–43
   methods used in, 38–40
   MSS designs and, 15–16
   of political culture, 198, 199(table), 201, 204–205, 217
   public opinion research and, 267–268
   See also Comparative analysis; Intraregional comparisons
Culture. *See* Political culture
Curran, James, 228

Dandavati, Annie, 122
Data gathering
   in cross-regional research, 50–53
   public opinion research and, 206, 216, 220(n25)
   See also Public opinion research; Statistical analysis
Data probe interview, 51–52
Datum S.A., 231, 233–234, 239, 243
Dealy, Glen Caudill, 197–198, 200
Debate, public, 228–229, 244–246

Deductive logic, 91, 92
Degree of competitiveness, 144
Delegative democracy, 147, 250(n12)
Democracy
    authoritarianism and, 73, 207–210
    civil society and, 174, 176–177
    corporatism and, 156
    cross-regional comparisons and, 17–18
    economic development and, 10
    educational funding and, 20–21
    political culture and, 207–213
    public opinion polls and, 228–230, 247–
        249, 275
    rational choice arguments and, 82, 84, 88,
        98, 101–102, 103(n1) social class and,
        17, 202–203, 222(n42)
    as theme for intraregional comparison,
        72–73, 75–76
Democratic Revolutionary Party (PRD),
    261, 269
Dependency theory
    described, 8–9
    downfall of, 9–10
    statistical analysis and, 12
Dependent variables, 40, 41
Determinism, 91
Development strategies
    cross-regional comparison of, 35–43
    defined, 55(nn 19, 20)
    as dependent and independent
        variables, 40–42
    described, 33–34
    five subtypes of, 54(n8)
Diamond, Larry, 208, 210
Díaz Guerrero, Rogelio, 258
"Difference" feminism, 112, 128(n1)
Distribution, state strength and, 167–168,
    178–179
Division of labor. See Labor
Domestic upgrading, 46
Dominant classes, civil society and, 172–
    173, 176, 178–179
Downs, Anthony, 97

East Asia
    cross-regional comparison with Latin
        America, 16, 35–50, 193(n49)
    development strategies in, 35–43
Eastern Europe
    perception of media in, 289
    results from surveys in, 282–289
    survey on economic conditions in, 282,
        284(figure), 285

survey on free market economy in, 285,
    286(figure)
    survey on household income in, 282,
        283(figure)
    survey on rate of economic reforms in,
        285, 287(figure)
    See also Europe; Russia
Ebel, Roland, 197
Economic development
    cross-regional studies of, 16, 35–43
    democracy and, 10
    global commodity chains and, 43–50
    international system and, 183–184
    public opinion research and, 282–285
    women's role and, 113, 118–120
    See also Political development; Regional
        development
Education, Latin American
    academic networks and, 61, 77–78
    authoritarianism and, 209–210, 224(n65)
    decline in, 19–20
Electoral behavior
    public opinion research and, 13–14, 261–
        264, 269–270
    rational choice arguments and, 88–89,
        104(n12)
    statistical research and, 12, 13–14
    See also Political behavior
Elshtain, Jean Bethke, 113
Embedded autonomy, 173–174
Encompassing comparisons
    cross-regional studies and, 16, 39
    defined, 3
    statistical analysis and, 7
EOI. See Export-oriented industrialization
EPZs. See Export-processing zones
Erickson, Kenneth P., 139
ESOMAR. See European Society for
    Opinion and Marketing Research
Este País (magazine), 258, 264
Europe
    corporatism in, 157(n1)
    cross-regional comparisons with Latin
        America, 16–18
    See also Eastern Europe
European Society for Opinion and
    Marketing Research (ESOMAR), 259,
    262
Evans, Peter, 52
Exclusionary political systems, 146, 149
Export-oriented industrialization (EOI)
    cross-regional comparisons of, 36–37,
        41–43
    primary vs. secondary phases of, 54(n8)

Export-processing assembly operations, 48–50
Export-processing zones (EPZs), 49–50
Export roles, 48–50
Expreso (newspaper), 234, 241
Extractive capacity, 166

Fagen, Richard, 10
Faletto, Enzo, 16
Family, survey research on, 198, 199(table), 219(n17)
Fascism, corporatism and, 160(n36)
Federalism, state strength and, 171
Feminism
    comparative politics and, 109
    evolution of, 112–117
    new social movements and, 120–122
    rational choice arguments and, 112, 127
    women in development studies and, 117–120, 123–125
    See also Gender methodologies; Women
Fishlow, Albert, 37
FLACSO. *See* Latin American Faculty for Social Science
Focus groups, 231, 251(n16), 281
FONDECYT. *See* National Fund for Science and Technology
Foreign investment, 46
Foucault, Michel, 228
Friendship, survey research on, 198, 199(table), 218(n12), 219(n17)
Fujimori, Alberto, 73, 225, 227, 230, 232–249, 258

Game theory, 99–100
García, Alan, 154, 234, 253(n56)
García, Henry Pease, 239
García Hamilton, José Ignacio, 208
GCCs. *See* Global commodity chains
Geddes, Barbara, 22, 32, 81, 296
Gender methodologies
    evaluating, 123–128
    evolution of, 112–117
    Latin American politics and, 109, 111–112, 126–127
    new social movements and, 120–122
    women in development studies and, 117–120, 123–125
    See also Feminism; Women
Geography, regional studies and, 66–67
Gereffi, Gary, 4, 16, 31, 33, 296
Germani, Gino, 197
Giddens, Anthony, 76
Gill, Anthony, 90

Gilligan, Carol, 113
Ginsberg, Benjamin, 228, 257
Glasnost, 278
Global commodity chains (GCCs)
    defined, 56(n33)
    described, 34, 45–47
    mapping, 47–48
    regional development and, 43–50
    world-systems theory and, 44–45
Globalization, comparative analysis and, 65–66
Global research designs, 7, 25(n12)
GNP. *See* Gross national product
Goals
    material interests and, 83–86
    rational choice arguments and, 81–82, 92
    stability of, 86
    state strength and, 166–168
Godoy, Leonel, 269
Gorbachev, Mikhail, 278
Gorriti, Gustavo, 237
Government
    legitimation of, through public opinion polls, 235–238
    rational choice arguments and, 96–99
    reaction to polls by Mexican, 259–264
    survey research on, 204, 213–215(tables), 220(nn 24, 30)
    See also Authoritarianism; Communism; Democracy
Granados Chapa, Miguel Angel, 269
Grondona, Mariano, 211
Gross national product (GNP), 267–268
Groups
    collective action and, 95–96
    focus, 231, 251(n16), 281
    political interest, 154–156
    rational choice arguments and, 105(n19)
Guilherme dos Santos, Wanderley, 11

Habermas, Jürgen, 115, 116, 117, 123, 228–229, 244, 257
Haggard, Stephan, 16
Hammergren, Linn, 141
Harrison, Lawrence, 208
Hartlyn, Jonathan, 144
Hartsock, Nancy, 113
Heclo, Hugh, 69–70
Heras, María de las, 263, 269
Herbst, Susan, 229
History, rational choice arguments and, 90–91
Huber, Evelyne, 11, 110, 296
Human rights, 74–75

Huntington, Samuel P., 10, 207

Ibero-Catholic traditions, 36, 37–38, 207
ICPSR. *See* Inter-University Consortium on
    Political and Social Research
IMF. *See* International Monetary Fund
Import-substituting industrialization (ISI)
    cross-regional comparisons of, 36–37,
        41–43
    intraregional comparison and, 64
    primary vs. secondary phases of, 54(n8)
In a Different Voice (Gilligan), 113
Inclusionary political systems, 146
Income distribution disparities, 53(n2)
Independent variables, 40–41
Individualizing comparisons
    cross-regional studies and, 39, 40, 42–43
    defined, 3
    statistical analysis and, 7
Industrial cycles, 46–47
Information, rational choice arguments
    and, 87–90
Inglehart, Ronald, 205, 267
Institutional configuration, 36
Institutional Revolutionary Party (PRI),
    258, 261–263, 264, 269, 270, 271–272
Institutional site, 143–144
Interest Conflict and Political Change in Brazil
    (Schmitter), 137
Interest group politics, 149, 150, 154–156
Interest intermediation, 142, 143, 144
Interest representation, 142
Intermestic relations, 66
International Monetary Fund (IMF), 36, 177,
    184
International system, state strength and,
    183–184, 188
Inter-University Consortium on Political
    and Social Research (ICPSR), 259
Interviews
    types of in-depth, 51–52
    See also Public opinion research
Intraregional comparisons
    approaches toward, 63–66
    authoritarianism as theme for, 73
    democracy as theme for, 72–73
    diversity in, 42–43
    extraregional references and, 79(n11)
    human rights as theme for, 74–75
    of military professionalism, 80(n17)
    of political culture, 201–204
    political development and, 75–76
    research designs and, 66–72
    research practices and, 76–78

    See also Comparative analysis; Cross-
        regional comparisons
Irigaray, Luce, 113
ISI. *See* Import-substituting
    industrialization

Jamaica
    international economy and, 183–184
    legal order in, 181, 192(n40)
Jamaica Bauxite Institute, 170, 183
Jaquette, Jane S., 11, 109, 111, 296
Jornada, La (newspaper), 260, 261, 269
Jowitt, Kenneth, 104(n12)

Katzenstein, Peter, 70
Kaufman, Robert R., 12, 143
Khrushchev, Nikita, 277
Kirkpatrick, Jeane, 213
Kish, Leslie, 271
Kristeva, Julia, 113
Krueger, Anne, 97

Labor
    civil society and, 175
    corporatism and, 146, 149, 155
    gender division of, 118–120, 127
    regional division of, 46
Labor organizations
    civil society and, 174–175, 180, 182
    corporatism and, 140–141, 146, 155,
        158(n23), 159(nn 24, 25), 181–182
Lafargue, Indalecio Perdomo, 10
Lagos, Gustavo, 212
Lapp, Nancy, 91
LASA. *See* Latin American Studies
    Association
LASDB. *See* Latin American Survey Data
    Bank
Latin American Council for Social Science
    (CLACSO), 20, 61
Latin American Faculty for Social Science
    (FLACSO), 61
Latin Americans, The (Dealy), 197
Latin American Studies Association
    (LASA), 262
Latin American Survey Data Bank
    (LASDB), 214, 224(n63)
Legal order, state strength and, 167–168
Legitimation
    civil society and, 177–178, 180, 181
    through public opinion polls, 235–238
    state strength and, 167–168
Lehmbruch, Gerhard, 145
Levine, Daniel, 204

Lewis, Oscar, 200
Liberal corporatism, 145, 149, 150
Lijphart, Arend, 2–3, 6
Linz, Juan, 101, 208, 210
Lipset, Seymour Martin, 208
Llosa, Mario Vargas, 231, 232, 238, 257
López Portillo, José, 264
Los Angeles Times, 258, 264
Lower class. See Working class
Lowi, Theodore J., 149
Low intensity citizenship, 163

Macropolitics, 73
Madres of the Plaza de Mayo, 114–115, 120, 121
Madrid, Miguel de la, 264
Majority rule, 93–94
Malloy, James M., 139
Manley, Michael, 175, 177
Manufacturing Miracles (Gereffi & Wyman), 37, 39, 42, 51
Maquiladora industries, 48, 49, 119
Marxism
    feminism and, 113, 118
    state power and, 164
    See also Communism
Material interests, rational choice arguments and, 83–86
McDonough, Peter, 11
McKelvey, Richard, 93
MDS. See Most-different-systems (MDS) designs
Media
    public opinion polls in Central and Eastern Europe and, 289
    public opinion polls in Mexico and, 258, 260–261
    public opinion polls in Peru and, 230–231, 238–241, 248–249, 251(n14), 253(n48), 255(n67)
    public opinion polls in Russia and, 276
Mejía Quintana, Oscar, 211
Menchú, Rigoberta, 114
Menem, Carlos, 73, 200, 211
Menéndez-Carrión, Amparo, 15, 21, 31–32, 59, 296
MERCOSUR. See Common Market of the South
Methodological individualism, 92
Mexican Association of Research Agencies (AMAI), 259
Mexican Society for Public Opinion Research (SMEOP), 262
Mexico
    beginning of public opinion research in, 257–259
    corporatism in, 155–156, 160(n40)
    cultural surveys in, 202–203, 209, 212, 213–215(tables), 220(n24)
    educational expenditures in, 19–20
    government reaction to polls in, 259–264, 271–272
    media influence in, 258, 260–261
    political culture in, 208–209, 222(n42)
    political impact of polls in, 259–264, 269–272
    professional survey groups in, 259, 262–263
    results of public opinion polls in, 264–268
    survey on economic conditions in, 264, 267(figure)
    survey on integrity of elections in, 267, 268(figure)
    survey on party preferences in, 264, 265(figure)
    survey on presidential approval in, 264, 266(figure)
Micropolitics, 72–73
Middle class
    democracy and, 17, 202–203
    social change and, 203–204
    See also Social class
Migrants, intraregional studies and, 65–66
Military regimes
    bureaucratic authoritarianism and, 171
    corporatism and, 137, 154–155, 162(n72)
    intraregional comparison of, 80(n17)
    Peruvian coup and, 237, 254(n60)
    political culture and, 210, 222(n49), 224(n61)
Military threats, state strength and, 183, 188
Mill, John Stuart, 4
Mills, C. Wright, 228, 245
Modernization theory
    described, 8
    renewed support for, 10
    women in development studies and, 117–118
Modern Social Politics in Britain and Sweden (Heclo), 69
Molyneux, Maxine, 115, 126
Monism
    corporatism and, 144, 160(n40)
    political culture as, 197, 218(n9)
Moore, Barrington, 3
Mora y Araujo, Manuel, 211
Morse, Richard M., 137
Most-different-systems (MDS) designs

cross-regional comparisons and, 15–16, 38–39
described, 4–6, 25(n7)
intraregional comparisons and, 68
Most-similar-systems (MSS) designs
cross-regional comparisons and, 15–16, 39
described, 4–6, 25(n7)
intraregional comparisons and, 68, 69–71
MSS. *See* Most-similar-systems (MSS) designs

Nacional, El (newspaper), 259, 262
NAFTA. *See* North American Free Trade Agreement
National Action Party (PAN), 261
National Bank for Economic and Social Development, 170
National Council on Science and Technology (CONACYT), 19–20
National Council on the Condition of Women, 122
National Fund for Science and Technology (FONDECYT), 20
Nation states, cross-regional comparisons and, 38–39
Nelson, Elizabeth, 263
Neocorporatism, 157(n1)
Newly industrializing countries (NICs)
cross-regional comparisons of, 35–50
income distribution disparities in, 53(n2)
News organizations. *See* Media
New York Times, 237, 258
Nexos (magazine), 258
NICs. *See* Newly industrializing countries
Noelle-Neumann, Elisabeth, 239
North American Free Trade Agreement (NAFTA), 17, 48–49, 59, 257, 258
Nun, José, 197

OAS. *See* Organization of American States
OBM. *See* Original brandname manufacturing
O'Donnell, Guillermo, 9, 100, 101, 140, 145–146, 149, 151–152, 163, 197
OECD. *See* Organization for Economic Cooperation and Development
OEM. *See* Original equipment manufacturing
Olson, Mancur, 94
Organic statism, 152
Organizational-level mapping, 47–48
Organization for Economic Cooperation and Development (OECD), 181

Organization of American States (OAS), 236–238, 242, 245
Organski, Kenneth, 197
Original brandname manufacturing (OBM), 48
Original equipment manufacturing (OEM), 48

Paired comparison studies, 15
PAN. *See* National Action Party
Papanek, Hanna, 133
Parliamentarism
cross-regional analysis and, 17
state strength and, 171–172
Parodi, Jorge, 248
Pateman, Carole, 196
PEAC. *See* Strategic Outlook
Peña, Ricardo de la, 262
Perestroika, 278
Pérez, Carlos Andrés, 181, 211, 237
Perón, Juan, 175
Peru
corporatism in, 141, 154, 159(n24)
democracy in, 228, 230, 236, 246–249, 255(n63)
Fujimori approval rating polls, 235(table), 243(table)
industrial communities in, 140
media influence in, 230–231, 238–241, 248–249, 253(n48), 254(n61)
military regime in, 237, 254(n60)
opposition to coup in, 238–242, 247, 254(n62)
polling industry in, 230–232, 247–249
poll on confidence in national institutions, 233(table)
postcoup polls in, 227–228, 235–243
precoup polls in, 232–235
public citizenry in, 244–246, 254(n57)
Peruano, El (newspaper), 236
Peruvian Association of Market Research Companies (APEIM), 231
Peruvian Public Opinion (POP), 236
Peruvian Research Company (CPI), 230–231
PHARE. *See* Aid for the Economic Reconstruction of Poland and Hungary
Philippines, state strength in, 185–186
Pluralism, 137, 143, 144, 149, 158(n7)
Policy formation, 143
Political analysis, state strength and, 165
Political behavior
game theory and, 99–100

rational choice arguments and, 83–86,
88–91, 93–94, 97–98, 104(n12)
See also Congressional behavior;
Electoral behavior
Political culture
authoritarianism and, 207–210
cross-regional comparisons of, 198,
199(table), 201, 204–205, 217
defined, 196
democracy and, 207–213
economic development and, 36
intraregional comparisons of, 201–204
literature on, 196–201
methods of studying, 201–207
military regimes and, 210, 222(n49),
224(n61)
public opinion research and, 196–198,
199(table), 200–207, 212–217, 219(n22)
social class and, 202–204
Political development
intraregional comparison and, 75–76
public opinion polls and, 228–230, 232–
238, 244–246, 275–276
See also Economic development
Political institutions
feminism and, 115–116, 128(n2)
rational choice arguments and, 96–99,
102–103, 105(n19), 107(n29)
state strength and, 169–170
Polls. *See* Public opinion research
POP. *See* Peruvian Public Opinion
Postmodernism, feminism and, 116–117,
124, 125, 126–127
PRD. *See* Democratic Revolutionary Party
Preferences
rational choice arguments and, 81–82
stability of, 86
Presidentialism
cross-regional analysis and, 17
state strength and, 171–172
Pressure politics, 143
PRI. *See* Institutional Revolutionary Party
Primary commodity exports, 48
Primary sampling units (PSUs), 279
Prisoner's dilemma game, 99–100
Privatizing corporatism, 145–146, 149, 150,
160(n43)
Producer-driven commodity chains, 45
Product-level mapping, 47
Proximity, intraregional comparisons and,
66–68
Przeworski, Adam, 4
PSUs. *See* Primary sampling units
Public choice, 83

Public debate, 228–229, 244–246
Public goods, 94–96
Public Man, The (Dealy), 197
Public opinion research
cross-regional comparisons and, 267–268
democracy and, 228–230, 247–249, 275
electoral behavior and, 13–14, 261–262,
263, 264, 269–270
government reaction to, 259–264, 271–272
guidelines for, 255(n67)
in-depth interviews and, 51–52
in Latin America, 12–13
manipulation of, 228–229, 244–245,
251(n14), 258
media and, 230–231, 238–241, 248–249,
251(n14), 253(n48), 255(n67), 258, 260–
262, 289
in Mexico, 257–272
in Peru, 230–249
political culture and, 196–198, 199(table),
200–204, 212–217, 219(n22)
political development and, 228–230, 232–
238, 242–243, 246–249
political impact of, 259–264, 269–272,
275–276
problems with, 209, 212, 217, 228–230,
238–241, 268–271
public debate and, 228–229, 244–246
public judgment and, 247–249
roles of, 271–272
in Russia, 275–292
strategic interviews and, 34–35, 52–53
uses of, 214, 224(nn 60, 61), 225–228
See also Data gathering; Statistical
analysis

Qualitative analysis. *See* Comparative
analysis
Quantitative analysis. *See* Statistical
analysis

Radcliffe, Sarah, 116
Radial subtype formation
conceptual stretching and, 149–150
corporatism and, 147, 148(figure), 149,
150
described, 147, 148(figure)
theoretical stretching and, 150
Radvanyi, Lazlo, 258
Ragin, Charles, 3, 15
Randall, Margaret, 114
Rangel, Carlos, 200
Rational choice arguments
aggregation effects and, 93–96

collective action problems and, 94–96
conservativism and, 83
defining features of, 92–93
described, 81–82
determinism and, 91
feminism and, 112, 127
game theory and, 99–100
history and context and, 90–91, 92
information and calculating
    requirements and, 87–90, 104(n8)
Latin American research and, 102–103
majority rule and, 93–94
material interests and, 83–86
misperceptions about, 82–92
political behavior and, 83–86, 88–91, 93–
    94, 97–98, 104(n12)
political institutions and, 96–99, 102–103,
    105(n19), 107(n29)
preferences and, 81–82, 86
strengths and weaknesses of, 100–102,
    105(n19)
Reagan, Ronald, 182, 200
Redistribution, 178–180
Regional development
export roles and, 48–50
global commodity chains and, 43–50
individualizing comparisons of, 42–43
regional divisions of labor and, 46
See also Economic development
Regional studies. See Area studies
Regions, defining, 66–68
Religion
authoritarianism and, 207–208, 224(n65)
survey research on, 198, 199(table)
Repression, 149, 182, 277
Reproduction of Mothering, The (Chodorow),
    113
República, La (newspaper), 239, 240
Research. See Academic research
Research Institute of Goskomstat, 279
Reyes Heroles, Frederico, 198
Riding, Alan, 200
Riker, William, 97
Rivera, Marcia, 20, 21
Rockefeller Foundation, 18
Rodríguez, José Luis, 17
ROMIR. See Russian Public Opinion and
    Market Research
Rueschemeyer, Dietrich, 17
Russia
development of public opinion research
    in, 276–278
impacts of public opinion research in,
    275–276

qualitative research in, 281
quantitative research in, 279–281
results from recent surveys in, 290–291
value of public opinion research in, 226,
    275, 291–292
See also Eastern Europe
Russian Public Opinion and Market
    Research (ROMIR), 278, 279, 281

Salinas de Gortari, Carlos, 200, 260, 264
Sartori, Giovanni, 149
Schamis, Hector E., 155
Schirmer, Jennifer, 122
Schive, Chi, 42
Schmitter, Philippe, 11, 22, 101, 137, 138,
    144, 151–152, 156
Schwartz, Thomas, 93
Scott, James, 112
Seaga, Edward, 181
Security forces, state strength and, 170–171
Seligson, Mitchell, 10, 208, 209
Sen, Amartya, 93, 123
Sen, Gita, 119
Sendero Luminoso, 232, 233, 245
Silva, Nelson do Valle, 21
Silva Michelena, José, 214
Silvert, Kalman, 197
Skidmore, Thomas, 15
SMEOP. See Mexican Society for Public
    Opinion Research
Smith, Brian H., 17
Smith, Peter H., 1, 209, 210, 296
Social class
civil society and, 172–173, 176, 178–179
democracy and, 17, 202–203, 222(n42)
political culture and, 202–204
See also Middle class; Upper class;
    Working class
Socialism
feminism and, 118
See also Communism
Social Origins of Dictatorship and Democracy
    (Moore), 3
Social Science Research Council Committee
    on States and Social Structures, 164
Social sciences
decline in academic funding for, 18–22
directions for Latin American research
    in, 8–18, 23–24
See also Academic research
Societal corporatism, 144–145, 147,
    148(figure)
Solberg, Carl, 15
South Korea

comparison to Latin America, 178, 218(n14)
state strength of, 185
Soviet Union. *See* Russia
Specification contracting, 48
Stable preferences, 86
Stalin, Joseph, 276–277
Stallings, Barbara, 9
State
comparative analysis of, 110
conceptualizations of, 165
Latin American politics and, 163–165
See also Political institutions; State strength
State action, civil society and, 174–175, 191(nn 30, 31)
State corporatism, 144–145, 147, 148(figure)
State strength
civil society and, 172–182, 185
conceptualizations of, 165–168
determinants of, 168–186
goals and, 166–168
international system and, 183–184, 188
measurement of, 186–189
structural characteristics of the state and, 169–172, 185
See also State
Statistical analysis
comparative analysis vs., 2–3, 7
critique of, 6
research on Latin America through, 2, 11–14
of Russian public opinion surveys, 279–281
types of, 7
See also Comparative analysis; Data gathering; Public opinion research
Statizing corporatism, 145–146, 149
Status production, 133(n39)
Stepan, Alfred, 101, 138, 146, 152
Stephens, Evelyne Huber, 17
Stephens, John D., 17
Strategic interviews, 34–35, 52–53
Strategic Outlook (PEAC), 260
Structural adjustment, 164
Structural characteristics, of state strength, 169–172, 186–187
Subordinate classes, civil society and, 173, 176, 178–180
Subregional comparisons, 71
Subtype formation, 146–150, 160(n50)
Survey research. *See* Public opinion research
Syndicalism, 144

TACIS. *See* Technical Assistance for the Community of Independent States
Taras, Raymond, 197
Technical Assistance for the Community of Independent States (TACIS), 285, 288, 292(n5)
Teune, Henry, 4
Thatcher, Margaret, 200
Theoretical debates, 8–11
Theoretical stretching, 150
Tiano, Susan, 208, 209
Tickner, Arlene B., 211
Tiempo (magazine), 258, 272(n3)
Tilly, Charles, 3, 6, 38–39
Torrado, Manuel, 231
Torres Guzmán, Alfredo, 231, 232, 234, 238, 240–241
Triangle manufacturing, 46
Tripartism, 173–174
Tsebelis, George, 100
Tullock, Gordon, 97, 98
Turner, Frederick C., 13, 21, 110, 195, 262, 297

UNCTC. *See* United Nations Centre on Transnational Corporations
UN Decade for Women (1975–1985), 114, 119
Unions, labor. *See* Labor organizations
United Nations Centre on Transnational Corporations (UNCTC), 57(n41)
United States, foreign area studies and, 21–22
United States Information Agency (USIA), 203, 205, 259
Universalizing comparisons
cross-regional studies and, 38–39, 40
defined, 3
statistical analysis and, 7
Upper class
democracy and, 202–203, 222(n42)
social change and, 203–204
See also Social class
USIA. *See* United States Information Agency

Values, attitudes vs., 196, 209
Vargas, Getúlio, 137, 175
Variation-finding comparisons
cross-regional studies and, 16, 39, 40
defined, 3
statistical analysis and, 7
VCIOM. *See* All-Russian Center of Public Opinion

Velasco, Juan José, 175
Venezuela, political culture in, 210–211,
    223(n50)
Verba, Sidney, 196, 197–198, 258
Very-large-scale integrated circuits (VLSI)
    industries, 42
Villarreal, René, 42
VLSI. *See* Very-large-scale integrated
    circuits (VLSI) industries
Voter behavior. *See* Electoral behavior
Voz y Voto (magazine), 258

Wade, Robert, 40–41
Waisman, Carlos, 6
Wallerstein, Immanuel, 16, 56(n33)
WAPOR. *See* World Association for Public
    Opinion Research
Weberian tradition, 165, 169
Welfare state, 186
Welsch, Friedrich, 211
Westwood, Sallie, 116
Whitehead, Laurence, 101
Wiarda, Howard J., 136, 150–151, 207, 208
Wickham-Crowley, Timothy, 15
WID. *See* Women in development (WID)
    studies
Wildavsky, Adam, 196
Wilkie, James W., 11
Wilson, Richard, 206
Women
    comparative politics and, 109
    gender methodologies and, 112–117

new social movements and, 120–122
    research on Latin American, 117–128
    women in development studies and,
        117–120, 123–125
    See also Feminism; Gender
        methodologies
Women in development (WID) studies
    criticisms of, 123–125
    described, 117–120
Women's Role in Economic Development
    (Boserup), 118
Work, survey research on, 199(table), 201
Working class
    corporatism for, 146
    democracy and, 17, 202–203
    social change and, 203–204
    See also Social class
World Association for Public Opinion
    Research (WAPOR), 259, 262–263
World Bank, 36
World-systems theory, 44–45
World Values Survey, 198, 199(table), 200,
    201, 202(table), 204–206, 212, 213–
    215(tables), 219(n17), 220(n30), 267
Wyman, Donald, 16, 37

Yankelovich, Daniel, 247
Yeltsin, Boris, 291

Zavala, Iván, 270
Zayuelas, Carmen, 214
Zimmerman, William, 18